WONDERS

Writings and Drawings for the Child in Us All

Edited By
JONATHAN COTT
& MARY GIMBEL

ROLLING STONE PRESS/SUMMIT BOOKS/NEW YORK

FIRST EDITION

1 2 3 4 5 6 7 8 9 10
LIBRARY OF CONGRESS CATALOGING IN PUBLICATION DATA

Main entry under title:

Wonders

SUMMARY: An anthology which includes poems, fables,
plays, short stories, and cartoons.
1.   Children's literature, American.   [1.   Literature—Collections.   2.   Short stories]   I.   Cott, Jonathan.
II.   Gimbel, Mary.
PZ5.W498   1980   810'.8'09282 [Fic]   80–17146
ISBN 0–671–40053–3

"Coyote Shows How He Can Lie" and "Whirlwind Woman" by
Barry Holstun Lopez originally appeared in *Giving Birth to
Thunder, Sleeping with His Daughter,* copyright © 1977 by
Barry Holstun Lopez, published by Sheed Andrews and McMeel,
Inc. Reprinted by permission of the author.
"Abiyoyo," by Pete Seeger, copyright © 1963, by Fall River
Music Inc. All rights reserved. Used by permission of Fall River
Music Inc.
Drawing by Saul Steinberg from *The Passport,* copyright © 1953,
by Saul Steinberg, published by Harper & Brothers. Originally
appeared in *The New Yorker.* Reprinted by permission of Saul
Steinberg.
"A Coupla Scalped Indians," by Ralph Ellison originally appeared
in *New World Writing,* copyright © 1956 by Ralph Ellison. Re-
printed by permission of William Morris Agency, Inc., on behalf
of the author.

ACKNOWLEDGMENTS

The editors would like to thank the following persons who helped make this book possible: Zita Allen, Paul Bresnick, Pauline Finkelstein, Angela Gaudioso, Bailey Gimbel, Leslie Gimbel, Ronny Johnson, Sarah Lazin, Pamela Lord, Irwin Shaw, James Silberman, Frances Waldman, and Jann and Jane Wenner.

Contents

Introduction I

Jonathan Cott

Creators of children's literature who have thought deeply about the nature of their endeavor—especially since late Victorian times when the demand for "instructing" gave way gradually to the desire for "delighting"—have often realized that one writes not so much for the child one used to be, as for the child one always is. As P. L. Travers has expressed it: "To be aware of having been a child—and who am I but the child I was, wounded, scarred and dirtied over, but still essentially that child, for essence cannot change—to be aware of and in touch with this fact is to have the whole long body of one's life at one's disposal, complete and unfragmented. You do not chop off a section of your imaginative substance and make a book specifically for children for—if you are honest—you have, in fact, no idea where childhood ends and maturity begins. It is all endless and all one."

The importance of this understanding has been attested to throughout history: "The great man is the man who hasn't lost the heart he had when he was a little child" (Mencius); "Genius is childhood recalled at will" (Baudelaire); "Childhood is the nearest to true life" (André Breton). And it is this awareness of the inseparability of what is "grown-up" from what is "childlike"—experienced at the root of all creative efforts—that has led many persons to refuse to recognize the value of a separate literature for children.

Before the mid-eighteenth-century writings of Thomas Boreman and John Newbery, which mark the inception of children's literature as a specialized and recognized commercial enterprise, children shared with adults what Professor Francelia Butler terms a literature of "dual interest." As Chekhov, in a letter to a friend, wrote: "I don't like what is known as children's literature; I don't recognize its validity. Children should be given only what is suitable for adults as well. Children enjoy reading Andersen . . . and Gogol, and so do adults. One shouldn't write for children; one should learn to choose works suitable for children from among those already written for adults—in other words, from genuine works of art."

Surprisingly, this attitude is as reminiscent of pre-eighteenth-century practice as it is a prescient indication of the kind of enlightened contemporary ideas we find expressed in a work like *Bibliophile in the Nursery* by William Targ: "A good children's book strikes a vibration in the soul that lasts a lifetime. And when a reader or collector achieves maturity and a special sense of values, he may recognize that the best books are really those that children have loved for many generations of lifetimes."

The Psalms of David, the Parables of Jesus, *The Flowers of St. Francis, Le Morte d'Arthur,* the poetry of Blake, George MacDonald's *The Golden Key,* the works of Lewis Carroll and Beatrix Potter, Tolstoy's Fables and Fairy Tales, *The Wind in the Willows, The Wizard of Oz, Babar the King*—all of these exist in one timeless and ageless universe, fulfilling the requirement, as stated by the critic of the *Quarterly Review* of 1844, that a children's book be a "union of the highest art with the simplest form."

C. S. Lewis must have had much the same thing in mind when he wrote that "a children's story is the best art form for something you have to say," adding: "We must write for children out of those elements in our own imagination which we share with children: differing from our child readers not by any less, or less serious, interest in the things we handle, but by the fact that we have other interests which children would not share with us. The matter of our story should be a part of the habitual furniture of our minds. . . . We must meet children as equals in that area of our nature where we are their equals."

It is interesting to see how children have proven themselves the equals of adults in the way they have taken over and adopted, and by so doing prolonged the life of, special works such as *The Pilgrim's Progress, Gulliver's Travels,* and *Huckleberry Finn*—in addition to the fairy and folk tales from around the world that were never originally intended for them. Conversely, innumerable writers for "adults," from Chaucer (*Treatise on Astrolabe*) to Barthelme (*The Slightly Irregular Fire Engine*) have also asserted their equality with children by creating works specifically for them. The past fifty years, for instance, saw the publication of books by, among others, Gertrude Stein, Aldous Huxley, James Joyce, C. S. Lewis, William Faulkner, E. E. Cummings, Eugene Ionesco, E. B. White, and Randall Jarrell. Yet with the exception of Lewis's Narnia series, White's *Charlotte's Web,* and Jarrell's *The Animal Family,* none of the above authors' books—excellent as many of them are—has attained the "classic" status of, say, Wanda Gág's *Millions of Cats,* Laura Ingalls Wilder's *Little House on the Prairie,* William Steig's *Sylvester and the Magic Pebble,* or Maurice Sendak's *In the Night Kitchen.*

Obviously, it is extremely difficult to create a great work for children; and some writers forget that an inspiring book for kids is almost always a vital and illuminating book for adults as well. The masterpieces of children's literature, simply, are small masterpieces of literature—regardless of the fame of their authors or the intended age of their readers. It is preposterous, for instance, to say that Beatrix Potter's works are best appreciated and understood by four- to seven-year-olds. But today, both the continuing specialization of children's literature as an industry—one controlled by publishers, booksellers, and librarians— and the categorization of literature into age brackets have, for the most part, effectively eliminated the encouragement and dissemination of much risky, imaginative, and experimental writing for children. And too often what is considered exemplary—*i.e.,* "inoffensive"—in this field is merely a devitalized and trivialized sense of childhood, leading to sentimental and patronizing books that are meant to satisfy only hypothetical children.

Since anyone who writes or illustrates or tells stories is potentially—for better or worse—a creator of children's literature, we decided to take a chance and send out about two hundred copies of the following letter:

> We are asking writers and artists to contribute a story, or a poem, or a fantasy, or a fable—whatever you have in mind—that you might like to tell a child (of any age).
>
> This book is a collection of pieces for children and adults, so you should feel free to create a short work (from one to twenty pages) that ultimately appeals to the child in you—regardless of the conventions of "children's literature."
>
> If you feel like illustrating your text, making a cartoon story, collaborating with a child or adult, creating a new version of a fairy tale or nursery rhyme, or writing a prose poem or satire—please do.

The result is this anthology.

No matter how the readers—whether young or old—of this collection decide to judge it, we, as editors, have been happy to have enabled writers and artists to redefine the notions of what children's literature can and "should" be. They have certainly disabused us of the misguided but widely-held notion that works for children must fit automatically into some kind of homogeneous "genre" or "subgenre." Children's literature is not a genre; it is as rich and varied as adult literature. And we have been fascinated by the multifarious ways in which the creators of this book have taken our suggestion and proceeded to provide examples—even if idiosyncratic ones—of folk and fairy tales, animal and transformation stories, trickster and cautionary fables, memoirs and myths, monologues and dialogues, lyrics and prose poems, epigrams and mock epics, cartoon strips and portraits. The writers and illustrators of this anthology have furthermore reflected and revealed themselves in ways both they and we might never have suspected or imagined, and they have done so in a fashion that, we hope, will inspire and encourage others to create their own children's literature.

Almost all of the selections in this collection were written and illustrated especially for it. A few of them originally appeared in now out-of-print, small-press editions; in poetry collections; or in local newspapers. In each of these cases, information concerning first publication is given in the biographical entries at the back of the book.

Introduction II
Mary Gimbel

New York editors listened skeptically to the idea of asking writers and artists to create works for children. ("Why would they do it?") Some literary agents warned us they would never allow their writers to join such a project. ("They've got nothing to gain.") With little encouragement and a sense that we were being presumptuous, we wrote two hundred people asking them for contributions. Why did people respond so generously?

Max Apple simply said, "As a man who tells five stories a night, I'd be glad to tell one for you." Hence the story about his stories that filled the hospital room of his newborn daughter, and, in turn, the various houses where he and his family have lived . . . until, as he says, "The new stories took up so much room we had to move to a bigger house."

Leslie Fiedler wrote us that thirty-five years ago he learned Japanese as an interpreter. During that time, he read a Japanese fairy tale that "continued to ring in my head, though I have otherwise lost the language completely. For a long time I tried to exorcize it by telling it over and over to my children. For many years my version grew longer and longer, then shorter and shorter, until now it seems *just right.* But as I have written and rewritten it, it has turned from a heroic poem into an antiheroic one, perhaps because the language I learned in reading it, I ended up using as an interpreter and interrogator of prisoners of war at the Battle of Iwo Jima. The endings of fairy tales are often changed as they are told and retold; but in every other case I know ('Goldilocks,' for instance, and 'Little Red Riding Hood'), they have become blither rather than grimmer. In this case, not so."

One novelist wanted to write something for this book, but needed time which he didn't have. Writing for children, he explained, is hard for writers. "Once, my daughter was sick and stayed home from school. When she was well, and returning, she asked me to write an excuse for her teacher. I sat down and wrote, 'Please excuse . . . ,' but I didn't like the phrase so I crumpled the paper and threw it on the floor. I began again: 'Jane has been home with. . . .' I didn't like that either and I tossed it out. The next two tries went the same way. Time passed. My daughter began to fret that she would miss the bus. I remained at my labor hoping the right phrase would come. Finally, I looked up. My whole family stood around my desk. They could scarcely believe what they saw: a floor littered with crumpled paper and a desperate man, a writer, who couldn't compose a simple note to the teacher. So you see, writing for children is hard."

Several writers contributed something in the hope that our calls and letters would cease. When Peter Matthiessen, the novelist and naturalist, became resigned to the fact that the above would not happen, he took his fishing rod to the beach on a clear October afternoon. He also took along an old paperback copy of *Under the Mountain Wall,* his book about New Guinea, as well as scotch tape and scissors. He settled down on the beach, fishing rod ready, keeping one eye on the water to watch for the flocks of terns or gulls that indicate the presence of fish. With the other eye, he cut from his book the passages about Tukum the Swineherd and pasted them together, creating a beautiful story about a lonely little boy who hoped to change his name to Mud.

For years, Norman Mailer has been reciting snatches of his rhyme to his various children, always accompanying the recitation with vivid body language . . . the knees bent, the cheeks puffed out, the stomach shoved forward for "Kalamazoo! Poo, poo!" Something in him is surely stirred at the mention of "East Haaaaartford!"—a powerful association he does not explain.

I bumped into Mailer occasionally over the last year, and each time we met he had a new line for his poem. He became a bard and hooted it out in high spirits, never less than delighted with his work. I wrote it down on the table cloth or on an envelope or on my hand. The thing evolved slowly. He had a deadline for a huge work-in-progress. He took his family away for the summer. He had numerous other commitments. He had said he would write something for our book, however, and he kept his word.

Another writer who received our original letter counted out numerous typographical errors. We were dismayed, but he said, "This letter, this hodgepodge, has put me entirely at my ease and quite relaxed me about the work I mean to do for you. But mind you, I only mean to do it so you'll leave me alone."

For the most part, the enthusiasm and good grace of our contributors was gratifying. Why did they agree to write for kids or about them or about the child in themselves? One worldly playwright said, "I'm beginning to think everything I write is for children." A novelist wrote that there had never seemed to him a difference between the tastes of children and of adults, and that both just wanted good stories. "Neither," he added sadly, "gets them very much anymore."

Jamaica Kincaid, the author of "Children"—a story about little girls who sail away in a navy blue boat named *Pam*—says, "Myself as a child is my favorite person. My childhood . . . I'd never give it up under any circumstances. It's the most interesting thing I have ever done."

When Saul Steinberg gave permission for us to print his drawing of the father holding up his daughter to see the moon, he said, "This drawing shows the courtesy of children. See how she holds herself . . . she becomes an object being elevated to a height. When we are grown up, if somebody lifts us up, we get panicky. We want consent or a contract; but the child, out of politeness and courtesy, lets herself be manipulated."

Helen Adam, the poet, wrote *In Harpy Land* and did the accompanying collages. Her sister, with whom she lives, thought the poem unsuitable for children. "She does not share my taste for the weird," said Helen Adam. "My sister finds children rather sensitive little creatures who ought to be reading charming funny things." *In Harpy Land* is a fantasy based on the myth of Kali, the Indian goddess of destruction. The Harpy queen ends up on God's right hand because she is, in fact, his darker side. "Without destruction, of course, life can't go on," declares Miss Adam.

P. L. Travers has said that children have strong stomachs; and as a child she herself had great affection for a book, found on her father's shelf, entitled *Twelve Deathbed Scenes.* "I read it so often I knew it by heart, each death being more lugubrious and edifying than the one before it. I used to long to die, on condition that I came alive again the next minute, to see if I, too, could pass away with equal misery and grandeur."

Novelists and artists and poets and essayists have contributed to this book. There are stories about African animals and about Victorian dolls; about growing old and about being born; about keeping rabbits in Japan, taking care of pigs in New Guinea; about Amerindian tricksters and Brooklyn draft dodgers. The range and variety of the authors and artists is reflected in the diversity of their contributions, and it demonstrates their willingness to express themselves in a new way for a new readership. For this, we thank them all.

THE DRUM

BY
Chinua Achebe

Long, long ago, when the world was young, all the animals lived in their families in one country. In those days, there were not many tortoises as there are today but only one tortoise, Mbe, the ancestor of all tortoises, and his wife Anum. Similarly there was Anunu, the father of all birds; there was Ebunu, the ram, and his wife Atulu; Enyi, the elephant; Agu, the leopard; Odum, the lion; and many others.

For many years, all these animals lived a happy life. The winds blew and the rains fell in their season and the crops grew and there was enough for everyone to eat and drink.

But one year the rain began to fail, the sun came out more than usual, and the dry season stretched far into the months that belonged to rain. The following year was much the same, and the year after that was even worse. The soil became so hot and dusty that seeds could no longer stay alive in it, let alone grow. The rivers and streams began to dry up. Drought had descended on the world. And with drought came famine.

The animals, who had always enjoyed three meals every day, began to eat only twice a day, and then once. By the third year most of them were lucky if they found one meal in three days. There was great sorrow in all the land.

One day, Tortoise set out from home in the early morning in search of wild fruits and berries. By noon the sun was beating down on the earth without mercy and Tortoise, tired and sweating, had not found even one berry yet. As he trudged along the burning foot-path, nothing else stirred or made the slightest sound. And so Tortoise heard his own footsteps on the hot sand and they seemed to say:

Aja mbene!
Mbe mbene!
Aja mbene!

Then a tall palm tree came into view. Tortoise's heart began to beat faster as he padded slowly toward its shade. He looked up at its long heavy trunk to its head and asked if it had any ripe palm fruit. In those days, trees and animals had one language and so understood one another. The palm tree replied that it had one ripe fruit. Though hungry and tired, Tortoise was angry and disappointed. One fruit! To climb that long and heavy trunk all the way into the clouds for one palm fruit! Tortoise also knew too well how palm fruits were surrounded by hard and sharp thorns. He knew how firm they could be and how difficult it was to pull them out before they were fully ripe. And there was yet another problem —how to know which of the hundreds of fruits in the bunch was the ripe one. Or should he simply go from one fruit to the next . . . and the next . . . bruising his fingers in the thorns until he chanced on the lone ripe fruit? Oh no! No! Tortoise would not do that kind of stupid thing! And what if he should fall down from that terrible height while he was searching the foolish bunch from thorn to thorn? Tortoise became truly angry with the tree and particularly with the land on which it grew. He cursed the hopeless and wretched soil, the tired and exhausted soil, the stupid soil that could do no better than a palm tree with one ripe fruit at its head! And he moved on. His anger seemed to have put a new strength into his walk. But very soon he slowed down again and then felt even more tired than before. The sands grew hotter under his feet. And the sound of his tired walk became louder and louder in his head:

Aja mbene!
Mbe mbene!
Aja mbene!

In due course, he came to another tree and asked how many ripe fruits it had. "Three," replied the tree. "Stupid land," cursed Tortoise, "good-for-nothing, useless land. Land that's fit only for Anunu, the bird, to dance upon. Shame! Four hundred kinds of shame on you!"

The next tree had ten fruits. Tortoise considered it for a while. Ten out of all those hundreds. It was still not worth it. What if he should miss his hold and fall from that great height? For ten tiny palm fruits. "Miserly land," he said, but he said it quietly under his breath. "Who knows, I may yet climb it if nothing better turns up," he thought.

But something much better did turn up: a moderately tall tree with thrice four hundred fruits! "How many did you say, good tree?" asked Tortoise wondering if he had heard right.

"Thrice four hundred," replied the tree.

Tortoise danced a little way up the road and then back again. He thought he heard faint sounds of a drum rising from this good and generous earth. Or perhaps it was only happiness beating the drum in his heart. Thrice four hundred! One thousand and two hundred fruits!

He began to climb. His energy had returned to him. Even the sun now seemed to beat the earth less harshly. Halfway up the tree, Tortoise felt a mild, pleasant wind begin to blow and cool him. He could now see the bunch clearly, with its thrice four hundred ripe fruits. Could he eat them all today or come back tomorrow? What if somebody else should come this way and discover the remnant of his banquet? Somebody like Anunu, the bird? No, it would be best to put everything in his stomach where it would be nice and safe. He chuckled aloud. "Thrice four hundred! A rather nice way of saying one thousand and two hundred!"

He had now climbed to the neck of the palm tree, right under the branch which supported the ripe bunch of fruits. He now climbed one step sideways and one step upward and came level with the ripe fruits. He stretched his hand and pulled out the first fruit and threw it into his mouth. It was the best and sweetest palm fruit he had ever tasted. It was not very large, but it was almost all flesh and no kernel. He picked another and another and another and crammed them into his mouth so that his cheeks bulged out on both sides. He chewed and chewed and swallowed the pleasant fresh juice and chewed and swallowed until all the juice was gone. Then he spat out the fiber and filled his mouth with five new fruits. Then he picked a sixth to hold in his hand. At the same time he tried to change his position on the tree slightly so as to get even closer to the fruits. In doing this the fruit slipped through his fingers and fell to the ground.

"I am sorry," said Tortoise, "but I will not allow even one of these marvelous fruits to get lost." And he began to climb down in search of the fallen fruit.

2 The fruit lay at the edge of a hole in the ground. "You see," said Tortoise to himself, "if I hadn't come down right away some little animal living in this hole might have come up and taken my fruit." As he stretched his hand to pick it up, it slid into the hole and lay just below the surface. Tortoise pushed in his hand to get it and it fell further in, just beyond reach but still quite visible. Tortoise noticed that the hole was really quite large and seemed to descend in steps.

"What is my name?" asked Tortoise of himself. "Am I not Tortoise who never gives up a fight halfway?"

He plunged into the hole and stretched his arm to grasp his fruit. His finger tip just touched it and it fell further down on the next step.

"Today is today," said Tortoise. "Wherever you go, my little fruit, Tortoise goes with you."

With the fruit always a little ahead of him, Tortoise descended deeper and deeper into the earth. Then all of a sudden he emerged out of the hole and found himself in a big clearing. There were huts and trees and farms. But the light was strangely mild and gave everything a tinge of yellow. Tortoise found a little boy standing close by, chewing something in his mouth.

"What are you chewing?" asked Tortoise.

"I am chewing a palm fruit," replied the boy. He spoke through the nose as if he had a head cold.

"Where did you find it?" asked Tortoise.

"I was sweeping our yard and it fell right here, out of the sky."

"I see," said Tortoise. "I suppose I too fell out of the sky?"

"Yes, sir," said the boy.

"Well, I didn't. And I have more news for you. I am Tortoise, the owner of the fruit you have just eaten."

"I am sorry, sir."

"No need to be sorry, my boy. Just find my fruit right now or I am taking you away to my country."

The little boy began to cry and his parents and others rushed out from the huts and asked what was the matter. They all spoke through the nose.

"Your boy ate my palm fruit and I have asked him to give it back to me or else. . . ."

"And who are you, if we may ask?"

"I am Tortoise who never gives up a battle half-way."

"I believe I have heard of you. We are spirits and this is our town. You are welcome, Tortoise." He turned to the boy and asked: "Did you eat Tortoise's palm fruit?" The boy said yes, with tears in his eyes. "I didn't know it was his."

"This is a simple matter," said the spirit. "We have many palm trees here," he said to Tortoise, "and we shall give you ten fruits for the one you lost."

"Oh no," said Tortoise. "My own fruit or else your boy goes with me." The boy screamed and wailed when he heard this. "Quiet!" said his father, and then turned again to Tortoise. "All right, we shall give you a whole head of palm fruits for your single fruit."

"I don't want to be offensive, but really you are wasting my time," replied Tortoise. "My fruit or the boy. Finish!"

At this the boy fled, screaming, into one of the huts. "Stop!" shouted Tortoise, running after him.

"Come on, my friend," said the elderly spirit, barring his way. "Don't scare the poor boy. We will give you something which is better than all the palm trees in the world."

"And what may that be?"

"A drum."

"A drum? Do I look like a drummer to you? Look here, my good friends, I have been very patient. . . ."

"You have indeed," said the spirit, "and we like you for it. The drum I will give you is no ordinary drum. Take it from me and you will be glad you did."

"All right," said Tortoise, "I shall accept the drum, but only because of your gentle manner and good words. But tell your boy to be careful in future and not gobble up any palm fruit that drops out of the sky. Where's the drum?"

They brought a strange little drum and its drumstick. Tortoise hung the drum from his shoulder by its strap and was about to beat it. But the spirit quickly held his hand.

"Not here," he said. "Beat it gently when you get back to the world. And if it doesn't surprise you, I'll be surprised!"

Tortoise said good-bye to the spirits and began to climb up to the world of white light.

At the foot of the palm tree, he beat the spirit drum. The sound that came out of it was unlike the sound of any drum he had ever heard:

Kpam putu! Kpam putu!
Igba nni n'ofe!
Gidi gada! Gidi gada!
Aneli n'anu!

Immediately, a table loaded with food was set before him. All the good foods he had ever eaten and those he had only dreamed of lay profusely around. Yams and cassavas, rice and beans, millets, fish, and meat stew, egusi and okra soup, and pots of palm wine. Tortoise ate as he had never eaten in all his life and drank a whole pot of palm wine. When he finally rose to go, he could hardly walk. He took three or four unsteady steps and then remembered the palm tree that had brought him all these good fortunes. He walked back to it and patted its trunk fondly and said "Thank you" five or six times, and set out for home with his drum. After a few steps he remembered the hole in the ground and went back and knelt down and whispered "Thank you" seven times into it. Then he began the journey home, whistling happily all the way.

3

At first, Tortoise thought he should keep the drum secret from the animals. But after one week of feasting with his wife in the innermost room of their home, another thought came to him. "If I feed the animals at this time when they are all about to perish from hunger, they will honor my name and perhaps even make me their king. That would be really nice!"

The only problem with this idea was that he could not say how long the food in the drum would last. Although, after one week, it still showed no sign at all of diminishing, yet who knows what would happen if the whole country began to feed from it? In the end, Tortoise could not resist the thought of becoming a popular hero among the animals and perhaps their king. And if the food in the magic drum should run out, why, he could always go back to the spirits for another drum. They must have stacks and stacks of them.

So the next day an invitation went out to all the animals in the country. The messenger was Anunu, the bird, and his message was to tell all the animals to assemble in Tortoise's compound tomorrow at lunchtime.

"Tell them," said Tortoise importantly and mysteriously, "that I have a message for them from the land of spirits."

"From the land of spirits?" asked Anunu, greatly surprised.

"That's right," said Tortoise, "from the very land of spirits. Tell that to every one of them, to every single animal in the kingdom."

"In the kingdom? What kingdom?" asked Anunu, more puzzled than ever.

"Oh dear, dear, dear! My thoughts are running away with me this morning," said Tortoise. "No, my good friend, it was a slip of the tongue, as the saying is. I did not mean to say *kingdom* but *country*. All the animals in the country. Here at my palace, I mean place. Lunchtime tomorrow. Business: a very important message from spirit land. Now, run along my dear friend and I'll see you all tomorrow."

As he flew away, Anunu thought how very odd Tortoise was becoming these days.

"I hope he is not opening his old bag of tricks again," he said. "I wouldn't want to be part of it. . . . Perhaps I should ignore his message and just fly home to my nest and endure my hunger in peace." But there was something about Tortoise's manner which had convinced Anunu that he was serious. What was even more striking had been the appearance of Tortoise and his wife. They seemed so well-fed. And a man who looked so well at this time deserved to be listened to even if he was known to be something of a crook. So Anunu took Tortoise's message to all the animals in the country. Few animals honored Tortoise's invitation. Some of the others thought it must be one of his practical jokes and stayed home. A few were even angry. They thought that the very mention of lunchtime at this time of general starvation was a cruel joke. And some were too weak and hungry to give any thought to the matter.

The few who came took their seats under the shade of a ragged old tree in Tortoise's compound. Monkey was there out of curiosity; Lizard came because his compound was just next door; Leopard was there determined to thrash Tortoise if the invitation should prove to be a hoax. And there were a handful of others who had one odd reason or another for coming.

When it became clear that no newcomers could be expected, Tortoise rose to speak. He began with a well-known proverb: *"If you underrate the little pot on the cooking stand, it will boil over and put out the fire.* I know that I am only a tiny fellow compared to such giants as Elephant, Rhinoceros, Buffalo, and the rest. And that, perhaps, is why so many have ignored my invitation. But little fellows sometimes have their uses."

"Please get on to the point," growled Leopard.

"Oh I will, my dear Leopard, presently," said Tortoise, "but it is always wise to prepare the ground before sowing the seed. Our wise men have also told us that eating without asking questions causes dying without being sick."

"We have had enough jokes about eating from you," said Hedgehog, bristling with anger, "and I am getting quite impatient."

"All right, good people. Let me come to the point. The hunger in the land is something we all know about. We have all suffered from it for three years. And so, the other day, I said to myself: *All the animals in the country will perish unless somebody comes forward to save them. Somebody who is prepared to risk his own life for the sake of his fellows.* And so I decided that that person has to be myself. . . ."

Some of the animals laughed at the thought. Tortoise as savior! What a joke.

"Go on, savior," said Monkey.

"And so I said good-bye to my wife, because I did not think I would return home alive," continued Tortoise. "And I did not tell her where I was going, because I knew she would have tried to stop me."

"And where were you going, Crazy?" asked Goat.

"I was going to the land of the spirits."

The animals roared with laughter. Goat is right, they thought. The fellow has gone crazy. Hunger has finally touched his brain. But Tortoise was now so overpowered by the story he was weaving that he did not even hear the mocking laughter.

"And so I journeyed for seven days and seven nights and crossed seven rivers and traversed seven grasslands. And finally I arrived in the kingdom of the spirits and was taken to their king."

"Poor fellow," said Leopard, "his mind is gone."
And he rose and left.

"To cut a long story short," said Tortoise, "I told the king of spirits that my people were dying of hunger in my country and I must find a cure or else die trying. The king then spoke. He said he had never seen a person who loved his people so much that he would brave the journey from the world of living creatures to the kingdom of spirits. He said his first thought had been to kill me. But my words and my courage had changed his mind. So he called a big feast in my honor to which he invited all his noblemen and their ladies. And he made a long speech in my praise and ended it by giving me a chieftaincy title. He called me Chief Tortoise Who Never Stops a Fight Halfway."

The animals were no longer laughing or talking. Something in Tortoise's face and voice held their attention firmly.

"I could go on all afternoon telling you about all the honors that king heaped on me. But I shall reserve that story for another day. You must all be hungry and we should attend to that first."

The animals stared at one another in total surprise.

"But before our feast, I should tell you that the food you are going to eat comes from my brother and friend, the King of Spirits, to you my beloved people of the Kingdom . . . I mean to say, the Country of Animals."

He turned around and walked slowly like a great chief to his hut. The animals sat in complete silence, watching. He soon returned carrying a strange drum from its strap on his left shoulder. He did not say another word when he got to his place before the little crowd. He just tapped the drum with the bent drumstick:

> *Kpam putu! Kpam putu!*
> *Igba nni n'ofe!*
> *Gidi gada! Gidi gada!*
> *Aneli n'anu!*

The way the animals went at the food was truly remarkable! They could have been starving for thirty years! Rat fell straight into the pot of egusi soup and was badly scalded, and Goat jumped with all four feet into the huge bowl of yams. Many of the dishes were overturned in the scramble and one or two smashed altogether and their contents snatched greedily from the ground. But after a while the animals realized that there was enough food around for the whole country to share peacefully. And so they settled down and gorged themselves without fighting.

4 The next day the whole country was at Tortoise's door at daybreak. He heard the tremendous noise of their presence and was happy. But he was not going to be rushed, he would do things at his own pace and in his own good time. He knew that that was the only way to make the animals accept his importance. A chief does not hurry. So Tortoise lay in bed listening to the hungry voice of the country and smiling contentedly.

After a very long while the confused noise of the animals stopped and a chant like the roar of the ocean took its place:

WE! WANT! TOR! TOISE!
WE! WANT! TOR! TOISE!

Tortoise's heart was touched by this appeal. He got up from his bed, washed his face and hands, and went out to meet his people.

WE! WANT! THE! DRUM!
WE! WANT! THE! DRUM!

"You will see the drum presently," said Tortoise, waving his hand to obtain silence. "You will see the drum, my good people. But first we must hear how the drum came into our hands. Those of you who answered my call yesterday already know the story. But they were only a handful of people. Today, I am happy to see that we have the whole country. I want you all to hear the story as it happened, not as hearsay."

And he told the story of his self-sacrificing journey again. Those who had heard it yesterday noticed little differences here and there in today's telling. For instance, Tortoise now said that when he told his wife he was going to the land of spirits she burst into tears. But nobody worried about such little details. The important thing, surely, was that he had gone to the land of spirits on behalf of his people and brought home a priceless gift which was there for all to see.

Because of the much larger numbers present at the second feast, it was far rowdier than the first. Indeed, it became a total riot. But again, as on the first day, some kind of order returned when the guests finally realized how large the feast was.

Every day the animals returned to Tortoise's compound and ate and drank and went home singing his praise. They called him Savior, Great Chief, the One Who Speaks for His People. Then one day a very drunken singer called him King Tortoise! Thereafter the great Chant of the Animals became:

> *WE! WANT! OUR! KING!!*
> *WE! WANT! OUR! KING!!*
> *OUR! KING! OF! KINGS!!*

A day was set for the coronation. Silk robes were ordered from the Country of Insects and a crown from the Country of Fishes. Tortoise's compound was bedecked with flags and bunting. And Toad rehearsed the anthem he had composed with the Choir of State day and night.

Coronation morning! The day broke with a salute of twenty-one guns. The animals assembled for the pre-coronation breakfast. The toad and his choir rendered endlessly the new anthem: *Our Great and Gloroise King Tortoise.*

Tortoise had decided that as king there were certain things he should no longer do, such as beating a drum. And so he had appointed Elephant his royal drummer. And thus it came about that on coronation morning as all the animals assembled for breakfast, Elephant picked up the magic drum for the first time and gave it a gentle tap with the drumstick. And such was Elephant's gentle tap that it ripped the hide from wood to wood! The little drum was broken!

And such was the cry that went up from the animals that King-elect Tortoise, who was not supposed to show himself to his people until the ceremonies at noon, rushed out in his loincloth. And he immediately saw the disaster. After the first shock, he took control of the situation. He sent two young animals to collect the latex of a certain tree and bring it to him. Meanwhile, he made a short speech to his people and asked them to remain calm. "This is only a temporary setback which we shall soon overcome," he said. "Our ceremony must proceed as planned. Nothing must shake us from our purpose."

The two animals returned with the latex and Tortoise applied it very skillfully to the broken membrane of the drum and put it in the sun to dry. The animals watched him in gloom and silence.

"Be of good cheer," said Tortoise to them. "Everything will be all right, and we shall smile again."

The glue was now dry and the drum seemed in reasonably good shape. Tortoise picked it up under his arm and looked at the crowd of animals. They were so still they seemed to be holding their breath. He tapped the drum with more care than he had ever shown it. An indistinct whirring sound came out. Then a grain of rice dropped out; a crumb of yam and a strand of meat followed, and then two drops of palm wine and a drop of egusi soup. The animals broke into a loud cry like a lot of children.

Tortoise made a short, moving speech to them in which he promised that as soon as his coronation was over he would return to his friend, the King of Spirits, and get another drum. "Let us proceed with the ceremonies as planned!"

But the crowd was beginning to break up. A voice was heard to ask: "Proceed on an empty stomach? Go and get the drum and then we shall proceed."

"Well spoken!" replied many voices. "The drum first and then the coronation. What's the good of a king without a food drum?"

And the animals began to leave Tortoise's compound in groups of three and four.

5

At the first crow of the cock, Tortoise was on his way to the land of spirits. By noon he was at the foot of the palm tree of thrice four hundred fruits. "Good palm tree, do you have any ripe fruits?" he asked breathlessly. The tree said nothing. "I think you have something. Anyhow, I shall come up and see for myself," said Tortoise, and began to climb. As soon as he got to the top of the tree he picked one fruit and let it fall to the ground. Then he descended. The fruit had fallen a good distance from the hole in the ground. Tortoise rolled it gently with his foot toward the hole and then pushed it in. He knelt down and reached into the hole. And, to his annoyance, the fruit lay perfectly within his reach. He cursed it and pushed it further down and then climbed in. Again it was within easy reach and again he called it a useless fruit and pushed it further and continued to curse and push all the way into spirit land. The little spirit boy was standing by with his long broom looking at the palm fruit when Tortoise jumped out of the hole. As soon as the boy saw him, he fled toward the huts.

"Don't run away from me my little friend," said Tortoise in his gentlest voice. The boy stopped, turned around, and gazed at Tortoise suspiciously.

"Don't be afraid of me, little fellow. I was only teasing you the other day. I enjoy teasing children; but I mean no harm. I am actually a great lover of children, as you will see when you come to know me better. . . . I hope your parents are home because I have come specially to thank them for that marvelous little drum. My people were so happy with it that they made me their king. And so I have come back to thank your father. Is he home?"

"Yes sir," said the boy. "He is in the hut. Shall I call him?"

"Don't worry," said Tortoise. "I shall walk over with you. But before I forget, I did bring a little present for you. I know you like palm fruits and so I brought you the sweetest fruit in the whole wide world. It dropped from my hand as I was coming down. Did you see it by any chance?"

"It's right there behind you."

"Of course it is. I'm getting old, you know, and my eyes are no longer what they used to be. . . . Here we are. It's a little present from me to you."

The boy hesitated at first. But Tortoise, in his sweetest manner, persuaded him to accept the fruit.

"Come on," said Tortoise. "Pop it into your mouth and tell me if it's not the sweetest palm fruit you ever tasted."

The boy's eyes glowed as he munched the fruit. He was enjoying it so much that he did not notice the change in Tortoise's face.

"Stupid boy! When will you ever learn? My fruit, if you please!" shouted Tortoise, glaring ferociously at the boy and grabbing hold of his leg. The boy screamed in fear as he tried to break loose from Tortoise's iron grip.

"Oh no," said Tortoise, "you are going home with me this time without fail."

As before, the elders, hearing the boy's cry, rushed out of the huts.

"I see," said the boy's father. "It's our old friend, Tortoise, playing with the boy."

"I am not playing, sir," said Tortoise stiffly.

"What's the matter then?"

"In spite of my warning, you have not taught your boy to respect other people's palm fruits. That's what the matter is. And I have just told him that nothing—repeat, nothing—will stop me from dragging him to my country by the ears."

"Please cool down, my good friend," said the spirit. "I am sure we can settle the matter more peacefully than that. . . . What about . . . erm . . . another drum."

Tortoise pretended to think about it for a while with his head thrown back and his face turned upward.

"All right," he announced at long last. "But I want everybody to understand that this is the very last time I shall be persuaded to accept a drum for my flute—I mean to say, my fruit."

"We understand that perfectly well," said the spirit.

"Show me the drum!" said Tortoise in the tone of an emperor.

"This way, sir," said the spirit as he led the way to the back of one of the huts. It was just as Tortoise had imagined. There were scores of drums of various sizes hanging from wooden pegs driven into the mud wall.

"The choice is yours, sir," said the spirit with a wave of the arm toward the drums. Tortoise was overjoyed at the way things were turning out. The last time he was given a miserable little drum with a delicate skin. Now he had a chance to pick a drum befitting a king. So he marched up to the end of the hanging row of drums, looking at each as he passed, and finally pointing at the largest one of all.

"Fine," said the spirit, "that one it shall be. Will somebody get it down for our friend?"

So Tortoise took the drum from one of the spirits and hung it on his shoulder. He picked up the curved drumstick, said farewell to the spirits, and set out for home.

6

Tortoise was so pleased with himself that he whistled all the way up the seven great steps that led from the underworld. Out of the hole, at the foot of the palm tree, he paused to catch his breath. Then he realized that he was very hungry. He wanted to eat badly, but he also wanted to rush home and resume his interrupted coronation. He looked up at the sky for time and found to his surprise that the sun was still overhead just as it was when he went down the hole. Was it the same day or was it tomorrow or yesterday? He couldn't say. But whatever day, it was noon. So there was time to eat and also get home to his installation. He lifted the drum, which he had set down to rest his shoulder, and beat it gently: A strange and frightening noise issued from it—an ear-splitting scream followed by a short chant of hoarse male voices:

> *Pial'awo pialu mbala!*
> *Ufio!!*
> *Pial'awo pialu mbala!*
> *Ufio!!*

What happened next was even more frightening and strange. Masked spirits with bundles of whips appeared from nowhere and began rushing and jumping around and hitting at everything in their way. And they were soon followed by swarms of bees and wasps stinging away. Tortoise was so beaten and stung that he fell to the ground and passed out altogether and remained unconscious for a long time. When he opened his eyes again, it was night. And he was so bruised and swollen that his shell could hardly contain him. "What happened? And where am I?" he wondered. Slowly his memory began to come back to him, and with it a great fear. Where was the drum? And where were the masked spirits? Were they waiting in the darkness for him to wake up? Perhaps they were asleep and he should sneak away now before they woke up.

But his effort to move caused him such sharp pains that he fainted again, and did not wake up until the afternoon of the next day.

When he came to, he took in the situation quietly with his eyes. The wicked drum lay innocently now where he had dropped it. And heaps of broken whips lay scattered around. Everything else was normal: the palm tree of thrice four hundred fruits, a few ragged trees, a scorched countryside, a cloudless sky, and a burning sun. Satisfied that there was no immediate danger, Tortoise stretched his limbs and found that he could just about manage to crawl home slowly and pain-fully. But there was really no reason to hurry now, he thought. He had more time than he could use. So he went back to sleep for another two days to think things over and plan his future.

Tortoise's return to the Country of the Animals with the first drum had taken place at night. He had planned it that way so that no one would see him. But coming home now with the second drum he chose the middle of the afternoon. As he walked slowly and deliberately toward his compound lugging the great drum, he was seen by many animals. Some of them went out happily to greet him and escort him home, while others rushed away to their friends to report the news. By the evening, Tortoise's compound was full again and as noisy as usual. Very soon the chanting of the animals began.

> *WE! WANT! TOR! TOISE!!*
> *WE! WANT! TOR! TOISE!!*
> *WE! WANT! OUR! KING!!*
> *OUR! KING! OF! KINGS!!*

Tortoise, who had retired early to bed, got up again and went outside to speak to the animals. As soon as he emerged through the door of his hut the animals sent up a huge, deafening roar of applause. Tortoise held up his hand and there was immediate silence. He began to speak in a tired voice.

"My good people," he said, "I have made the journey as I promised you. And I have brought you a drum, a king of drums."

The animals clapped and cheered and jumped up and down. Tortoise held up his hand again.

"I had thought to rest tonight and then present the drum to you in the morning. . . ."

> *WE! WANT! IT! NOW!!*
> *WE! WANT! IT! NOW!!*
> *THE! KING! OF! DRUMS!!*

"But I see that you are impatient to see the drum," continued Tortoise, "and I can't say that I blame you. After all, you have tasted no food for many days now. So I will present the drum to you shortly." There was a huge ovation when he said this. He held up his hand and then continued.

"But I would be failing in my duty if I did not tell you something of the difficulties I had getting this drum. Some of you have already asked about the wounds all over my body. Well, my good people, you may remember I told you that it was no easy matter traveling to the land of spirits. There are terrible monsters and demons along the way. I braved them all for your sake and took whatever punishment they gave. I shall say no more at present because I am very tired and must take my rest. . . . But you may go ahead and have your dinner. I know I can trust you to conduct the dinner in an orderly fashion. In view of the accident we had with the last drum, I suggest that you appoint from among yourselves a new drummer with a lighter touch than our beloved Elephant." This produced much laughter among the animals. Tortoise left them laughing and went back to his hut and soon returned with the large new drum. The animals cheered wildly. "Enjoy yourselves," said Tortoise as he withdrew, waving. And he barred the door of his hut after him.

The animals elected Monkey the new State Drummer. But they did not want to offend Elephant too much and so they made him State Trumpeter and Retired Drummer. Everyone was satisfied. Monkey came forward and lifted the drum to his shoulder. The animals gave him a loud cheer. He bowed to them in return. And then he picked up the drumstick with great dignity and tapped the drum.

When Tortoise barred the door to his hut, he did not retire to bed as he said he would. Instead, he took his wife hurriedly out of the compound through a back exit deep into the bush behind his compound wall. His wife was surprised, but Tortoise dragged her along. "This is no time to explain," he said to her. "Everything will be clear to you later." And so they went deeper into the bush until they came to a huge rock in a dry riverbed and took cover under it.

As for the animals, what they saw that evening has never been fully told. Suffice it to say that they dragged themselves out of Tortoise's compound howling and bleeding. They scattered in every direction of the world and have never stopped running.

IN HARPY LAND

BY
Helen Adam

COLLAGES BY
HELEN ADAM

In Harpy Land, in Harpy Land,
The grapes are guarded with rose spines,
The roses revel on the vines.
Amazing roses on the vines
In Harpy Land!
And there the dreadful Harpy Queen,
My promised bride in world unseen,
Beckons me to her dark demesne,
With bloodstained hand.

Thick feathers when the Harpies fly
Smother the air, and shroud the sky.
All beauty fades for all must die.
To dust life blows.
In vain I travel time and space.
At any time, in every place,

Always I see the Harpy face

Behind the rose.

When she walks in the Harpy Wood
The trees cry out, and drip with blood.
The River Styx begins to flood
And trembling runs.
Out of its stream at dead of night
The day star rises blazing bright.
She is the priestess of that light
That dulls the sun's.

Across the River Styx I rowed.
A coal-black beauty was my load.
I led her to the Queen's abode
Hand warm in hand.
The Queen was drunk with Pluto's wine.
She stole my love by candle-shine.

Dark roses nod on every vine
In Harpy Land.

Learning I lack, but this I know
All things exist, and change, and grow,
Only for her to overthrow.
She flirts her wings

O'er battlefields of sumptuous red.

In charnel pits her feasts are spread.
She takes the outlawed to her bed,
And slaves, and kings.

Whate'er she plays with she destroys,
Delicious girls,

and laughing boys.

"The seeing eye," the singing voice,
The dancing feet.

No prayer avails, no strength of ours,
Not "Principalities and powers."

The whole creation she devours
It is her meat.

She changed me to a humble dog,

Then to a moth,

Then to a frog.

She burned me like a forest log
With lasting fire.
She flung my ashes east and west.
She flung my ashes east and west.
Still I was blest, still I was blest,
Who knew her for the loveliest,

The world's desire.

Oh! Harpy Land, Oh! Harpy Land,
Where Heaven and Hell go hand in hand.

The damned are blest. The blest are damned,
Still hand-in-hand.
At dead of night the day star shines
And there are roses on the vines.
The grapes are guarded with rose spines
In Harpy Land.
Bitter as death her grapes that grow
On thorny briars set thick, but Oh!
Her golden roses open slow,
Divinely bland.

And I am warned that if I wait
Till trumpets sound at Heaven's Gate,

I'll see her where she sits in state
At God's right hand.

SUCCESS:
AN ADMONITORY FABLE FOR YOUNG GIRLS

BY

Alice Adams

O nce in San Francisco there was
a little girl named Molly, who lived alone with her mother, Monica, who
was divorced. Their small house was quite near a large park, called the
Julius Kahn Playground, which had views of the Golden Gate Bridge,
as well as swings and slides and a sandbox and a huge playing field.

The park was fun, and Molly spent a lot of time
there, but her best, favorite days were when she and Monica went to art
museums, all over the city. Even when Molly was really little her mother
took her to see the great halls of paintings, which Molly loved. "At one
time I thought I wanted to be a painter," Monica sighed, as they wandered
through the De Young Museum, the Palace of the Legion of Honor, and
the San Francisco Museum of Art.

In kindergarten, like everyone else, Molly her-
self took up finger painting and crayon drawing, and she liked it very
much. She drew the Golden Gate Bridge, with fog coming through under
it, and cable cars, and the island for monkeys in the Fleishhacker Zoo. Her
teachers said her drawings were good, and they tacked them up on the
bulletin board.

Then six different things happened at once,
more or less, which were not exactly connected, but later, in Molly's
mind, they were always linked.

One, at the beginning of a certain summer,
Molly's two front baby teeth came out.

Two, Molly and Monica spent three weeks in a
cabin on Lake Tahoe, where Molly did drawings of the lake and the
mountains on the other side, some chipmunks and birds.

Three, a friend of Monica's came over and saw what Molly had done, and she said that Molly was sensational, so talented, maybe a genius.

Four, Monica told Molly not to take everything that people said too seriously.

Five, when they got home it turned out that Monica had forgotten to pack the art work that Molly had done.

The sixth and last event of that summer was that new teeth began to come in where the baby teeth had been, and the new ones looked as though they were going to be just slightly crooked, Monica said.

Molly, of course, thought about everything that had happened, feeling good about some things, bad about others, but she did not reach any serious conclusions. She went on going to school, working on paintings and drawings and sometimes modeling clay, and playing in the park in the afternoons. Sometimes Monica still took her to art shows, but Monica was more and more busy with Friends and Lovers.

Then one day at school the art teacher announced that she would be available for extra time and work on Thursday afternoons, if anyone wanted to stay, and she smiled at Molly, who understood that she was being especially invited.

At supper that night, Monica told her mother what she would be doing on Thursday afternoons, from now on. Monica smiled and said how nice, but then she remembered something else, and she frowned and said, "But you can't go this Thursday. I made an appointment at the orthodontist's for you, and actually he may want to see you on some following Thursdays. He's very busy."

"*I don't want an orthodontist . . . I want to paint!!!!!!!*"

This was the loudest thing that Molly had ever said, and they were both surprised.

Monica said, "But darling, we really have to see about your teeth. They have to be straight——"

"*I don't need straight teeth . . . I need to paint!!!!!!!*"

"But darling, when you're older—men . . . jobs . . . good impressions——"

"*I don't want men or jobs. Paint!!!!! I want to be a painter.*"

A terrible scene; we will skip the rest of it, and just say that Molly won.

She never went to the orthodontist, and she grew up with crooked teeth and a talent for painting, and, perhaps most important of all, with terrific, unshakable determination.

She became a successful painter, and a happy, good-looking woman, loved by her Lovers and Friends. The only person who ever objected to her teeth was, interestingly, a famous Art Critic named Irving (who, like her mother, had once wanted to be a painter). Irving said, "You know, if it weren't for your teeth, you'd be a beautiful woman," and he was equally rude about her painting. Molly didn't care.

MORAL: Do not listen to people who once wanted to do what you are doing very well.

THE FOUR APPLES

BY

Max Apple

J essica popped out of Debby's tummy and said, "Tell me a story, Dad." While a nurse wiped the other world from her eyes, I started to tell. All the kids from my own child-hood appeared. There was Bad Bernie throwing stones at people, Marky Fixler riding his purple bike, and his little brother Gonzalez trying to pedal a scooter alongside him. My sisters were there, too, dressing me up in their old clothes and pushing me around in a buggy. The stories made so much noise that the doctor told us to leave the hospital.

But the stories followed us home. They filled up the playpen and the yard. When Jessica ate, she mixed them with baby food and smeared her face and laughed. She threw the rubber-coated spoon at me and yelled "More stories."

So I told her about my grandma and the grand-ma stories brought in people with beards and funny clothes from Europe, people who were bakers and farmers and fishermen. And they made us feel lazy for not working as hard as they did. The new stories took up so much room that we had to move to a bigger house. Then just when all the stories and Jessica and Debby and I got comfortable in our new house, just then Sam popped out of Debby's tummy and said "Tell me a story, my own story not Jessica's, and make it about garbage, and tell it right this minute."

So for Sam, all the witches and monsters and heroes that I knew came to our house and they all made noises like the garbage truck and they all thought it was fine to crawl around without a diaper. All the witches and monsters and heroes liked to get together with Sam and Jessica to play water city. They turned the kitchen floor into the ocean so they could swim between the refrigerator and the stove. But when Sam got to be two, he said, "Enough baby stuff." He took out a long straw and sucked water city clean. He bought himself a TV with an antenna that reached the moon. He and Jessica found an old convertible and hired Mr. Rogers to drive it. They tied me to the back seat with spaghetti and fed me cheese sandwiches and beer as long as I kept telling them stories. When I complained, they pulled out the radio and stuck me into the dashboard.

Debby said "Enough stories, let them go to bed." Even Mr. Rogers got tired of driving so he swallowed the car and hid in the TV. Jessica and Sam hated bedtime until they discovered the secret of the thumb. Now they know that if they suck their thumb and curl their hair the stories will keep right on all night unless they have to stop for some water or apple juice. During the night, the stories crawl on the walls and hang from the ceiling. In the daytime, they make yucky food good. You can squeeze them into a lunchbox or let them get big and take over the whole playground. They're faster than running shoes.

When Jessica and Sam wake up, they put on clean clothes and push the old stories out the door. There, George the dog licks and smells them before he sends them down the street to Sally or Ilana, who are always sending us their stories, too.

At nursery school the kids trade stories like stocks and bonds. Jessica grows rich and corners the market. She hires Sam to protect her wealth. He stuffs a water pistol into his training pants. She and her staff of girls circle the playground gossiping, practicing numbers. They hold hands and are quiet around the boys. The stories pile up like snow. They fill the school, too. Finally, when Jessica learns to read, she files the stories into books where they fit just right. "It's a miracle," she tells Sam, but he's still suspicious. He saw three capital R's running down the page and had to squirt them. It's his job to tear out some of the pages and turn them upside down. He is very good at his work. Jessica tapes the words back in place.

Now that most of the stories behave and stay in the books, we have lots of room in the house. I tell only five new ones at bedtime. The kids suck their thumbs and turn those five into a hundred.

Debby comes home from work. She tells me her stories. I suck my pen and turn hers into new ones. Sam and Jessica roll off the mattress, George barks at the wind, the stories bounce off the walls.

WHO WILL GO TO HEAVEN?

A FABLE BY
Isaac Asimov

A certain sage was roused from contemplation by the arrival of a young man seeking enlightenment.

"Who will go to Heaven, Master?" asked the young man, reverently.

"Everyone, my son," said the sage.

The young man was astonished. 'What? Are none to be sent to the place of fire and torment?"

"Not one."

"But surely that is impossible."

"Not at all. It can be demonstrated very simply."

"Please do so, Master."

"Gladly, my son. I think it is fair to assume that at least one person will so live as to be worthy of Heaven."

"Certainly."

"And that one, in Heaven, will be perfectly happy."

"Undoubtedly."

"And surely the happiness would be tarnished, however slightly, and thus become less than perfect, if his or her friends and loved ones are absent; all the more so if he or she knows them to be in Hell."

"So it would seem to me, Master."

"Therefore, since we are agreed that in Heaven he or she will be perfectly happy, that must be because his or her friends and loved ones, without exception, are with him or her. If there are any of those among them who in their own right deserve to be in Hell, that does not matter, since the merits of the Good must surely outweigh the demerits of the Bad."

The young man nodded. "Yes, it is more important to reward the Good than to punish the Bad."

"And each of those friends and loved ones, may have friends and loved ones in addition to those of the original person in Heaven. So those, too, must be brought. And they will have friends and loved ones, and so on. And thus, finally, all human beings will be in Heaven, for who has ever lived who has never been befriended, never been loved."

"But then, if Hell is empty and has always been empty, Master, what purpose does it serve?"

"None. From which we reason that there is no Hell."

The young man frowned. "But if there is no Hell, and if all are translated to Heaven, for what purpose have we been placed on Earth? If this is not a testing ground to determine who deserves salvation and who damnation, what purpose our life?"

"From which we reason it has some other purpose."

"But, Master, if the purpose is not to judge who is worthy of Heaven, what is the use of Heaven?"

"From which we deduce, my son, that there is no Heaven either."

THE STORY OF BEOWULF

RETOLD BY

Gordon Ball

Once there was a young warrior named Beowulf. He lived nearly fifteen hundred years ago in the land of the Geats, which is now the southern part of Sweden bordering the Baltic Sea. Beowulf was the nephew of the King of Geatland, Hygelac, and so great things were expected of him: He was groomed to be a noble warrior and leader, an heir to the throne. Yet in his early youth he did not demonstrate great eagerness for battle, nor was he overly bold.

As Beowulf grew to manhood, a neighbor across the waters was afflicted by grievous trouble. King Hrothgar of Denmark, who had built the mightiest of castles, Hereot, was threatened nightly by a savage monster who came after dark to prey on his men, whom he often gobbled alive.

For twelve years the monster, whose name was Grendel, held such vicious sway over Hrothgar and his once-mighty men that they were scarcely able to sleep in peace.

When Beowulf heard of the hardship of Hrothgar and his warriors, he determined to aid them. With the approval of the king's counselors, he chose fourteen men and set sail with them for the land of the Danes.

When they arrived on the Danish coast, a coast guard spied them from his lookout, and wondered who these men in bright battle dress might be. He jumped onto his horse and galloped down to meet them. As he did so, he noticed that one of them commanded a special presence, so resplendent was he in his armor, so noble was he in his bearing. This one man was, of course, Beowulf.

The guard asked the fifteen men who they were

and what they intended. At the same time, he singled out Beowulf; he said he'd never seen a greater looking man on earth.

Beowulf answered him. He explained forthrightly that they were Geats and their mission was to relieve the Danes of their terrible, long-standing burden. This impressed the guard, and he led them to the magnificent hall, to Hrothgar's Hereot, the most splendid castle then built by man.

At Hereot, Beowulf and his men were greeted warmly by Hrothgar, who immediately ordered a feast prepared in the great banquet hall. The Geats and the Danes, Beowulf and his men and Hrothgar and his Queen and their men, all sat down together. As they drank mead and ate, the king's poet sang and recited poetry to the accompaniment of his harp. All were merry, and hope rose within long-stricken Hereot.

But one of the king's counselors, Unferth, became contentious after drinking much mead, and remonstrated Beowulf. "You, Beowulf," he challenged the young leader of the Geats, "are not of the caliber you'd like us to think. I know for a fact that when you were younger you engaged in a swimming endurance contest with another young man named Breca, from which Breca, not yourself, emerged the victor. You have by no means proven yourself a match for the likes of Grendel."

At these words Beowulf bridled some, but the noble Geat contained his anger. Without rancor, he pointed out that Unferth was drunk, and told the Danes of the swimming contest in his own words. He admitted it was a foolhardy, reckless exploit undertaken when he was in his teens, but he explained that he and Breca were side-by-side for five days and nights until the surging icy sea separated them. A sea monster clasped Beowulf and drew him into the deep, where other monsters waited. But Beowulf slew not only his captor but all of the flesh-hungry monsters with just a short knife and his bare hands. When he at last surfaced, the currents took him to another land, to Frisia. Breca had also safely reached shore, but he did not have to endure such rigors, such great challenges to his life. "Nor," concluded Beowulf, turning to his challenger, "have I heard the same of you."

This shut up Unferth. With much graciousness, Queen Welthow dispensed more mead, honoring the visiting warriors and their leader. As the night grew long, the banqueting ended and hosts and guests took to their bedding. As Beowulf removed his armor, he told his men that he would face Grendel unarmed, without shield or blade, so as not to take unfair advantage. Had any of the Danish host heard of this intention, they would of course have cautioned strongly against it, but they were already a-bed. Thus Beowulf lay down, shieldless and armorless, near the great door of the castle, to sleep and to await the coming of Grendel, the wicked ravager of men.

From the marshland, through the misty moors, his gleaming eyes lighting his way, Grendel skulked toward the great hall whose night joys he'd so often put to an abrupt end. As he came to the great door, he pulled it loose from its hinges with one quick tug of his clawed hand. Immediately, he saw one of Beowulf's companions resting by the door, and immediately, with his claws and jaws, he tore the young warrior apart and swallowed him at once.

Excited at the prospect of more prey, he approached the next Geat lit by the terrible light from his eyes. But for once, Grendel would not have his way; as soon as his claws dug into the resting warrior, he felt his own body seized in a grip he'd never known a man to give. Grendel had met Beowulf.

The two buffeted and tossed, tumbled and turned in furious battle that shook the walls of the castle. The Danes and the Geats both were roused, as if by an earthquake. In the darkness, they could see only what was lit by Grendel's eye-gleam. Beowulf continued to hold the monster in the mighty grip from which Grendel had known at the outset he would never escape with his life, try as he might. Yet the wicked ravager of men did manage to wrest himself free, but not without paying a mortal price: His shoulder snapped clean off in Beowulf's tight hands. The beaten monster ran, armless and bleeding, out from Hereot, across the dark moors, toward the sea pool where he and his lady lived at the end of the marshland.

High was hung the terrible arm, shoulder, and claw of Grendel when all of Hereot realized its visiting warrior had made good his boast. In the morning, many were the people from neighboring lands who came to witness the proof: Grendel had been defeated.

That night, there was much rejoicing at Hereot; King Hrothgar presented Beowulf and each of his companions with many gifts of armor, of jewels and rings. The poet sang as the Danes and Geats celebrated, drinking.

Meanwhile, across the moors, Grendel's lady brooded most sorely on the loss of her mate. Grendel had returned to their sea lair mortally wounded. Vowing vengeance, she crept from the marshes to Hereot.

When she arrived, the banquet-filled Danes and Geats lay asleep in the restful arms of triumph. This was the first time in twelve years that the Danes were without dread of a monster, but their relief was premature. Before they could reach their swords, she seized one of them, whose name was Aeschere; he was the King's dearest companion. As she fled their onslaught with her victim, she managed to wrest Grendel's claw from the rafters.

The Danes and Geats gathered together to lament this new misfortune and consider what to do next. King Hrothgar wept, but Beowulf cautioned him: "End your sorrow. Vengeance is better than eternal mourning. Each of us who lives his life on this earth will come to his end. It is best while living to fight for the glory of one's name; fame after death is the noblest goal."

They were Germanic warriors and they knew Beowulf spoke their true code. Seeking their vengeance, the Danes and Geats set out across the moors. Hrothgar's counselors had told him that people near the moors had once seen a pair of monsters, one looking to be male, the other female, stalking nearby. They were said to live in the sea at the end of the land, where wolves lived amid windy cliffs and trees overhung great precipices. The sea itself, his counselors told him, burned at night like a great torch.

They followed the monster's tracks through this treacherous region. As they came to the sea, the Danes trembled: High above the water on a rocky cliff was the head of Aeschere.

Fantastic sea monsters and snakes sported about on the water's surface: This was their home, when they were not harassing voyages across the wide seas. With his bow and arrow, mighty Beowulf shot one of them. He then fastened on all of his armor, and Unferth, the King's counselor who at first had challenged him, gave him a fine, magical sword named Hrunting. As he dove into the murky sea, Beowulf knew that this might be his fiercest battle yet.

Hours passed as he swam beneath the water's surface, until he discovered, in the muddy bottom, the terrible she-monster herself. She grasped Beowulf tight, but her claws could not pierce his armor. Holding him in her grip, she carried him to the cave hall that was her home. Beowulf landed a blow with the mighty sword, Hrunting, straight on her head, but it was futile. He threw it down and resolved to use his hands, but she had the advantage; she had him on his back. She struck at him with a dagger, but his armor protected him.

Suddenly, Beowulf saw hanging nearby on the cave's wall a great old sword, the work of giants long ago. With one quick reach he had it in hand and sent it cutting straight through his she-foe's neck. She fell back, blood-covered and lifeless.

Beowulf walked along the wall and saw the dead body of Grendel propped up in a corner. In a final act of vengeance, he cut the monster's head from his body and carried it out through the sea hall. The blade of the great ancient sword, having done its work, melted like ice, leaving only the hilt.

Meanwhile, up above the water the Danes and Geats had watched with sadder and sadder eyes as the morning passed without sign of their hero; only bloody bubbles rose to the surface to greet them. The Danes decided to leave the Geats to await their leader's body alone.

Then, when the sun was high overhead, Beowulf broke through the surface of the sea, clutching both the hilt of the sword and Grendel's huge, heavy head. The Geats rejoiced and thanked God. Before they could return to Hereot, they had to jam a spear through Grendel's head so that four men, two on each side, could carry it. Less would not do.

Back at Hereot, Beowulf explained that he had survived only through God's help, and presented the golden hilt to Hrothgar, telling the Danes they no longer needed to fear either monster.

King Hrothgar examined the hilt, on which was carved in runic letters the story of the Flood, of the battle between Good and Evil. Holding the hilt in his hand, Hrothgar addressed Beowulf. He praised his noble valor. He knew Beowulf would become leader of all his people, but warned him not to follow the example of the Danish king Heremod, who out of material wealth and pride became dissatisfied with his power, wanted more of it, hoarded his rings and treasures instead of giving them, and finally slew his counselors and companions. Hrothgar told Beowulf to place faith only in what was eternal, and reminded him that all men die, whether by sword, sickness, fire, disease, or old age.

He thanked Beowulf and invited him to their final feast, after which everyone went quickly to sleep, for at dawn the Geats would sail for home.

In the morning, Beowulf and Hrothgar exchanged parting words, and the king bestowed upon the Prince of the Geats still more gifts. As the Geats approached their ship, Beowulf presented the coast guard who'd first met them with a gold sword.

Soon, Beowulf and his men reached the land of their kin, and Beowulf presented himself at the throne of his uncle, King Hygelac. Beowulf reported his exploits in the most modest terms, and brought in the treasure he had won for his lord—the shining armor and four fine horses Hrothgar had given him as well. To the Queen, Beowulf gave a neck ornament given him by Hrothgar's Queen.

Great was the banquet that followed in the court of the Geats.

Time passed; Hygelac died; his wife, Hygd, Beowulf's aunt, asked him to become king. Beowulf declined, because he knew there was a son, Heardred, to whom he felt the crown should go. Heardred became king, but died in battle against the Swedes. Beowulf then did ascend to throne, and ruled well for fifty years, until a dragon was disturbed and began to wreak terror on the Geats.

A household retainer who was fleeing his lord discovered a barrow or cave tower within the woods. Entering, he saw a store of great treasure, which had been hidden by men a thousand years ago who placed a curse on anyone who plundered it. At the sight the retainer was awe-struck, and panicked. Impulsively, he seized a jeweled cup and returned to his master, offering it to him as a compact.

But the dragon discovered the theft and began to stalk the countryside, breathing fire, uprooting trees. Beowulf's own castle burned to the ground. The dragon had been peaceable until the theft; no one knew of his existence, for he slept near his treasure by day and by night raised his mighty wings and flew for joy in the sky. Now, after the theft, he waged fierce war against the family of man.

Beowulf, though now quite old, knew that he would have to face the dragon to save his land and people. He ordered an iron shield built especially for this battle, for he knew that a wooden one would be turned to ashes by the dragon's fiery breath. Choosing a dozen men to go with him, Beowulf headed for the dragon's barrow. As he did so, he felt age in his body, which was not as strong as his armor. He turned to his followers and recited his career, everything he had worked for, then asked them to stand nearby, atop a hill, as he approached the barrow.

The dragon had sensed his coming, and sprang out from his dwelling. His ferocious flames instantly scorched Beowulf's iron shield. The leader of the Geats knew that for once fate was not with him, yet he fought with great resolution. He struck the dragon's side with his sword, and it drew blood, but not without beginning to crack.

Wounded, the dragon leaped in pain, sending more flames from his furious mouth. The Geatish warriors, on seeing the great multicolored dragon and the poor figure Beowulf cut against it, did not come to the aid of their lord, but instead fled toward nearby woods. All did so except one, that is. His name was Wiglaf, and he was a distant relative of the King. He started to flee with the others, but checked himself and called to them. He reminded them of the boasts they'd made when drinking in the mead hall, of Beowulf giving them the swords and armor with which they were now fleeing. He urged them to aid their brave lord in his time of need, but none turned to come with him.

Wiglaf quickly leaped into the midst of battle with Beowulf, fighting side by side, dodging the dragon's deadly fumes. Wiglaf's wooden shield turned to ashes, and he leaped under Beowulf's. The King took one mighty swing with his sword against the beast's head, and though it wounded the dragon even more, the sword broke apart. The dragon retaliated by digging his tusks deep into the neck of Beowulf, whose blood fell like rain.

Wiglaf then quickly moved under the dragon's belly and plunged his own ancestral sword into the great foe's soft underside. The dragon's flames began to subside. Beowulf, bleeding, drew his dagger and cut the beast in half; it fell dead.

But the King of the Geats was wounded; he could tell from the swelling in his neck that the dragon's fangs were poisonous. As he lay dying, Beowulf asked that Wiglaf run for the treasure, that he might gaze upon what he'd won for his people before departing.

When Wiglaf returned with all the gleaming treasure he could carry, Beowulf lay gasping for breath. Wiglaf sprinkled water on his King, reviving him enough to speak. Beowulf gave thanks to his Lord for all He'd given him, and he asked Wiglaf that a monument, a tower, be built which would contain his ashes. It would be on the highest promontory next to the sea, called Beowulf's Tower, visible from afar, a guide and inspiration for all men at sea. Beowulf gave Wiglaf his helmet, ring, and armor, then followed the path of his ancestors.

Wiglaf stood alone; Beowulf lay dead to one side and the dragon to the other. Those men who had fled the battle returned from the forest, ashamed. Wiglaf admonished them, ruefully, for their disgraceful act. He then ordered a messenger to ride to the rest of the Geatish warriors, who were waiting across the cliff for word of their King.

The rider reached them and gave them the news, predicting terrible fighting from their nearby enemies, the Franks, the Frisians, and the Swedes, once they learned the Geats were without Beowulf, who had kept enemies away for fifty years. Grievous was the messenger's prophecy: warriors would no longer waken to the harp but to the dark raven, eager for the spoils of slaughter.

The warriors followed the messenger back to the shoreline next to the barrow, where they saw the two lifeless bodies. Wiglaf addressed them, told them of Beowulf's wish for a tower. He ordered the funeral pyre be made ready, and then led seven of the Geats to the dragon's barrow. With the light of a torch, they saw gold and silver rotting in the earth, and many cups, plates, and rings. They carried out as much as they could, then rolled the dragon into the sea. They loaded the treasure on the wagon carrying the body of their King, and brought it down to the shore, to the pyre.

The pyre was stacked high with wood, and hung with helmets and armor. The warriors, weeping, laid Beowulf atop the wood and kindled the fire. Lamentations rose to the sky, mingled with the swirling flames and smoke. An old woman with braided hair sang a song of woe and misfortune to come as the fire consumed all that was left of Beowulf.

The Geats then built the tower in ten days, sealing inside the ashes of their departed lord. In it they also placed all the treasure won from the dragon's barrow—it was all returned to earth, to remain as useless as it ever was. Twelve of the most noble Geats rode solemnly around the tower, praising their lord, who was bettered by no man. There had never been a leader so gentle to his people, and so eager for praise.

TWO POEMS

BY
Paulé Bartón

THIRST SONG

There was a slow donkey
day. Oh the boy
went to the water bird
to beg a drink.

"Just one feather
of your good water, please?"
he said. But the water bird
soaked into the ground.

It was a sad day.
The boy's heart
donkeyed down to the sea.

SONG OF DUSK

All there is left of the sun is now
in the beard of my goat, the small
brushfire of my goat's beard.
This is why he rubs it in the sand.

All over the island goats
are putting out the sun.

—Translated by Howard Norman

THE ELEPHANTS' GRAVEYARD

BY
Peter Beard

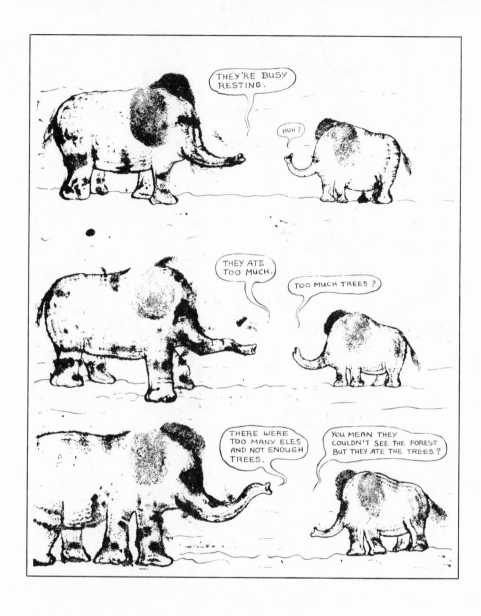

A BITING DOG

BY
Ann Beattie
ILLUSTRATED BY
DAVID GATES

A biting dog approaches a non-violent dog. The nonviolent dog lies down and plays dead. The biting dog sniffs and walks away. The other dog is really dead.

A man dies and is buried. A biting dog comes faithfully each morning to lie by the man's headstone. The dead man was not the biting dog's master.

Can you find three biting dogs in this picture?

A rare-record collector is on his way home, having just purchased a mint copy of "Zulu's Ball" by King Oliver and his Creole Jazz Band. Passing an alley, he is rushed by a biting dog. He drops the record. The biting dog rounds the corner, with a maniacal grin on his face.

Interrogation of a conscientious objector:
Q. Do you mean that if a biting dog came at you, you would not defend yourself?
A: I would try to reason with it.

DANGEROUS ENEMIES

BY

Bill Berkson

ILLUSTRATED BY
BILL BERKSON

Larry Fagin and I were calmly walking along. He was humming some march and swinging his stick. Suddenly, as if from nowhere, a dog appeared, then another, and still another—in all about fifteen sheep dogs, who began barking at us. Larry imprudently flung a stone at them and they immediately sprang at us.

They were Kurd sheep dogs, very vicious, and in another moment they would have torn us apart if I had not instinctively pulled Larry down and made him sit beside me on the road. Just because we sat down the dogs stopped barking and springing at us; surrounding us, they also sat down.

KITTY

BY

Paul Bowles

Kitty lived in a medium-sized house with a big garden around it. She loved some things, like picnics and going to the circus, and she hated other things, like school and going to the dentist's.

One day she asked her mother: "Why is my name Kitty?"

"Your name is really Catherine," her mother said. "We just call you Kitty."

This reply did not satisfy Kitty, and she decided that her mother did not want to tell her the truth. This made her think even more about her name. Finally, she thought she had the answer. Her name was Kitty because some day she was going to grow up into a cat. She felt proud of herself for having found this out, and she began to look into the mirror to see if perhaps she was beginning to look like a cat, or at least like a kitten.

For a long time she could see nothing at all but her own pink face. But one day when she went up to the glass she could hardly believe what she saw, for around her mouth tiny gray whiskers were beginning to sprout. She jumped up and down with delight, and waited for her mother to say something about them. Her mother, however, had no time for such things, and so she noticed nothing.

Each day when Kitty looked at her reflection she saw more wonderful changes. Slowly the whiskers grew longer and stood out farther from her face, and a soft gray fur started to cover her skin. Her ears grew pointed and she had soft pads on the palms of her hands and the soles of her feet. All this seemed too good to be true, and Kitty was sad to find that nobody had said a word about the marvelous change in her. One day as she was playing she turned to her mother and said: "Meow. I'm Kitty. Do you like the color of my fur?"

"I don't know," her mother said. "What color is it?"

"It's gray!"

"Oh, gray. Very pretty," said her mother, and Kitty saw with a sinking heart that she did not care what color the fur was.

After that, she tried to make several neighbors remark on her fine whiskers, her velvety ears, and her short fluffy tail, and they all agreed that these things were very nice, and then paid no more attention to them. Kitty did not care too much. If *they* could not see how different she had become, at least she herself could.

One summer morning when Kitty awoke, she discovered that her fingernails and toenails had been replaced by splendid new pearly gray claws that she could stick out or pull in as she chose. She jumped out of bed and ran into the garden. It was still very early. Her mother and father were asleep, but there were some birds walking around on the lawn.

She slipped behind some bushes and watched. After a long time, she began to crawl forward. The branches caught her nightgown, so she tore it off. When one of the birds came very close to her, she sprang forward and caught it. And at that moment she knew that she was no longer a girl at all, and that she would never have to be one again.

The bird tasted good, but she decided not to eat it. Instead, she rolled on her back in the sun and licked her paws. Then she sat up and washed her face. After a while, she thought she would go over to Mrs. Tinsley's house and see if she could get some breakfast, so she climbed up to the top of the wall and ran quickly along it to the roof of the garage. From there, she scrambled down the trellis into Mrs. Tinsley's backyard. She heard sounds in the kitchen, so she went up to the screen door and looked in. Then she said: "Meow." She had to keep saying it for quite a while before Mrs. Tinsley came and saw her.

"Well, if that isn't the cutest kitten!" Mrs. Tinsley said, and she called to her husband and her sister. They came and saw the small gray kitten with one paw raised, scratching at the screen. Of course they let her in, and soon Kitty was lapping up a saucer full of milk. She spent the day sleeping, curled up on a cushion, and in the evening she was given a bowl of delicious raw liver.

After dinner, she decided to go back home. Mr. Tinsley saw her at the kitchen door, but instead of opening the door for her, he picked her up and locked her into the cellar. This was not at all what Kitty wanted, and she cried all night.

In the morning, they let her go upstairs and gave her a big bowl of milk. When she had drunk it, she waited in the kitchen until Mrs. Tinsley opened the door to go out into the yard. Then she ran as fast as she could between Mrs. Tinsley's feet and climbed up onto the roof of the garage. She looked down at Mrs. Tinsley, who was calling: "Kitty, Kitty, Kitty." Then she turned and ran the other way. Soon she was in her own garden. She went up to all the doors and looked in. There were policemen inside the house with her mother and father. They were holding Kitty's torn nightgown in their hands, and her mother was crying and sobbing. No one paid the slightest attention to Kitty.

She went sadly back to Mrs. Tinsley's house, and there she stayed for many weeks. Sometimes she would go over to her own house and peek again through the doors, and often she saw her mother or her father. But they looked very different from the way they had looked before, and even if they noticed her, they never came to the door to let her in.

It was nice not having to go to school, and Mr. and Mrs. Tinsley were very good to her, but Kitty loved her mother and father more than she could love anyone else, and she wanted to be with them.

Mr. and Mrs. Tinsley let her go out whenever she pleased now, because she always came back. She would go to her house at night and look in through the window to see her father sitting alone reading the paper. This was how she knew that her mother had gone away. Even if she cried and pushed her claws against the window, her father paid no attention to her, and she knew that he would never let her in. Only her mother would do that. She would come and open the door and take her in her arms and rub the fur on her forehead and kiss her.

One day several months later when Kitty climbed over the wall into her own garden, she saw her mother sitting in a chair outside. She looked much better, almost the way she used to look. Kitty walked slowly toward her mother over the grass, holding her tail in the air. Her mother sat up straighter, watching as she came nearer. Then she put out her hand and wriggled her fingers at Kitty. "Well, the pretty pussycat," she said. "Where did *you* come from?"

Kitty went near enough so that her mother could rub her head and scratch her cheeks. She waved her tail and purred with delight as she felt her mother's fingers stroking her fur. Then she jumped up into her mother's lap and lay curled up there, working her claws joyously in and out. After a long time, her mother lifted her up and held her against her face, and then she carried her into the house.

That evening, Kitty lay happily in her mother's lap. She did not want to try her father's lap because she was afraid he might push her off. Besides, she could see that it would not be very comfortable.

Kitty knew that her mother already loved her, and that her father would learn to love her. At last she was living exactly the life she always had wished for. Sometimes, she thought it would be nice if she could make them understand that she was really Kitty, but she knew there was no way of doing that. She never heard them say the word *Kitty* again. Instead, because her fur was so long and fine that when she moved she seemed to be floating, they named her Feather. She had no lessons to worry about, she never had to go to the dentist's, and she no longer had to wonder whether her mother was telling her the truth or not, because she knew the truth. She was Kitty, and she was happy.

NIGHT

BY

Joe Brainard

Day, you have gone and done it again!

Night is a set period of time—just like day—only darker: to say nothing of *black!*

Night is when all the carrots we have eaten are supposed to help us see better.

Night is when the stars come out to dazzle us, should we happen to be looking up.

Night is when the moon comes out to govern the stars. And to shimmer upon our lakes, and other large bodies of water, in long horizontal "strips" that tingle and glitter, with each little ripple, of each little wave, about which so many songs have been written, if too numerous to remember.

What *I* remember most about night when *I* was a kid is scary noises. Cold sheets in the winter time. Soft pajamas with feet. And—sometimes—playing "Doctor" when a friend would spend the night.

I remember "Sleep tight, and don't let the bedbugs bite." And wonderful dreams of being able to fly.

I remember, more often than not, falling asleep before I got to "Amen."

I remember the sliver of light that comes into your room from the crack under the door from the light out in the hall.

I remember the "z-z-z" of saws sawing wood in balloons in cartoon strips.

I remember being scared to death, in summer camp, that I'd forget I was on the top bunk in the morning and . . . well, you can imagine: (bonk!).

I remember counting to ten before making myself jump out of bed on cold mornings.

I remember begging to be able to stay up for "Just five more minutes, *please!*"

I remember that little jerk you give (like falling through space) just before going to sleep.

I remember the sand man, and the tooth fairy. But I don't think I ever really believed in them. Do you?

And—golly—I just remembered: I haven't woken up with my eyelashes glued together with that sticky stuff from the corner of your eyes in . . . I don't know how long.

All this, of course, was a long time ago. Before you were born. Before outer-space travel. Before men on the moon. Before we discovered that all there really is up there is dust and rocks. (Z-z-z.) Perhaps the moon had more of a face then. Especially if you squinted.

But do things really change all that much? You tell me.

My name is Joe Brainard (Howdy Folks!) and I'm thirty-six years old. But let me warn you in advance that you never really feel like a "grown-up." Any more than you probably feel like a "kid." At least, I never did. Except, of course, when it was convenient to. (If you know what I mean.) At any rate, enough of this chit-chat. Let's go back to our subject: *Night.*

Night is when ghost stories are told around campfires. Usually after a weenie roast. With black marshmallows all warm and mushy inside.

Night is when—looking out of windows—we sometimes jump at seeing ourselves.

Night is when thunder and lightning has a way of . . . scaring the shit out of us!

Night is when babies in cradles get to be la-la-byed, nipples inserted into mouths. When angry parents have to keep getting up in the middle of the night because the little brat wants *another* glass of "wa-wa."

A time for father to read newspapers in comfortable chairs. And to pet the dog at his feet who brought him his slippers. Or—be it wife—heavier petting may be required (snicker-snicker) if behind closed doors. *If* she doesn't have a headache.

Night is a time for families in living rooms all across this great nation of ours to gather in around the boob tube to complain about "poor programming." To fiddle around with tuning knobs. To adjust antennas. To fight (or draw straws?) over which program to watch. And to rush to the kitchen for munchies during commercial station breaks.

Night is a time for baby-sitters, and homework, and cocktail parties: where the adults meet to "let it all hang out." Where everybody stands up to mingle. And everybody talks to each other all at once. Smoke fills the room. (Cough-cough.) They rattle their ice cubes around in their glasses, when they don't know what else to do. And they laugh a lot. Especially when a lampshade makes its appearance as a hat. Which usually means it's time to go. (The party's over.) Time to go home and get some shut-eye. So tomorrow won't be a total wipe-out. Because— you know—a day is not for keeps either.

And so, be it work, or school, or what have you—the important thing is simply to enjoy it. To get out of a day all that you can. Even to make a real effort, if that's what it takes. Because time sure does fly. And life is much too precious to waste. Because—as we know—it's not for keeps either!

THE
ANCIENT SADNESS
OF ROBINS

BY
Harold Brodkey

ILLUSTRATED BY
HAROLD BRODKEY

Robins give an altered call when it rains.
—D. Gruenau

Robins ornament
a lawn, a noon, a firmament.
> They perch and preen
> and summer-sing
and in the summer rain
> they alter notes for sadder sound
> while leaves drip rain upon the ground
> and the gray-speckled air is frail
> and threaded through with moody song.

IN OUR TOWN

BY

Michael Brownstein

Men walk more slowly than women in our town because there is less for them to see. They run their fingers across the surfaces of the shop windows and doorframes like blind persons, although of course they aren't blind. It's just that with their eyes they're employed throughout their lives in "seeing straight." Seeing straight is the livelihood of men in our town—they support their families, go on vacations, and build a secure future for their children by looking narrowly ahead. Thus, all the rest of us know what they're doing at any given time and can plot the future based on the impeccable performances of these men in their present moment. This, incidentally, is where the word *straightforward* comes from. In our town, the highest value is accorded to those who are literally and precisely straightforward. As long as they stand looking straight ahead (it's almost like a game and, indeed, started originally, I am told, as one of the earliest assaults on the *Guinness Book of World Records*), the town can plot its future in a fairly confident manner and thereby make the estimates necessary for dealing successfully with any needs or problems that might arise. This seems to work out well enough.

Next summer, for example, instead of the annual Fourth of July town picnic and fireworks display at the park down by the river, specially strong red, white, and blue nylon fishnets will be draped over the entire area. All our homes and schools and offices will be covered tightly. Then the Vegetarians from across the ocean will come, landing in their sleek jet airplanes, and in a quiet ceremony just outside the town limits will carry on their age-old debate whether or not Vegetarians are allowed to eat fish. Not a single firecracker will be allowed to go off. After a final roll call and voice vote, accompanied by the playing of the Vegetarian National Anthem on reed flutes and rhubarb-leaf drums, they will decide if they will eat us. Sentiment in our town, as far as I can make out, is that we hope they don't eat us just yet, because there's a general feeling that one important piece of business affecting all of us still has to be resolved. After that the Vegetarians will be free to pass the tartar sauce and forks!

But this piece of business is actually a sensitive problem everyone believes will take a long while to solve. And that's the problem of what the women in our town should be doing while all the men stare straight ahead. Some say girls from the seventh grade up should be trained to see as much as possible, since the boys are narrowing down and narrowing down.

"Let them look over the place, stare wildly at everything inside shop windows and doorframes, and generally peer at whatever they want," some citizens say. "Girls have a golden opportunity to become our finest detectives! They'll be the golden retrievers of our future, leading lives of unparalleled adventure and discovery. The women would be tomorrow's heroes for their men!"

Others, however, are of the opinion that starting even earlier than the boys, in the fifth or even fourth grade, girls should be trained to carry on their mothers' traditional occupation of filling shop windows with bright, colorful objects and standing in striking or soothing poses in the doorways of their homes. That way, men can continue to be straightforward, reassured by the sense they'll have as they stare straight ahead of all the colorful things taking place around them. Men will continue, therefore, to develop the peripheral vision they first became aware of by playing basketball in their youth. Proponents of this argument are quite insistent on this point. If the men in our town do not sense wonderful things going on around them, even if they cannot see them, who knows how they might react! The uncertainty would be demoralizing, they might even break rank and run in all directions, and then where would we be? How would the town be able to decide what the future will bring and make the necessary plans? How would we be able to "take precautions"?

Personally, I think, in spite of the numerous vocal supporters of this latter viewpoint, that when the final vote is tallied, girls will be allowed to look wherever they like, in spite of any problems this will cause. Not too many people are willing to admit it, but there always has existed a very strong desire here for something different —for change of any kind. In fact, as far as I can tell, the only reason we haven't decided all this a long time ago is that we know the Fourth of July would be at most 364 days away, and then we'd find ourselves at the mercy of the Vegetarians and their awful verdict. We're not at all prepared for the possibility of our whole town and everybody in it being transformed into one gigantic fish. Nobody's crazy about being eaten alive at this point. Our sense of modesty somehow just won't allow it.

MISS MINNIE AND HER NEW HAIRDO

BY

Ed Bullins

Miss Minnie lives in the Bronx. She is a little girl whose father named her Miss Minnie. When it came time for Miss Minnie to begin school, she thought that her hair would look best in a "natural" style.

"You are too young for an Afro," her mother told her.

"Awww, honey, Minnie would look adorable in one," her father later told her mother.

But her mother was convinced that Minnie wasn't ready yet for that fashion.

So Miss Minnie started school and she liked it. She learned to draw with the crayons. And she learned to paint with the water-colors. And to sing her ABC's and to drink all her milk and take a nap before the big yellow school bus came to take her home.

She was very happy at her school until one day a new student came. The new student was very pretty and had bright eyes. She also had an Afro hairstyle and looked very charming.

Miss Minnie made friends quickly with the new little girl but didn't tell her that she wanted a "natural" hairdo, too.

"No, Minnie," her mother told her that night. "I don't want to talk to you again about it. You are too young for a 'natural.' "

The next morning, before the school bus came to get her, Miss Minnie got the scissors from her mother's sewing box. Her mother was in the bathroom bathing her little brother, Baby Boy, so she did not know that Minnie was cutting her hair.

When Miss Minnie's mother came into the room, she saw that Minnie had cut a patch from the center of her hair clear to the scalp.

"Oh, Minnie, what am I going to do? You've ruined your hair," her mother said. Then Mother took the scissors and cut off all of Minnie's hair to even it out, not even leaving a little fuzz on top.

That day Miss Minnie stayed home from school. Mother didn't feel well; she cried and cried. And Miss Minnie kept feeling her bald head and looking at herself in the mirror.

"She's pretty!" Daddy said to Minnie's mother that night.

"Oh, don't say that," her mother said. "Her hair's ruined."

"No, honey," her father said. "She's really attractive. And besides, it's the new style."

Miss Minnie's mother and father were happy then. They bought some ice cream and had a little party for Miss Minnie and her new hairdo. Baby Boy ate his ice cream fast and then tried to reach Minnie's. When Miss Minnie pulled her bowl away, Baby Boy struck Minnie on her bald head with his large spoon. But that didn't hurt too much. And Minnie forgave him. It was a nice party.

Next day when the bus came, Miss Minnie was waiting, wearing her large, floppy, red Minnie Mouse hat that her daddy had bought her. When she got to school, Miss Minnie's teacher told everyone to take their hats and coats off. Minnie took her hat off and everyone gasped. Some of the students even tried to touch her head. But then the teacher said:

"Minnie! How pretty you look with your new hairstyle. Did you know that many African women wear their hair in that fashion? Even the Egyptian queens wore their heads like that. My, my, Minnie, you look as beautiful as Cleopatra, the Queen of the Nile."

Miss Minnie liked what her teacher said. Her classmates said they liked her bald head. And her friend with the "natural" said that she wished that she had a bald head just like Minnie's.

That evening, Miss Minnie told her mother how happy she was that she didn't get an Afro. And her mother kissed her and showed her two little gold earrings that she had just bought for Miss Minnie, since she had become quite a little lady of fashion and could now wear her own jewelry as most little queens do.

NICANOR

BY

Reed Bye

Nicanor of the Yellow Plume
rides into a meadow, flowers
like lusty bravos waving.
He dismounts to take a nap,
his horse stands over eating daisies.
A hawk "makes lazy circles" high above.
When the breeze turns cool & the light darkens
Nicanor wakes and rides away
with a grateful nod to the meadow.

A fish for dinner.
A swim in the river, Nicanor
surrenders the magnificent Plume,
the current carrying it away downstream.
He remains
years without horse or girlfriend,
his heart fills up with love.

He learns the ways of the owl
with enormous yellow eyes.
To move silently in the air.
In the river he could be a fish.

The following years, in which he leaves
the river to travel
remain clouded in speculation.
Some say he roamed the icy tundra
for six years living on lichen.

All anyone knows, without knowing why
is that it was this time
                    the carved bone figurines
referred to as Nik-O-Noor by the northern people
found their niche in the igloo wall.
Here is a song these people sing
as they prepare the oil they burn in their lamps,
whose little flames, like the low arctic sun,
remind them of Nicanor's Yellow Plume,
his generous spirit:

> Hail, hail Nik-O-Noor
> though you have gone away
> We still sing this song to you
> on long, dark winter days
>
> When we are feeling tired
> and the walrus have all run
> We see your yellow feather poking
> over the horizon
>
> When we are feeling hungry
> our tempers growing short
> And the fish swims off with the harpoon
> and we have to eat the gorse
>
> We remember you then Nik-O-Noor
> how they say you smiled
> On bad days when the fishline broke
> with the weather getting wild
>
> We don't forget you Nik-O-Noor
> we've grown out of your care
> And it grows in us everyday
> your plume is in the air

THE
YOUNG
BLASPHEMER

BY

Hortense Calisher

Our bible, hung leathery
With lamentation,
Lifted me
Rung by Sunday rung
Into our nation,
The family——

Where I walked, blessed
With sorrow,
And being thorough
Jew,
With my cousin Jesus, who
Was also Christ.

WHEN

BY

Andrei Codrescu

Once upon a time when there was no time,
when no one had any need for time because there was plenty of it,
when time was an idea whose time hadn't come,
when the pear tree produced peaches or toy trucks,
when fleas jumped into the sky wearing very heavy shoes,
when everybody ate what they cooked and scientists were always sick
because they had to eat bombs,
when dogs and cats were on the best of terms
and men and women never fought pitched battles
under the pitched tent,
when children never took baths because they were always swimming,
there lived a very old storyteller
in a village high in the mountains
who told a very long story
day and night.
No one knew when he had begun telling this story
because he was always telling it
and you could drop by his house and listen to some of it
and then come back when you were old yourself
and listen to some more of it.
When I heard him the story hadn't even begun because he was
still busy telling when the story began.
Maybe, one day, we should drop in on him and listen some more,
maybe he has begun.
We will, okay, one day, when we have the time.

EATING CROW

BY

John N. Cole

It began with the automobile. Before the motorcar, there were horses. Every now and then as they trotted along country roads and city streets, pulling sulkies, carts, and carriages, a horse would squish a beetle or an ant. But, by and large, the casual mortality rate on the road was low during the age of horses. Not even the most flighty mare or the most plodding draft horse really wanted to put its hoof on a fellow creature. If a puppy, or rabbit, or chicken ran into the road, a horse would do everything it could (sometimes including upsetting the cart) to avoid a collision.

Not so with the auto. From the day the first four-wheeled machine went chattering and rattling and chuffing along the road, animals everywhere were threatened. There are few existing records, but it is known at least one (dead) chicken was found in the brass radiator grille of the first Bugatti ever tested on a road leading to Milan. About the same time, Henry Ford was being yelled at by an irate farmer who wanted to know what the inventor was going to do about the piglet that had been struck (dead) by the right front wheel of Mr. Ford's first model T.

Mr. Ford gave the farmer a share of stock in the Ford Motor Company and told him not to worry about his piglet. "There are more important things afoot," Mr. Ford said, and went back to work perfecting the Model T gear linkage.

Soon, Fords were rolling off the assembly lines. While Bugattis were still being built by hand, Fords were being mass-produced as America led the way toward showing the rest of the world how an industrial giant could be created in an essentially agricultural society. Taking their cue from Ford, Buicks, Hupmobiles, Studebakers, and Stutz Bearcats also came rolling off the assembly lines. In a few years, so many farm animals and so many wild creatures were getting splatted on the highways that no one gave it a thought anymore. After a while, the idea that a farmer was given a share of stock in the Ford Motor Company because his piglet had been struck (dead) seemed like a joke.

Guinea hens, roosters, spaniels, coon cats, turkeys, ewes, and wandering squab were being kabonged into never-never land any time they left the farm and tried to cross the road. And, if a highway wound through the woods or meadows, chipmunks, black snakes, partridge, porcupines, and stinky skunks were flattened like doormats whenever they ventured from their natural habitat.

From coast to coast the great American automobile went thumping and crunching and splatting its way through America's wild and domestic animal families. Soon, for everyone except the crows, the sight of carcasses on the asphalt became a way of life.

For the crows, the carcasses were a windfall. As scavengers—and smart ones, at that—the crows soon learned that America's automakers had served them up a new protein bonanza.

In the age of the horse, and for all time before, crows had a difficult time finding good meat. They would try robbing the nests of other birds; fresh eggs, after all, are a tasty protein source. But spunky smaller birds, like the kingbird and the redwing, raised so much ruckus whenever a crow tried stealing eggs that, more often than not, the crow would give it up and fly away, trying to pretend nothing much was happening even though the kingbirds and the redwings were dive bombing, trying to put out the crow's eyes with their sharp, little beaks.

Crows could only take so much of that. And they obviously weren't big enough to tackle a live coon cat, or a wild porcupine. They learned to live within the limits of their own reality, eating grain, an egg every now and then, and perhaps an ant or a beetle whenever they could find one that had been squished inadvertently by a horse.

Then one morning, crows heard a new chattering and rattling and chuffing along the country roads, and it wasn't long before every crow in America knew where to go when it needed some high-protein meat. Crows soon learned to live by the side of the road. Instead of having to go out and hunt for their breakfast, they had only to wait for a merry Oldsmobile to come whooshing along and put the bumpers to a gray squirrel or a cottontail. Then, for crows, the pickings were good.

Soon, Americans had more cars than all the rest of the world put together. This was a nation on wheels, and nobody liked it better than the crows. The animals being kayoed right and left didn't cotton to it much, but there wasn't much they could do about it after they had been compressed by a Firestone Steel-Cord Radial 500.

Just as human beings had done over the generations—as each generation was better nourished—crows began to grow. The new diet, the abundance of food with the decrease in hard labor which the mass-production system had brought, enabled each of the crow's succeeding generations to be a trifle larger than the last. Wingspans were a bit broader and bodies a bit heavier, year after year. As long as Darts and Chargers and Cougars and Impalas roared along the thruways, crows didn't have to worry about a thing. The best crow diet was being served up to them every day on concrete platters.

Measured against human concepts of time, the change in the overall size of crows was hardly noticed. Every now and then, a person who had a particular interest in crows, an ornithologist perhaps, would say something like, "Evelyn, have you noticed? Crows seem to be getting larger." But that was about as far as it got. The crows didn't grow fast enough to make the headlines, or the Walter Cronkite news.

But make no mistake about it, they were not only getting larger, but bigger, too. There were many times back in the seventies and eighties when amateur birdwatchers reported the sighting of bald eagles (the national bird, thought to be in danger of extinction) when really what they had seen was one of the larger crows.

It was almost the turn of the century when the ornithologist said, "Evelyn, I swear to God, I saw a crow today that looked bigger than an eagle."

"That's nice, Gerhardt," Evelyn said.

Yet, just as Gerhardt was about to begin to apply for a government grant to pursue a year's research into the apparent increase in the stature of the common crow, the birds fell upon hard times. Oil had at last run out. Saudi Arabia, the North Slope, the North Sea, the Canadian Tarpits, the Mexico Bonanza, and the Continental Shelf—all the oil fields everywhere on the globe had been discovered and depleted. There was simply no more oil to be had.

This information did make the Walter Cronkite news, and as soon as it did the price of gasoline went to $200 a gallon. As expected, this kept most of middle-class America off the roads. Only trucks, buses, and the Rolls-Royces and Mercedes of the power elite were still rolling. Death rates among wild and domestic animals dipped sharply. Some crows were saying the bottom had dropped out of the meat supply altogether. They used terms like *catastrophe* and *crash* to describe what was happening.

Once generations have become accustomed to a particular way of life, succeeding generations are likely to have a diffi-cult time adapting to any change in those ways. And so it was for the crows. They were most reluctant to start heading back to the grain fields, or hanging around nests trying to deal with kingbirds and redwings. In-stead, they kept standing by the side of the road, waiting, waiting for an eighteen-wheeler or a Mercedes to come along and, hopefully, splat an instant dinner.

But travel in this troubled nation was severely curtailed. Along with the traumas brought by the end of the Petroleum Age—unemployment, depression, an end to the record industry—thou-sands of huge crows stood mutely by deserted highways, black totems commemorating a dark time.

Ms. Diana Dale noticed the crows more than most Americans. She had taken over her father's two filling stations that faced each other across the New York Thruway; he'd retired just three years before the oil ran out. An attractive, but small, slim blonde, she stayed on the job simply because she didn't know what else to do. The gas pumpers and mechanics who had once worked at the stations had left, and Ms. Dale tended both places. She had plenty of time to cross the thruway when she heard a car coming east when she was on the side headed west, and vice versa. That's how barren the highways had become. On a busy day, Ms. Dale might hear ten trucks, two buses, and three Rolls-Royces go by.

A crow watched her one morning as she de-bated whether to cross the thruway. She could hear a truck coming east from Cleveland, but at the same time she thought she heard a Mercedes heading west from Albany. "If the truck does stop," she told herself, "it will buy more fuel than the Mercedes. I'll cross to the other side."

But the Mercedes was driving faster than she had guessed. She could see it coming along at an impressive clip. "I'll have to wait," she said. "Darn, I'll probably miss the truck, too."

As she stood there beside the thruway, the crow that had been watching flew about twenty-five feet in the air, timed his dive perfectly, and hit Ms. Diana Dale in the small of her slim back with both of his crow feet. She stumbled off the curb directly into the path of the speeding Mercedes. She was left there as flattened and squashed as any box turtle or woodchuck.

The members of the power elite in the Mercedes knew what a terrible thing had happened, but they were afraid to stop on the lonely road. They were unarmed and they thought there might be more killer crows nearby. When they reached the Buffalo exit, they called Washington from the nearest Pancake Kitchen.

In a short while, the President declared a state of national emergency and, on the next day, Congress voted to approve a declaration of war against the giant killer crows.

"In a way," the President told his Cabinet, "this tragedy is a break for us. War against the crows will take everyone's minds off the end of the Petroleum Age and the current economic instability."

In about a month, there was hardly a crow left alive. Citizen casualties were listed as "light."

MORAL: There's no such thing as a free lunch.

AN ESKIMO CHILD'S CAUTIONARY TALE

BY

Robert Coles and
Robert Emmet Coles

When we went to Alaska, in 1972, for the first time, we spent time in a small Eskimo community on the Kobuk River. We talked with a number of children, and began to get some sense of how boys and girls live in the far North, where the winters are long and fierce, the summers brief and strongly unsettling: endless days, all too many mosquitoes and flies, spells of clinging humidity. The Eskimo children became teachers of ours. They were learning how to become hunters and fishermen, and wanted to share with us their skills, intelligence, competence. They wanted to tell us of their world, its assets and liabilities, even as we were asked questions about our own background and way of life. We were told about, really, a subsistence economy—not yet taken over by Big Oil or the welfare system of food stamps, surplus commodities, social security checks, all brought by the weekly visit of a bush pilot's small plane to a somewhat primitive landing strip carved out of the desolate tundra.

One Eskimo girl, about ten years old, paid especially careful attention to us. She heard us out patiently—our questions, one after the other. She watched us closely—our casual but substantial clothing, our relatively elaborate gear, our intense desire to find out everything, absorb a whole world as quickly and exactly as possible. After a while, several days in fact, we began to feel a bit "oriented." We knew how things worked in the settlement; we had caught hold of its rhythms, its manner of contending with a harsh but not unenjoyable life. We were beginning to feel more confident, more at home among our hosts, and, to be honest, rather pleased with ourselves—so far away from our own town, and already acquainted in a few short (or rather quite long!) days with a community of Eskimos.

But the girl who had been one of our "informants," and who had shown us more forbearance than we knew to appreciate, finally decided to help us out with a story. We had been asking her all sorts of questions, and she had come up with answers, one after the other. She told us now, ever so politely, to stop: "You both don't have to learn any more! You've captured us! The white man always gets what he wants! He is the biggest hunter of them all. We catch fish. We get rabbits or ducks. When we are even smaller than I am, we practice with lemmings; we chase them, and they go to the sea even faster than they usually do. But we are no match for the white man. He is like a big animal, a polar bear, who is strong and gets a scent and won't be stopped until he gets what he wants—his catch. He sees what he wants to see. He only listens to what he wants to hear. If he sees or hears something he doesn't understand, he makes a lot of noise and hopes it will soon go away. If not, he has his teeth—his bullets.

"The best thing for an Eskimo is to stay away. There are salmon. There are geese. There are even whales, if we get ambitious. The polar bear is not for us; he is dangerous, because he wants more than he needs. He wants whatever he can get. And he thinks a lot of himself, more than the rest of us do. That is what makes him most dangerous of all. The missionaries come and tell us about pride. Well, the polar bear knows pride. I think the missionaries do, too! A strong scent and pride—they are an enemy the Eskimo had best respect! There is a big weakness, though: the polar bear knows he is so strong, and thinks he is so smart—that he can end up tricking himself. He beats his breast with his paws—Mr. Big—and the ice floes corner him and he gets crushed. He follows his scent, and he finds another animal teasing him, baiting him, shooting at him. If you are smart and strong, you have your own trouble, and you can stumble in your own way."

Having pursued with cunning (we thought) and greed (we were made to realize) our scent (The Eskimo), we had been appraised, taken aim at, told off. We tried, thereafter, to restrain ourselves, to keep our noses off too many scents, to keep our paws by our sides—no bragging and strutting about and loud-mouthed, self-congratu-latory cries. But each animal has its compulsions, its drives, its "character" or "nature," and so the immediately foregoing avowal or claim is no doubt highly suspect—more of the polar bear's swagger (albeit cleverly sub-dued).

THE
DONATION

BY

Betty Comden

The doll was given to me when
I was about eight years old by my Aunt Cal, on her return from a summer
vacation in Europe. "My 'fake' aunt," I would explain to my friends
proudly, "not my mother or my father's sister, but my mother's best
friend from high school." Aunt Cal had begun taking her summer jaunts
through Europe with my mother, years before this, when they had gone
on together from high school to the Maxwell Training School for
Teachers, and then into the public school system. My mother taught for
several years in Brooklyn, then married, and as most young ladies did at
that time, she stopped working to be a wife and mother. Aunt Cal continued teaching and traveling as Miss Seelman all her life, a teacher adored
by her pupils, many of whom remained her friends long after graduation,
and an inspired leader of young people at the Henry Street Settlement
House.

I also adored her. She had white, white hair,
always cut short, an olive skin, bright eyes, blue, I think, that crinkled at
the corners, and a quick, even smile. Her voice was low, and beautifully
modulated, and her speech patrician but not affected. When I was older
I realized that she must have had a profound influence on my mother,
who had arrived at Ellis Island from Russia when she was eight, speaking
no English at all. On the first day of school she had been sent off with
her name and address pinned to her coat. The cultured, reserved girls,
whose families had been Americans for many generations, like Caroline
Seelman and Mary F. Starkey, whom she met just a few years later at the
Girls' High School, were the girls who became my mother's closest
friends. Clearly, she had sought out the ones whose characteristics she

admired and wanted to emulate. Her voice too was low, beautifully modulated, her diction clear, her manner reserved, and her posture regal. When she sat in a chair, she always allowed several inches between its back and her own. Growing up, I was gently abjured from making unnecessary gestures, touching my hair and face after my toilette was considered finished, and indulging in emphatic inflections. My unusual mother, warm and loving, and formidable, was often, in the beauty of her composure, mistaken for an Englishwoman.

When Aunt Cal visited, she always wore something for me to try on and play with. She had many long chiffon scarves, mainly blues and greens in elaborate floral patterns, and strings of beads, lapis lazuli and silver, carnelian, amber, and my favorite, made of wood covered with crushed tiny beads in a swirling multicolored design. These I was allowed to appropriate for the length of her visit, and many were the undersea ballets and Arabian Nights tableaux my mother and Aunt Cal had to witness over the years. Sometimes her scarves were the billowing waves, and sometimes they were veilings to conceal my sacred face from the unclean in the marketplace. My father could not escape these theatricals either, for sometimes Aunt Cal came to dinner with my parents, and I was allowed to be the dinner floor show until they went off to the Philharmonic concert at the Brooklyn Academy of Music.

When I first saw the doll she brought me, I realized at once that it was something very special. "This comes all the way from Alsace-Lorraine," she said. "That is how the ladies dress there." The doll was about six inches tall, but seemed larger to me at the time. Covering the entire top of her head was a flat black bow, stitched down the center like hair parted in the middle, the halves of the ribbon standing out stiffly on either side of the head. The bodice of her dress was black with a white lace insert at the throat, and the sleeves were striped in many colors. She held her arms close to her body, the hands disappearing somewhere under the bodice. The skirt was a round black satiny bell, broken in front by a tiny striped apron. The skirt was long, and if you turned the doll upside down, there were no feet or shoes, just the flat circular surface the doll stood on. What was extraordinary was her face. She was an old woman. The face was wrinkled and tan, the cheeks lined and sunken, the eyes realistically small and somber. I found her odd and beautiful. I had never seen an old lady doll and none of my friends had either. On birthdays and Hanukahs my grandfather would bring me a huge French china doll, and so by this time I had a number of these gorgeous creatures with pink cheeks, long lashes fringing eyes that closed when you laid the doll down, silky curly hair, and jointed bodies made of something very hard that hurt when you hugged them. They wore perfect starched dresses and underthings, and little black buttoned shoes, and often a gold locket around the neck. Grandpa would appear with a long box and say solemnly that he had brought me a fish. It was a running joke and we both knew it, and enjoyed the ritual of pretended disappointment and revulsion, plus stifled giggles, yet I remember always feeling a slight shudder of apprehension as I opened the box, which subsided only when I had actually seen those little black Mary-Janes peeking through the tissue paper at one end. My other dolls were two soft raggedy individuals, a boy and a girl, named F'day and F'dunk, and a mottle-faced baby named Anna Katerina. Not knowing the properties of her composition face, I had washed it with maternal thoroughness and soap and water, removing the paint and leaving her with a permanent case of the measles. But my little old-lady doll from Alsace-Lorraine became my treasure. I felt privileged to possess her, and treated her with deep respect. I could not cuddle her or presume to tuck her in at night, but I took her to the windowsill for an outing every day, and stood her carefully in a special place on a shelf every night.

Our apartment house was directly across from a small park one block square. The long ground floor we occupied fronted on the street with what we knew not as the living room or parlor, but simply as the "front" room. From there going back along two consecutive hallways were the rest of the rooms, looking out on an alley, and beyond them a kitchen and tiny "back" room with a view of the backyard, complete with clotheslines, cats on a fence, and, from time to time, singers who would serenade in broken, harsh voices until coins were thrown down to them wrapped in bits of newspaper. The park across the street had one long, beautiful meadow, marked with "Keep Off" signs. Sometimes my brother and the other boys on the block would be playing stick ball or association in the gutter, and a cop would come, summoned by the old ladies from four forbidding stone houses remaining from better days among the somewhat newer post-World War I apartment houses with names like Joffre Court. The boys would leave the gutter, climb the park fence, and resume their game on the forbidden meadow, from where a genuinely frightening park man, brandishing a stick, would come and chase them back into the gutter. Then the cop would come back and there would be a lot of fast running. I once saw a policeman confiscate a kid's baseball, and as the whole group, including me and a few other tolerated girls gathered in a fascinated, horrified circle, he took out a knife and carefully dissected the ball, first cutting the stitches and removing the two interlocking bell-shaped pieces of leather. This skimming revealed a tightly compressed mass of tangled string which he flicked apart with the tip of the knife and scattered, seeming to fill the whole gutter with the baseball's intestines. Soon it all unraveled and fell away, leaving a tiny rubber center, the heart. This he flicked into the air with his thumbnail. We dispersed silently as from a funeral.

The other half of the park was composed of a hill good for sledding in winter, and rolling in spring, and the Brooklyn Children's Museum. This lovely Victorian edifice, with its green-streaked, oxidized roof, was not only a museum to me, but also a library, a theater, and a horror house. The library windows had faded cretonne window seats where I could curl up on rainy days first with Louisa May Alcott and Gene Stratton Porter, and later with Eliot, Dickens, and Twain. The theater was the auditorium, which showed historical movies on Saturday mornings, the one I remember best being a stately silent about Alexander Hamilton. The horror house was the bird room. There were many nature exhibits, and it was in the bird room that I developed my lifelong fear of large birds from the gigantic all-seeing, all-knowing stuffed condor which dominated the main case past which I would dash, breath held, eyes tightly shut, and heart pounding. The wonderland of the museum, where I spent a great deal of time, was the doll collection. There were cases and cases of dolls of all sizes from all over the world and from all periods of history. They were stunningly arrayed in the native costumes of their countries and times, and some were arranged in dioramas and rooms furnished in detail to give them the perfect settings: Spanish, French, English, German, Portuguese, Dutch, Italian, African, Chinese, Japanese. I would stare long and lovingly at them, and could almost feel myself going through the glass to be with them. I knew what countries they came from but I wondered how the Museum had managed to get hold of them. I asked my mother and she said she supposed the Museum had people who traveled and collected for them, but that most dolls had been donated by various citizens who wanted to share their possessions with everyone in the city.

The word *donated* rang in my ears. I thought it was beautiful. I became engulfed in noble feelings. I too would "donate." I would share with everyone in the city. It would be a painful sacrifice, but I would make it. The poor dear Museum, for all its great collections, had no doll from Alsace-Lorraine. But I had. There must be millions of little girls like me, I reasoned, and educated adults as well, who had never seen one, and would never know how the ladies dressed there unless I donated to the Museum my doll from Alsace-Lorraine.

I announced my intentions to my mother, who looked surprised and asked me if I were sure I wanted to part with my doll. I stood tall and noble and said yes I was sure. At the same moment, I thought of the doll I loved so much, and wished I could retract my reckless statement. If my mother felt any uneasiness about this I did not sense it at the time, but spent the next few days until our appointment at the Museum going through all kinds of conflicting emotions; joy, pride, sadness, regret, an impulse to mislay the doll, an impulse to run away from home with her. I loved the doll, but truly felt it was the right thing to share her with others.

The day of the appointment came. I dressed carefully in my best dress, brown velvet with smocking and ecru lace collar and cuffs, and over it reluctantly my unattractive coat and leggings and hat of brown chinchilla, not the priceless feathery fur, but a sturdy, bumpy cloth made to last for several seasons. The precious doll was taken from her shelf, wrapped in tissue paper, and put into a shoe box. I whispered to her that I would come often to visit her, and that she must realize that she would now be able to bring pleasure and knowledge to thousands. Though trembling nervously when my mother and I were mounting the stairs to the curator's office, I felt the same warm glow of noble renunciation "The White Sister," as played by Lillian Gish, must have felt giving up her soldier lover for her vows. Sadly but proudly I handed over the box to the tall, thin-lipped lady who was the curator. She opened the box, turned back the tissue paper, looked at my doll, and said, "I'm afraid we can't accept this. You see, it's not really a doll at all. It's a pincushion." She poked a thin finger into the revered old lady's bell-shaped skirt, turned her upside down, and tapped the flat surface where there should have been feet. "It's a tourist souvenir, you see, sold by the thousands," she said cheerfully, handing it back to me.

I have no memory of going home. I do remember the waves of humiliation, rejection, and rage that rocked me into nausea. My mother tried to comfort me, saying "Nothing's changed, dear. She's still as beautiful as she was, and now you can have her all to yourself again." But something had changed. When I took the doll out of the box at home and looked at her again, she seemed smaller, and I was embarrassed by the absence of feet and shoes, and indeed, hands. I stood her on my dresser. I took a pin and tentatively stuck it into the stuffed bell which was her lower half. She did not mind. But I did. I grabbed my cuddly, raggedy F'day and F'dunk and, hugging them to me, curled up on my bed and cried.

HOW I
LOST
TUESDAY

BY

Evan S. Connell

ILLUSTRATED BY
EVAN S. CONNELL

When I was a kid, I used to go to camp near Estes Park, Colorado, and one summer a bunch of us climbed Long's Peak—which is 14,256 feet high. You don't need ropes or ice axes, but it's an eighteen-mile hike so you have to start early and you don't get back till after dark.

This is a drawing of the east side of Long's Peak, which they call the east face. It's about two or three thousand feet straight up and down.

Professional mountaineers are the only ones who try to climb the east face. Everybody else hikes around to the other side because it isn't as steep.

The top of the mountain looks like a field of boulders and if you want to you can walk right up to the edge of the east face and look down. I remember thinking that if anybody sailed a balsa-wood glider from up there it would probably take at least an hour to glide down into the valley.

Well, a few years ago when I happened to be in Colorado, I decided to climb Long's Peak again. But this time, I thought, I really would sail a glider off the top, so I went to a dimestore and bought one. It would be easy to carry because it came in a little cardboard box. And I bought a Hershey bar to eat when I got to the top of the mountain. Then, early the next morning, I started walking. It was a nice warm day.

After a couple of hours I heard somebody on the trail and pretty soon a high school boy caught up with me. He said he'd been mountain climbing in Colorado all summer but he'd never climbed Long's Peak. I told him I had when I was twelve years old.

We hiked along together and the trail began to get steeper and then it began zig-zagging back and forth. The pine trees got smaller and smaller as we climbed higher, and the air got thinner. It seemed as though we were always out of breath.

I could tell he was trying to climb a little faster than I was, just to prove he could beat me, which made me sort of mad. When I was a kid I beat everybody else to the top of Long's Peak and I didn't want to come in second this time, so I started climbing fast enough to stay ahead of him.

Then he began cutting corners instead of following the trail back and forth, so I did too.

The pine trees kept getting smaller and both of

us were breathing hard, and finally—even though neither of us had said anything—we knew it was a race.

After a while, we had climbed up above the trees. Practically nothing lives that high up—just a few shrubs and some little furry brown animals called marmots. The wind blows all the time and it's not anyplace you'd want to spend the night.

Then, as we climbed up still higher, there weren't any shrubs or marmots. There was nothing except lichen, which is a sort of crusty greenish-brown stuff that feels like a dried-out washcloth and grows on rocks.

Finally, I could see that in fifteen or twenty minutes we'd get to the top. We were scrambling up the mountain side by side—both of us puffing like steam engines—but neither of us wanted to stop even for a few seconds because that would give the other guy a big lead.

Well, I began to think that what we were doing was pretty silly. If we had challenged each other to a race it would have been different, but we were just about ruining ourselves racing up the mountain while we pretended it was nothing unusual.

The more I thought about that the sillier it seemed. After all, the longer you go on pretending the harder it is to stop.

So I just quit. I don't know who would have won if I'd kept on climbing as fast as I could. It would have been close.

Anyway, he got there first. He reached the top of Long's Peak a minute or two ahead of me, but of course he couldn't brag about winning because nobody had said it was a race.

So finally, after all that climbing, there we were.

When you get to the top of a mountain, there's not much to do except sit on a boulder and look around. You could see a long way, though—at least a hundred miles. You could look down on more mountains than you could count—some of them thousands of feet below. And even further down you could see glaciers and icy blue lakes and the dark green pine trees.

Well, after I'd looked around and rested for a while, I decided to have lunch. I unzipped my leather jacket and took the Hershey bar out of my pocket, but it had gotten so soft it would have been easier to eat with a spoon. I had a messy, sticky lunch.

Then I took the glider out of the box and assembled it. There was a rubber band to hold the wings in position and slots in the rear of the fuselage where you attached the tail.

The wind was blowing like a hurricane and since I didn't want to go sailing off the east face myself, I crawled over to the edge on my hands and knees. I looked down just once. That was enough. It looked like about ten miles straight down. I turned around and crawled away. Just being close to the edge could make you dizzy.

I set the glider's wings in what I thought should be the right position, so it was all ready to go. Then I took a pencil out of my pocket and printed my initials on the tail. I don't know why I did that—it just seemed like a good idea. Then I aimed the glider toward the edge and gave it a shove.

I expected it to sail away from the cliff and go spiraling slowly down and down into the valley, but that isn't what happened. The wind tossed the glider every which way and threw it against the cliff and probably broke it. I never did see where it went because I didn't want to lean over the edge. A few scraps of balsa wood didn't seem that important.

So everything had gone wrong. I had carried a glider all the way up the mountain, but it wouldn't sail anywhere in that wind. And my Hershey bar had melted. And the high school boy had won the race because I felt silly about racing.

Here I am on top of Long's Peak after all those disappointments. The drawing makes me look sort of disgusted. Actually, I was just tired. We'd been climbing for three or four hours.

Pretty soon it was time to start back, because we didn't want to get caught up there after dark.

We walked down the trail together until we came to the ranger station and the parking area, where we said good-bye. Then I got in my car and drove to the hotel.

It was almost nine o'clock at night when I reached the hotel. I hadn't had anything to eat all day except a melted Hershey and I was hungry, but the dining room was closed. I thought about going someplace else for dinner, but I was too tired. I felt as though I'd been racing up Mount Everest. I went straight to bed.

I woke up once because some people were talking in the hall outside my room. Then I fell asleep again.

When I finally got out of bed, I was surprised to see that it was past noon. I didn't think I'd slept that long.

In the coffee shop I bought a newspaper to read while I was waiting for breakfast, but then I noticed it wasn't Tuesday's paper—it was a Wednesday paper. That didn't make sense. I had left the hotel Monday morning to climb Long's Peak and I got back Monday night, which meant this had to be Tuesday because Tuesday always follows Monday.

I couldn't understand why I had gotten a Wednesday paper. At last I said to the cashier, "Excuse me, what day of the week is this?"

She said it was Wednesday. She knew I had been looking at the newspaper, so she must have thought I was cracked.

I guess when I woke up and heard people talking in the hall that must have been Tuesday, and the next time I woke up it was Wednesday. I had been asleep thirty-nine hours.

It didn't make any difference, because I hadn't planned to do anything special on Tuesday. Just the same, I felt sort of cheated. Even though there are plenty of days, you don't like to lose one.

BLUE FOOTBALL

BY

Peter Cook

"I'm a Blue Football" said Timothy Frears.
"No you're not" said his father, and kicked him upstairs.
"I'm a Blue Football" his mother was told,
"I'm rubber inside and I'm sixty years old."
"If you're rubber inside" his mother announced,
"I can't understand why you've never been bounced."
She opened the window and threw him below,
Down into the garden and what do you know,
He bounced down the pathway and over the gate,
Then he bounced on a bus, number one-forty-eight.
He bounced up and down for a while on the top
And only bounced off when the bus had to stop.
It stopped at the Palace, he bounced very hard,
Right over the railings and way past the Guard.
The sentries could scarcely believe what they'd seen
When Timothy landed on top of the Queen.
She was combing her locks when he dropped on her head,
"I'm sorry, Your Majesty" Timothy said,
"But I'm a Blue Football, I'm rubber inside."
"Of course you are dear" the good lady replied,
"You must meet my husband, he'd love to meet you,
The Duke's keen on footballs, especially blue."
She sent off some servants, the Duke was soon found,
And the Queen and the Duke kicked him gently around.
"Goodness me" said the Queen when the game was all done,
"Kicking Blue Footballs is really great fun.

After all of that kicking, it's only polite
To give you some tea and make you a Knight."
She pulled at a bell on a long silken cord
And ordered some scones and her best knighting sword;
And after they all had had plenty to eat
Young Timothy knelt at the Queen's royal feet.
She dubbed him Sir Timothy Football The First,
But the sword on his shoulder made Timothy burst.
He flew into pieces all over the room:
The Queen smiled faintly and summoned a groom.
"Those swords are too sharp" she said to the man,
"Get all my best doctors as quick as you can."
The doctors arrived with their needles and thread,
And sewed him together, his chest and his head,
His arms and his legs, his knees and his feet,
In under an hour he was nearly complete.
But one piece was missing and the Duke said "Oh dear,
You'll have to go home without your left ear."
"Are you sure you had both when you came?" asked the Queen.
"Never mind" said Sir Tim, "it's just one less to clean."
Apart from one ear he was quite good as new.
The doctors advised him just what he should do.
Eat plenty of yoghurt, fresh raisins, and yeast,
And cut down on bouncing for two weeks at least.
The Queen shook his hand and climbed into a car,
She was meeting a Chieftain from West Zanzibar.
The Duke waved good-bye and said "Never fear,
I promise I'll keep an eye out for your ear."
His mother and father asked where he had been,
So he told them about being kicked by the Queen,
And how he had burst when she made him a Knight,
How the doctors had sewn him together all right;
They couldn't believe him but did think it queer
That he should come home with only one ear.
Then seven days later a messenger came
And asked for Sir Timothy Football by name.
"I've got an ear here, the object was found
By Her Majesty's corgi whilst sniffing around.

So please ascertain if this ear is the one
And then we can get it back onto your son."
When they came back from the doctor's that night,
Sir Timothy said, "You see I was right,
I am a Blue Football and rubber inside."
"So you are" said his father, his voice filled with pride,
"And your mother and I must be footballs as well."
And they all started bouncing; that's all there's to tell.

HARRY, IKE AND JACK AT THE COUNTY FAIR

BY

Robert Coover

Harry, Ike, and Jack
Went to the county fair;
Harry didn't pay,
Ike didn't care.

Harry had a great time
And rode on every ride;
Jack watched the shows,
While Ike played outside.

Harry tried his strength
And did quite well;
Ike did even better
And Jack rang the bell.

Harry stole a hotdog,
Jack had an ice;
Ike bought an apple pie
And Harry ate a slice.

Harry, Ike, and Jack
Went to supervise
The livestock judging:
Harry won first prize.

Harry and the judge
Got into a fight;
Jack calmed them down,
Ike stayed out of sight.

Harry rode the Whip,
Jack the Carousel;
Ike bought a flag
To wear in his lapel.

Harry whistled at the girls,
Jack was more discreet;
But all the girls liked Ike:
They said he was so sweet.

Ike bought a cherry pop
And Harry drank it all;
Jack threw baseballs
And won a kewpie doll.

Harry, Ike, and Jack
Rode the Loop-the-Loop;
Jack and Harry laughed
When Ike lost his soup.

Harry tossed horseshoes
And won a fountain pen;
Ike got lost
But Jack found him again.

Harry had the best damn time
In the whole dominion;
Jack was just a trifle bored,
Ike had no opinion.

Harry pinned a tin star
On Ike but it rusted;
Jack bought a red balloon
Which somebody busted.

Harry hiked home
From the county fair;
Jack got a ride,
Ike didn't care.

TWO POEMS

BY
Gregory Corso

AS A BOY
I monitored the stairs
altar'd the mass
flew rooftop birds
Kissed the moon in a barrel of rain
E'en tagged the tail of light
. . . O what wingéd wows

AS A MAN I SAW MY BOY
An angel all the way
without wings
with human smile
and nothing to say

A LINDEN TREE ON A SUNNY CANAL

BY

Jonathan Cott

Lights are moving up and down the branches,
visiting the leaves.
It is midafternoon,
and they are happy to be shaded from the sun.
The leaves are shiny.
The lights are crossing on their way
to pick each other up.
As the water moves,
there are more lights.
They look alike
but move faster and together.
They are getting dizzy.
Everything is rocking!
Passing through their friends
they vanish into brightness.

HAIKAT

BY
Myrna Davis

ILLUSTRATED BY
PAUL DAVIS

Suddenly head in air
staring intently
at no thing I can see

MONSTERS:
A one-act play for children to perform for adults

BY
George Dennison

Cast:

BECKY ⎱ (eight-to-nine-year-old girls)
NELLIE ⎰

GHOST

MONSTER

NIGHTMARE (a two-headed horse)

GOBLIN

PROFESSOR WITCH (played by an adult)

GREEN GLOB

Late at night, an attic bedroom with an open window between two beds. The girls are dressed in pajamas and are sitting together on one of the beds.

NELLIE: Monsters come from places you don't know about. Like . . . you know . . . long, long ago . . . out of the swamps and all that . . . and they're so ugly it makes you scream . . . and then they come down the street at night . . . and they hold their arms up and drag their feet, but you can't escape them . . . they GET YOU!

BECKY: Yeah, but they come from anywhere. It could be anyplace. It could be a crack in the ground right in back of the house, and while you're watching television a hand comes up out of the crack, only not really a hand, it's green slime with eyes in it, and it yuks along over the ground, and yuks right up the side of the house. . . .

NELLIE: Yeah, and it comes up the stairs without any sound at all, just *s-s-s-s-s-s-s* . . . and it slups under the door, and you look around and your whole room is full of slimy mud, and it has hands and eyes . . . and you scream, but nobody hears you because the slime goes *schlupp!* and all the tables and chairs go *glug, glug* . . . and you're standing up in bed screaming, and the slime comes after you, and the bed goes *glug* . . . and you're stuck on the windowsill. . . .

BOTH (*a play scream that is partly real*): Aghhh!

BECKY: That's worse than *anything!* That's worse than a ghost. . . .

NELLIE: Yeah. . . .

BECKY: Ghosts are pretty bad, though. . . .

NELLIE: They're dead people who can't stay dead.

BECKY: They come out of graves in scary places when it's late at night and foggy, and they drift along like nothin' at all . . . and you better not live in the place they died . . . you wake up all of a sudden, and you hear a voice, and then you see this shimmery thing . . . and then you see a face . . . "What are you doin' in my bed?? Ooooooooo. . . ."

NELLIE: Shhh! I hear something!
(*They listen.*)

NELLIE: What would you do if a ghost came in?
(*They scream playfully and hug each other in fright.*)

BECKY: What if a ghost and a monster *both* came in? Maybe they'd scare each other and run away.

NELLIE: Oh no. A monster can't scare a ghost. You can hit a ghost right on the head with a hammer and it goes right through, it doesn't even bother him. And a ghost can't scare a monster. I don't *think.*

BECKY: Shhh!

NELLIE: What?

BECKY: I hear something!

NELLIE: What?!

BECKY: On the stairs!

NELLIE: Aghhh! I hear it too. . . .
   (*Enter* GHOST, *left.*)

BOTH GIRLS: Aghhhh! A ghost!
   (*Enter* MONSTER, *right.*)

BOTH GIRLS: Aghhh! A monster!

MONSTER: Hiyah, ghost! How ya been?

GHOST: Hey! Look who's here! Whatta ya say, Monster! How's tricks?
   (*They shake hands.*)

MONSTER: I been gettin' on. What about you?

GHOST: Yeah, not bad, not bad.

MONSTER: Hey, what's this I hear, they tore down the Old Fergusson
   place?

GHOST: Yeah . . . well . . . you know . . . win a few, lose a few. I ain't
   worried.

MONSTER: Right. Well . . . okay, Ghost . . . take it easy.

GHOST: Yeah. Great. Nice talkin' to you, monster. See you 'round.

MONSTER: So long, ghost. . . .

GHOST: So long, monster.
   (*Both exit.*)

BECKY: Wow! Was that a close one!

NELLIE: What if they saw us!?

BECKY: Which one were you scared of most?

NELLIE: I don't know. The monster could choke you and eat you . . . but
   the ghost is so . . . so . . . oooh . . . *yuk!*
   (*They look in the wings and come front.*)

BECKY: They didn't scare each other one single bit. They shook hands.
   (*A* TWO-HEADED HORSE *looks in the window, vanishes.*)

NELLIE: Yeah. They just shook hands! "Pleased to meet you." "Pleased to meet you." I was more scared of the ghost. I never dreamed of a monster, but I really did dream of a ghost once. It was really creepy. I could see right through it. First I thought I was dreaming, then I thought it was right there in the room. I screamed so hard I woke everybody up.

(*The* TWO-HEADED HORSE *appears at the window.*)

BECKY: That was a nightmare, Nellie. I had a lot o' nightmares once. Everybody has them. When I was a little kid, I used to think they came in the window.

(*The* HORSE *climbs in the window and prances behind them.*)

BECKY (*continuing*): You're just dreaming away and all of a sudden . . . you know . . . something *happens,* you don't know *what* it is, it sneaks up on you and . . . and you can't help it, you just start *screaming.*

(*The* HORSE *stamps its foot, whinnies.*)

BOTH GIRLS: Aaaghhhh! A nightmare! A nightmare!

(*The* HORSE *chases them. They run around and around, screaming. Then the* GIRLS *flee to a corner. The* HORSE *keeps going in a circle. The* GHOST *comes in.*)

GHOST: Hey-y-y-y! Nightmare! Whatta ya say! Gimme a ride!

HORSE: (*Whinnies*)

(*The* GHOST *holds the* HORSE's *tail and gallops behind him. The* MONSTER *comes in.*)

MONSTER: Giddyup! Giddyup! Yahoo!

(ALL THREE *gallop in a circle.*)

GHOST: Faster! Faster! Giddyup!

MONSTER: Yahoo!

HORSE: (*Whinnies*)

(*The* GHOST, MONSTER, *and* HORSE *all run off together. The* GIRLS *are hugging each other in the corner.*)

BECKY: Nightmares! Ghosts! Monsters! Help!

NELLIE: The next thing you know, we'll see a goblin!

(*A small* GOBLIN, *head down, runs across as fast as possible and exits.*)

BECKY: Where are the good fairies? Where are the elves?
(GHOST *runs across, exits.*)

BOTH GIRLS: Aaaaghhh! Aaaaghhh!
(MONSTER *runs across, exits.*)

BOTH GIRLS: Aaaaghhh! Help!
(HORSE *runs across, exits.* GOBLIN *runs across, exits.*)

BOTH GIRLS: Aaaaghhh! Aaaaghhh!

BECKY: Where's that good guy that came out of Aladdin's lamp?

NELLIE: We need a fairy godmother! Help!

BOTH: Help! Help!

BECKY: Fairy godmother! Help!

NELLIE: Fairy godmother!
(*There is a puff of smoke in the room. When the smoke clears, the* PROFESSOR WITCH *is standing there. He wears a derby, smokes a cigar, and has a long bushy beard. He carries a shopping bag in each hand, speaks with a German accent.*)

BECKY: Are *you* our fairy godmother?

PROFESSOR: Of course not! I am the Professor Witch. I have come to explain everything to you. That is my business, explaining everything.

BECKY: Oh yeah, bozo? Well we don't need explanations, *see*—we need help.

PROFESSOR: An explanation *is* help. Listen closely. My words are worth a nickel a piece, maybe more. Are you listening? Very well. What you are suffering from is an explosion of the unconscious into the conscious mind. Do you know what this means, *the unconscious?* I will tell you. Are you listening? What you think about—that's not it. What you *don't* think about and even so it happens anyway, or especially happens on account of that—that's it.

BOTH GIRLS: What!!??

PROFESSOR: Suppose I have a glass of water. In the bottom of the glass there is sludge. Now I shake the water. What happens? Up comes the sludge, right?

BECKY: Oh yeah! Well I don't have any sludge in me, bozo!

NELLIE: Me neither, mister bozo witch.

PROFESSOR: Of course, you have sludge in you. We all have sludge. If I shook you, it would come out your ears. But I am not going to shake you. I am going to tell you a secret and give you a present. Come here.
(The PROFESSOR *hands each one a shopping bag, whispers in their ears. They exit. He addresses the audience.)*

We will see what happens to these ghosts, these nightmares, these ridiculous hobgoblins. You too listen to my words. The price is going up. What are these creatures of the night but the wishes of the day that got tired of hanging around and went underground? There are no monsters, no ghosts. Of course sometimes we do find certain manifestations of evil . . . certain presences that appear at night in places like this. . . .
(He speaks with growing anxiety.)

One can be calm, however. There is no need to be afraid. The top of the house represents the top of the mind. Nothing unexpected happens there. Of course . . . sometimes the very thing you *know* is going to happen . . . scares you half to death. . . .
(The GIRLS *rush on dressed as witches and wearing witch masks.)*

PROFESSOR: Witches!!! Aaaaaghhhh!
(He rushes off, screaming.)

BOTH GIRLS: Come back! Come back!
(They lift their masks.)

BECKY: What did he do *that* for?
(She calls into the wings.)

Professor Witch! Come back! We need you!

NELLIE: Come back, Professor Bozo. Help!

BECKY: What if the ghost comes back?

NELLIE: Shhh! I hear something!
(She rushes across the stage, looks off, runs back.)

It's the ghost, Becky! He's coming! What'll we do?

BECKY: It's too late! We gotta scare 'im! Put on your mask! Rush right at him. Yell as loud as you can! Come on!
(*They put on their masks.* GHOST *enters. They rush at him, yelling.*)

GHOST: Hey-y-y-y! Look who's here! A couple o' groovy witches! Wow! You look great! Don't go away. Lemme call the guys. Where you been all this time? (*He shouts*) Hey-y-y, you guys! C'mere! See what we got! You new around here, hunh? Wow!
(*Enter* HORSE, MONSTER, GOBLIN.)

I want you guys to meet a couple o' great new witches. This is Monster. This is Nightmare. This little guy here is Goblin. He's small, but don't mess wid 'im, right Goblin?
(*They shake hands, "pleased to meet you," etc.* HORSE *whinnies.*)

So . . . where you witches been all this time?

MONSTER: How come we never seen you, hunh? Whatta you been doin'?

BECKY: We don't come from around here.

NELLIE: We come from California.

MONSTER: What is it? Sump'm happen out there? You get in trouble out there? Whatta you doin' way out here?

GHOST: Hey! Let up, Monster. You know what I want? I mean . . . whatta ya say . . . I mean, give us a few fancy curses, hunh? Kind o'thing we don't hear much around here. Yuh know?

MONSTER: Yeah. Yeah.

NELLIE: Who should we curse?

GHOST: Whatta yuh mean, *who?* Anybody! What difference it make? Just pretend there's some guy standin' here. Let 'im have it. Come on.

BECKY: Curses on you! Yaa-a-a-a! Drop dead!

NELLIE: May you be cursed today and tomorrow and every day until you drop dead screaming.
(*Pause.*)

GHOST (*ominously*): Is that all?

BECKY: Isn't that enough?

GHOST: How long you been in this business?

NELLIE: Oh, about . . . about. . . .
(BECKY *and* NELLIE *whisper.*)

BECKY: About fifteen years.

GHOST: And that's all you got for curses? I dunno. You don't sound like real witches to me.

MONSTER: They *ain't* real witches.

NELLIE: We're real witches. We really are. We just thought . . . uh . . . you guys probably already knew all the curses.

GHOST: Well I heard a few, I heard a few. I'm not bad myself, y'know. Sometimes when I'm hauntin' a place really heavy, I stand at the foot o' the bed, y'know, and I say, "You are cursed in your sleep and cursed in your waking. May your food turn to worms in your mouth. May everything you drink burn your throat like acid. . . ." Goes on like that, y'know. Keep 'em up all night if I want.

NELLIE: We got one like that, too. May your knees split open and your feet drop off!

GHOST: Hey! Good! Good!

BECKY: May you lose both eyeballs in your soup!

NELLIE: May every breath you take burn your nose like fire!

BECKY: May you walk backward when you try to go straight ahead! May you bump into everything! May you fall downstairs! May the whole house fall on you!

MONSTER: Yeah! Yeah!

GHOST: Go! Go!

NELLIE: May everything you say become a snake, and it crawls in your ear and chews your brain!

MONSTER: Yeah!

BECKY: May you slam the door on your hand and your whole arm comes off! May everybody hate you! May they stuff you in the blender!

GHOST: You got it! Go!

NELLIE: May you jump into bed but you fall down a hole instead, and your voice goes *A-a-a-a-g-hhh* (*a descending scream*) and you keep falling . . . falling . . . and you can't see a speck of light . . .

BECKY: . . . and you hear a noise and it's a great big rock they tossed in after you . . .

NELLIE: . . . and it comes closer and closer . . .

BECKY: . . . and you HIT the bottom!

NELLIE: . . . and the rock SQUASHES you like a bug!

MONSTER: Yeah!

GHOST: Wow!

GOBLIN: Those curses might even scare The Glob!
     (*Silence. Agitation.*)

GHOST: Don't mention The Glob.

MONSTER: Ain't no curses gonna work against The Glob.

NELLIE: What works against The Glob?

GHOST: Only one thing.

BECKY: What's that?

GHOST: Runnin' fast.

NELLIE: You mean you guys are *scared* o' something!?

BECKY: What is The Glob, anyway?

GHOST: Don't say that name. The Glob is The Glob.

GOBLIN: He's green.
     (*All are uneasy. They look this way and that.*)

GHOST: Sometimes he comes when you ain't lookin' for him. And sometimes he comes when you are lookin' for him.

MONSTER: He comes when he wants to come. He don't care what you're doin'.

GOBLIN: Shhh! I hear something!
     (*They listen.*)

BECKY (*whispering*): What does he sound like?

GHOST (*whispering*): Like nothin' at all, just *whssshhh* on the stairs. . . .

MONSTER (*whispering*): He sounds like The Glob.

GOBLIN: I hear 'im! It's him! He's gonna get us!!!
(*Enter* THE GLOB.)

ALL: Aaaaaghhh!!! The Glob!!!
(NELLIE *crouches by one of the beds.* ALL THE OTHERS *rush out the opposite wing.* THE GLOB *exits, pursuing them.*)

NELLIE: Becky! Becky! Why did you run away?! Ohhhh . . . what if The Glob gets her?
(BECKY *climbs in the window.*)

BECKY: No Glob's gonna get *me!*

NELLIE: Becky! How did you get away?

BECKY: I just scooted to the side and he kept chasin' the other guys.

NELLIE: What if he comes back?

BECKY: He's too busy. We better keep watch, though. I'm takin' off these witch things. They're too hot.

NELLIE: Me too. Do you think Professor Witch wants them back?
(*They remove their costumes and pile them on the floor.*)

BECKY: No . . . he's too scared.
(But NELLIE *calls into the wings*)

NELLIE: Professor Bozo Witch, you can have your things!

BECKY: Do you think he's still there?
(BECKY *sits on one bed,* NELLIE *on the other.*)

NELLIE: I wish a real fairy godmother would come and bring us some apple cider and cookies. Aren't you *hungry,* Becky?

BECKY: I'm starved! Hey! I just remembered! I've got two cookies left over from lunch. They're in my lunchbox, and my lunchbox is . . . right . . . down . . . *here!*
(BECKY *produces the lunchbox from under the bed, takes a cookie, gives* NELLIE *one. They recline on their beds, eating.*)

NELLIE: Oh boy! Now I think I'll live.

BECKY: We better take turns standing watch.

NELLIE: Okay.
(PROFESSOR WITCH *enters quietly.*)

BECKY: But maybe we shouldn't take turns. Maybe we should do it both together.

NELLIE: Okay.
(PROFESSOR WITCH *tiptoes to the bed, looks at the girls, who are* asleep.)

PROFESSOR: Sound asleep. Ridiculous to be frightened. What could be more embarrassing? Two girls, not very big. The grand total of their ages is not even eighteen.
(*He turns over the witch costumes with the point of his shoe.*)

Some black rags. Cardboard hats. I must learn to control myself. In the meantime . . . since I am actually their fairy godmother. . . .
(*He tiptoes to the wall behind their beds, and with his finger to his lips pulls a scroll across the back wall and fastens it in place. It is large enough to cover the window completely. It is painted like the night sky, blue-black, with stars and moon. He tiptoes out.*)

LESTER

BY

Rosalyn Drexler

Lester Frink was an eight-year-old boy. He did not want to fight evil, he did not want to fight fires, he did not want to be a rock star . . . he wanted to stay in bed. His mother was worried, his father was worried, and his sister was worried. Even the superintendent of his building was worried.

"I haven't seen Lester running down the steps lately; is anything wrong?" he asked Lester's mother.

"Wrong? Not terribly," she answered, unwilling to let the man know just how worried she really was. "He goes to the toilet, eats, and reads his comic books . . . but then he gets right back into bed, pulls the covers up to his chin, and shuts his eyes. I'm sure it's only a passing phase." She looked heavenward, as if the Passing Phase were a bird heading south.

"Why don't you take a walk around the block?" Mrs. Frink asked Lester hopefully.

"Nope," he answered glumly, "I don't like the smell of garbage, I don't like dirt, I don't like bums, and I don't like my friends . . . they're stupid!"

"Stupid? What have they to be stupid about?" she mused, then opened the windows—a little at the top and a little at the bottom, so the air could circulate. "This room is as musty as an old closet; you need air." Her chest expanded as she demonstrated the need for air. "See, it's much better with the windows open."

Lester watched her as if she were in a movie. It was a daily movie, its subtleties known only to him: slight changes in vocal modulation, a costume variation, the shifting of light from one hour to the next, special multiphonic sound coming through the walls. . . . For the movie to be over, Lester had only to close his eyes and stuff his fingers into his ears; then he'd think something wonderful: the ocean (that he had never seen) and a soft beach. By concentrating, he could almost feel the clean sand between his fingers, the cool water between his toes.

One day, the day after Lester had refused to let his mother change the sheets on his bed, Mrs. Frink brought a tall, friendly gentleman to visit with him.

"Hi there, Lester," the visitor began. He did not know that Lester had already become a smooth, shiny pebble, half-hidden in the sand . . . a no-name perfect pebble.

"Answer the man," Mrs. Frink implored. "He's come all the way from West Eighty-eighth Street to see you."

Lester shifted his position on the pillow; the tide was coming in. It left him stranded there with only a broken sign that read: Private Beach . . . Keep Off!

"If you don't mind, I'll just stay a while," the visitor said. "Would you like to play with these?" Out of his briefcase, he took four rubber toys that had a funny smell and could bend in any direction. They looked like tiny people and their faces were dusty pink. Lester ignored them.

Finally the man left. He took his miniature family with him.

Holding an empty dinner plate, Lester's mother said to his father: "At least he eats. He prefers seafood now. . . . It used to be pizza."

"But he eats with his mouth closed," Mr. Frink stormed. "It's strange; his nose seems smaller, and his head rounder. The boy no longer resembles me, he looks like . . ." he hesitated, afraid to voice his fears.

"Go ahead, say it," his wife encouraged, taking his hand staunchly.

"He looks like a face painted on a large, gift-shop pebble," Mr. Frink blurted out.

"Yes, I've noticed that myself," his wife added hesitantly. "His appearance is hardly human. I didn't want to cause you concern, but he's been sleeping with his arms and legs tucked under him. Twice a day I have to exercise his limbs to keep them supple . . . just in case he wants to use them again."

"What does the doctor say?" Lester's father asked.

"He's concerned, but says there's been some progress."

"What progress?"

"Lester wiggles his toes when the doctor asks him to wiggle his toes," Mrs. Frink replied brightly.

"Some progress," Mr. Frink said. "You know as well as I do that our son always wiggles his toes."

Lester's older sister, Kathy, who was thirteen years old, also noticed Lester's resemblance to a stone and treated him as if he were one: "Oh there he is, my pretty little pebble. I'm gonna carry that dumby-pumby to the bath and wash his dumby-pumby face till it shines."

Lester did not let on that he liked the way she treated him . . . in fact, he loved it, and almost became a boy again. . . .

The pleasant visitor returned, and pulled his chair up to Lester's bed: "Now that we're friends," he said mistakenly, "why don't we confide in each other; I'll tell you my secrets and you tell me yours. Okay? Me first. Well, Lester, I have an angry rash under my left armpit. Nobody knows that but you and me." He waited expectantly.

Lester watched him perched on the edge of his chair, a tape recorder in his lap. Lester said nothing. He was a pebble. He rolled off the bed. His mother and the visitor got him back in.

"His coordination is poor . . . it may be a nerve disorder," the man said. Lester's mother opened her mouth to let out a silent scream. "But I can make him better," the man promised swiftly, "with mega-vitamins, a spinal adjustment, and daily use of this super-tough musical knee-knocker." Mrs. Frink put on a brave smile.

"Oh," she whispered, "has it come to that? Any chance of a spontaneous remission?"

The doctor shook his head as if to say: "Who knows?"

Lester enjoyed the new movie. It had dramatic tension. The cast, though not glamorous, was star-studded enough for him: mommy, daddy, sister, and the mysterious stranger. His own name came up often enough for him to suspect that the story of *his* life was unfolding and that he was a celebrity.

Summertime came, but there was no air-conditioner or fan in Lester's room. Money had run out. Mr. Frink, out of work, was waiting to hear whether or not he had been hired by a California oil drilling company.

"Poor child," Mrs. Frink said, applying cold compresses to Lester's warm forehead. "Cooler weather will be here soon." Then she kissed his cheek. Surprisingly, it was glacial.

"I've got it. I've got the job," Mr. Frink shouted on a Tuesday in August. "We must get ready. The company is paying for the entire move, and has already found the perfect home for us in Santa Monica."

The house was on the beach. At last Lester's dream was real. This small miracle helped him to be real again, too: At first he bent his knees and elbows, then he sat up, and at last left his faithful bed, to walk, slowly at first, to the ocean. It was wonderful: birds flew overhead, the air smelled like fish and old socks, shells and seaweed lined the uneven shore, the cold water washed his toes, and other children shouted and tumbled happily, not far from Lester on their private beaches.

Since he was no longer a pebble, Lester had fun collecting them in a shoebox, making designs in the sand with them, tossing them into the ocean as far as he could. On one creative occasion, he painted a face onto an especially large pebble . . . it did not look like him.

So, Lester lived happily ever after, except that he still had a few stupid friends (who doesn't?) who made fun of his name, changing it from Lester to Lister and rhyming it with blister:

> *Lester Lister*
> *fester blister*
> *fell in love*
> *with his own sister*
> *when his parents weren't home*
> *And with her he was alone*
> *Lester Lister kiss'd her.*

But happily, he found other friends too, who liked throwing a frisbee, riding bicycles, and watching television much more than making fun of his name.

"How crucial a change of scene can be," Mrs. Frink remarked.

HER SECRET MOLECULE

BY

Ann Druyan

The London Underground shuts down around midnight, and the Metro conductors of Paris are tucked in by two. But someone is always awake in New York City, so the subway trains rock and roll all night long. Through the darkest hours they go barreling from borough to borough, and on more than one occasion they have been the scene of important events.

On a stuffy, moonless August night in that city, Arabia Crimmins decided to flee her screaming family. She was nine, thin, poor, and furious.

Arabia had tried everything: pillows, towels, and even some flannel pajama bottoms with the legs tied around her head. But no material was tough enough to prevent her parents' sharp words from cutting through to her ears.

"E-nough," she howled as she jumped down the metal-tipped steps of her broken house with her legs stick-straight and her feet together, so that every noisy stomp sent home pain right up through her calves. She wasn't sure what she would do when she got to the heavy front door until she heard her angry Papa's voice.

"You never do this," he was shouting at her Mama.

"You never do that," Mama yelled back. It helped Arabia to make up her mind.

"E-nough equals E-nough everytime," she thought. "So I'll be going." She budged open the door and raced through the still air to the nearest subway station on the Independent Line. There was nobody there to stop her or to make change, and that was just fine because she already had a token. In a few minutes the F train, an express, roared into the station and parted its doors before her.

The car she entered was deserted except for a *Daily News* which had come apart, a fat lady in a deep sleep, and an empty, rolling soda bottle.

Arabia took a seat directly across from the woman and stared at her enormous purple legs. This lady looked terrible. She wore weird green men's corduroy sneakers with slits cut in them to make even more room for her oozing hippo feet. Her shredded stockings were held up by rubber bands just below her knees. Her shirt, her skirt, and her teeth were stained with brown spots. There were a couple of straight hairs on her chin. She was jiggling and nodding with the motion of the train as she slept with her chunky fingers looped through the paper twine handles of the shopping bags that sat on either side of her. One of the bags had the name "Bigelow's" printed on it. Another read, "Kutscher's Butchers Since 1951. Our Meat's So Tender Don't Bother to Chew."

When the F train arrived at the Union Turnpike station the horrible woman opened her eyes.

"Hey little sweetie," she called to Arabia, "I knew you'd come. And just in time. I'm Fanny Kassman and tonight my life is ending."

"You look okay to me," Arabia lied.

"Don't tell a former inventor's wife when she's dying," Fanny said cheerfully. "I'm dying all right. But it's not so bad because you finally showed up." She rubbed her sticky mouth and added, "It's been a long time since I've spoken a word to anyone at all."

"Must be some mistake," Arabia insisted. "I never met you before."

"No, you're right there," Fanny agreed. "We never have met. But I have a treasure for you just the same."

"What is it?"

"Not so fast," said Fanny. "Aren't you a child and isn't it the middle of the night? Two or something?"

"I couldn't stand it another minute. Had to go. My name's Arabia."

"Hello, hello. You'll be going right home after I give you my treasure. Sure you will."

Arabia looked doubtful. "What is this treasure anyway?"

"I call it my special molecule. But first I need your solemn promise."

"Promise what?" asked Arabia. "I'm not promising to go home. Uh-uh. No way."

"That's your business," sloppy Fanny replied. "Go. Stay. Do whatever you think is best. But promise me that you will use your new power to fight fear in all its forms."

Arabia quickly switched her gaze to the grave Pope's face on the front page of the disheveled paper on the grimy train floor.

"Promise me, little girl, that you will take on the governments and the corporations and anybody who pushes the people around." Fanny leaned forward and slapped her hands down on her red potato knees. "I know that the reunification of all living things is no small order. But I don't expect you to do it unaided. I have something here that will help."

Fanny carefully reached into the Kutscher's Butchers bag with both hands and pulled out a family-sized Hellmann's mayonnaise jar. She gestured for Arabia to come closer.

"My late husband, Mel, made this," Fanny confided proudly. She unscrewed the blue-and-white top and removed the creased wax paper that covered the jar's mouth, affording additional protection. Inside was a churning sea of marbleized reds and golds. "It would have revolutionized the swimming pool industry," she observed. "It would have made charcoal obsolete. But Mel didn't have a bunch of degrees. He didn't have connections." Fanny looked disgusted.

"What am I supposed to do with it?" Arabia asked, putting her hands out for balance as the F train came to a sudden and ungraceful halt in the many-tracked Queens Plaza station.

Fanny put the Bigelow's bag on the floor so that Arabia could sit down next to her.

"This is my secret molecule, Arabia," Fanny whispered into her ear. "I'm giving it to you. It has many magical powers. Who knows how many?" she said, her cloudy stare rising to the handles that hang down for standees. "But one thing I know for sure: the ants worship it. A drop on a Q-tip and they come running. At your service.

"Call them," Fanny urged. "And they will come out from behind the sinks and refrigerators of the world. From out of a billion cracks in a million sidewalks they will rush to you. The little brown house ants will leave off scaling sugar bowls and crawling around pieces of cheese. The pinching carpenters will head for you. The fiery red stingers, the ones that build the giant hills in Africa, they'll find a way to get to you."

Arabia, amazed, turned to Fanny and looked her right in the eye.

"You'll be their general and people will listen. I'm counting on you, Arabia. Remake the world so it will be impossible for anyone to be as alone as I am. Redistribute the wealth. Don't pay any attention to their old excuses. Change the world so much that even Fanny Kassman wouldn't recognize it. Now go home."

Arabia, her arms around the bag with the Hellmann's jar inside, left Fanny at Lexington Avenue. She thought she heard Fanny calling, "Don't forget the whales," before the F train carried her away, forever.

The tired girl boarded the steep escalator and came down again on the uptown side of the tracks. A pretzel man sitting on a bench looked up at her and just shook his head.

When she got home she was not surprised to find that her absence had gone completely unnoticed. They had finished their fight and turned off the lights.

Arabia opened the jar and set it down on the sooty windowsill next to her bed. The paint on the windowsill had cracks in the shape of a cow. The beautiful mixture was still surging to the pull of some unseen moon. She stuck in a bobby pin, captured a drop in its crook, tapped it down where the cow's eye would have been . . . and she waited.

In a minute the first ant came padding by from his home on the outside ledge. He headed straight for the golden droplet. Rearing up on his hind legs that were only as thick as a hair, he began waving his antennae in an orderly fashion. He was quickly joined by many others. Eight lined up neatly behind him and the tenth made a right turn.

"Oh, Fanny," she called out in wonder. She was leaning so close that there was only an eyelash length between them. The streetlight dazzled off their tiny blacks backs. Two dozen of them were now linked, antenna to ankle, in an ant chorus line that formed an unmistakable "R."

"Oh, Fanny, it will be different," she promised as they continued to gather, and she didn't blink or swallow until they spelled "READY."

THE HONEY MOON BEES AND THE BUSY MAN'S GARDEN

BY

Robert Duncan

Once upon a time there was a busy man who had a garden which took all his time. He was up at four and in bed at ten, all day long tending and weeding, planting and seeding, watering and keeping his garden neat, picking the green bugs off of each leaf and pruning the new shoots to improve every twig, every branch, every leafy lively vegetable and every climbing designing vine and every beautiful special flower in his yard.

He had hedges to trim and in the bright sun workd all day cutting every stray scratching twig away and constantly restoring the beautiful shaped planed surfaces of hedgy green. He had hedges in box shapes and round ball shapes and he had splendid big hedges taller than he was that made walls and he had great green animals in neatly trimmd shaped hedges, a peacock, a lion, a dove, and a pyramid.

He had rows of perfect rose bushes that were like bouquets on the tops of regular trunks, and he had red and pink and yellow roses on four-foot-long stems. He had briar roses and wood roses and night roses and tear roses.

He had tulips, even in every season, of every hue.

He was up at four and at work all the long days and the shorter days too, spraying his garden or making little ditches where streams of water ran or arranging rocks to make attractive grottos, setting out new little plants or taking in delicate plants before the cold weather.

Now you see that it was really his garden that kept the busy man busy. It was in fact the wonderful garden of the busy man's busyness.

The busy man was always sending away for new plants. He had catalogs and he sat up in bed busy checking them over and writing away for rare flowers and all sorts of leafy, twiggy, green things he had never heard of before. So one day he saw an ad for a moon bean. And he sent off immediately a wire for some seeds. And so it happened that he planted a bed, at a far corner of the garden, of moon beans.

He waterd them carefully, he prepared their bed with leaf mold and all kinds of fertilizer. He waited and waited. But nothing happend. The busy man wanted more and more to see what his moon beans would look like. There had been no picture in the catalog, you see, and he was very excited, and then he was very eager and wondering what the moon beans would look like, and then he was worried when nothing happened and grew, and then he was unhappy. Then he was always wishing and at last, one day, he thot only of his moon bean garden.

The roses and the hedges, the tulips and chrysanthemums were neglected. The grass began to grow up wherever it wanted to and the borders all became unruly.

The busy man thot only of his moon bean garden. It seemd to him that it was at last the very important thing he had been busy for. One day then as he sat longing and despairing and not giving up, he started to cry.

He cried and he cried then. O my moon beans my moon beans, he wept, and the tears fell all around him where he sat.

Wherever his tears fell a tiny blue sprout showd, like a tear starting at the corner of an eye, and ran out in tendrils of silver and yellow all over the patch like tears running out over a cheek. He did not see them at first. He was so busy weeping. When he finally took out his handkerchief and dried his eyes, there all about him growing and sprouting were hundreds of moon beans.

He was overjoyd. He sat and he sat watching them grow and as they grew he began to hear a faraway faint singing. The singing was the moonlight but he could not see by it he was hearing by it. He was hearing more of it. The moon beans were singing not growing. They were buzzing and humming. The ground was alive with them, with golden rustling seeds that were really bees.

The man did not go in for dinner that night. It was so wonderful sitting in the far corner of the garden. All of his busyness anyway had gone into the bees, you see. He had cried and cried and lost all sense of being busy. Now he was content to sit and listen.

He was beginning by listening to their song to see very clearly. It was the dark of the moon, a very dark night. But the moon bees were a moving humming lantern in the garden.

He saw by their light the hedges that were growing every which way so that he could hardly see the peacock for the wild hedge it was, he could hardly see the lion in his hedge. And all the new shapes seemd wonderful to him. He saw the roses scraggly and thorny and unkempt, shedding their petals all over the ground. And O O O, the little bugs and the pale yellow slugs everywhere. Snail trails of silvery moon webs glistend in the lamplight.

All my garden is wildly ruind, he exclaimd with joy. How wonderfully strange it has grown.

And as he saw the whole garden by the magical moon bean lantern, the whole flock of moon bees swarmed and rose, singing and drunk with their own singing, and flew up up up up up up into the faraway black night, up into the sky to the moon, filling it to fullness, to the full round moon lantern shining down upon the happy man in his unruly garden.

So, said the father of the little girl, when you come to the honey moon, you will find it round and full like a hive with the honey moon bees.

FIRST WINE

BY
Jack Dunphy

Aunt Frances's white cat Matilda was reflected in the sideboard when he passed through the dining room into the parlor after supper. He would be followed by Happy, in his polished black oxfords, dark blue serge trousers, and white shirt. The cat, though male, was called Matilda because he was such a high flier, Aunt Frances said.

Leaving Matilda behind in the parlor thinking up devilment, Happy would turn back and walk through the dining room and into the kitchen again, then back to the parlor again, back and forth, back and forth, in his pigeon-toed way, his hands in his pockets, until bedtime.

Till then I had only seen Happy sit down at mealtimes, when he ate, and once, when I saw him downtown on Market Street driving his American Express truck through the traffic with one of the many kinds of grins on his face that he always wore. Where he came from nobody knew. I once asked Aunt Frances and she told me it was a mystery. That in itself was wonderful enough to me; but, then, the fact that Happy had been engaged to Aunt Frances's daughter, who had died at a very young age of consumption, made me really wonder at him; since Happy, although extraordinarily dramatic, did not seem to realize he was.

Aunt Frances Fitzgerald was everything I wanted. She could be facetious, sardonic, sarcastic, impressively philosophical, funny and sad, always generous, always my friend as long as I would need her; which I did not think would be for too long then, since I was growing up and would soon move far away from Ingersoll Street.

Since Aunt Frances was a widow, there were just Happy and herself and high-flying Matilda in the little two-storied row house with its sand-soaped white marble front steps next to the corner.

On the corner was Hampton's Grocery Store, with its casks

and crates, its barrels and sacks, its mélange of odors of peanut butter and coffee, and almost dried-out winter apples, faded and wrinkled as the proprietors themselves, oriental in their self-effacement: two white aprons gleaming out of the cool dark store: man and wife, but come to looking so much alike one another with the passing of the years, that Aunt Frances suspected them of being twins!

"Twins, Aunt Frances?"

"Brother and sister," Aunt Frances Fitzgerald told me, looking this way and that up and down Ingersoll Street with a Don't-let-on-I-told-you air about her that drove me wild!

"This is just between ourselves, Jackie. Are you alone? I don't want that Johnny Ervine coming in here with you. Now you drink this down. There you go."

Dandelion wine!

Ah, I've had wine since, but nothing comes back to me like Aunt Frances Fitzgerald's dandelion wine. It cannot be repeated, nor rediscovered, though I know it must be somewhere, since its perfume seduces me of a sudden, down through the years, in the most unlikely places, far as far from Ingersoll Street.

Today, for instance, this fragrant field, tantalizingly like Aunt Frances's house because it smells the way her house used to smell. I see no dandelion, though. Or if I do, and take some up and hold it to my nose, it doesn't smell like much of anything to me. Indian Bread, Queen Anne's Lace, Milkweed. I go around to all of them in turn, but they give me nothing by themselves, though together they tease and tantalize me with something like, yet not altogether like, what I used to drink as a very little boy.

"This'll wet your whistle."

It did. But it's only a smell now, mystifying me, in lonely fields.

We were a new little family and our house was half-empty. Aunt Frances lived only three doors away, but for all that her house was in another country. It was the essence of coziness. Its atmosphere was thoughtful and reminiscent. Compared to my mother, Aunt Frances was a gypsy, darkly dressed. She never wore jewelry. It was her imagination Aunt Frances kept polished and put on the way ordinary women do their bracelets and beads.

Being wild herself, she favored wild things. I was wild, Matilda was wild, Happy, who never sat down except when he was fed, or driving his truck, had never been tamed.

Later, when we moved away from Ingersoll Street, I visited

Aunt Frances, and slept in the same bed with Happy. He used to make himself small and quiet as a domino. Really, I had the bed to myself. Did she, though, Aunt Frances, when she took off her dress and black cotton stockings, and let down her black hair, open the connecting door between their rooms and slip into bed with Happy, to console him for the loss of her daughter? If she did, there was no sign of it.

Her secrecy was enormous. Why not? Seeing life as she did, vigilance was imperative.

"I have all the friends I need. I don't want anymore. My days of making friends are over."

Friends she had, and they were all young males. They used to sit around her dining room table drinking dandelion wine. Happy's glass would be set next to Aunt Frances's. He would take a sip, standing at her elbow, then put his glass down on the table near hers again and continue to prowl. He was blond, with a ruddy complexion, his hair parted on the side and always neatly combed. Aunt Frances waited until he came out of the kitchen, then she would follow him with her eyes as he passed on his way into the parlor to Matilda. He never talked to Matilda, but he used to look at him, bending over him, his hands in his pockets, and his face getting very red from the rush of blood, but he would never open his mouth. He smiled, and Matilda did something with his face, but all they ever did was look at one another. Then Happy would remember Aunt Frances and his walk and he would continue prowling.

There were pictures of Aunt Frances's daughter everywhere. A porcelain shoe with a cushion inside for pins was hers. Her clothes were gone, though, and in their place in the closet Happy hung his clothes. They were few and looked lonely hanging there alongside so much unused space.

Aunt Frances's daughter did not look like her in any of her pictures, but like Mr. Fitzgerald. They looked like brother and sister, weak and different, not at all like Aunt Frances. Aunt Frances talked about them in a low voice. We'd be sitting on her front steps. Aunt Frances sat on the side of the step where she could catch Happy's shadow on the window screen as he turned around in the parlor on his way back into the kitchen.

When we moved away from Ingersoll Street and I used to visit Aunt Frances for a week at a time, her hair had begun to turn gray, and she no longer gave me any dandelion wine. It was still being made, fermenting in barrels down in the cellar. Her young male friends had grown a little older. They sat around the dining room table. The sideboard still reflected Matilda. Happy was the same.

"I have all the friends I want. I don't want anymore. New friends wouldn't appeal to me."

We no longer sat gossiping on her doorstep together. Once, I remember, I ran off, just ran off somewhere, running for the sake of running, jumping as I ran, from side to side, hurdling. I left Ingersoll Street behind me and passed Robert Morris Grade School. I was down near College Wall when I gave myself a reason for running away from Ingersoll Street in the first place. Johnny Irvine had moved away from Ingersoll Street and was now living in a dark, brown, four-story row house across from College Wall.

Johnny was glad to see me. They had an aunt living with them who shared the rent. Mr. Irvine, a trolley car conductor, had died. Johnny and his mother and the aunt lived in the four-storied house in a relieved sort of way, as though they were on a continual picnic. They were always getting lost and coming on one another suddenly in the strange rooms and laughing. Johnny and I got wet through chasing one another from floor to floor. From a window at the top of the house we could see over College Wall into Girard College.

"I can go there now, since my father's dead," Johnny told me.

"Will you wear a uniform?" I asked him.

"If I want," he replied.

For a minute he looked grown up to me. I knew then that someday I would not see him anymore.

"Let's exchange hats," I said.

So we did. And ties.

"Don't forget to get back your hat and right tie, John," his mother said at the front door when I was saying good-bye.

We had forgotten.

Johnny screamed and laughed, tearing my tie from around his own throat and attempting to fix it on me.

"You can't tie anybody else's tie for them, John," his mother said.

Her appearance was always iron-gray, and she wore brown dresses with white collars. Johnny, red-faced and sweaty, laughed at her. He had a mad, high laugh, and Mrs. Irvine did not laugh at all. What I adored about Mrs. Irvine was to hear her say "Don't be a hog, John." She pronounced *hog* "hawg" and it sounded delicious to my ears.

"Good-bye Johnny, good-bye Johnny," I repeated over and over again, "good-bye Johnny," as I ran along College Wall. I ran backward and made so much noise that I failed to hear anything else. Johnny had gone in. His mother had pulled him inside.

"Don't be a *hawg!*"

I stopped and listened, hoping she would say it again. I loved to hear it so, but what I heard instead was my own name.

Aunt Frances came running toward me along College Wall in her carpet slippers and black cotton stockings. She had slipped into a coat, but was obviously too upset to think of closing and buttoning it. It probably didn't even occur to her that she had not changed into shoes for the street.

She was frantic. I hardly knew her. She was altogether different from the way I remembered her when we used to sit on her white front steps gossiping together.

"Where have you been? I'm near out of my mind worrying about you? Where have you been?"

"Why, to see Johnny. He lives near here."

"Johnny who? I never heard of anything so careless and crazy. Lives where?"

"Why, Johnny Irvine. He lives across from College Wall."

"Good riddance to him. I had no idea where they moved to. I don't see why you should. I thought you'd got lost. I had half a mind to call the cops. I swore you were lost."

"How lost, Aunt Frances? This is my old neighborhood. I know the streets by heart. I couldn't get lost in them even if I tried."

"That's what you think. Well, don't try, is all I can say. Or else you might find yourself lost again."

"But I haven't been lost, I tell you."

"Well, be that as it may, come on, get a move on. Happy's waiting on supper for you."

She began to run ahead of me, kicking her feet in their carpet slippers out to the side of her like flippers. It struck me so funny that I began to laugh. I laughed like Johnny Irvine, laughed like I'd like to strangle or bust.

"What are you laughing at? Come on, I tell you. Didn't I say Happy's waiting? How did I know that you were lost and I'd have to come so far as College Wall looking for you?"

She looked at me and took hold of my hand. I saw she was smiling. She liked to be given a hard time. She liked it when Matilda leaped on her polished dining room table and skidded across it before tearing out through the house across the street to kill himself for sure this time, since he was deaf, and getting deafer. She liked it. She just liked it, that's all. The harder the better.

"Anyway," I said, "I wasn't lost."

"You were."

"I wasn't."

"You look as if you were."

"I don't feel as if I was."

"You do to me," she said. "Feel lost, I mean."

She put her arm around me and drew me to her, so that I felt little again, and really as if I had been lost. I looked at the back of her neck for the curls that used to escape from her pile of black hair and they were gray and made me sad.

"Gosh it was terrible," I said.

"What was terrible?"

"Being lost."

Easter Vacation I arrived at the little house near the corner on Ingersoll Street later in the day than I had planned. Big Tom Kelly, Fritzie Kuh, Francis Xavier O'Shea, with one or two others of Aunt Frances's male companions, were seated around her dining room table drinking wine with her. I'd telephoned I was coming, but Aunt Frances seemed surprised anyway. Tom Kelly, who had made such a fuss of me when I lived on the street, was strained when he greeted me.

I felt strange with him, too.

I could not swear and show-off to Tom anymore, nor would he have wanted me to, being a quiet-going, serious young man; Aunt Frances's friend, primarily, and speaking only when she spoke, and not before.

I was wondering where the house's old welcoming ways had

got to when Happy stopped before me in his evening promenade and took my Boston bag from me and carried it upstairs to the room we shared.

Dear Happy!

Late the next morning, Aunt Frances stood at the stove frying me up a stack of buckwheat cakes. The sun was warm enough to leave the kitchen door open and to allow Matilda to sit outside on the wooden doorstep cleaning himself, while keeping an eye out for pigeons. It seemed to me that Matilda never closed his eyes. Deafer than ever, he was always on the watch, like a rabbit.

Aunt Frances took up a polishing rag and left me alone with my buckwheat cakes. She did not watch me eat as many as I could and keep count anymore. I sat at the kitchen table, toying with a buckwheat cake, and missing her. I wondered why people change and why it should matter.

"Aunt Frances?"

"I'm right here, honey."

"Remember when Matilda caught the pigeon, Aunt Frances? Aunt Frances, are you there? Can you hear me?"

"I'm here, I'm here."

Her voice sounded faint; she was under something, cleaning.

"I'll never forget that," I said.

"What did you say, Jackie? Do you want more flapjacks?"

She came back into the kitchen.

"I was thinking of the time Matilda caught the pigeon in the snow and came along the back fence with it hanging out of his mouth. Do you remember, Aunt Frances?"

"I should think so. You don't want more buckwheat cakes then, do you? There was a time I couldn't keep up with you, you ate them so fast."

"I'd love some more."

I didn't really, but the cellar door was open, bringing the old smells of dandelion wine up from below, and I wanted Aunt Frances to stay with me in the kitchen, because they went together. So she mixed me up another batch of buck, smiling her sweet way, and looking at me, and counting the flapjacks I ate the way she used to, one after another, as many as I could, to please her. There was still a pile when the doorbell rang, and someone pounded at the front door at the same time, and I sat there at the table in the kitchen, my heart fluttering in my breast like a bird in a rain puddle; for I knew who was at the door, though I dared not say.

Aunt Frances took exactly three years to go to the door and come back to the kitchen.

"It's that Johnny Irvine. Don't let him in. I thought they moved."

"Johnny! How did you know I was here, Johnny?"

"Because it's Easter Vacation, dopey!"

He grabbed my hat, and I took his easily, and we made for The Basin at the top of the other Ingersoll Street a block away.

It's all houses now, but then there was this two-story-high mound of orange-colored earth, with a pond full of debris in the middle, that we called The Basin.

"I see a dead cat," said Johnny, as soon as we slid down into The Basin and were rushing around the edge of the pond. I said I didn't see anything.

"You're always seeing dead cats in The Basin."

"I almost ate one, too."

"You didn't."

"I did. My father brought home this rabbit that turned out to be a cat, and we did *almost* eat it."

"I see a bird, and you don't!" I said.

"I do, too."

"Where?"

"Somewhere."

"Give me back my hat."

"Catch me first."

Johnny ran off laughing in his shrill way. His foot slipped into the pond and he got wet up to his knee.

"Lordy!" he said. "Now look what you made me do."

Just then I got my hat from him and he chased me, and I slipped into the pond and got wet up to *both* my knees. Johnny regarded me enviously. For once he didn't laugh. "Give me back my hat," he demanded sullenly.

I threw his cap in the water, he jumped for it, and got wet up to both his knees.

"I'm wetter than you," he said. "That makes me King of The Basin."

"You're not! I am! I was born King of The Basin!"

"I was double-born King of The Basin!"

We fought 'round and 'round the edge of the pond and got wetter and wetter. When the sun pulled out of The Basin and began to sink down among the houses in West Philadelphia, Johnny and I stood facing one another, shivering.

"What'll I say when I get home?" Johnny asked me, as we climbed up out of The Basin.

"Say it rained," I told him.

"No, I'll say you pushed me into the pond."

"I once saw it rain on only one side of the street somewhere, Johnny. So it's not really a lie. It could happen."

"No," Johnny said, at the top of The Basin, "I'll say you pushed me."

He descended The Basin toward College Wall, and I stood where I was, looking after him, until I could not see him anymore.

"I'm King of The Basin!" I shouted.

Then I remembered that Johnny would tell his mother that I had pushed him into the pond on purpose and I felt cold and wet. It was different with Johnny, his mother watched him so, even how he ate: "Don't be a *hawg*, John!" I probably wouldn't hear her say that anymore now, I thought. So I said it to myself all the way to Aunt Frances's. "Don't be a *hawg*, John, don't be a *hawg*!" But it wasn't the same.

Aunt Frances did not appear to notice me coming in. She was polishing her daughter's pictures and Mr. Fitzgerald's. She did this every day. I slipped upstairs and got out of my wet clothes and put them somewhere where only Happy would see them. I knew he wouldn't say anything. They looked funny, though, hanging wet and muddy next to Happy's blue serge jacket in the part of his closet that was always empty, waiting for almost anybody to come along and share it with him.

I had other clothes with me, even another pair of pants. I was nearly dressed when the telephone rang and I felt I could guess who it was. Aunt Frances didn't talk very long to the party, and when she hung up you could hear the click all over the house. I was sure the caller had been Mrs. Irvine and wondered whether Aunt Frances would tell me or not. It wasn't like she was really my aunt, because if she'd really been my aunt she would have *had* to tell me, since that's what they say families are for: to take care of one another.

Aunt Frances came upstairs, her carpet slippers slapping

the steps one-two, one-two, like that, and her dress rustling. She passed Happy's room, where I sat on the edge of the bed waiting for her, and went into the adjoining room, her own. I counted ten, then to twenty, and closed the closet so my wet clothes wouldn't show and went downstairs in my stocking feet.

I don't know why, but everything looked suddenly new to me, different, and as if I might be seeing them for the last time. Yet there was nothing I felt I could pick up and hold and say good-bye to. I knew enough not to try and pick up Matilda. It was the house I would have liked to hold, hug, in my arms. How could I do that? Houses can't be held.

The cellar door was still open. I went down and sat on the stairs surveying the open vats. The song of the fermentation of the dandelion wine came to me and I drank wine in my imagination as I used to do in reality when it snowed to heaven outside, and a darkly dressed figure —three doors from my own—would call me into her vestibule.

"Here you are, Jackie. This'll make Jack Frost melt in your bones."

"Who's Jack Frost?"

"Never you mind. You drink this down now. And don't tell anybody. Especially not that Johnny Irvine. Because I don't trust him."

"But why, Aunt Frances? Why don't you trust Johnny? I do."

"Well, you shouldn't."

"Why not?"

"Because he's deceitful. There he is now, clamoring outside the door for you. Go out to him. I don't want him in here."

"Yes, but he's *not* that, Aunt Frances. He's just not."

"Why not?"

"Why, because *I'm* not. We're alike in everything, everything there is. So if he's that, then I am too."

"Deceitful? You? Never."

"But I want to be, Aunt Frances! I want to be if Johnny Irvine is."

"Jackie? Jackie? Don't tell me he's gone out."

I sat still on the cellar stairs in my stocking feet. I didn't feel like answering. I didn't feel like company.

"Jackie? Jackie? Don't tell me he's gone out again."

She saw me, finally, and came down the cellar stairs flapflapping her carpet slippers, and sat down on the step beside me. The last light of day showed at the two little oblong-shaped cellar windows looking out on the brick pavement in front of Aunt Frances's house.

"Listen to the wine," Aunt Frances said, quietly. "It's talking."

"What's it saying, Aunt Frances?"

"I'm not sure what it's saying to *you*. It says different things to different people."

"What's it saying to *you?*"

Aunt Frances slid down on the step below me and cocked her ear over the vat nearest us, and listened.

"Hello, hello," she said. "Bubble and squeak."

"Bubble and squeak?"

"Just before the bubbles break, they squeak. Then they say, Hello, hello!"

"Never good-bye, Aunt Frances?"

"No. Never."

"That's nice."

I put my head down to where I touched hers, and she smelled of dandelion wine.

"I didn't push him into the pond up at The Basin today, Aunt Frances."

She was stone; noble.

Nor did she turn prying eyes on my misery, but let me suffer in my own way, unmolested by advice, unencumbered by a helping hand, grazing on my own freedom among the thistles and the thorns.

TO ALPHA DRYDEN EBERHART: ON BEING SEVENTY-FIVE

BY

Richard Eberhart

When you were in high school, in the old red brick
Building, a bomb in the form of a firecracker
Went off under your seat in the schoolroom. The
Teacher thought you were the culprit, you were
Summoned and you were expelled, although your sense
Of fairness to a friend kept you from telling
That another had set off the report. Then up rose
Our fair and gentle mother, roused to go before
The school committee to attest that her son was
Not a bad boy. Bravo for her. It took courage,
But she stood by you as a youth of good character,
No revolutionary. Over half a century later
I recall this prank, its gusto, and the high sense
Of life that inhered in you and in our mother.

Another memory, when we used to go down in the meadow
Somewhere near the river, and snare gophers. We had no
Sense of their pain or of our injustice. We were boys
Out for sport. A circle of string was placed over the hole,
Run back maybe thirty feet and there on our bellies
We youths would wait for a long time for an unwary head

To pop up into sight. Zing, and we would strangle the creature,
Stand up and swing him around our heads in gusty triumph.
Then we would skin him and nail him to a board and
Salt him, and in a while have a number of such trophies.

A COUPLA SCALPED INDIANS

BY

Ralph Ellison

They had a small, loud-playing band and as we moved through the trees I could hear the notes of the horns bursting like bright metallic bubbles against the sky. It was a far-away and sparklike sound, shooting through the late afternoon quiet of the hill; very clear now and definitely music, band music. I was relieved. I had been hearing it for several minutes as we moved through the woods but the pain down there had made all my senses so deceptively sharp that I had decided that the sound was simply a musical ringing in my ears. But now I was doubly sure, for Buster stopped and looked at me, squinching up his eyes with his head cocked to one side. He was wearing a blue cloth headband with a turkey feather stuck over his ear, and I could see it flutter in the breeze.

"You hear what I hear, man?" he said.

"I *been* hearing it," I said.

"Damn! We better haul it outta these woods so we can see something. Why didn't you say something to a man?"

We moved again, hurrying along. Until suddenly we were out of the woods, standing at a point of the hill where the path dropped down to the town, our eyes searching. It was close to sun-down and below me I could see the red clay of the path cutting through the woods and moving past a white, lightning-blasted tree to join the river road, and the narrow road shifting past Aunt Mackie's old shack and on, beyond the road and the shack, I could see the dull mysterious movement of the river. The horns were blasting brighter now, though still far away, sounding like somebody flipping bright handfuls of new small change against the sky. I listened and followed the river swiftly with my eyes as it wound through the trees and on past the buildings and houses of the town—until there, there at the farther edge of the town, past the tall smokestack and the great silver sphere of the gas storage tower, floated the tent, spread white and cloudlike with its bright ropes of fluttering flags.

That's when we started running. It was a dog-trotting Indian run, because we were both wearing packs and were tired from the tests we had been taking in the woods and in Indian Lake. But now the bright blare of the horns made us forget our tiredness and pain and we bounded down the path like young goats in the twilight, our army-surplus mess kits and canteens rattling against us.

"We late, man," Buster said. "I told you we was gon' fool around and be late. But naw, you had to cook that damn sage hen with mud on him just like it says in the book. We coulda barbecued a damn elephant while we was waiting for a tough sucker like that to get done. . . ."

His voice grumbled on like a trombone with a big, fat, pot-shaped mute stuck in it and I ran on without answering. We had tried to take the cooking test by using a sage hen instead of a chicken because Buster said Indians didn't eat chicken. So we'd taken time to flush a sage hen and kill him with a slingshot. Besides, he was the one who insisted that we try the running endurance test, the swimming test, *and* the cooking test all in one day. Sure it had taken time. I knew it would take time; especially with our having no Scout Master. We didn't even have a troop, only the Boy Scout's Handbook that Buster had found, and—as we'd figured—our hardest problem had been working out the tests for ourselves. He had no right to argue anyway, since he'd beaten me in all the tests—although I'd passed them too. And he was the one who insisted that we start taking them today, even though we were both still sore and wearing our bandages, and I was still carrying some of the catgut stitches around in me. I had wanted to wait a few days until I was healed but Mister Know-it-all Buster challenged me by saying that a real stud Indian could take the tests even right after the doctor had just finished sewing on him. So, since we were more interested in being *Indian* scouts than simply *boy* scouts, here I was running toward the spring carnival instead of being already there. I wondered how Buster knew so much about what an Indian would do, anyway. We certainly hadn't read anything about what the doctor had done to us. He'd probably made it up and I had let him urge me into going to the woods even though I had to slip out of the house. The doctor had told Miss Janey (she's the lady who takes care of me) to keep me quiet for a few days and she dead-aimed to do it. You would've thought from the way she carried on that she was the one who had the operation—only that's one kind of operation no woman ever gets to brag about.

Anyway, Buster and me had been in the woods and now we were plunging down the hill through the fast-falling dark to the carnival. I had begun to throb and the bandage was chafing, but as we rounded a curve I could see the tent and the flares and the gathering crowd. There was a breeze coming up the hill against us now and I could almost smell that cotton candy, the hamburgers, and the kerosene smell of the flares. We stopped to rest and Buster stood very straight and pointed down below, making a big sweep with his arm like an Indian chief in the movies when he's up on a hill telling his braves and the Great Spirit that he's getting ready to attack a wagon train.

"Heap big . . . teepee . . . down yonder," he said in Indian talk. "Smoke signal say . . . Blackfeet . . . make . . . heap much . . . stink, buck-dancing in tennis shoes!"

"Ugh," I said, bowing my suddenly war-bonneted head, "ugh!"

Buster swept his arm from east to west, his face impassive. "Smoke medicine say . . . heap . . . *big* stink! Hot toe jam!" He struck his palm with his fist and I looked at his puffed-out cheeks and giggled.

"Smoke medicine say you tell heap big lie," I said. "Let's get on down there."

We ran past some trees, Buster's canteen jangling. Around us it was quiet except for the roosting birds.

"Man," I said, "you making as much noise as a team of mules in full harness. Don't no Indian scout make all that racket when he runs."

"No scout-um now," he said. "Me go make heap much pow-wow at stinkydog carnival!"

"Yeah, but you'll get yourself scalped, making all that noise in the woods," I said. "Those other Indians don't give a damn 'bout no carnival—what does a carnival mean to them? They'll scalp the hell outta you!"

"Scalp?" he said, talking Colored now. "Hell, man—that damn doctor scalped me last week. Damn near took my whole head off!"

I almost fell with laughing. "Have mercy, Lord," I laughed, "we're just a coupla poor scalped Indians!"

We laughed, Buster stumbled about, grabbing a tree for support. The doctor had said that it would make us men and Buster had said, hell, he was a man already—what he wanted was to be an Indian. We hadn't thought about it making us scalped ones.

"You right, man," Buster said. "Since he done scalped so much of my head away I must be crazy as a fool. That's why I'm in such a hurry to get down yonder with the other crazy folks. I want to be right in the middle of 'em when they really start raising hell."

"Oh, you'll be there, Chief Baldhead," I said.

He looked at me blankly. "What you think ole Doc done with our scalps?"

"Made him a tripe stew, man."

"You nuts," Buster said, "he probably used 'em for fish bait."

"He did, I'm going to sue him for one trillion, zillion dollars, cash," I said.

"Maybe he gave 'em to ole Aunt Mackie, man. I bet with them she could work some out*rageous* spells!"

"Man," I said, suddenly shivering, "don't talk about that old woman, she's evil."

"Hell, everybody's so scared of her. I just wish she'd mess with me or my daddy, I'd fix her."

I said nothing—I was afraid. For though I had seen the old woman about town all my life she remained to me like the moon, mysterious in her very familiarity; and in the sound of her name there was terror:

Ho, Aunt Mackie, talker-with-spirits, prophetess-of-disaster, odd-dweller-alone in a riverside shack surrounded by sunflowers, morning glories, and strange magical weeds (Yao, as Buster during our Indian phase, would have put it, Yao!); *Old Aunt Mackie, wizen-faced walker-with-a-stick, shrill-voiced ranter in the night, round-eyed malicious one, given to dramatic trances and fiery flights of rage; Aunt Mackie, preacher of wild sermons on the busy streets of the town, hot-voiced chaser of children, snuff-dipper, visionary; wearer of greasy headrags, wrinkled gingham aprons, and old men's shoes; Aunt Mackie, nobody's sister but still Aunt Mackie to us all* (Ho, yao!); *teller of fortunes, concocter of powerful, body-rending spells* (Yao, Yao!); *Aunt Mackie, the remote one though always seen about us; night-consulted adviser to farmers on crops and cattle* (Yao!); *herb-healer, root-doctor, and town-confounding oracle to wildcat drillers seeking oil in the earth—*(Yaaaah-

Ho!). It was all there in her name and before her name I shivered. Once uttered, for me the palaver was finished; I resigned it to Buster, the tough one.

Even some of the grown folks, both black and white, were afraid of Aunt Mackie, and all the kids except Buster. Buster lived on the outskirts of the town and was as unimpressed by Aunt Mackie as by the truant officer and others whom the rest of us regarded with awe. And because I was his buddy I was ashamed of my fear.

Usually I had extra courage when I was with him. Like the time two years before when we had gone into the woods with only our slingshots, a piece of fatback, and a skillet and had lived three days on the rabbits we killed and the wild berries we picked and the ears of corn we raided from farmers' fields. We slept each rolled in his quilt and in the night Buster had told bright stories of the world we'd find when we were grown-up and gone from hometown and family. I had no family, only Miss Janey, who took me after my mother died (I didn't know my father), so that getting away always appealed to me, and the coming time of which Buster liked to talk loomed in the darkness around me rich with pastel promise. And although we heard a bear go lumbering through the woods nearby and the eerie howling of a coyote in the dark, yes, and had been swept by the soft swift flight of an owl, Buster was unafraid and I had grown brave in the grace of his courage.

But to me Aunt Mackie was a threat of a different order, and I paid her the respect of fear.

"Listen to those horns," Buster said. And now the sound came through the trees like colored marbles glinting in the summer sun.

We ran again. And now keeping pace with Buster I felt good; for I meant to be there too, at the carnival; right in the middle of all that confusion and sweating and laughing and all the strange sights to see.

"Listen to 'em now, man," Buster said. "Those fools is starting to shout amazing grace on those horns. Let's step on the gas!"

The scene danced below us as we ran. Suddenly there was a towering Ferris wheel revolving slowly out of the dark, its red and blue lights glowing like drops of dew dazzling a big spider web when you see it in the early morning. And we heard the beckoning blare of the band now shot through with the small, insistent, buckshot voices of the barkers.

"Listen to that trombone, man," I said.

"Sounds like he's playing the dozens with the whole wide world."

"What's he saying, Buster?"

"He's saying. 'Ya'll's mamas don't wear 'em. Is strictly without 'em. Don't know nothing 'bout 'em. . . .'"

"Don't know about what, man?"

"Draw's, fool; he's talking 'bout draw's!"

"How you know, man?"

"I hear him talking, don't I?"

"Sure, but you been scalped, remember? You crazy. How he know about those peoples' mamas?" I said.

"Says he saw 'em with his great big ole eye."

"Damn! He must be a Peeping Tom. How about those other horns?"

"Now that there tuba's saying:

> 'They don't play 'em, I know they don't.
> They don't play 'em, I know they won't.
> They just don't play no nasty dirty twelves. . . .' "

"Man, you *are* a scalped-headed fool. How about that trumpet?"

"Him? That fool's a soldier, he's really signifying. Saying,

> 'So ya'll don't play 'em, hey?
> So ya'll *won't* play 'em, hey?
> Well pat your feet and clap your hands,
> 'Cause I'm going to play 'em to the promised land. . . .'

"Man, the white folks know what that fool is signifying on that horn they'd run him clear on out the world. Trumpet's got a real *nasty* mouth."

"Why you call him a soldier, man?" I said.

" 'Cause he's slipping 'em in the twelves and choosing 'em, all at the same time. Talking 'bout they mamas and offering to fight 'em. Now he ain't like that ole clarinet; clarinet so sweet-talking he just *eases* you in the dozens."

"Say, Buster," I said, seriously now. "You know, we gotta stop cussing and playing the dozens if we're going to be boy scouts. Those white boys don't play that mess."

"You doggone right they don't," he said, the turkey feather vibrating above his ear. "Those guys can't take it, man. Besides, who wants to be just like them? Me, *I'm* gon' be a scout and play the twelves too! You have to, with some of these old jokers we know. You don't know what to say when they start easing you, you never have no peace. You have to outtalk 'em, outrun 'em, or outfight 'em and I don't aim to be running and fighting all the time. N'mind those white boys."

We moved on through the growing dark. Already I could

see a few stars and suddenly there was the moon. It emerged blade-like from behind a thin veil of cloud, just as I heard a new sound and looked about me with quick uneasiness. Off to our left I heard a dog, a big one. I slowed, seeing the outlines of a picket fence and the odd-shaped shadows that lurked in Aunt Mackie's yard.

"What's the matter, man?" Buster said.

"Listen," I said. "That's Aunt Mackie's dog. Last year I was passing here and he sneaked up and bit me through the fence when I wasn't even thinking about him. . . ."

"Hush, man," Buster whispered, "I hear the sonofabitch back in there now. You leave him to me."

We moved by inches now, hearing the dog barking in the dark. Then we were going past and he was throwing his heavy body against the fence, straining at his chain. We hesitated, Buster's hand on my arm. I undid my heavy canteen belt and held it, suddenly light in my fingers. In my right I gripped the hatchet which I'd brought along.

"We'd better go back and take the other path," I whispered.

"Just stand still, man," Buster said.

The dog hit the fence again, barking hoarsely; and in the interval following the echoing crash I could hear the distant music of the band.

"Come on," I said, "let's go 'round."

"Hell, no! We're going straight! I ain't letting no damn dog scare me, Aunt Mackie or no Aunt Mackie. Come on!"

Trembling, I moved with him toward the roaring dog, then felt him stop again, and I could hear him removing his pack and taking out something wrapped in paper.

"Here," he said, "you take my stuff and come on."

I took his gear and went behind him, hearing his voice suddenly hot with fear and anger saying, "Here, you 'gator-mouthed egg-sucker, see how you like this sage hen," just as I tripped over the straps of his pack and went down. Then I was crawling franti-cally, trying to untangle myself and hearing the dog growling as he crunched something in his jaws. "Eat it, you buzzard," Buster was saying, "See if you tough as he is," as I tried to stand, stumbling and sending an old cooking range crashing in the dark. Part of the fence was gone and in my panic I had crawled into the yard. Now I could hear the dog bark threateningly and leap the length of his chain toward me, then back to the sage hen; toward me, a swift leaping form snatched backward by the heavy chain, turning to mouth savagely on the mangled bird. Moving away I floundered over the stove and pieces of crating, against giant sun-flower stalks, trying to get back to Buster when I saw the lighted window and realized that I had crawled to the very shack itself. That's when I pressed against the weathered-satin side of the shack and came erect. And there, framed by the window in the lamp-lit room, I saw the woman.

A brown naked woman, whose black hair hung beneath her shoulders. I could see the long graceful curve of her back as she moved in some sort of slow dance, bending forward and back; her arms and body moving as though gathering in something which I couldn't see but which she drew to her with pleasure; a young, girlish body with slender, well-rounded hips. *But who?* flashed through my mind as I heard Buster's *Hey, man; where'd you go? You done run out on me?* from back in the dark. And I willed to move, to hurry away—but in that instant she chose to pick up a glass from a wobbly old round white table and to drink, turning slowly as she stood with backward-tilted head, slowly turning in the lamplight and drinking slowly as she turned, slowly; until I could see the full-faced glowing of her feminine form.

And I was frozen there, watching the uneven movement of her breasts beneath the glistening course of the liquid, spilling down her body in twin streams drawn by the easy tiding of her breathing. Then the glass came down and my knees flowed beneath me like water. The air seemed to explode soundlessly. I shook my head but she, the image, would not go away and I wanted suddenly to laugh wildly and to scream. For above the smooth shoulders of the girlish form I saw the wrinkled face of old Aunt Mackie.

Now I had never seen a naked woman before, only very little girls or once or twice a skinny one my own age, who looked like a boy with the boy part missing. And even though I'd seen a few calendar drawings, they were not alive like this, nor images of someone you'd thought familiar through having seen them passing through the streets of the town; nor like this inconsistent, with wrinkled face mismatched with glowing form. So that mixed with my fear of punishment for peeping there was added the terror of her mystery. And yet I could not move away. I was fascinated, hearing the growling dog and feeling a warm pain grow beneath my bandage—along with the newly risen terror that this deceptive old woman could cause me to feel this way, that she could be so young beneath her old baggy clothes.

She was dancing again now, still unaware of my eyes, the lamplight playing on her body as she swayed and enfolded the air or invisible ghosts or whatever it was, within her arms. Each time she moved, her hair, which was black as night now that it was no longer hidden beneath a greasy headrag, swung heavily about her shoulders. And as she moved to the side I could see the gentle tossing of her breasts beneath her upraised arms. *It just can't be,* I thought, *it just can't* and moved closer, determined to see and to know. But I had forgotten the hatchet in my hand until it struck the side of the house and I saw her turn quickly toward the window, her face evil as she swayed. I was rigid as stone, hearing the growling dog mangling the bird and knowing that I should run even as she moved toward the window, her shadow flying before her, her hair now wild as snakes writhing on a dead tree during a springtime flood. Then I could hear Buster's hoarse-voiced, *Hey, man! where in hell are you?* even as she pointed at me and screamed, sending me moving backward and I was aware of the sickle-bladed moon flying like a lightning flash as I fell, still gripping my hatchet, and struck my head in the dark.

When I started out of it, someone was holding me and I lay in light and looked up to see her face above me. Then it all flooded swiftly back and I was aware again of the contrast between smooth body and wrinkled face and experienced a sudden warm yet painful thrill. She held me close. Her breath came to me, sweetly alcoholic as she mumbled something about, "Little devil, lips that touch wine shall never touch mine! That's what I told him, understand me? Never," she said loudly, "You understand?"

"Yes, ma'm. . . ."

"Never, never, NEVER!"

"No, ma'm," I said, seeing her study me with narrowed eyes.

"You young but you young'uns understand, devilish as you is. What you doing messing 'round in my yard?"

"I got lost," I said. "I was coming from taking some boy scout tests and I was trying to get by your dog."

"So that's what I heard," she said. "He bite you?"

"No, ma'm."

"Course not, he don't bite on the new moon. No, I think you come in my yard to spy on me."

"No, ma'm, I didn't," I said. "I just happened to see the light when I was stumbling around trying to find my way."

"You got a pretty big hatchet there," she said, looking down at my hand. "What you plan to do with it?"

"It's a kind of boy scout ax," I said. "I used it to come through the woods. . . ."

She looked at me dubiously. "So," she said, "you're a heavy hatchet man and you stopped to peep. Well, what I want to know is, is you a drinking man? Have your lips ever touched wine?"

"Wine? No, ma'm."

"So you ain't a drinking man, but do you belong to church?"

"Yes, ma'm."

"And have you been saved and ain't no back-slider?"

"Yessum."

"Well," she said, pursing her lips, "I guess you can kiss me."

"MA'M?"

"That's what I said. You passed all the tests and you was peeping in my window. . . ."

She was holding me there on a cot, her arms around me as though I were a three-year-old, smiling like a girl. I could see her fine white teeth and the long hairs on her chin and it was like a bad dream. "You peeped," she said, "now you got to do the rest. I said kiss me, or I'll fix you. . . ."

I saw her face come close and felt her warm breath and closed my eyes, trying to force myself. *It's just like kissing some sweaty woman at church,* I told myself, *some friend of Miss Janey's.* But it didn't help and I could feel her drawing me and I found her lips with mine. It was dry and firm and winey and I could hear her sigh. "Again," she said, and once more my lips found hers. And suddenly she drew me to her and I could feel her breasts soft against me as once more she sighed.

"That was a nice boy," she said, her voice kind, and I opened my eyes. "That's enough now, you're both too young and too old, but you're brave. A regular lil' chocolate hero."

And now she moved and I realized for the first time that my hand had found its way to her breast. I moved it guiltily, my face flaming as she stood.

"You're a good brave boy," she said, looking at me from deep in her eyes, "but you forget what happened here tonight."

I sat up as she stood looking down upon me with a mysterious smile. And I could see her body up close now, in the dim yellow light; see the surprising silkiness of black hair mixed here and there with gray, and suddenly I was crying and hating myself for the compelling need. I looked at my hatchet lying on the floor now and wondered how she'd gotten me into the shack as the tears blurred my eyes.

"What's the matter, boy?" she said. And I had no words to answer.

"What's the matter, I say!"

"I'm hurting in my operation," I said desperately, knowing that my tears were too complicated to put into any words I knew.

"Operation? Where?"

I looked away.

"Where you hurting, boy?" she demanded.

I looked into her eyes and they seemed to flood through me, until reluctantly I pointed toward my pain.

"Open it, so's I can see," she said. "You know I'm a healer, don't you?"

I bowed my head, still hesitating.

"Well open it then. How'm I going to see with all those clothes on you?"

My face burned like fire now and the pain seemed to ease as a dampness grew beneath the bandage. But she would not be denied and I undid myself and saw a red stain on the gauze. I lay there ashamed to raise my eyes.

"Hmmmmmmm," she said, "a fishing worm with a headache!" And I couldn't believe my ears. Then she was looking into my eyes and grinning.

"Pruned," she cackled in her high, old woman's voice, "pruned. Boy, you have been pruned. I'm a doctor but no tree surgeon— No, lay still a second."

She paused and I saw her hand come forward, three clawlike fingers taking me gently as she examined the bandage.

And I was both ashamed and angry and now I stared at her out of a quick resentment and a defiant pride. *I'm a man,* I said within myself. *Just the same I am a man!* But I could only stare at her face briefly as she looked at me with a gleam in her eyes. Then my eyes fell and I forced myself to look boldly at her now, very brown in the lamplight, with all the complicated apparatus within the globular curvatures of flesh and vessel exposed to my eyes. I was filled then with a deeper sense of the mystery of it too, for now it was as though the nakedness was nothing more than another veil; much like the old baggy dresses she always wore. Then across the curvature of her stomach I saw a long, puckered, crescent-shaped scar.

"How old are you, boy?" she said, her eyes suddenly round.

"Eleven," I said. And it was as though I had fired a shot.

"Eleven! Git out of here," she screamed, stumbling backward, her eyes wide upon me as she felt for the glass on the table to drink. Then she snatched an old gray robe from a chair, fumbling for the tie cord which wasn't there. I moved, my eyes upon her as I knelt for my hatchet and felt the pain come sharp. Then I straightened, trying to arrange my knickers.

"You go now, you little rascal," she said. "Hurry and git out of here. And if I ever hear of you saying anything about me I'll fix your daddy and your mammy too. I'll fix 'em, you hear?"

"Yes, ma'am," I said, feeling that I had suddenly lost the courage of my manhood, now that my bandage was hidden and her secret body gone behind her old gray robe. But how could she fix my father when I didn't have one? Or my mother, when she was dead?

I moved, backing out of the door into the dark. Then she slammed the door and I saw the light grow intense in the window and there was her face looking out at me and I could not tell if she frowned or smiled but in the glow of the lamp the wrinkles were not there. I stumbled over the packs now and gathered them up, leaving.

This time the dog raised up, huge in the dark, his green eyes glowing as he gave me a low, disinterested growl. *Buster really must have fixed you,* I thought. *But where'd he go?* Then I was past the fence into the road.

I wanted to run but was afraid of starting the pain again, and as I moved I kept seeing her as she'd appeared with her back turned toward me, the sweet undrunken movements that she made. It had been like someone dancing by herself and yet like praying without kneeling down. Then she had turned, exposing her familiar face. I moved faster now and suddenly all my senses seemed to sing alive. I heard a night bird's song, the lucid call of a quail arose. And from off to my right in the river there came the leap of a moon-mad fish and I could see the spray arch up and away. There was wisteria in the air and the scent of moon-flowers. And now moving through the dark I recalled the warm, intriguing smell of her body and suddenly, with the shout of the carnival coming to me again, the whole thing became thin and dreamlike. The images flowed in my mind, became shadowy, no part was left to fit another. But still there was my pain and here was I, running through the dark toward the small, loud-playing band. It was real, I knew, and I stopped in the path and looked back, seeing the black outlines of the shack and the thin moon above. Behind the shack the hill arose with the shadowy woods and I knew the lake was still hidden there, reflecting the moon. All was real.

And for a moment I felt much older, as though I had lived swiftly long years into the future and had been as swiftly pushed back again. I tried to remember how it had been when I kissed her, but on my lips my tongue found only the faintest trace of wine. But for that it was gone, and I thought forever, except the memory of the scraggly hairs on her chin. Then I was again aware of the imperious calling of the horns and moved again toward the carnival. Where was that other scalped Indian, where had Buster gone?

RONALD ASKS A FAVOR

BY

Gloria Emerson

onald was afraid of quite a few things but he knew better than to tell anyone. For example, Ronald felt very nervous in his own neighborhood in New York City, which was called Harlem. Every day his mother reminded him to come home the minute school was over and not to play in the streets or talk to anyone. So he did. The bigger boys, and some grown-up men, often made a fearful amount of noise after it was dark and it worried all the women in Ronald's building. Sometimes there was real trouble, not just noise. Ronald saw a man snatch the big, black, old handbag of Mrs. Johnson and the loss made her cry for three days. Another time, Ronald saw a dead man lying in the street, blood on the back of his army jacket, and another man stole the shoes from the corpse. And a mean child put a dead cat in the elevator of Ronald's building and the sight of it made Henrietta Washburn howl and sob for twenty minutes even though she was all of twelve years old. Nice things did not happen in the neighborhood. The people felt squeezed by the little rooms they lived in. The women looked anxious all the time and the men seemed sad, as if they had lost something important and could not exactly remember what it was.

Ronald, who was not yet eight, hardly had any hope for himself. The effort to be cheerful only made him cranky or tired so he rarely tried. He did not like going to school because nothing he learned there made much sense to him. He wanted to be a farmer who grew corn and round beans, who had one or two pigs, and maybe a mule who would be his friend. Ronald also dreamed of raising small frogs, hundreds and hundreds of small frogs, because he loved the way they hopped. He was not sure what a farmer did with frogs, but he wanted them anyway.

Each summer, Ronald and his older brother, Jackson, went to visit their grandparents in Virginia who owned a small farm. It had taken him twenty-four years to get the money for the land, the grandfather said to Ronald. There was a barnyard, a crop of corn, beans, and a little tobacco, three huge and old trees which Ronald could climb, and a creek where he pretended to fish. The summers were so fine they seemed only an hour long and he dreaded the family's return to Harlem, and that school, and the twitching that came when he walked down the city streets. When Ronald felt most sad, he would shut his eyes and try to see his very own frogs, but it did not always calm him down.

Of course, when he shut his eyes in class it made the teacher cross and she complained to Ronald's mother that he was a lazy pupil. Ronald was sent to tutoring school in Harlem to improve his writing and his arithmetic. He hated having to sit still for another two hours, after all that time in school, and it alarmed him to have to walk home by himself for six blocks when it was dark. The lady tutor saw the problem and said: "Ronald, it's not such a bad neighborhood."

"It is for me," Ronald said. Her face turned quite pink. The truth is that she lived quite far away, and took taxis home from Harlem, all of which Ronald knew. In any case, it made him feel worse when people tried to buck him up, and not even his mother could make him feel better. She had stopped saying to Ronald that he would start growing very suddenly and catch up. For Ronald was six inches shorter than Jackson, his older brother, and he barely came to the elbow of his father. At home and sometimes in school he felt like a midget. Ronald thought that if he could be a farmer with all those frogs it would not matter if he was small and fat and behind in school. The frogs would hardly care. The corn would not care.

But then, when his misery seemed hard enough to bear, a horrible thing happened. The elevator in Ronald's building began to speak. It was an ordinary building, twenty-two stories high, which looked exactly like six or seven others all with grand names—The George Washington, The Abraham Lincoln, The Theodore Roosevelt. He knew they were buildings for people who did not have much money, for people who were very different from the family in *The Brady Bunch* (his favorite program on television).

The first time the elevator began to speak,

Ronald suspected nothing. He had failed a test in arithmetic that morning. He pushed the button for the eighteenth floor and waited to go up. All his life, the elevator had risen, but not now. First it made a little moan.

"I can't take it anymore," the elevator said. It reminded Ronald of the voice of his tutor, for it was hard and hurried and slightly hoarse. Suddenly the elevator began to wobble, to move up slowly.

"It's too much. I don't even get decent care in this building and look at the shape I'm in," the elevator said. Ronald was so petrified he thought he might start crying the way Henrietta Washburn did, but his father said he must always act like a man and leave the tears to women and little girls. Ronald's legs felt like soup, so he sat down on the floor of the elevator and hid his face in his arms. When the elevator doors finally opened, he ran to the apartment and told his brother what he had heard. "You're bananas," Jackson said, and brushed him away because he was watching *The Odd Couple* on television and did not believe a word Ronald was saying. Ronald could hardly eat supper, which was prepared by his father before he went off to work at night. The father fixed their meal because Ronald's mother did not come home from work until eight p.m.

After the first shock, Ronald could not bear to be alone in the elevator, but it was out of the question to walk down, or walk up, the eighteen flights of stairs. Besides, his mother had said never to use the stairs because "not nice" people sat there, or robbers were running up or down them. Ronald's mother was not happy in the building and she had stopped trying to keep the halls clean, or wash the hall floor. Of course the elevator looked terrible. LUIS IS A PIG and ARTHUR STEALS were written on the walls with magic markers, and the buttons for all the floors looked as if they had been hit with a hammer.

Ronald changed. He had nightmares and ate less. He could not remember how frogs leaped or what corn looked like on his grandfather's farm. Each time he stepped into the elevator he felt like a baby, with no power to protect himself. Then the voice came at him again.

"I'm not very strong now," the elevator said, with a deep shudder. "I'm supposed to be able to carry five hundred pounds, but my cables are wearing out and my doors won't close nicely and my nervous system is very damaged." Ronald thought the elevator might be crying, for it made a strange honking noise. He held his breath, which did no good at all. From that day on, Ronald waited for other people to ride in the elevator with him. He grew sulky and watched too much television and ignored his homework. It suddenly occurred to him that it was not just the elevator that spoke but other objects as well. There was a television commercial that had a package of margarine saying it was butter, another with a cat that had a very deep voice, and still another in which a bottle of cleaning stuff (which his mother used in the kitchen) said in a bossy way how good it was. The possibilities made him sick. Did his bed talk? Did the couch? Did the desk in school? Would he have to hear them all? Ronald prayed that he might go deaf and began to pretend he could not hear, which made everyone even more cross with him.

One night, when he was asleep, he heard people shouting in the hall, then someone pounding on the elevator doors, and, lastly, a faint shriek. Ronald thought it might have been the elevator which gave the shriek. He knew the elevator hated rough stuff and that its doors ached when they were hit or held open too long. That summer, two girls in the elevator, who pretended to be grown-up, were robbed of the rings they wore on every finger and sixteen dollars. Ronald was in the car with them, but when the two men entered on the fifth floor and held up the girls, he hid behind the fattest one so he would not have to hand over the dollar he always kept in his left sneaker. When the men got out, warning the girls to be quiet, Ronald thought he heard the elevator complaining, but the girls were wailing so he could not be sure.

Afterward the elevator spoke often to Ronald, calling him "little boy." It became clear that no one else heard this voice even if the car was crowded. The elevator sometimes said it did not blame the people in the building for the rough way they behaved, the elevator certainly knew their lives were not easy, that many of the men were out of work, and the prices of food were outrageous. The elevator said many of the same things that his father said, so Ronald whispered "Yes, yes" to the elevator in case some response was expected.

Ronald began begging his mother to let him go to Virginia to live with his grandparents; he promised to work very hard in school and be a good boy if only she would let him go. Ronald's mother said: "We'll see," which meant no. There was nothing for him to do but ask the elevator a most unusual favor. He got up early one morning and went to speak to it in his pajamas.

"Elevator?" Ronald said, very unsure of how such a strange conversation would go. There was no answer so he rode up and down in it for a while, then stopped the elevator between two floors (which was forbidden, of course). "Elevator, are you there?" Ronald said faintly.

"Of course I am here. You are in me," the elevator answered in a cross, sleepy voice. Ronald was so nervous his voice squeaked and his hands felt wet. "Listen, elevator," Ronald mumbled, "I have a favor to ask." He explained how unhappy he was in the city and how much he wanted to live in Virginia, but that his parents would not move unless the elevator made his mother feel life in the building had become too spooky.

"Well, she certainly isn't very happy here," the elevator said. "She's always complaining to Mrs. Johnson, the lady whose handbag was taken. All I hear are complaints or threats. No wonder I feel so terrible myself."

"I want you to scare her just a little, to show her that you really are not safe, then maybe she will want to live in Virginia," Ronald said, shyly. The elevator became quite huffy and said that it was an outrageous idea, that it worked very hard to function decently, and that Ronald was a wicked boy to suggest such a thing. Ronald began to cry and the elevator became silent.

But some bad news in his family soon made him feel better. His mother was suddenly fired from her job (he did not know what she did, only that it made her very tired) along with many other people who were given no warning. He could hear his parents talking together in their bedroom, in the special low voices they used when they were worrying about money.

His mother stayed home and cleaned too much and looked in the newspapers and frowned a lot. Ronald made a final plea to the elevator, which was looking dirtier and more damaged than ever. It answered him in a very weary voice. "All right, all right," the elevator said. "I'm feeling dreadful and I can't last much longer so I might as well do one good deed." The next day Ronald was very alert in school and so excitable that his teacher felt his head to see whether he was feverish. At the tutoring center, he read a story about Willie Mays so quickly, and with expression, that his tutor smiled. What Ronald felt for the first time made him almost dizzy. It was hope. He did not even feel scared walking home.

His mother was lying down when he got home so his father was fixing supper. While they were eating, the father told Ronald and Jackson that the elevator had fallen three floors when their mother was in it, and she was so upset she had a headache so-do-not-make-any-noise. And then, not much longer after that, the elevator stalled when Ronald's father was in it and it made him late for work.

The family moved to Virginia because, as Ronald's mother put it, the city was making them nervous wrecks. At first they lived with the grandparents, and even when the house was crowded, Ronald did not mind. In fact, he was so happy he did not even want to go to sleep at night and he almost never watched *The Brady Bunch* because it seemed stupid to him now. He did all the things he wanted to do, and his grandfather even paid him for his chores so he began to save money to buy frogs. He never told anyone about the elevator, and how it spoke, and how it helped him. He did say something about it to the first frog he bought, but it no longer worried him, you see, so he forgot about it. But there was a curious thing about Ronald. Even when he grew up, and became quite tall just like his father, he would always avoid big buildings and elevators, saying to his own children it was wiser to use the stairs.

LANDSCAPE

BY
Larry Fagin

ILLUSTRATED BY
GEORGE SCHNEEMAN

The little white dog wags his tail

The red mill turns silently

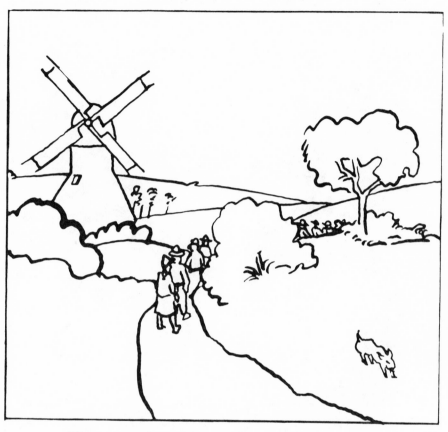

The movie line is a mile long

The sleepyheads toy with their food

The Japanese gardener flies to pieces

Orange soda blows in the wind

A lettuce leaf floats by

ABCDEF

BY
Jules Feiffer

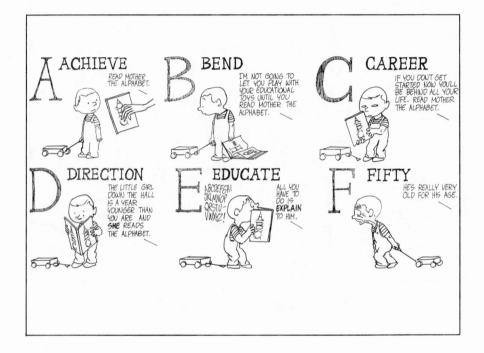

BOOGERS

BY
David Felton
ILLUSTRATED BY
AARON FELTON

I t was a terrific, toe-tapping, bell-clear blossom and blue-sky morning outside Watson Elementary School, but inside, Professor Titus Sphincter, the most boring man on earth, was as usual doing his best to miss the point.

"Through the ages," he intoned in a voice muffled by saliva and tweed, "philosophers have pondered the mysterious riddle of appearance and reality. Are things what they seem? Do we really exist? What's in a name?"

What garbage, thought Ignatius "Pig" Newton as he gazed from his window seat at the beautiful spring day. He was in excellent spirits. That morning he'd wolfed down his favorite breakfast of Tang, Froot Loops, and raw bacon. He was wearing his favorite Elton John T-shirt, which just yesterday he'd found, after a seven-week search, underneath the rabbit hutch. And right now his fingers had retrieved from his right nostril a huge, juicy, gray-green booger of the ideal consistency for molding into various shapes. Yes, it was an almost perfect day except for the relentless drone of Mr. Sphincter and the fact that Pig Newton was forced to sit there and suffer it.

"Speaking of appearance and reality," continued the professor, "perhaps Mr. Newton would like to explain to the class the reality of that . . . that *thing* he is holding in his fingers."

Pig Newton turned abruptly to the front of the classroom and was struck by a bank of eyes staring back at him, the eyes of his fellow students, but most prominently, the eyes of Mr. Sphincter, glowering through his bifocals with a fiendish twinkle.

"Well sir, it appears to be," said Pig, "a booger. Yes, I'm almost certain."

"I see . . . and what, may I ask, do you plan to do with it?"

Mr. Sphincter snickered. The class tittered. Pig Newton fumbled and faltered.

"I guess, well, I'll probably just roll it around in my fingers until it disappears." Actually, Pig knew this wasn't quite the case. Most likely he would roll it around until it was solid enough to drop to the floor.

"Most likely," said Mr. Sphincter, "you will roll it around until it is solid enough to drop to the floor, and someone will have to clean it up. Isn't that so?"

"Yes sir."

"May I suggest, therefore, since we all agree littering is unacceptable behavior, that you eat it."

"What?"

"Eat the booger."

"That's disgusting!"

"*You're* disgusting, Mr. Newton. It is simply bad manners to pick your nose. It is particularly bad manners to pick your nose during my lecture. You have offended us all, and therefore I insist that you now, in front of us all, eat it. That's right, just chew it up and swallow it, yum yum." Like many adults of Pig's acquaintance, Mr. Sphincter was capable of the highest authority in the lowest circumstances.

The young boy felt trapped and humiliated. He studied the booger for a moment, then with a force only intense loathing could produce, flicked it toward Mr. Sphincter. It landed on the man's bifocals. The class laughed and cheered. Aghast, the professor snapped backward as if hit by a bullet, then lunged down the aisle, grabbed Pig, and shoved him against the door. "Out! Get out!" he shouted in an hysterical wheeze. "Report immediately to Dr. Brain!"

Although Pig Newton had never met Dr. Mucus M. Brain, the school principal, he'd never regretted the fact. Students only met Dr. Brain when they were in trouble, he knew that. And he figured anyone who would employ a nerd like Mr. Sphincter must be some kind of bad news. Thus, as he knocked on the door of Dr. Brain's office, he felt a strange unpleasantness in his stomach. He wished he hadn't eaten that raw bacon so fast.

"Come in." The voice was deep but friendly and came from a face more relaxed and warm than Pig had expected. Dr. Brain sat behind a tastefully arranged oak desk. His hair was white and distinguished. His hands were folded in a wise manner.

"Ah, Mr. Newton," he said, "please sit down. What brings you here?"

"It was Mr. Sphincter's idea." Pig realized that wasn't sufficient. "Uh, well, he sent me down here 'cause I was . . . picking my nose." Dr. Brain still looked puzzled. "Uh, well, I picked my nose and then I flicked the booger at Mr. Sphincter."

The principal nodded and raised his thick gray eyebrows.

Pig squirmed defensively. "But he wanted me to eat it! While the whole class watched, he wanted me to—"

"Yes, yes, I see." Smiling to himself, Dr. Brain opened a folder on his desk, scanned it briefly, and looked at the boy. "They call you Pig."

"Some call me Pig. Some call me Iggy Piggy."

"Doesn't that bother you?"

Pig shrugged. "It beats Ignatius."

"Yes, of course." Dr. Brain leaned forward and got to the point. "You know why they call you Pig, don't you?"

Pig said nothing.

"Well, *look* at you. Your hair's uncombed and seems matted in a peculiar way. Your fly's unbuttoned. Your shoes are untied. Your T-shirt looks like it hasn't been washed in seven weeks and, frankly, smells *very* strange. And . . . you pick your nose."

"But Dr. Brain," said Pig, "you're talking about appearances. What has all that got to do with the way I really am, the way I am *inside*?"

"Are you saying," the principal inquired wryly, "that using a Kleenex would rob you of your soul?"

Pig was in no mood for drollery. "What I'm saying, sir, is that what I did was natural, logical, and efficient. It harmed no one. What I'm saying is that in this world we all have a choice between picking our nose or having a head full of boogers. What I'm saying is that I, and every kid I know, are sick and tired of endless lectures, sermons, put-downs, and reprimands . . . from boogerheads!"

"My, my." Dr. Brain took a deep breath. "You are certainly an angry young man, Mr. Newton. And that's not bad, not bad at all. Our civilization owes a great deal to angry young men and women—builders, explorers, artists. But the point is, they saved their anger for the important things. Your crusade today is not important." The principal winked at the boy. "In other words, none of these people ever broke new ground by defending their right to break wind."

Pig Newton giggled. It was the kind of joke he liked.

"Now Pig, I want you to take the day off. I want you to think about what I've said, see if it doesn't make sense. And then tomorrow I want you to clean up your act, stop picking your nose, and apologize to Mr. Sphincter." Dr. Brain beamed at him from across the desk. "Have a nice day."

At least Pig now had an opportunity to enjoy

the beautiful spring weather, but as he walked along a grove of flowering apple trees, he was not in an enjoyable mood. He was confused. What Dr. Brain had said did kind of make sense. But yield to the boogerheads? Apologize to Mr. Sphincter? It left a bad taste in his mouth.

Suddenly, under one of the trees, Pig spotted Barf Wellington, an immensely fat youngster generally considered ten times more offensive than Pig. He was so offensive he was not permitted within a half-mile radius of the school. He was so offensive that the flies which invariably accompanied Pig completely avoided Barf. Naturally, the two boys were the best of friends.

"Hey, Pig, how's it goin'?" greeted Barf. "You look down, man."

"Yeah, I just come from Dr. Brain's office. He told me to stop picking my nose. Told me to apologize to that cretin Mr. Sphincter. He's right, I suppose."

With a small handful of rocks he'd collected, Barf started pelting a family of stinkbugs. "Think of it this way," he said. "You're not a neat person, are you."

"No, of course not. Neither are you."

"Do you make your bed in the morning?"

"No."

"Why not?"

Pig thought for a moment. "Well, it just gets unmade at night and you have to make it again the *next* morning. And the morning after that."

"Exactly," said Barf. "Neatness is always an exercise in futility. How about raking leaves? You like to do that?"

"Yyyyyech!"

"Same thing. Leaves just keep fallin'."

"What are you driving at?" asked the bewildered Pig.

"Well, ain't it the same way with picking your nose? It's an act of neatness. You get one booger, a few hours later you have to reach for another one."

Pig's eyes lit up. "Wow, I think you got something there."

"Fruitless, man, fruitless." Affectionately Barf put his arm around the cleaner boy's shoulders. "You see, Pig, the truth is, we are all boogerheads, every one of us. We nosepickers just don't like to accept the fact."

Pig reached out his hand. "Hey, Barf, thanks a lot. I'll see ya later."

"Keep your nose clean, man."

His heart singing, Pig Newton raced back to school. He had to tell Dr. Brain. Everything was cool. He would obey the rules, he would apologize to Mr. Sphincter, but he would do it for his own secret reasons.

Pig flung open the door of Dr. Brain's office. And then a smile exploded across his face, the greatest smile he had ever smiled, a smile that reached clear to the back of his neck.

Dr. Brain was picking his nose!

"Ahem," said Pig.

Dr. Brain looked up, his face turned red. He

whipped the finger from his nose and tried to regain his composure. "Uh, yes, Mr. Newton, can I do anything for you?"

"Yes, as a matter of fact, you can," said Pig, already starting to laugh.

"What's that?"

"Eat it, Dr. Brain."

"*What?*"

"Eat it." The tears rolled down Pig's face. "And tell Mr. Sphincter to eat it too!"

Shrieking with delight, Pig Newton bolted outside and clicked his heels twice in the air. He'd never been so happy. As the wisdom soared through his grubby body, he felt a tremendous sense of freedom. Now he saw the world differently. He would listen to all the lectures and sermons that the boogerheads called knowledge, but he would listen to them *differently*. And he would think differently every time he read a story with a moral to it.

MOMOTARO, OR THE PEACHBOY: A JAPANESE FAIRY TALE

BY
Leslie Fiedler

I

THE FINDING OF THE PEACH

An old wood chopper
And his old, old wife
Lived in the forest
For all of their life.

And the name of the chopper
Was Chopper;
And the name of his wife
Was Wife;
And the name of the days
They lived was Day;
And the name of the nights
Was Night;
But the name of the sum
Of them all was Pain,
For they had borne no child
To bear their name.

Till crouched one day
By the bank of a stream,
Washing her wash
And dreaming her dream,

The old woman saw
A giant peach,
Afloat on the water
Just out of her reach.

Over and over,
It turned in the Sun
Singing a song
Or humming a hum:

"Domburi, Domburi
Reach out your hand;
What is born in the Water
May live on the Land!
What begins as a Peach
May end as a Man.
So wet your feet
And catch, if you can."

Like a Child,
She clutched it,
Clutched at the Peach.
Something to fondle?
Or something to eat?
Like a Child, she held it
Tight to her breast;
But knowing no Names,
How could she guess
What to call it, or
What would come next.

"Peach," she called it,
Carrying it home
To where the Old Man
Waited alone.

II

THE CUTTING OF THE PEACH

"I'll cut it," said the Old Man,
Since cutting was his trade,
"Let's eat what luck has brought us,
Why should we be afraid?"

But his Wife was lost in wonder;
And talk, though not her trade,
Was what she did when she was not
Hanging in a glade
Their wash or the wash of Others,
Or mending what was frayed.

"Hold off," she cried, "or let me,
Who've held it to my breast,
Draw the knife across its skin
As soft as a caress—
I've felt its heart against my heart,
And a mother's touch is best."

"A mother," he cried angrily,
For hunger gnawed his gut,
"What have you borne but empty words.
Be still and let me cut."

But even as they argued
The peach was split, uncleft;
Without a stroke from either one,
It parted right and left.

And there within its bloody heart
They saw a red-gold boy,
A child as red-gold as the fruit,
Whose cry drowned out their joy.

"The child I could not bear," she said,
Was brought us by the river—

A token like a fallen leaf
For us to keep forever."

"Peachboy is his given name,"
She said, "We have no choice."

"*One* name like him is given,"
He said, "But I rejoice
Another name is ours to give,
And his to bear forever;
Since he is Peachboy Son of Us
Who fetched him from the river."

III

THE COMING OF THE DEMONS

He grew between the two of them,
Like some astounding tree,
Whose only blossom was his face,
Its stem and leaf both he.

Till Demons came one evil day
And blackened with their wings
The noontime sky above their heads
And hushed the birds that sing;
And breathed upon the burgeoning wheat
And turned the seed to dust,
And ate the living cattle up
And chased the maids in lust.

Then Peachboy rose up taller
So that his thrusting head
Split the thatch to let him watch
The demons as they fled.

"I know you now," he cried aloud,
"I know, too, who I am,
For until he has spied his demons
No boy can become a man."

"Bake Milletseed cakes, dear Mother,
Kibidango to fill my sack,
And I'll load your lap with treasure,
When I come riding back."

"But all the skills you taught me, Dad,
And all your sage advice,
Now turn to dirty water,
Like a sheet of rotten ice;
For I must become a father,
Though I was not born a Son
I will beget myself upon myself,
Before my tale is done!"

"Oh, I'll be rich, dear Mother,
When the demons all are dead,
And I will buy you a palace
And a beautiful silken bed.
And Dad will sit in a rocker,
And rust will nibble his ax;
And the house you live in will be my house,
When I come riding back."

"Please take my ax on your journey;
It has killed a thousand trees,
Taller by far than demons,
Lords of the earth and the breeze."

"No, no," said the boy, "dear Father,
I will take the household knife
You raised to cut the red-gold fruit
That fed my secret life."

"Take me with you, Peachboy,
Take me, if you can."

"Be still, for a dog or a monkey
Is more use than an old, old man;
A bird or dog or a monkey
More use than a dying man."

IV

THE JOURNEY

The sun behind, the dark ahead,
As if he fled the day,
He set out in search of evening
Along the Demons' Way;
And all the beasts of the forest,
Smelling them hot from the pan,
Longed for his *kibidango,*
The best in all Japan.

First the bird from the highest treetop
Called to him by name,
"Where are you going, Peachboy,
On what journey or quest for fame?"

"I go to the Island of Demons
To conquer their evil King,
And make my dream a story,
A song that the minstrels sing."

"Give me one *kibidango*
And I will fly with you,
Until on the Island of Demons
Your song and mine are through.
And I will call you Master
And serve your every whim;
For I, too, have dreamed a journey,
And know that we shall win."

"Take and eat and fly with me,
For it seems that I have heard
That no man can be a Hero
Until he has talked to a bird."

Then the monkey called out from hiding,
"Peachboy, let me eat, too,
And I will swing from the branches
To spy out the world for you.

And I will call you Master,
And serve your every whim,
For I, too, have dreamed a journey,
And know that we shall win."

"Come eat my *kibidango,*
For it seems to me I've heard
That the man who would be a hero
Must be monkey as well as bird."

The Inu-san barked from the bushes,
The dog who has always served man,
"I smell *kibidango,* dear Peachboy,
The best in all Japan.
I will serve you for food not glory,
Since like others I have my own tale
Which I chase in the hope of an ending,
Though I know I will never prevail.
And I will call you master, too,
And serve your every whim,
Though I have dreamed another dream
And know no one can win."

"Take and eat and come with me,
For it seems that I have heard
That the hero must heed the bark of a dog
As well as the song of a bird."

"I love you all, dear brothers,"
The Peachboy said to the three,
"For teaching me here in the forest
That, unlike the fruit of a tree,
I must hide and whimper and scamper,
And chatter and scratch my fleas,
And nip and slaver and growl
And ride the tide of the breeze.

"No man can be a mother,
To this I am resigned;
But though I was born from the heart of a peach,
You three are born from mine."

V

THE DEFEAT

How easy to conquer the Demons
Once he had encountered the beasts.
They lay in a drunken stupor
After a round of feasts,
Lie always in drunken slumber,
And only dream of the feasts;
From which they arise without waking,
To pillage the poor in their sleep.

On the back of the dog he lay hidden,
Fording their moat at high noon;
And the monkey rode on his shoulder,
And the bird flew over the moon,
Singing, "Conquer them all, Momotaro,
While they lie in their beds in a swoon;
For they dream that they dream they are dreaming
In a dream not even their own:
Warp and woof are a web of your weaving,
The test you begged as a boon.
They'll die, if you like, without waking.
Fade out like the vanishing gloom."

But he cried a great cry to arouse them,
And they rushed from the hush in his head,
To fall one by one on the pavement
As the coming of morning flushed red;
And red as the red of the morning
Were the drops of their blood that he shed.

Till their King alone loomed before him,
A mountain of motionless stone
Eyeless and bloodless, undying,
Unborn on his carved granite throne;
Enthroned for all time in carved granite,
With eyes of unseeing stone.
Then his knife dropped unused to the pavement,
And a chill froze the boy to the bone;
For the unseeing face of the mountain
Was his own flower face turned to stone.

Seeing which, the three beasts in panic
Scrabbled and scratched at his eyes,
Biting hard the soft flesh of their master,
As if he were the foe and the prize.

But "Enough!" cried a voice from the mountain,
"The battle is over and done!"
"Begone!" cried a voice from its caverns,
"What there is to be gained you have won!"

And the Peachboy woke at the roadside,
A league from the place he was born,
Astride a great horse with a scepter
And a spear and a shield and a horn,
And a crown on his head gold as sunrise,
And behind him a treasure was borne
On percherons, palfreys, and asses
And the backs of men better unborn;
While a crowd on both sides of the roadway,
Defined a path to his door,
Where his parents waited to greet him
Their heads bowed down low to the floor.

"Rise up!" he cried out in horror,
"You need not bow down to your son."
His voice was the voice of the thunder,
And his head darkened the disk of the sun,
So all fled save his father and mother,
Who lay dead as he roared, "But I've *won!*"

WAYNE'S ADVENTURE

BY

Dick Gallup

This is a story about a little boy named Wayne. He lived in a white house with a green door.

Once, Wayne was having a bad day. So he filled his pockets with cookies and ran away.

Wayne walked and walked. The sun was going down and it was getting dark. He found a tree to eat his cookies under. Then he ate all the crumbs and went to sleep.

The next morning he started walking again. He passed trees and cows and horses and fences. He went on walking for three days. And every day the trees and cows and horses and fences looked a little smaller. On the third day his shoelaces came untied. When Wayne bent down to tie them again, he found that his feet were a long way from his fingers. Wayne had grown very tall! Yes, he was tall. He was so tall that the bird flew right under his nose, and the clouds in the sky tickled his ears.

It was very different, being big. Wayne found that he could do a lot of things you can't do when you are small.

He could be a giraffe: dancing around a little with his feet, way down there, while he nibbled at the leaves at the very top of the trees. Eating leaves is like lying around eating the grass. It doesn't especially taste good, but it feels good, just doing it.

He could run and jump, real hard, and leave the biggest, deepest, scariest footprints you ever saw. Scary giant footprints. Fee—Fi—Fo—Fum! And monster footprints. And dinosaur footprints. He had a great big stick that could be a spear or an arrow or a cannon. One day it rained. Wayne's scary footprints filled with rainwater and turned into lakes, and he sailed leaf boats in them.

Wayne could do wonderful things on the shores of his lakes. He could make the biggest mud pies in the whole world. And he made a mud castle big enough for twenty little girls and all their dolls and all their servants to bring them their tea. Wayne was hoping some little girls would come along and try it out. They never did. While he was waiting for them, he dug some channels with his big stick and put all the scary footprint lakes together into one big lake. Then he built a dam to hold the water back. Then he used branches and sticks and more mud to make a fort in case the Indians came along. They never did, so Wayne had to be the Indians, too.

One day, Wayne wanted to see his mother and father again. He started walking home. After a while, he came to a river. He stepped over a bridge and walked along in the middle of the river, wiggling his toes in the bottom and splashing. Far away, he could see a tiny little town and a tiny little house next to the river. It was his house!

When he got there, he lay down across the baseball field and two vacant lots, curled his arm around his mother's flower garden (being very careful of the roses), and stuck his head down next to his house. He almost poked his eye with the television antenna on the roof.

His house was still white and it still had a green door, but it was awfully little! He reached out with his finger and gently tapped with his fingernail on the front door. The whole house shook!

His mother opened the door. "Who's there?" she said, in a little voice. In the tiniest whisper he could manage, Wayne said, "It's Wayne." All the same, his breath was so big it blew a pile of leaves and an old newspaper up the street.

Wayne's mother and father stuck their heads out of the door and looked up. There was a giant face, and it really did look like Wayne.

Wayne said, "I've come back," and he smiled.

Wayne wanted to give them a kiss, but he didn't know exactly how to do it. Finally, Wayne's father brought out a ladder. He propped it against Wayne's finger. He and Wayne's mother climbed up onto Wayne's finger and walked into the palm of his hand. It tickled. Wayne picked them up, way up into the sky above the rooftops, and gave them a kiss. He couldn't kiss them in any particular place because they were so little. He just sort of kissed them all over. Wayne's father and mother each took a finger and hugged it.

They said, "We're happy that you're back, Wayne. We really missed you."

Wayne was awfully happy to see them again. He put them on top of his head and told them to hold on to his hair. He stood up, carefully, with one foot in his street and the other foot one block away. On top of his head, right over his eyebrows, there was a little Wayne's-Mother's-Head and a little Wayne's-Father's-Head peeking out.

"We're going for a walk," said Wayne. And they did.

After a while, Wayne got tired of walking. He sat down and leaned against a tree. His mother and farther scrambled out of his hair into the branches.

"You are a good boy, Wayne," they said. "We love you." Then Wayne's father looked at his watch. "We've got to be going. Are you coming home with us?"

"I don't think so," said Wayne, "I wouldn't fit into my bed anymore. I'm too big."

"We'll write to you," said his parents. He carried them to a train station, and they waved good-bye from the train.

The next day, Wayne wanted to get little again. It was fun to be big, but he wanted to sleep in his own bed. He thought about it while he ate his breakfast. Then he stood up, and tried to push himself down. He put both his hands on top of his head and pushed as hard as he could. Nothing happened.

Next he tried to blow all the air out of himself, like a balloon when you untie the string. He blew and blew. He made such a big breeze that people for miles around said to each other, "I think a storm is coming." And they all shut their windows and got out their umbrellas. Wayne blew until he got so dizzy he fell down. But he was still just as big.

After that, he just stood around with his head in the treetops, feeling bad. There was no use trying to get little anymore. He had tried every way. He thought of playing giraffe again, but he just didn't feel like it. So he watched the birds building their nests on the branches, and the little caterpillars weaving their cocoons around themselves. Cocoons are great things to make. You weave one all around you, tight and snug, when you're a fuzzy little caterpillar, and when you're inside it you turn into a beautiful butterfly. Then you fly away.

Now, Wayne had always wished he could fly. He decided then and there to make a cocoon for himself and see if he could become a sort of boy-butterfly. He got ready a lot of wet mud and leaves. Then he lay down on the ground and covered every inch of himself with it, the arms last of all. It was the biggest cocoon in the whole world, because it covered up a giant Wayne. Inside, it was very dark, but warm and snug, like getting under the covers on a cold night.

Wayne got very tired building his cocoon. It was very comfortable and he fell asleep and slept for a long time inside the mud cocoon while it got hard and dry in the sun. He must have slept for two or three weeks.

When he woke up, it was as dark as before. But now he couldn't feel the cocoon next to his skin anymore. He heard little car noises way overhead. After he had walked a long way, feeling around in the dark, he came to a wall. Then he found a little crack in it where the sunlight came through. Wayne helped the crack get bigger with his fingers, and wiggled out.

From outside it looked like a big gray tunnel. There was a six-lane highway on top of it, with cars coming and going.

Wayne was walking along slowly.

Suddenly, ouch!—He tripped and fell over a little root sticking out of the ground. He rubbed his toes. They were little toes!—little and round at the ends and easy to reach with his fingers. Wayne was little again! He was so happy he started singing his favorite song, and ran and walked and ran again, just feeling good.

Under a shady tree he found an old man fishing beside a big lake.

"Hello," said Wayne, "I don't know where I am."

"This is the Wayne Lake," said the old man. "Have some fish with me?"

Wayne sat down and ate very politely with the old man, putting a big leaf in his lap for a napkin.

"That's the Wayne Tunnel, over that way," the old man went on. "It was built by a giant named Wayne. Maybe you've seen him?"

Wayne's mouth was full of fish, so he couldn't answer.

"Some people say Wayne is asleep in his tunnel. But most people think he built it just for fun and left it there. It was a nice place to put a highway, wasn't it?" said the old man.

"My name is Wayne," said Wayne. "I was asleep in the tunnel for a long time. I was using it for a cocoon. I was going to be a butterfly."

"You've got mud all over your back," said the old man.

"That should be my wings," said Wayne. "I guess it doesn't work very well if you use mud."

"I guess not," said the old man. "Have some baked beans?"

"I'd rather go home, if you don't mind," said Wayne, wiping his mouth with his leaf.

"Okay, Wayne," said the old man, "I'll take you in my truck."

They drove back to town on the new Wayne highway in the old man's big blue truck. The old man let Wayne play the radio.

When Wayne got home, dinner was on the table. He had cake and ice cream both afterward, and Wayne's mother and father each read him a story while he went to sleep. It was one of the best days ever.

IN A WORLD
OF
JUST DESSERTS

BY

Willard Gaylin

AUTHOR'S NOTE: *This story takes place a long, long, long, long, long, long time ago—before Muhammad Ali, Ali Khan, or the Cannes Film Festival; before Johnny Cash or instant credit; before Faith Baldwin, Bob Hope, or charity bazaars; before Watergate or Water Beds—before Walter Cronkite! The narrator of this story is a little boy called Playtoes (or Playtoe for short), who lived in a little town called Athens. People in Athens speak a different language than you and I—and I have taken certain liberties with the use of dialect. It is necessary to steer a scholarly balance between giving the reader sufficient local color so he knows he is in a strange, faraway place, yet not enough so he gets sick to his stomach. I do not want any letters from outraged children telling me that halfway through the story I forgot the dialect. Everything that is done to you here is done on purpose; and don't you forget it.*

Y ou don't know about me without out you have read a book by the name of *The Adventures of the Shadows in the Cave*; but that ain't no matter. My name is Playtoe and this is a story about me and my best friend, Prissy Walker. Playtoe ain't my real name (my real for-sure name is Billy Joe Peckerwood)—but everybody knows that Athens is in Georgia, and everybody knows that in the South nobody is called by their real name. That name got hung on me when I was just a little critter for a disgustin habit which I had (no different from all of my friends, but which for no fairness I got stuck with) and which I won't go into now, particularly since this is a sweet tale about desserts.

Prissy Walker and me are best friends, though if truth be told, Prissy is a changeable polecat with both the sweetest and baddest mouth in all of Dixie. His baptize name was Parsifal, but he got tagged with the name Prissy because of a mean religious streak that otherwise spoilt his good character. One minute he was a good ol' boy smokin corn and playin hooky behind the barn, and the next minute with no more warnin than a summer storm he'd be suckin up to Jesus like a born-again you know what. For all that, Prissy and me, we was good pals.

Well, we better get on with this story or we ain't never gonna get it told. One day, me and Prissy were havin dinner with Prissy's Uncle Sock'rtease and his Aunt Tippy. "Sock'rtease" was what me and Prissy called his uncle—except never to his face, his real name bein' Colonel Beauregard Bullfeathers.

Uncle Sock'rtease was a gay ol' hound who loved playin with little boys. But his idea of play—like many gay ol' hounds—was pinchin or punchin or teasin. As a result, me and Prissy called him "Uncle Sock'r-tease."

Well, this story is gettin longer all the time, and I'm gonna cut through the main meal and get right down to the sweet part, which of course is the desserts, which of course is what this is all about.

One day, Prissy Walker and I was havin dinner with his Uncle Sock'rtease and his Aunt Tippy—a Tennessee Terwilliger (and don't she ever let you know it!) and a Southern Baptist lady of the meanest kind—and there I was pokin around this food, and I knew I could never get any of it into me. It was an ol' family dish called moosacow, or somethin like that, and it looked like a whole damn moose had to be buried away somewhere in there, it bein all brown and gooey and ugly. I never was much for havin foods all mushed together so's you couldn't tell what was where. Well, I just kept shovin it back and forth, hopin it would begin to look smaller.

"You haven't touched your moosacow, Playtoe," said Aunt Tippy.

"No, ma'am," I said, "I ain't all that hungry; don't it look good though!"

And so on, and so on—jest pourin out the molasses by the bucket. Then, soft and slippery like a preacher workin the purse, I jest oozed out: "I think I might jest wait for desserts."

Well, that sure pinched her Baptist heart. The idea of jest havin sweet desserts all through life started a four-hour speech, or so it seemed to me, where you'd have thunk that greens was God and puddin the Devil. Still, I jest know'd I couldn't get that stuff down without upchuckin right there on the table, so I jest kept sayin over and over all I wanted was jest desserts. And she kept sayin over and over, "We can't live in a world of just desserts."

Sure enough, as if his Aunt Tippy wasn't after me enough, Prissy got the religious spasm right then and there, and said, "If the good Lord had intended this to be a world of just desserts, he wouldn't have created okra, grits, or eggplant."

"Sweet Jesus," said Uncle Sock'rtease, as he pinched Prissy's prat under the table, "let me teach you two a thing or two."

Everybody got very quiet at that point. When Uncle Sock'rtease reckons to teach a thing or two, you got two chances. If you're lucky you get a story, if you're unlucky you get a butt-bustin game he invented, a terrible game where he asks all the questions and no matter what you come up with it's always wrong. And worst, he never will tell you the right answers no matter how much you beg from him. Prissy and me, a long time ago, decided they were no answers to any of those damnation questions. It was jest his way of teasin. The way he pushed back from the chair though, we had a feelin we was gettin a story, and he wasn't bad at storytellin. Sure enough, he started:

"This story takes place a long, long, long, long, long, long time ago, before Frosty Flakes, Frosty the Snowman, or frosted hair. Before Big Mac or Little League. Before Bubble Yum or Billy Beer—before the Beatles! In the sovereign state of Louisiana in La Fontaine Parish, just up the river from New Orleans, lived a no-good, Cajun grasshopper, known only as Lassie-gal. Cheek to jowl in the same plantation lived a maiden ant named Ms. Beulah Formi. While Lassie-gal was a no-account critter, Ms. Beulah Formi was all-account good. While Lassie-gal was sashaying around playing in the hot summer sun, sowing her wild oats, Ms. Beulah Formi was busy—butt up—all the hot days, sowing her crops for the cold, long winter she knew would come. While Lassie-gal was crashing high-tone parties at the Odd Fellows' or Elaine's, Ms. Beulah Formi was working from sunup to sundown, areaping her crops."

"As ye sow, so shall ye reap," said Prissy, surprisin hisself at the words that jest slipped out.

Nobody paid no mind to the interruption. Nobody blamed Prissy. Religion to him was like hiccups to other folk. It jest come over him, uncontrollable like. "Testament tics" is what Uncle Sock'rtease called it.

"Well, anyway," Uncle Sock'rtease continued, "for four months that little ant just crawled back and forth, back and forth, working her tail off. It was enough to make you tired just watching. But Lassie-gal wasn't watching. Too busy raising hell to raise crops.

"And then Labor Day came; and the good times were over, and the free-loading and barbeques were put away till Confederate Memorial Day.

"Ms. Beulah finished off her last jar of pickled watermelon rind, sealed it tight, proudly surveyed a cellarful of vittles, enough to last beyond Confederate Memorial Day, even unto the Fourth of July. Then Ms. Beulah dragged her weary bones to the door of her split-level, storm-proofed, semi-attached, three-and-one-half room condominium to say a last good-bye to the poor, unfortunate critter that frittered away the summer days on fun and foolishness and now had to face a cold and hungry winter. Well—just at that same spooky second, when Ms. Beulah stepped into her front yard—a drunken porno peddler, passing by, dropped a plain brown-paper-covered copy of *Popeye and Olive Oyl*—the unexpurgated edition—right on Ms. Beulah Formi, squashing her right into the ground.

"Lassie-gal wept for her dear friend for a moment, but since there wasn't enough left of her to make a proper burial, Lassie-gal stepped around the mess and into Ms. Beulah's split-level, storm-proofed, semi-attached, three-and-one-half room condominium, closing the door behind her to a long winter of rest and relaxation and a larder filled with the good efforts of her dear, departed friend.

" 'Hot spit,' she said—admiring her deceased neighbor's efforts. 'Danged if that hard-working, Christian lady weren't right after all. Always after me to read my chapters and verses. The good book said, "The Lord will provide"—and he shore has!' "

Everybody waited for Uncle Sock'rtease to go on, but one good look at that smirky cat-that-swallowed-the-catfish look on his face, and it was clear as a mountain lake that the damnfool story was over.

"I don't believe it," said Aunt Tippy. "I don't believe you'd tell a story like that in front of the innocent ears of these two tads."

"What's wrong with the story?" asked Uncle Sock'rtease.

"Everything," said Aunt Tippy.

"Surely, my dear Tippy, you don't mean Every Thing," said Uncle Sock'rtease. "Come, let us examine that statement."

Well, they was off! Prissy give me a look—and we both knowed then that Aunt Tippy was hooked, landed, gutted, and spitted right then and there whether she knowed it or not. She had taken the bait and was caught on that dangblasted twenty-question game of Uncle Sock'rtease's.

They was after each other for like an hour—he playin out his line till she was one tired ol trout of a Terwilliger.

My head was hurtin from all those crazy questions. When Uncle Sock'rtease was goin at you—you couldn't say *piss* without you had to splain it, yet you knowed he passed enough in his ol life to drown in, let alone knowin what it was. And if you was fool enough to start about *good* or *bad* or *rights 'n wrongs,* he would shake you up like an ol hound with a dead jackrabbit.

Well, Aunt Tippy she kept askin for it—saying words like *immoral* and *indecent,* and Uncle Sock'rtease he kept askin those questions with no answers.

We knowed it was almost over when she stopped calling him Bullfeathers and switched to Colonel.

"Colonel," said Aunt Tippy, all the starch taken out, "that ending was just not fair."

"Fair or just?" asked Uncle Sock'rtease.

"Fair."

"Well, you know what Li'l Jimmy Peanut said about life not being fair."

"Lord," said Aunt Tippy, "you ain't going to start quoting the flakiest cracker in Georgia, are you Colonel? All right—forget *fair.* It's not just. That no-good Lassie-gal didn't *deserve* to harvest the fruits of that good woman's labor."

That word *deserve* was the hocus-pocus Uncle Sock'rtease was waitin for, and he jest melted down like brown sugar on hot grits.

"No, she didn't," agreed Uncle Sock'rtease. "And that poor ant after working all summer didn't *deserve* to get squashed like a bug on the day before her retirement."

Then, Uncle Sock'rtease got that look that meant the 'possum's treed and said, "I know what's bothering you, Tippy. You don't like the story because you really—after all—do believe in a world of just deserts."

Well, Aunt Tippy snorted and fumed, Prissy giggled to himself, and I was as happy as a tick in a plowboy's ear because all the while Uncle Sock'rtease was tellin the story, which had us all bobbin and whirlin and payin no mind to what was really goin on, he was scrapin all that moosacow stuff into the garbage, stackin things in the dishwasher, and making ready for the sweet end of the meal.

"And now that we have settled that," he said, "I want you boys to come in the kitchen and see a surprise, cause I just invented something for you."

Now I know this part is goin to be hard to swallow cause Uncle Sock'rtease bein a philosopher ain't supposed to do nothin useful (Aunt Tippy always said, "Philosophy bakes no bread"), but I was there, and I seen it, and cross my heart it's true. We moseyed into the kitchen and there was this big chunk of beautiful, red, shivery, clean, cold and sweet stuff.

"This is for you, boys, and it's no more than you deserve," he said. "It's called 'red-jello-with-no-fruit-in-it'! It ain't good for you and it ain't got no vitamins, and it don't build muscle and it don't make you smart. It's just dessert, and that's the way it should be."

And that's the way it was that day with me and Prissy Walker and his Uncle Sock'rtease and his Aunt Tippy.

MAGIC SPELL

BY

Allen Ginsberg

There once was a boy who lived in a wooden house uphill from the red brick mills along the Passaic River in Paterson, New Jersey, near the Great Falls. He was lonely and wandered over the concrete bridge above the raceway where purple water spilled from the silk-dye works into a pool where naked boys swam in summer heat sunny afternoons between the factory walls.

His friend Earl up the block protected him from bullies who slapped the little kids without clothes and threatened to push them off the concrete edge of the swimming place on one end overlooking a rusty scrapyard filled with old cars.

He wished he had a Magic Spell and was King in ermine robes with gold crown, so that he could make Earl his Grand Wizard. He lost track of his protector Earl after he got out of Grammar School.

He grew up and went to India and studied Magic Spells. He sang *Hare Krishna Krishna Krishna Krishna Hare Hare Hare Rama Hare Rama Rama Rama Rama Hare Hare** for several years for protection. Then he sang *Om Namah Shivaye.*† That got him excited and everyone who heard him sang along, excited. Everyone got high, and then went home. But to get excited they had to sing the Magic Spell over and over. Then they got tired of being excited.

He grew older, and found it bothersome to sing long Magic Spells all the time, even though the new one he sang, *Gate*

---

* Sing-song to the Preserver of the universe.
† Sing-song to the Changer of the universe.

Gate Paragate Parasamgate Bodhi Svaha,* had a snappy rhythm and meant that no one had to get excited anymore, they could relax. Still, it was long and sounded mysterious.

War came and he went around singing a new Magic Spell that was easy to remember. When the tear gas drifted by in city parks and young, long-haired boys and girls yelled at policemen trying to chase them away, he walked around singing *OM* as loud as he could. That was okay, but it still sounded mysterious and though everyone knew it was a Magic Spell, nobody knew exactly what it meant.

War ended and he said *Ah.* That was it. It was a natural Magic Spell, everyone understood saying *Ah,* just like Fourth of July appreciating fireworks. His beard grew white and he looked like a wise king and said *Ah* at every opportunity.

Ah was like a breath of air. In fact, you had to breathe out to say it, and he was breathing all the time just like everyone else. One day he stopped saying *Ah,* but kept on breathing out. He discovered he was aware of the Magic Spell every few minutes, just by breathing out. Other people were breathing but they weren't aware of the Magic Spell in their breath most of the time, only sometimes when they remembered they were breathing out into space.

So he went around and looked people in the eyes, aware that he was breathing. They all treated him as if he were a king anyway, so he didn't need a crown or a robe. In bald middle age he asked advice from everyone he met so he found many Grand Wizards and they all helped rule the Earth.

He settled in New York City. Sometimes he goes back to Paterson, New Jersey, and visits the pool between the factories. He stands there silent and breathes.

* Gone out, Gone out, All gone out, All over gone, Wake Mind, so Ah.

PRICKLED PICKLES DON'T SMILE

BY

Nikki Giovanni

Never tickle
a prickled pickle
cause prickled pickles
Don't smile

Never goad
a loaded toad
when he has to walk
A whole mile

Froggies go courting
with weather reporting
that indicates
There are no snows

But always remember
the month of december
is very hard
On your nose

TEDDY
THE
SPY

BY

Herbert Gold

ILLUSTRATED BY
ARI, NINA, AND ETHAN GOLD

Teddy needed to be something special. Powerful. Different.

He looked around in books, on the teevee, and in his toy box, which he called Frog's House. He found helicopters, trains, puppets, cars, and a few old pieces of gum. Nothing he really wanted to be. He found a torn balloon under his father's pillow. He didn't want to be that, either.

Teddy knew he couldn't be a filthy awful monster, because only a few get to be filthy awful monsters. He saw one in a dream. He decided not to be like that: horns, fire, scales, claws. There was no chimney and the fire came out of the mouth. Very unattractive.

A spy was different. He noticed one in a black raincoat with loops for holding stuff and a belt for keeping his middle together. His mother and father were watching the spy on television. A spy finds things out—secrets, maps to treasure or dungeons, formulas for bombs or frozen yoghurt. Things other people don't want him to know.

Teddy could be a spy. He wore a white towel instead of a black raincoat. He held his invisible see-a-scope in his left hand and kept his right hand free for emergencies. He used it to hold up the towel.

Now he went spying a little around the house. He looked under his mother's and dad's bed. Ahah, he was in business. Ahah, the spy found one sock which his father was looking for last Sunday.

"Where did you find that?" his mother asked.

Teddy only smiled. Spies don't tell. They don't speak no matter how much they are tortured by their mothers asking, *Where on earth did you find that?* Spies need their rest, however, and Teddy went to bed.

Sleep. A bag of loose dreams bounced around on Teddy's nose. He sneezed. He curled on his side. Sleep. Sleep.

There was a dream which made him dream he had waked up. Hey, Teddy! Hey!

The Filthy Awful Monster pointed his fire at Teddy and said: "Where did you find something, I don't remember what?"

Teddy knew the monster lived in his dream, his mother and father lived everywhere else, and only he was a spy in both places. "I won't tell," he told the monster.

"Arrrgh!" roared the monster.

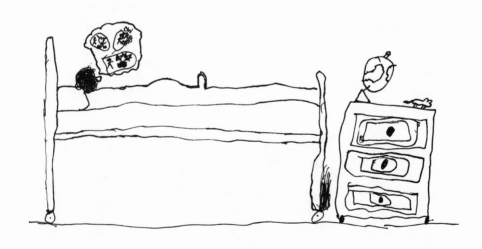

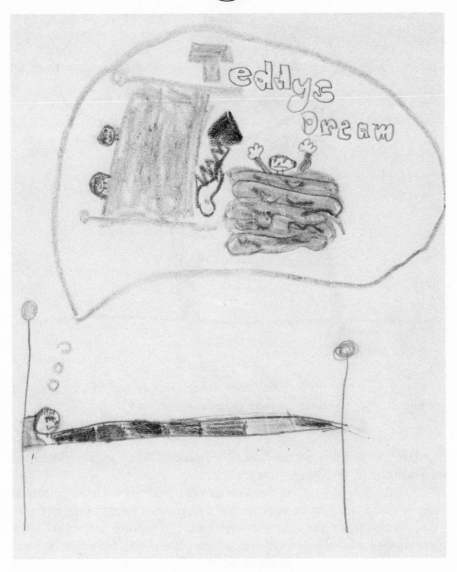

So loud it really woke Teddy up and he ran to his parents' room. "I'm scared," he said.

"Of what?" his mother said.

"Monsters."

"Oh, just like television," his dad said. "Think of it as a rotten program and turn it off."

"I was asleep," Teddy said.

"You were dreaming," his mother said.

"That's not teevee," Teddy said. "Can I sleep on the floor in your room? In case the program comes back?"

"Oh, what a bunch of . . ." said his dad.

It wasn't like teevee at all. They put some blankets and a pillow on the floor. They tucked Teddy in. He missed his own bed a little, very little—not at all. Zzzzz.

It was a convenient place to sleep. Huge brown shoes to guard him. The monster looked everywhere, even in Frog's House. The monster didn't know how to find him. His mother and father were there in case the monster slithered around the shoes, burning the laces with his breath. And Teddy was near the place where he had found the sock—a good spot in the spying business.

His father snored a little.

His mother breathed deeply. It wasn't quite snoring, but it made noise anyway. She said she didn't snore, but Teddy's father snored. Okay, she breathed powerfully and he breathed snorefully. Teddy kept his eyes open.

Teddy the spy lay awake on the floor. He peeked between some shoes and under the bed, but there were no more secrets unless you count a few belly button fuzzballs, a lost wad of Kleenex, and a squeezed blue tube which couldn't have been toothpaste. Kachew. And a sneeze.

He listened in the dark. He heard the house creak. He listened for sounds of slithering and the singeing of hottened breath.

No slither.

No fiery rush of throat smoke.

Yawn. Teddy missed his dreams. He decided to fall asleep again and spy out a monster. He felt brave. He felt wide awake. He felt sleepy. So he crept through the house, following noises where they led him.

No Filthy Awful here in the bedroom.

No Filthy Awful there in the kitchen.

No monster on the stairs, either.

If he was a spy, he had better keep on looking. He kept on looking. Even in Frog's House. Even the monster's filthy, awful shadow was gone.

The night was passing. The birds were cheeping in the trees. The monster said, "Ahah."

Teddy said, "Arrrgh."

"You scared me," said the monster, shrinking in the heat from Teddy's breath.

"I found you again," said Teddy.

"ARRRGH," said the awful monster.

"I'm a spy and a magician!" said Teddy. "I'll change you into something. Channel Forty-four!"

The monster slithered toward Teddy. Its claws

made a scraping noise on the floor. There was too much fire in its mouth—licking, snoring, crackling flames.

"Channel Forty-four!" Teddy cried. "PBS! PBS! My magic words!"

The monster sagged. The fire went out. The claws softened. Teddy had changed him into a woolly, fuzzy, droopy sock.

He woke up rather pleased with his victory over the monster. He was in his own room. He was not only a spy, but also a magician. The best place to meet filthy awful monsters and change them into socks was in his own bed.

"Peebee Ess," he said. "I kind of like that dumb secret word."

He got up feeling hungry and dressed himself almost as quickly as he could undress himself.

"What on earth did you say?" his mother asked at breakfast. (Orange juice, Unnatural Way Granola with added vitamins, banana with a Chiquita sticker for the heck of it, toast, raisins, milk. He mixed it around with his spoon and considered future action.)

"Huh?" his father asked. He hadn't drunk his coffee yet. Before his coffee he said, "Huh," to answer questions, or asked, "Huh?" if he wanted to know something. You had to give him the question again.

"Nothing," Teddy said. "I was just thinking."
Spies don't have to tell everything.

LIKELY AND THE DRAGON: A Play for Marionettes

BY

Paul Goodman

Cast:

LIKELY

MATTY

LAURA

    children of seven to nine

LARRY, Likely's brother, aged about two

TEXAS, an old horse

VOICE OF MAMA

DREAD VOICE

GHOST OF TEXAS

DRAGON

PUNCH and JUDY (in left and right shutters)

Scene 1. *A field.* LIKELY, MATTY, LAURA, *and* LARRY.

LIKELY: Let's climb up on Texas!

LARRY: Yeoow!

LAURA: Here, Texas!

MATTY: Come. Texas. Good Texas.

LIKELY: Get the ladder, Matty. Here he comes.

(*Exit* MATTY.)

LAURA: Here Texas, here Texas!

LIKELY: See how the cornflowers are shining in the field. Let's pick flowers.

(*Enter old* TEXAS.)

LARRY: Yeoow!

LAURA: Whoa, Texas.

LIKELY: Stand still, Texas. Here comes Matty with the ladder.

(TEXAS *patiently backs up. He patiently lets himself be used, perhaps only rolling his eyes in distress.*)

LIKELY: Stand still, Texas, while we climb on.

(*They lean the ladder against his side.*)

LIKELY: First! I'm first. I'll sit on his neck. Whoa, Texas! don't you budge.

(*She climbs.* MATTY *climbs.*)

MATTY: I'll jump. (*He jumps.*)

(LAURA *stands trembling on* TEXAS's *back.*)

OTHERS: Jump. Jump!

LAURA: I'm scared.

OTHERS: Jump!

(*She falls off.*)

LARRY: Me! Up! Up! (*He blocks the ladder.*)

MATTY: Get out o' the way, you monkey. Likely, make your brother get away, he's blocking the ladder.

LIKELY: Get out o' the way, Larry, you pest. Why don't you go home? You're too small to climb. Go home! Tell Mama I sent you home.

(MATTY *pulls him off,* LARRY *bawls. The others climb and jump.*)

(*Suddenly* TEXAS *moves forward.*)

LIKELY: Whoa, Texas.

LAURA: He's moving, help!

MATTY: Whoa, horse. Stand still. You're knocking the ladder over.

(TEXAS *moves two steps, whinnies once, and falls down dead.*)

ALL: Oh!

LARRY: Up! Up! Tex, up!

LIKELY: Stand up, Texas. Good horse.

MATTY: Good Texas. Stand up so we can climb on your back again.

(*Pause.*) (LARRY *begins to cry sadly.*)

LIKELY: He's dead. He can't get up anymore.

(*Spirit flies from* TEXAS's *mouth.*)

Look, there goes his ghost.

MATTY: Texas is dead.

LAURA: Poor Texas.

LIKELY: He can't get up anymore.

(*They begin to chant.*)

ALL:
Texas is dead
Poor Texas
He can't get up anymore.

(*The song continues. They bring flowers and scatter them on* TEXAS. *They move in a slow circle around.*)

LARRY (*shrieks*): I'm scared. (*He runs away.*)

(MATTY *and* LAURA *follow.* LIKELY *is left alone.*)

LIKELY (*murmur*): Good Texas. Stand up, Texas. That's a good Texas. He can't stand up. He can't stand up anymore. Ohhhh—poor horse Texas.

(*She begins to weep. She picks up flowers, and rejects them.*)

The flowers are dead. Oh, everything is dying. The summer flowers are withered

(*Autumn leaves begin to fall; the music continues.*)

and the autumn leaves are beginning to fall. The leaves are slowly falling in the field.

(*Great tears fall across the scene.*)

And now my tears are falling from the sky. I can't see! I can't see!

(*The music stops. She weeps in silence.*)

PUNCH: What's the matter, little girl? Why are you crying?

JUDY: She's crying because the horse died, silly. You'd better let her alone or she'll get mad. Sometimes people like to cry by themselves.

PUNCH: I can't leave her there crying, it breaks my heart. What's the matter, Likely?

LIKELY (*passionately*): Everything is dying. All the things I love are going to die. Texas is dead already. My Mama is going to die too and my little brother Larry. But I'm going to die before he does, 'cause I'm older than he is.

(*At this, she bursts into wild sobs.*)

PUNCH (*sententiously*): Don't cry, Likely. God ain't going to die.

LIKELY: What! Everybody's going to die. I see it plain as day.

PUNCH: No. God is and God always was and God always will be.

LIKELY: Say that again.

PUNCH: I said, God is and God always was and God always will be.

LIKELY (*in anger and pain*): Ow! that's horrible. God doesn't have a birthday. God never had a birthday, he never had a birthday party. I'm scared of God. Ow!

(*She runs away.*)

(*Curtain.*)

JUDY: See, smarty? I told you to let her alone. Now you've made it worse than ever.

PUNCH: I did the best I could.

JUDY: That's not good enough.

Scene 2. *A city street with trees.*

PUNCH: Now we are back in the city and Likely is happy again. Here she comes now. She and her mother are out for a walk with little brother Larry. Likely is skating. Those big legs belong to Mommy.

(MAMA'*s legs.* LARRY *pulled in a red wagon.* LIKELY *skating.*)

LIKELY (*skating*):   *This* foot—*that* foot
                        that's the way we skate
                        wheee, quick as the wind.

Look! There goes the red bird in the tree. Look, Mommy.

(*A bird darts across.*)

MAMA'S VOICE: Where? I can't see it.

LIKELY: There! There it goes! It's a tanager.

VOICE: How do you know it's a tanager?

LIKELY: By the markings, of course. Can't you see it's a tanager?

VOICE: I can't even see the bird. How can I see it's a tanager?

LARRY (*standing up in the wagon*): Yeoow!

LIKELY: Little brother can see it. Only he thinks it's a tomato. Zip! now it's in *that* tree.

VOICE: I still can't see it. Oh dear.

LIKELY: Now you can't see him because he flew away. But don't be disappointed. He'll come back tomorrow. That's where his nest is.

VOICE: Yes, I see the nest.

LIKELY: Hi! There go my friends. Hi Matty! Hi Laura! Wait, I'll skate with you. *This* foot—*that* foot.

(*Exit.*)

LARRY (*standing in wagon*): Bye, Likee.

(*She reappears.*)

LIKELY: Do you know, there are five ways of going places. There's walking, running, skipping, and jumping; that's four. And there's rolling on iron wheels quick as the wind, that's five. *This* foot—*that* foot.

(*Exit.*)

LARRY: Bye, Likee.

MAMA'S VOICE: *Likely!*

(*She reappears.*)

LIKELY: Yes, Mommy.

VOICE: Likely, will you watch Larry a minute while I step in at the tailor's?

LIKELY: Oh, but I was going skating with Matty and Laura. See, there, they're going away.

VOICE: I'll be only ten minutes. But if you don't want to, I'll take him in with me. I thought that you might want to take care of him.

(*Pause.*)

LIKELY: Oh, all right. Sure.

(*Exeunt legs.*)

LIKELY (*to Larry*): Sit down, you. You'll fall and break your head.

LARRY: No. Larry stand. Up! Up!

LIKELY: Sit down! (*She sits him down. He bawls.*)

I hate you, lousy Larry. Why do I have to take care of you? But if I don't, Mommy will be displeased. And it's only for ten minutes. . . . Yah, you can't even talk. I'd rather play with Matty, who can talk.

Lousy Larry, lousy Larry,
lousy Larry, I hate you.
I'll chop you up in pieces
and plant them under a tree.

And when the tree grows tall
I'll put them together again
and he will be Prince Charming,
and *then* I'll marry him!

PUNCH: Ow! Such awful language from such a nice girl. I'm surprised and shocked. Does she really hate her little brother? She's just fooling, ain't she?

JUDY: The hell she's fooling! She hates him like poison. All boys and girls hate their baby brothers and sisters. They're jealous. Mommy has to take care of the baby, she hasn't time to watch *them* out of the window as she used.

PUNCH: Ts. Ts. That's too bad. I suppose it can't be helped.

JUDY: No, stupid, it can't be helped. Here come the others back.

(MATTY *and* LAURA *fly by.*)

LARRY: Yeoow!

MATTY: Hi.

LAURA: Hi.

(*They vanish and reappear.*)

MATTY: Come skate with us.

LIKELY: I can't. I got to take care of *him.*

(*They vanish and come back.*)

LIKELY: I have an idea! Let's drag Larry in the wagon!

LAURA: We'll be horses. I'm Texas.

LIKELY: No, I'm Texas, it was my idea.

MATTY: Whoever heard of horses on skates. *I'm* Texas, do you hear?

(*They grab the rope and begin to drag.*)

LIKELY: We'd better go slow or he'll fall out.

LARRY: Yeow!

MATTY: Giddyap. Faster.

LIKELY: *This* foot—*that* foot—

LARRY: Yeow!

LAURA: He loves it.

MATTY: He loves to go fast.

LIKELY: He'll fall out and hurt himself.

LARRY: Yeow! Fast! Fast!

MATTY: Wheee, Texas!

(*The skates make a terrible noise.*)

LIKELY: *This* foot—*that* foot—
                     wheee—quick as the wind.

(*BANG! The wagon turns over and* LARRY *falls out. Pause. After a moment,* LARRY *lets out a yowl.*)

(MAMA's *legs appear.* LARRY *flies up—to her arms.*)

VOICE: What's the matter. Oh, poor child. His nose is bleeding. Is this the way you take care of him?

MATTY: He wanted to go faster and faster.

LIKELY: No. It was all my fault. I knew he'd fall out and get hurt, but I dragged him too fast anyway. Now I'm not angry with him any more.

LAURA: His nose isn't bleeding anymore.

LIKELY: How brave he is, just like my Papa. He cried out only once. Poor Larry. Now I love him. He's so brave. Let me kiss him.

VOICE: No. I'm displeased. Now you can go and skate if you want to.

LIKELY: I don't want to skate. (*Exit, dragging her feet.*)

(*Curtain.*)

Scene 3. LIKELY's *bedroom.*

(LIKELY *preparing for bed. She arranges clothes, pulls down the shade. Music.*)

LIKELY: Mommy isn't angry with me anymore. She never is for long. I can rely on it.

(*Lights out. A lullaby.*)

SINGING VOICE:
    The ending of my song is silence,
    the ending of company being alone.
    So sleep. So sleep.

    Come, come, come sleep; my tired heart
    has, hunting and building, turned to stone.
    The ending of my song is silence,
    the ending of company being alone.

LIKELY: It is a sad, pretty song.

VOICE: I will not stir till someone gives me
help and courage not my own.
The ending of my song is silence,
the ending of company being alone.

      So sleep. So sleep.

  (LIKELY *is asleep.*)

PUNCH: Shhh!

JUDY: Shhh!

PUNCH: She's asleep.

JUDY: Why don't you shut up, or you'll wake her up.

PUNCH: I'm scared.

JUDY: What are you scared of, you booby?

PUNCH: Something terrible is going to happen. All the children will be
frightened.

  (*He gives a little shriek.*)

JUDY (*angrily*): Shhh!

PUNCH: Maybe we oughtn't to show it after all?

JUDY: Nonsense! Children like to be frightened—anyway it's only a
play and it's only a dream.

PUNCH: Children! Don't be frightened because it's only a dream and it's
only a play. And anyway, it all comes out happy in the end.

  (*There is a* DREAD VOICE.)

DREAD VOICE: *Likely!*

  (*She stirs.*)

DREAD VOICE: *Likely!*

  (*She sits up.*)

DREAD VOICE: *Likely!*

LIKELY: What is it?

DREAD VOICE (*slowly*): You—killed—your—brother—Larry.

LIKELY: No, no! I didn't kill him! He's in the next room.

(*She calls.*)

Larry! Larry!

(*Pause.*)

LIKELY (*faint shriek*): Help! Help! Who will come to help me?

(*There is a blue light. Enter the* GHOST OF TEXAS, *winged and with skates.*)

PUNCH: It's a ghost!

JUDY: It's Texas!

GHOST OF TEXAS (*in a friendly baritone*): Don't be afraid, little Likely. I'm a friendly ghost and I've come to help you because you were as kind to me as you knew how. Your brother Larry isn't dead. Soon we'll bring him back.

LIKELY: But where *is* Larry? I called him in the next room, but he didn't answer.

TEXAS: You sent him away beyond the Horizon, where the Sun gets swallowed up at night. But the Sun comes again, he comes again.

LIKELY (*tearfully*): I didn't mean to send him away. I didn't really hate him. I want my poor little brother back.

TEXAS: Don't feel bad; you didn't do anything very wrong. All boys and girls hate their little brothers and sisters. It can't be helped. Mommy has to take care of them because they're so small and can't do anything for themselves. Then she can't pay as much attention to you and watch you out the window as she used. It can't be helped. It can't be helped. But don't worry about it—Mommy understands how you feel, and she loves you more than ever.

LIKELY: Yes, she loves me more than ever and she sings me to sleep with sad, pretty songs. But how can I go and bring back Larry?

TEXAS: Around the Horizon lies the Dragon of the Horizon.

LIKELY: A Dragon! What Dragon? I'm afraid of Dragons. I know what the horizon is, it is the circle all around where the sky comes down to the earth.

TEXAS: Yes. Around this circle lies a monster Dragon who bites his tail with his mouth, so he makes a big ring. He is and always was. Now that Dragon—don't be frightened—has swallowed Larry down, but we will go and fight him and cut him open, and out will step Larry bigger and better than ever.

LIKELY: Let's go. I'm not afraid anymore. As long as there is something that must be done, I'm not afraid. How are we going to get to the Horizon?

TEXAS (*patiently*): You may ride on my back.

LIKELY: Oh!

(*She hesitates.*)

TEXAS: Climb up! Climb up just as you used to.

LIKELY: I don't like to say anything personal, but won't you fall down and die?

TEXAS: No. I'm not going to die anymore.

(TEXAS *stands up to the bed and* LIKELY *climbs on his back.*)

TEXAS: I have wings on my shoulders to fly into the sky, and skates on my hooves to roll past the stars.

LIKELY: Yeow! Yeow! Giddyap.

(*Curtain.*)

Scene 4. *Across the sky.*

(*They are mounted in the sky. The houses of the stars move past.*)

PUNCH (*looking up in awe*): Oh!

JUDY: Heavens! Where are they now?

(*A Lion in heaven.*)

PUNCH: This is the Lion's house. All of the sky is divided into the houses of the stars, and this is where the Lion rears and roars.

JUDY: Roars? I can't hear anything.

PUNCH: He roars quietly. Nobody can hear him, in the dead of night.

(*A Hunter.*)

JUDY: Hm. Who is this?

PUNCH: This is the mighty Hunter. He is hunting the Lion across the sky. But as the Hunter moves on the Lion moves on, so that one never catches the other.

JUDY: That's stupid! What's the use of hunting him if he can never catch him?

PUNCH: No, no, not stupid. That's how it must be, across the top of heaven.

(*A Crown.*)

JUDY: What's this?

PUNCH: This is the starry Crown, overhead for us all if we look up to it. This is the Crown in Heaven for the winner.

(TEXAS *and* LIKELY *drift into and out of view. There are abstract figures.*)

PUNCH: Do you know what they are doing? They are playing heavenly hopscotch.

JUDY: Hopscotch? How is that?

PUNCH: All the sky is divided into the houses of the different starry animals, the Lion's house, the Crab's house, and the rest. Now these houses are the same as the squares in the game of hopscotch, each one of which has a different number. Into each square you must throw your stone, or keys, or ring—it must be something your very own, that you wear close to your body—you throw your pebble and visit each house in turn.

JUDY: Why must we do it?

PUNCH: Then you have crossed the sky and you can come home and be happy. This is why children play the game, but they don't remember why anymore.

(*A shooting star.*)

JUDY: Oh!

PUNCH: That's a shooting star. It brings good luck. (*Excited:*) Look! Look!

(*The Horizon Line.*)

JUDY: What on earth is *that?*

PUNCH: They have come to the Horizon. There is the sleeping Sun. And now they are entering the blood-red land of the Dragon. I'm scared.

(*He slams his shutter.*)

JUDY: So am I. (*Slams hers.*)

LIKELY (*in a loud voice*): I'm not! I'll fight this Dragon and cut him open, and get back my little brother.

(PUNCH *and* JUDY *peep out timorously.*)

Scene 5. *The blood-red land of the Dragon, a strand on an endless sea.*

VOICE FROM WITHIN THE DRAGON: Let me out! Let me out!

LIKELY: We're coming.

TEXAS: This is the Dragon that is and always was. You see he is biting his tail, so he makes a closed ring.

VOICE: Let me out!

LIKELY: That's my brother Larry's voice, crying "Let me out." I'm coming, Larry! . . . How am I supposed to fight this Dragon?

(*The* DRAGON *thrashes and fumes, etc. There is a wind and weird voices. Speech comes in gusts and gasps.*)

Ugh, I don't like the looks of it, but I'm not afraid.

TEXAS: I'll dress you as a knight in armor and give you a sword and a shield.

(*He dubs her with the sword.*)

Likely, don't be afraid. Every girl and boy, not only you, must fight with this fearful Dragon. Here is your shield.

LIKELY: I don't like this shield. It has a Winter Sun on it, trying bravely to shine through a snowfall. How heavy the helmet is!

(*He puts the helmet on her. She cries in fright.*)

I hate this helmet. Inside, I can see only a little light through it, and the people outside can't see my face at all. I like to see plain, without these bars in front.

TEXAS: Poor child. Here is the sword.

LIKELY: Ohohoh—now I *am* afraid. I'm not afraid of the Dragon, I'm afraid of the armor.

(*She shakes.*)

(*The* DRAGON *bellows.*)

VOICE (*shrieks*): Let me out.

(LIKELY *advances nervously, flourishing the sword.*)

PUNCH: Hurrah for Likely. We're not afraid.

JUDY: Hush up, you make her nervous.

(*The* DRAGON *swipes her with his claw and sends her flying. The helmet rolls off.*)

TEXAS: (*in terror*): Owow! *All is lost!*

LIKELY (*springing to her feet and throwing away the shield*): *Nothing is lost!* The armor was too heavy for me. I'll throw it away. Let me fight him my own way, freely moving my arms and legs.

(*She cries out, stretching high her arms.*)

Help me! Help me, O helping hand!

(*A real hand appears from above and gives her the sword.*)

(*She steps up confidently to the* DRAGON, *who bellows and spits fire.*)

LIKELY: You can't frighten me with thunder and lightning, Dragon of the Horizon.

(*They fight.*)

I am sorry to hurt you, monster, but you must give me back my brother Larry.

(*She cuts off the* DRAGON's *head.*)

(The DRAGON *shrieks.)*

(The light fades toward sunrise.)

HEAD OF THE DRAGON: Thank you, Likely. Now I can leave off biting my tail. Now I can go and swim in the sea.

(The HEAD *goes off like a walking fish and dives into the sea.)*

LIKELY: Larry, come out!

(She cuts open the belly. Out steps LARRY, *happy and new.)*

LARRY: Happy birthday! It's God's birthday. God has a birthday every couple of weeks. Sometimes, when all's well, he has a birthday every morning at sunrise.

LIKELY: Larry! How well you can talk!

LARRY *(proudly)*: Yes, now I can talk as well as anybody and better than some. Texas! Here Texas! Good Texas!

TEXAS: Climb up! Climb up! We have to get back by sunrise. And here comes the sunrise.

(They spring onto the horse's back.)

(They move toward the Horizon, where the Sun rises at a bound.)

SUN: Home free! Home free!

PUNCH: There! I told you there was nothing to be afraid of and everything would turn out all right.

JUDY: Rats! You were more scared than anybody.

(TEXAS *and the* CHILDREN *are flying through the pale dawn sky.)*

LIKELY: Texas, you are old and wise and we love you dearly. But you don't know how to fight dragons. You must never put on heavy armor, but swing your arms and legs with all your hard might and cry out loudly for a helping hand.

(Curtain.)

Scene 6. LIKELY's *bedroom in sunshine.*

(She is sitting up in bed.)

LIKELY: It's a bright day and all's well.

(*Enter* LARRY, *pulling the wagon charged with a great cake and candle.*)

> Happy birthday to you!
> Happy birthday to you!
> Happy birthday, dear world,
> happy birthday to you.

PUNCH AND JUDY (*echo*):

> Happy birthday, dear world,
> happy birthday to you.

ALL:

> Stand up, stand up, stand up and show us your
>   smiling face;
> stand up, stand up, stand up and show us your
>   face.

(*The Sun shows in through the window.*)

LIKELY: Why is there only one candle on the world's birthday cake? The world must be older than that.

LARRY: No. That's the *extra* candle, the one to grow on. That's the only one that counts.

LIKELY:

> I don't hold back for foolish fears,
> but I fly into the next moment.
> Or I sit still and let the next moment come to
>   me.

LARRY: Here come Matty and Laura.

LIKELY: I love Matty, he's my favorite boy. (*She flies and kisses him.*)

LARRY: Kiss me, too.

LIKELY: Yes, I love you, too.

(*There is a dance of general kissing.*)

MATTY: Say, you aren't going to have birthday cake for breakfast, are you? That's no way to eat.

LIKELY: Oh, it makes no difference about the cake. It's not the cake but the shining candle that makes the birthday party. Larry, bring on the toast and cereal.

(LARRY *drags on in the wagon a huge heap of toast, lit by a candle.*)

LIKELY: See, you can have a candle on a bowl of toast and cereal and it's a birthday party—if all is well.

PUNCH: Where is Texas?

JUDY: Texas is present in his absence.

(*Curtain.*)

IN THE CITY OF PARIS

BY

Hannah Green

ILLUSTRATED BY
JOHN WESLEY

In the city of Paris there are many garden parks with trees and grass and beds of flowers and little gravel paths and iron fences all around painted black with little gates at every corner and sometimes in the middle too, and on each gate there is a sign: ALL DOGS ARE STRICTLY FORBIDDEN, EVEN THOSE ON LEASHES.

There are angels in the parks of Paris and little elves in tulip beds, perfect egg-shaped tulip beds. There are pigeons in the grass, alas, and cats slip in right through the fence rails, but all dogs are strictly forbidden, even those on *leashes*.

Giraffes may nibble the leaves off the trees and children somersault where they please, girls can turn cartwheels, and a large hippopotamus can just wander in and sit down in a sandbox and say what you may there's no room left for a soul to dig a hole, make a castle, or even a pie. But all dogs are strictly forbidden, even those on leashes.

Helicopters can fly right down and let out pretty girls and boys with peacocks and parrots and monkeys for pets, but all dogs are strictly forbidden, even those on leashes. Lions may walk the gravel paths and tigers may circle the trees, but policemen in their uniforms walk up and down to see that no dog comes strolling in, even on a leash.

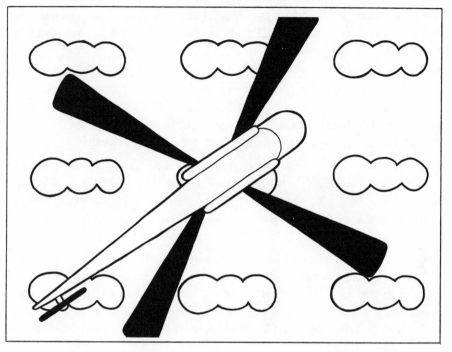

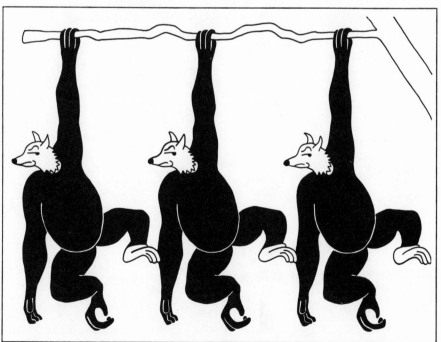

Birds fly in to sing their songs, the nightingales sing all day long, toads hop here and, slowly, there; and in bigger parks, the parks with ponds, ducks may float and frogs may croak and children come to sail their boats, but all dogs are strictly forbidden, even those on leashes.

Balloons descend, baboons swing in, migrating pigs and horses, of course, not to mention the gnus, the gnats, and the bats, and the laughing hyenas who create a disturbance as little scholars walk neatly by with their books in leather bags on their backs, going home from school, and all dogs are strictly forbidden, even those on leashes.

Unicorns are sometimes seen in the shade of certain trees, and ladies vanished centuries past, and rabbits sniffing the flowers of spring while poets carved in stone look on, but policemen in their uniforms walk up and down to see that no dog may enter here, even on a leash.

Grass blades glisten in the sunshine, and babies smile up at the sky when clouds float over as white as white doves and the saint with his head in his hand appears, but if you're a dog, a dog on a leash, you get tied to the fence right outside the gate, lie down and be good, that's life, for the law is: ALL DOGS ARE STRICTLY FORBIDDEN, EVEN THOSE ON LEASHES.

JUST A LITTLE CLOSER TO THE LORD

BY

Winston Groom

ILLUSTRATED BY
PAT OLIPHANT

There is a tiny town along the coast of the Carolinas called Widgeville. It is situated between a river and a swamp and the land around it is very flat and good for growing rice, which is what the people in Widgeville do, grow rice, and when they are not growing rice they keep to themselves and go to church and do not have much to do with the outside world.

Two types of people live in Widgeville, black people and white people, and they have lived there for hundreds of years. The white people are short and squat and have blue eyes and blond hair and speak in a dialect that is not like any dialect heard in that part of the country—or, for that matter, in any other part of the world. It is said that they are descendants of Englishmen who survived a mysterious shipwreck off Cape Hatteras in 1652.

The black people are tall and thin and fiercely black and they talk with an accent that is clipped and short and very difficult to understand, and it is said that their ancestors were of an ancient and powerful tribe that was kidnapped from a remote mountain region in Africa and sold into slavery. But black and white alike, the Widgeville people live together in harmony, growing rice, going to church, and speaking in their peculiar accents.

All but one.

His name is Walking Hand and he is very old and does not speak at all and some people believe that he is the Devil.

Walking Hand simply appeared one day and began roaming the streets and highways around Widgeville, carrying a preposterously battered black suitcase. Sometimes, early in the morning, he would materialize at the head of the little main street, follow it to the end, and turn off down a lane to the highway near the river. Later, near sunset, he would return by the same route and go off down a dirt road that ended near the swamp. Occasionally, his journey would be made at night, a tall, stark figure shuffling quietly down the streets, which would scare the bejesus out of anyone who happened upon him unexpectedly.

It had been nearly a year since he came and in all that time he had never said a word to anyone.

Just how this Devil business got started, nobody could remember exactly. Perhaps, seeing him on the street, someone commented that he certainly "looked like the Devil," which was interpreted in different ways until it finally became the consensus that if Walking Hand wasn't exactly the Devil, he was at least under the Devil's spell—doomed for the rest of his days to roam in silence, without apparent food or shelter.

In fact, he did present a frightening appearance.

He was gaunt and tall with sunken, amber eyes that stared straight ahead and did not blink. He had a long, slack jaw and a large, bulbous nose. He might have been bald, or white-haired, but no one knew because he always wore a dark slouch hat.

And he never, ever, smiled.

Now, whether by coincidence or design, the Widgeville rice crop was experiencing an awful setback that year; there wasn't enough water in the river to flood the fields and the tender green shoots began to wither and die under the summer sun. Since the rice crop supported the town, its loss could mean the end of everything and the Widgeville people were anxious and afraid. They began to go to church more often, both to pray and to discuss their problem, since the churches, black and white alike, served as meeting houses as well as places of worship.

It was during one of these meetings that someone remembered the river had begun to fall at almost precisely the same time Walking Hand appeared in their town.

A low and uneasy murmur ran through the Widgeville community during the next few days. If before they had believed that Walking Hand was in some way in league with the Devil, this feeling was all the stronger now, and the discussions began to center on him, and what role he might be playing in the drought.

"He is cursed by Satan and we are cursed by him!" cried Ebenezer Gooch, alderman in the black church.

"You can see the Devil in his eyes," declared Jonathan Boswell, deacon of the white church.

But they were afraid and confused about what to do next. Of course, the Devil was certainly not as powerful as God, but he was certainly not to be trifled with by mere mortal men. And if Walking Hand was indeed the Devil's disciple, then he most assuredly had some of the Devil's powers. If, for instance, they ordered him to leave town, or tried to overpower him, and failed, he might very well place an even meaner curse upon them.

Then they discovered that Walking Hand actually *was* the Devil, for who else would live in the swamp?

The swamp was a dark and forbidding place at the outskirts of town and the closest most of the Widgeville people ever came to it was when they went to dump their garbage at the trash heap at its edge. It was covered in a brown, tea-colored water, out of which rose fallen branches and rotting stumps, and choking green water plants. Beneath all of this, in the muck and quicksand, lived snakes, alligators, snapping turtles, and the Lord (and the Devil as well) only knew what else. Tall stark trees grew in the swamp, their branches gnarled like terrible fingers in the sky. Many of them were draped with huge clumps of Spanish moss, some so large and deformed that they resembled ghostlike, human forms.

But the eeriest thing of all was the opossums.

The opossums hung by their tails from the branches of the trees, upside down, and at night their eyes could be seen shining like myriad tiny lights, sometimes a dozen in a single tree, slowly consuming the foliage, hanging like bats and looking like rats.

The Widgeville people hated the opossums and feared them.

Since they were nocturnal creatures by inclination, whenever an opossum was seen in the daylight it was assumed that it was rabid or mad—and at the very least a bad omen.

One evening, three of the village boys followed Walking Hand on his sunset return, hiding behind him in the bushes and shrubs, and reported back in gasping breaths that he had disappeared into the darkest and most remote regions of the swamp. If there was doubt about his identity before, this news made it all the more certain because the swamp was unquestionably the Devil's lair.

That same night, a meeting was called in Widgeville. It was

held in the white church, which was a little larger than the black church, and it was packed to the last row with black and white people alike.

"The Devil is in our midst," said Percival Widge, for whose ancestors the town had been named. (Actually there were only six family names in the entire village: Widge, Boswell, and Slocum were the white names; Gooch, Cantwell, and James were the black names. Everybody else was kin to them.)

"What shall we do?" the others cried.

Ebenezer Gooch raised his finger into the air. "We must rid ourselves of him. It is the only way."

Much discussion followed, a vote was taken, and it was decided that the following Sunday the town would approach Walking Hand and politely ask him to leave. These were good, God-fearing people in Widgeville, and they would not seek to harm him, but if he refused, other steps would have to be taken, for God-fearing people could not tolerate the Devil in their midst.

During the next few days, Walking Hand was shunned like an awful disease. People who saw him coming down the street would immediately cross to the other side. Mothers would shuttle their children inside when he passed by, and lock the doors and pull the shades. By the time Sunday arrived, an electric sense of excitement and anticipation had filled the town.

Then there came an omen. One of the Widge boys saw it first.

High atop a telephone pole in the center of town a large opossum had perched.

In broad daylight, no less.

It was gripping the pole tightly with its clawed feet. Its skinny white tail was wrapped snakelike around the glass insulator and its pointed snout opened and closed rhythmically, baring a set of sharp, gleaming teeth.

The Widge boy shouted and ran for his house. Other people, on their way to church, began to gather around.

Mothers clutched their children to their skirts in case the opossum decided to lap upon them. The men wore strong, dark frowns and muttered among themselves as to what it might mean. Plainly it was an omen, but what kind of omen, no one could say.

"Why is it so ugly, Mama?" cried Martin Gooch.

"Can I have its skin?" said one of the Slocum boys.

"I get it, I saw him first!" exclaimed Tommy Widge.

"Be quiet, all of you!" Mrs. Gooch said.

Without warning, from behind the crowd, a stone sailed up toward the opossum. It missed by several feet and fell with a clatter on the roof of a house across the street. Eyes turned. One of the Slocum boys was preparing for another throw.

"Don't! Don't do that!" exclaimed Ebenezer Gooch. "We must all of us decide."

"Let's get rid of it," one of the men said. "We must stand firmly."

"It might have the rabies!" another cried. "It might jump down and bite someone."

A second rock flew up at the telephone pole, bouncing off a foot or so below the opossum's perch—and then another, and another, whistling by its head. The opossum did not jump or flinch,

but remained frozen in the same position, facing in the direction of the swamp. From that height it could probably see the trees and the dark slews and perhaps even smell the musky, damp odor.

Now there was no stopping them. Everyone, men, women, and children, were picking up rocks and throwing them. Some missed only by inches, others by yards, but none yet had actually struck the opossum. Then from the back of the mob a voice rang out like a clap of thunder.

"Stop!" the voice commanded.

The people spun around. There was Walking Hand, looking as fearsome and devilish as ever. A gasp ran through the crowd. He was standing ramrod straight, his black suitcase on the ground beside him. Some of the people began to back away, and others fingered the rocks in their hands menacingly.

Behind them, high on the pole, the opossum remained motionless except for an intense working of its beady eyes. The warm summer breeze ruffled its matted fur and it looked tired and sad, as though it knew it was never meant for telephone poles and street lamps and automobiles.

Walking Hand strode through the crowd. He seized a rung on the telephone pole and began to climb. When he neared the top, he reached out and the opossum neatly curled its tail around his wrist. Then, slowly, he came down, each step taken carefully, his arm held out level with the ground, the opossum hanging from it by its tail, upside down.

When he reached the ground the crowd was facing Walking Hand. Ebenezer Gooch, with Jonathan Boswell at his side, stepped forward and confronted him.

"Sir," said Ebenezer Gooch, "you have caused us a great deal of trouble. From the day you came to our town we have had no water for our crops. The rice is dying and we will all be poor. We do not know what you want, or why you are here, but we must ask you to leave."

Walking Hand did not reply. His eyes were fixed on Elenezer Gooch and Jonathan Boswell, and they glowed in his head like two hot coals.

"If you do not go," Jonathan Boswell said, "we will be forced to take steps. You roam our roads and streets, you frighten our children. . . ." He was about to continue when a cry from the back of the crowd interrupted him.

"Hey! Look at this!" said an excited voice. They turned and the crowd parted. Several of the children were kneeling around the battered black suitcase. They had opened it and spread the contents on the ground.

There was a neatly folded brownish shirt that had obviously been washed in swamp water. There was also a handkerchief and a pair of socks. There was a bag of mulberries and a sack of wild rice and a bottle of water. There was also an ancient and well-worn Bible. Pressed, dried leaves marked places in the Book of Psalms.

At the very bottom of the suitcase was a box of watercolors and brushes. The watercolors had been made from swamp berries and herbs and the brushes carefully woven of dried swamp grass. Beneath all of this was a stack of several dozen flat, thin layers of tree bark, each about a foot square.

"Hey! That's me!" exclaimed one of the Widge boys, "and you, too, sister, and mother and father!" He could hardly contain his excitement. He held the bark high for all to see. "It's our house, too." Sure enough, it was the Widge house, with the entire family posed in front behind a little white picket fence—even the Widge dog was in the painting. Everyone gathered in close and began examining the other pieces of

bark. On each one was a portrait of a Widgeville family in front of their own house.

"Oh, that's us!" someone said. "They're so real. They almost look like photographs."

And slowly, as each family looked at the paintings of itself, a hush fell over the crowd, for each saw in his or her own face a deep and radiant beauty that they had never recognized was there before. The fact was, that the Widgeville people had always believed they were ugly— the whites because they were short and squat and different from people in other towns around them, and the blacks merely because they were black. But here in the portraits they saw themselves for the first time as an outsider might see them, each face framed with a glow of hope and loveliness that bloomed from the paintings almost magically.

There was one piece of bark left in the suitcase. It was not a portrait of anyone, but a drawing of the town and the rice fields as they might have appeared from high in the sky. And there were strange markings on this drawing, in the rice fields, that did not in fact exist on the ground.

They turned back toward Walking Hand. The opossum had uncurled its tail from his arm and crawled along it to his shoulder where it sat comfortably, gently nuzzling his ear.

"But what does this mean?" Jonathan Boswell asked haltingly. "Are you trying to mark us . . . for something?" He searched for words. "First you ruin our crops . . . and then the omen . . . and now *these*" He gestured at the paintings and the drawing of the fields. "Are you making records of us?"

Walking Hand spoke for the second time.

"I am a painter," he said, "and I came here because I admired your lovely town. I have ruined no crops, but I believe I have a solution that can save them. Every day I have walked from the swamp to the river and taken measurements. I believe that if your men will dig a canal across the rice fields you will be able to irrigate your land and no longer have to depend on the uncertainties of the tides. I intended to leave all of this with you. The drawing shows how the canal might be dug."

The people of Widgeville began to shift uneasily and lower their heads in shame, and there was a long silence, except for the rustling of the warm summer wind in the trees. Then a tiny voice came from the front of the crowd. It was Martin Gooch.

"But . . . we thought you were the Devil," he said hesitantly, and with a touch of disappointment, "because you live in the swamp. And then the omen . . . why did it come? Why did he climb up there?"

Walking Hand spoke for the third and final time.

"I am only a painter and a lover of God's creatures. And this," he said, gently petting the opossum's fur, "is not an omen. He came because he wanted to see the town, or he might have been hungry.

"Why he climbed, I do not know. Perhaps he wanted to get a little closer to the Lord."

With that, Walking Hand strode down the main street toward the swamp, leaving the suitcase and the paintings behind. They all watched until he had vanished down the path, and the only sound was the soft sighing of the wind in the trees.

Later, near sunset, the people of Widgeville went down to the edge of the swamp and sat on the bank, waiting for dark. Night fell like a hundred midnights, and with it the opossums came out to feed in the trees. In the blackness, their eyes glowed and twinkled like fireflies.

Then, at precisely the stroke of twelve, a large, orange pair of eyes appeared high in the tallest tree in the swamp. These eyes did not blink; instead they stared out ferociously at the Widgeville people, but with a certain inquisitiveness—the better to watch them, perhaps, or just to get a little closer to the Lord—no one ever knew, and no one ever would.

THE CAT THAT THOUGHT HE WAS A STORY

BY

Donald Hall

Once there was a cat that thought he was a story. He wandered all over the place, smiling to himself and thinking what a good story he probably was. He didn't *know*, because nobody had ever told him.

The cat came up to a garbage can. "Hello," he said. "Would you tell me, please?"

The garbage can was irritable because of some flies. "Tell you what? Tell you what?" he said. "Can't just tell you anything."

"Just *tell* me," said the cat. "I'm a story."

"Go away," said the garbage can. "You're nothing but a plain old cat."

The cat was angry at this response. He could have jumped on the garbage can and knocked it over, but he walked away with his tail up.

Pretty soon the cat saw a hedge of boxwood that was at least a hundred years old. The hedge looked dreamy, as if it might like a story. "Hedge, will you please tell me?" said the cat.

"How can I tell you, my dear, when I don't have my glasses on?" said the old hedge.

"I'll get you your glasses," said the cat.

"I don't have any glasses," said the hedge.

"Oh," said the cat, and wandered away.

He was getting discouraged. Then out in the garage he saw the automobile, and it looked more friendly than most things. "Will you tell me?" he said.

"Sure," said the automobile, "if you'll play me."

"What?" said the cat.

"I'm a violin," said the automobile.

The cat, who didn't like nuts, got out of there in a hurry.

He guessed it was useless to ask to be told. He decided to give up.

He went across the street into the library where there was a children's section with empty spaces. Because he was a story, he curled up on one of the shelves and looked out at the books across from him. The librarian was a kind lady and didn't say shoo. In fact, she pretended he wasn't there at all, which is just what the cat wanted. He sat there a long time.

Then a little boy came in and took him home and read him.

THE KID MEETS BIG MAC

BY

Oakley Hall

All the while Big Mac and that gang of his were growing and spreading out and doing their evil, which, when you come right down to it, was the destruction of everything decent in the world—all the while a pure devil like Big Mac was taking over more and more until there seemed no end to it, not far away, and getting his growth, was the Kid.

Except that it does seem that the Big Macs are always a step ahead of the Kid, who is forever having to hurry to catch up, and maybe just never quite does, which is why things are the way they usually are.

There are different versions of the Kid's birth and kin. It is said that he was treated so cruel by a stepfather that he ran away to join the gypsies, or else was sold to them for fifteen dollars. That was where he learned the crafts and tricks that served him well later on. These gypsies traveled up and down putting on shows in mining camps, knife-throwing exhibitions and roping, which the Kid was especially good at, fortune-telling, monte games, bull-and-bear fights, and such. If the Kid had a special friend among the band, it was a big grizzly named the Duke of Cumberland. The Kid tended to him, and it was said he could all but talk with that big bear, who later on sometimes would turn up to the Kid's advantage when the Kid got into stiff trouble.

Those were times when miners were hard set against foreigners. Fellows with the wrong color skin or slant of eye were run out of the district, some of them tarred-and-feathered, or worse. In one place a mob came against the Kid's band of gypsies, with ropes, so it looked like bad trouble. But they reckoned without the Kid. He sneaked through the crowd, told the Duke what was wanted, and let him out of his cage. Well, wasn't that a fine show, the grizzly chasing miners every which way, with a yelling and puking to beat anything. The reason they were puking was because they had got into a barrel of gypsy popskull liquor that was still on the ferment, and the bear chasing them put the stuff to churning in their bellies. They say that camp still stinks of puke to this day. Anyway, the Kid was just a lad when he first showed what he was made of, and got his friends out of trouble as slick as you please.

There is another story of the Kid's beginnings that has him found floating down the river in a tiny coffin, with a ring hung on a chain around his neck. A mine owner's wife adopted him. She already had a daughter, a beautiful fair-haired child named Flora, and the Kid and Flora were brought up as brother and sister. But the mine owner lost his holdings, he and his wife died of the influenza, and the Kid and Flora were orphaned. They were taken in by a man named Jasperson, who ran an orphan school in that place, and was a kind man, though strict. By that time the Kid had given his ring to Flora to wear. It was supposed to have "properties," and it had more than that, as will be seen.

There was also a Blackfoot boy at the school. One day, the river being in flood, he slipped in and was just managing to hold onto a branch to keep from being swept down and drowned in the falls, when the Kid happened by, though on the other side of the river. It did look like Jimmy Blackfoot was a goner, but the Kid was equal to the occasion, as always.

He was carrying a hank of rope with which he'd been practicing roping tricks, and, quick as lightning, he slung a loop over a high branch of a cottonwood there and started running around and around the tree, winding the rope up on it. When it was all wound up he began running the other way with the rope unwinding and swinging him off the ground and spiraling farther and farther out over the river until he was flying over the far bank, where he let go. He staggered around half-drunk for a bit, from all that circling, but just in time he got hold of Jimmy Blackfoot's collar and pulled him to safety. You can believe that lad was grateful, and he was the Kid's faithful sidekick from then on.

It was said that the Kid would fall into his terrible rages even as a little chap. It was like he would be burning up with a fever. They would have to pop him into a barrel of stream water they kept under a tree there, along with two other barrels. The water in the first barrel would come to a boil and spurt up. Then they'd plunge him into the second barrel, where the water wouldn't boil, though it would turn hot enough to make a man yell if he put his hand in it. The third barrel would only turn warm enough for bath water.

The Kid would run crazy like that especially if Flora was being fussed. Once at the school an older boy was scaring her threatening to take away the ring the Kid had given her, and the Kid went after him like that. The bully, who was twice the kid's size, lit out of there for his life. He was halfway across the river before he realized he was running on water, and he was not one the Kid bothered to save from the falls downstream.

When the Kid was older, he was chief boy at Mr. Jasperson's school, and a great help to the schoolmaster. Once when the school had gone for an outing on the train, he saved the other children of the school from Big Mac's clutches. It was his first meeting with Big Mac.

Big Mac's crew had jammed a log across the rails so the coaches were cut off from the locomotive and dumped over on their sides. When those passengers and the orphans from the school climbed out through the windows, they found they were captives of Big Mac's evil band.

Big Mac was sitting on his big black looking over the scene, with half a dozen riders ranged around him. He slumped in the saddle with the corners of his mouth slashed down and his eyes sleepy like he'd seen everything there was to see and here it all came past again. His chins ran down to his neck, his belly hung out before him, and his black hat was turned down all around to keep the sun off his face that was scabby with sun sores and bristling with beard.

People were so affrighted of Big Mac in those days it was like a sickness on them, and even strong men armed could do no more than herd like a bunch of sheep, women crying out, insulted and worse by those desperados, and Mr. Jasperson and the Kid trying to keep the orphans from the school together and their spirits up. Jimmy Blackfoot was especially downcast because he had lost in the wrecked coach the sacred bow and quiver of vermilion-painted arrows his father, who was a chief, had given him. Flora was frightened that those road agents would see the Kid's ring and take it from her.

Everyone was set to marching north, very smart, those that couldn't keep up helped along with a slash from a blacksnake whip, and the men and older boys, like the Kid, with their hands tied behind them. That march was pure hell, and that night, which they spent herded into an old corral, the same. But in the dark the Kid managed to sit close to Flora, and whispered to her where to press on the ring she wore so that a tiny blade, curved like a trigger, slid out. With this she sawed at the rope that tied his hands until he was free. He slipped out of that place quiet as a shadow and was gone. There were a few from the school that thought he had run out on them.

Come daybreak, they were started on again, and that day there was terrible suffering, everybody whipped along by those blacksnakes, and some of the older folks left behind to perish of thirst in that desert country. It was clear that Mr. Jasperson's orphans would begin dropping out soon, but just when everything looked hopeless there was a shout, and off to the east and coming hard was a cloud of dust, so big, and rising so tall, that it must be cavalry, or a posse at least. Everybody began pointing and rejoicing, though not too loud for fear of those riders of King Mac's. The dust came closer, and the riders began conferring one with another, the whole bunch finally gathering around Big Mac, big as any three ordinary men; all at once they all lit out together.

The big dust cloud came on, and the smaller cloud of Big Mac's crew faded off. Then weren't those passengers from the train, who had been captives bound for who knows what abominations, and now were free, running and cheering to meet their saviors? But it wasn't cavalry or a posse, it was a herd of longhorns with branches tied on them to scrape up a great dust. And all over the place, waving his hat to hurry along his blown cow pony and chouse those steers into a staggering run, was no one else but the Kid!

It seemed that every woman in that bunch, whether she was a schoolgirl or a grandmother, had to kiss that boy with his shock of fair hair, and those eyes so blue it was said you could chin yourself on a glance from them; though it was Flora that kissed him the longest. And every man had to shake his hand, though it was Jimmy Blackfoot who shook it hardest, and slapped him on the shoulder time and again. But the Kid told them there was no time to be lost. They must hurry back to the railroad to the relief train in case it came to Big Mac to circle around on them. So they turned back in as great a hurry as they had come this far, the Kid chasing back and forth on one side of the column and the other, hustling them along waving his hat.

And they were not finished yet with Big Mac, treacherous as a rattlesnake that will slip roundabout for another strike. Just in sight of the backing engine and crane that had been sent out to right the cars and repair the track, when that raggedy, cheering bunch of men, women, and children broke into a run, all of them afoot except one sickly girl up on that scarecrow pony of the Kid's, women scampering with their skirts hoisted, and Flora and Jimmy Blackfoot holding the hands of the youngest children—just then down off a hill came a pack of riders yelling and quirting and kicking up a storm of red dust, and it was a near thing whether Big Mac's men would cut those poor refugees off from the relief train or not.

But there'd been a couple of sheriff's deputies sent out along, and though they hadn't much enthusiasm for getting into a shooting scrape with Big Mac, they did let off a shot or two, upon which that unholy dozen turned tail, though once behind a ridge they dismounted and began sniping. But meanwhile, everyone came to safety on the relief train, where there were rifles to pass out. Jimmy Blackfoot scouted through the upset car until he found his bow and arrows, while bullets smacked through windows and clanged on steel wheels with a sound like bells.

All the women were kissing and blessing the Kid for their salvation, and the men waiting in line to shake his hand some more, who was not one bit puffed up from all the praise. Just then there was a shout, and out in front of the wrecked coaches was Big Mac on his seventeen-hands gelding, black-hatted and wearing those fringed buckskins that made him look rippling with motion, like pine needles in a good breeze.

He bellowed out that he would like to see the fellow who had tricked him.

There was a good deal of palaver about this. Jasperson and one of the deputies warned the Kid, who was inclined to show himself, that there was no trusting Big Mac and never had been.

But Big Mac yelled that he was unarmed; they had his bond he had no iron about him. So the Kid shook off Flora's restraining hand, mounted up on the scarecrow horse, and shambled out to meet Big Mac. You could almost hear every last breath sucked in and held at the same instant, while the two horses faced nose to nose, the big black and the cow pony that could hardly hold his muzzle up from weariness. And mounted on them that barrel of a scab-faced, whiskered horror, and the handsome lad who couldn't have weighed a hundred pounds dripping wet.

Big Mac said, "You mean you are the one that contrived it? Or is this another trick on me, which is one too many?"

The Kid said he had contrived it.

Big Mac asked him his name, and the kid told him. Big Mac nodded like he was not apt to forget it, and said, "Well, you have beat me this time."

"Oh, I was pretty lucky," the Kid said, respectful enough.

"I wouldn't lean on my luck again," Big Mac told him.

To which the Kid replied that he had always been able to trust to his luck, but that probably Big Mac wouldn't see him again until he had got his growth. Big Mac could rest easy until that time.

Big Mac made a noise like the air going out of a balloon. He raised up in his stirrups so that he towered over the Kid, and all of a sudden there was a blacksnake whip in his hand that he had jerked out of his coatsleeve. The whip snapped around so fast no one could make out what had happened. The Kid didn't flinch and it seemed that by some miracle Big Mac had missed him. He sat his pony very straight watching Big Mac spurring away in a flurry of sniping shots from his men hidden behind the ridge, and Jimmy Blackfoot alongside one of the upset cars with a vermilion-shanked arrow nocked to the head, swearing under his breath in Indian for not knowing whether to loose it or not.

When the Kid came back behind the relief train, there were some that noticed his face was white as a fish's belly. Jasperson and one of the deputies got him into the cab of the locomotive and away from the people clamoring over him.

He sat down on a wood crate beside the firebox with a grunt. They helped him off with his shirt. There was a welt around his chest the size of two fingers, like a red snake coiled there, that fine young fellow marked by Big Mac's treachery. The deputy stroked some salve on while Jasperson waved his hands and fluttered like a mother hen. The boy never let out a whimper, staring straight ahead of him into the future with that blue gaze of his, and smiling just a little.

"Well, I guess that is one a piece," he said.

Just then, there was a scream and shouting. Three of those riders of Big Mac's had run in behind the cars, swept up Flora, and carried her off.

The Kid leaped off the wood crate with his fists clenched, his bare chest red as the welt around it, and his face bright scarlet. You could almost see the steam coming off him. He snatched up a rifle and was aboard the blown pony in an instant. Yelling like a crazy man, he spurred after those desperados who had borne the girl away.

He rushed over the ridge and down into a clearing behind it, where he reined up so hard the pony was pulled to his haunches, for he had ridden into an ambush. Big Mac sat his big black with his revolver drawn, and with him were the three others, Flora white-faced up before one of them on his saddle; all of them with guns trained on the Kid. Big Mac's buckskin fringes were shivering as he chuckled. It was said he avoided gunshot keeping himself always blurred with those fringes moving like that, so no one could take aim for his vitals because of the blurry motion.

"Drop your piece, if you please, my friend," Big Mac said, and the Kid had no choice but to throw down his rifle.

Just then the rider furthest over on the left side disappeared off his horse, which nobody noticed because their concern was elsewhere.

"I believe I can still show you a trick or two," Big Mac said, chuckling some more. "Maybe even after you have got your growth."

The Kid did not respond to this, and something that might have been a bird settled on the neck of the next-to-the-end rider, who went down with a horrid gurgle.

Next there was a twang, and an arrow with a vermilion shaft stood out on the neck of the rider who had Flora up before him, both his hands hanging onto it while he made a noise like a turkey gobbling. Lightning quick, Big Mac spurred forward to clap the muzzle of his revolver to the Kid's temple, his pig eyes switching this way and that as he shouted, "Call off your dogs or you are a dead man!"

Meanwhile, Flora's captor slowly toppled and fell, bearing her down with him, where she sprawled beside the dead road agent not quite as ladylike as she usually took care to be seen. And just then, with a growl, swarming out of the brush came a bear bounding like a great, hairy ball, to rise to his hind legs and make one swipe, with a pawful of claws like knives, at the haunch of the black gelding. The horse screamed like a woman, rearing, and then bore Big Mac from that place at a dead run, while the grizzly disappeared into the brush again and the Kid lit out after Big Mac, jerking his lariat loose from his saddle horn and swinging a loop.

The loop settled over Big Mac, and the Kid pulled the pony to its haunches to take the shock. Big Mac came out of the saddle with his fringes all a flutter to hang in the air for what seemed like half a minute before he smacked down with a jar to shake his grandmother.

As Big Mac staggered to his feet, panting and groaning and cursing, the Kid was running around him, winding the lariat around him and cinching it tight. Then he mounted again, and with Flora up on her captor's horse, and Big Mac at the rope end lurching rubber-legged behind, and Jimmy Blackfoot with his bow coming up to trot alongside, led that little procession back to the relief train, to turn Big Mac over to the deputies there, who were about as pleased to take him into custody as if he'd been a timber wolf on a leash.

And that was the run-in the Kid had with Big Mac before he got his growth.

TWO SHOES FOR ONE FOOT

BY

John Hawkes

ILLUSTRATED BY
SOPHIE HAWKES

In a small mill city in Bavaria, there lived some children who were afraid of a one-legged man called the Kommandant. He lived within walking distance of the shops and houses, so near that with the help of his crutch he often swung in the direction of their cobbled streets and little blackened windows and smoking chimneys. The Kommandant frightened the boys, of course, because he had only one leg, yet it was just for this, for their dreams of fleeing the single foot, that they talked of surprising him with their bravery and cleverness and skill. But they had no Teutonic helmets, no wooden swords; to the boys it would be nothing less than an exchange of heart for heart.

One evening while it was still light and before the frost became hard, they approached the Kommandant, stared at the straight trouser leg and at the folded trouser leg, and made him an offer. He heard them silently, then followed them, and they were careful not to walk too quickly. They took him by back streets and through an unproductive orchard to the house of the oldest boy, Heinrich; they led him directly inside, where he stood wearing his Kommandant's cap and leaning on his crutch. He looked closely at what the boys were offering for sale, at what they dared offer to no one but himself. The smallest of the boys darted forward suddenly and pulled the coverlet from the bed. The Kommandant stepped near the bed, which filled nearly the whole of the room.

Through the narrow single window the sunset was cold and red, a brutal light on the still figure now stretched before them.

"He is ours," whispered Heinrich, and the boys' eyes were the eyes one seeks at dusk under the roots of a tree, five pairs or more, in winter, staring up to the surface of the earth with that animal curiosity which shines from the pitiless lair. In this room only the bed, the Kommandant, the boys: and the boys stood there like brothers, each as familiar as Heinrich himself with the chipped walls, the hole in the floor, the place where he hung his jacket and put his shoes, all of them ragged and expectant in the intimacy of boys together.

"Come look, mein Herr," Heinrich whispered, and his companions also pressed closer. They tried not to touch the Kommandant's crutch. The boys waited for the bargain to be sealed as if they felt that no one else would come here or become aware in any way, ever, of what was happening in Heinrich's room while the sun set.

Upon the bed lay a man, heavy and fully dressed in a shirt and black suit of a good cut but tight across the chest, a man who appeared to be neither asleep nor dead, though the cloth and the hair were wet with the rains so frequent in this country.

"He is complete. He is not damaged, not at all damaged, Herr Kommandant," whispered Heinrich, and the eyes of his companions were the eyes of moles. "He is all here," Heinrich told him again in his soft, decisive voice.

"But look," said the Kommandant. "Look at his feet, boys. Where are the shoes?"

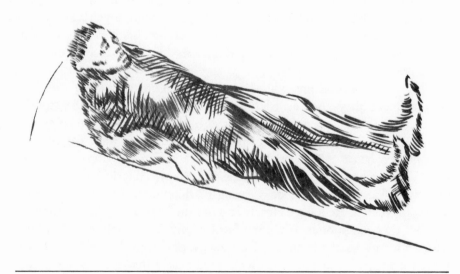

Heinrich smiled and went to the wooden rack where he kept his own worn pairs of boots. "On the rack, mein Herr. They were soiled, you can see for yourself; they were covered with blood. So I removed them. But they belong with him and they shall go with him." Without hesitating, he returned to the bed and placed the great swollen shoes on the coverlet next to the feet, exactly as if he had tipped the scales from a crafty, childish generosity.

"Good," said the Kommandant.

The sun fell sharply through the window and lit the buttons on the dead man's coat. The eyeglasses began to shine, but for a moment only. Following some curious law of growth, some urge dictated by its sap and fibers, the lowest branch of one of the few trees in the orchard, a tree planted too near the house, had reached to the window and pressed its crowded shape to the panes. Now, like an arm twisted in some invisible grip, it moved as much as it could and scratched painfully on the glass. The sun came into the room through the window and between the gray twigs of the branch that struggled and obscured the view. Beyond a few dead leaves and the dusty glass could be seen a layer of smoke from the mills, and further yet, under the red streaks of the sun, the gathering of the night itself.

"Good," murmured the Kommandant again, and frowned, considering the man on the bed. The eyeglasses were cracked and twisted, but they had been readjusted on the bridge of the nose. Though not expertly, the hair had been brushed into place.

"And Herr Kommandant," said the oldest boy, "he has papers also." Heinrich unfastened the top button, drew away the coat, and pointed. The papers protruded thick and white from the inside pocket until quickly Heinrich hid them away again and smoothed the lapel.

"He is cold," Heinrich said, peering up, smiling, indicating the heavy breast of the man. He continued to watch the Kommandant for some change in his face.

"Herr Herzenbrecher!" the smallest boy shouted. "He is Herr Herzenbrecher!"

The sun passed away, the orchard became dark, the boys shifted and one of them held the smallest idly by his hand. They could hear the sounds of all the things that woke Heinrich in the night. Now the buttons no longer flashed on the coat, the lifelike expression was shadowed on the dead man's face, his black waistcoat was tight and fastened awry over the belly still filled with air. Dusk in this city, despite the wireless and industry, was the time when the inhabitants feared to see the dead taking to the open roofs.

"But your bed? You bring him to your own bed?" asked the Kommandant.

"Oh," said Heinrich quickly, "it's all right. I have slept on the floor. But of course I covered him each night with the blanket until the sun rose." Then, by a slight gesture, a movement of his finger, calling attention to the watch chain and to the belt buckle which must have been loosened after the last meal, all the while staring at the Kommandant, Heinrich pursed his lips and asked, "Well? What do you think of him?"

A shrill whistle, like the furious sound that regulates life in prisons, came from far-off in the direction of the mills, and the iron machines began scraping in that distant end of the city. Heinrich waited. Suddenly the smallest boy snatched up the bloodied shoes

and ran with them into the orchard. "Look," he cried, "I have stolen his shoes! Look here, I have stolen Herr Herzenbrecher's shoes!" He ran under the trees, to and fro, laughing, fat, and his childish and impetuous and uneven flat steps came boldly back from the earth out there. He wet his stockings in the leaves. He hugged the shoes. "Two shoes for one foot," he shouted under the withered apple tree, "two shoes for one foot!" He was wrapped in the mist and bare-armed, hurrying between the hanging trees, squatting and hiding himself at every twisted trunk. "Two shoes. . . ." he tried to shout again, but the boys caught him and stopped his shrill humor with their white hands. He began to sniffle as they led him inside the house.

"If you are not good," said Heinrich, he will blow his breath on you. Now mein Herr," he said, forgetting to smile, forgetting to change the sternness in his voice, "what of our business?"

The Kommandant nodded and leaned closer, as if to sit on the edge of the bed. It was so dark now that the boys' heads were little skulls in the shadows, featureless except for the large dark charcoal smears of eyes and mouths. The body was larger in the darkness.

"We have washed him. Have we not done well, mein Herr?"

The Kommandant could hear the beating of the children's hearts. He tried to see what he could of the room, he smelled the coverlet and the leaves and the wet paper wadded under the coat. "Yes," he answered at last.

The smallest boy began to cry and struggled to run, knocking against his comrades, weeping and laughing at the same time. "Herr Herzenbrecher is bad, Heinrich. He is going to blow his breath on Heinrich."

"Hush," said Heinrich. "But would you care to look in his pockets, Herr Kommandant? Perhaps if you glance in one pocket anyway. . . ."

It started to rain. The rain filled the orchard outside with droplets that did not stream slantwise down the window but clouded it, dulling it with the harmless but telltale puffing of a dead storm; the kind of rain which, if it is a dark night and the sun has been red, drenches the coat of fur noiselessly and in a moment, before the dog can take cover. Such rain did not help the apple trees to grow.

Heinrich lit a candle and tilted it so that not a line in Herr Herzenbrecher's face could be missed. He noticed a clot of dirt on the trousers and brushed it off. For a long moment he admired Herr Herzenbrecher. Then he smiled and all the boys around the bed smiled also. "No one has ever found anything like Herr Herzenbrecher," he whispered. "Herr Herzenbrecher looks like my father. He looks like Hansel's father also. He is not a plaything, Kommandant, you can be sure."

The room was small for the Kommandant, and in it his crutch cast a dark shadow. The room so belonged to a child that it was hardly part of the house, but dusty, slowly sinking off its plumb, empty except for the boy living within and except for his friends who appeared out of the orchard, knowing so well the weather-beaten paths to it. The room itself, the wind, the boys. And now Herr Herzenbrecher. And now the Kommandant. The boys held each other by the hands, the limb of the apple tree moved against the window.

"But what of marks on his person?" asked the Kommandant. "Nothing of violence?"

"Oh yes," answered Heinrich shortly, "you will see." Heinrich put his fingers lightly on the dead man's shoulder. "However, they are not noticeable, mein Herr, and we covered them. Perhaps you will not even find them."

"Heinrich," asked the Kommandant slowly, "do you know how long the man has been dead?"

Heinrich stared and moved as if to blow out the candle; he hugged the smallest boy and pulled on his stockings; his face was whiter than ever.

"For as long as my Papa has been dead," answered Heinrich at last.

"But you have not thought of telling anyone about this man?"

"No, mein Herr."

"Nor of summoning the police?"

"No, mein Herr."

"But now you want to give him up," said the Kommandant.

"Mein Herr. We are only *offering* you Herr Herzenbrecher. He is ours. We found him. He has a gold watch. He is with us, and now we are all men."

"But this man is dead!"

"Comrades," whispered Heinrich, "assure the Kommandant that we know that Herr Herzenbrecher is dead."

"Mama, Mama, Mama," cried the smallest boy until Heinrich picked him up and, still holding him, and perspiring, spoke again to the one-legged man: "Are you thinking of his murderer, mein Herr?"

At that moment the window smashed and the branch, at last

finding entrance through the broken glass, intruded, nodding and twisting as if it had finally penetrated a wall of stone. . .

"Tell me," said the Kommandant, speaking as plainly and softly as he could, "do you know how Herr Herzenbrecher died?"

Heinrich's face shone like gold and became thin and bright with pleasure. But he remained silent.

"Well, do you know?" repeated the Kommandant.

"Yes. Of course. Mein Herr," Heinrich whispered then, staring at the window, "he died fighting, throwing himself upon a great animal armed with scales. Bravely."

The Kommandant frowned and leaned on his crutch. He stopped himself from speaking.

The whistle blew again beyond the orchard, beyond the electric cables tapping in the mist. There came a slight odor of apples through the rain. In the forward part of the house a bell tinkled sharply. Immediately Heinrich stepped away from the corpse, laughed awkwardly, and bowed before the officer.

"Pardon, mein Herr Kommandant. My grandmother is calling me to our supper. I must be with her. We eat together. But will you take him, your Honor?"

The Kommandant waited and then nodded, and then from his heavy leather purse he gave each boy a few marks and a few pfennigs.

Then Heinrich signaled. They scurried about and produced a long umbrella, a bundle containing a flattened hat and handwoven shawl, and a piece of cord with which they securely tied the shoes. All this they thrust upon the Kommandant.

The smallest boy pulled Heinrich to the door and shouted after the Kommandant, who was laboriously pushing his wooden cart into the darkness and rain: "Live well, Herr Herzenbrecher, live well!"

THE VALLEY DARK & DREAR (and How It Got Better)

BY
Bobbie Louise Hawkins

There was once a valley that got fed up with its situation and set out to improve its prospects. This is the story of what went wrong and how it got better.

The valley had begun as a regular, cheerful sort of a place with birds and sunshine and a rippling brook and deer grazing in dappled glades. It had been ideal. It had been the perfect place for a picnic.

Then a transient witch with an itchy foot who loved to travel made her home there for a while.

She changed everything.

She couldn't bear sunshine and cheer horrified her so she pulled out her magic paraphernalia and made the valley comfortable. Comfort for this particular witch meant gray skies with no birds and no butterflies, stagnant ponds with no fish and no small animals coming to drink, thorny bushes with no flowers, and poisonous vapors. And that was only the beginning. All the beings that hate sunshine, lizards and poisonous snakes and the slimiest toady things came to live there.

Now some people might feel through a misplaced sense of justice and a mistaken notion of democracy that those things have a right to live someplace and that the valley was perfect for them. But that line of thought doesn't include how the valley felt about it.

The valley hated the whole business.

One moment it was basking in sunlight and listening to birds sing and the next moment, Pow! black skies and slimy inhabitants.

The valley felt as if it had come down simultaneously with a rotten case of the flu, a powerful case of measles, and a general depression. Its life was ruined, and through no fault of its own.

Along about then the witch, as was her wont, moved on to ruin some other place by living there. Of course it didn't occur to her that that was what she was doing. She thought she was leaving a trail of improvement behind her.

And now we come to the part that makes this story unique. The valley could have accepted the ruin that had been foisted onto it. It was a valley with a will of its own. After sitting around on its hills for a considerable length of time it decided that the only way it was going to be helped was if it helped itself. So it shook itself in one long ripple like an earthquake and it went for a walk.

You can imagine the shock it was for anybody to see the valley coming toward them.

It was a big uneven hole extending farther than the eye could see with hills like moving elephants on the sides.

There was a lot of action going on. Everything had to keep up. The poisonous vapors had to move along without letting the inrushing wholesome air dissipate them. The thorn bushes just dug in and held on tight, but the stagnant ponds really had to concentrate to hold their shapes firm and not dislodge the slime and coagulated ooze on their surfaces. Snakes and toads and lizards and frogs rushed along gasping.

The witch had laid a spell strong enough to withstand a good shake so nothing got disturbed enough to make a difference.

It was enough to break the poor valley's heart the way people and animals and flowers ran when they saw it coming. Well, the people and the animals ran. The flowers just disappeared like winter had come and reappeared when the valley had passed like it was spring.

But that was no casual valley. It swallowed disappointment after disappointment and just kept going.

And now we come to the next problem.

The valley just wasn't made right for a travel-
ing life and it started going a little lame here and a little devitalized
there. Some of the trees just laid down and died and had to be carried
with their branches dragging and crashing and gouging holes in the
ground.

The valley got weaker and the worse for wear.
It was in a state of daily hardship. When it finally stopped to rest, it was
on its last legs.

And now we come to the good part.

By luck or whatever you want to call it the
valley stopped not more than fifty feet away from a small cottage belonging to the only person who could help it.

In the cottage lived an old jolly grandmother
who was also a witch but not so as anybody'd ever notice it.

When the valley arrived the old woman was
sitting in her rocking chair worrying about her granddaughter. The
golden-haired child she loved more than anything in the world had
stopped laughing. It had happened when the same witch that ruined the
valley had passed overhead dripping spell-dust.

The grandmother had tried and tried to make
the child laugh without suspecting that the child had a spell on her. She
thought the child was unhappy and needed amusing and she had gone
through all kinds of antics with that thought in mind.

And now we come to another complication.

The grandmother's attempts to make the child
laugh had been noticed by some of her neighbors, the wrong sort of
neighbors, the sort who are prone to read the worst into everything and
who poke their noses everywhere.

Only the week before the valley arrived those
neighbors had gone to the King and Queen of the country to complain
that there was an old woman living near them who had lost her wits.

"She was standing on her head juggling apples
with her feet," one neighbor said indignantly. "Her skirts were flapping
every which way and she was wearing red stockings!"

The Queen gasped at the idea.

"She was riding her goat bareback, playing a
jig on a fiddle while she balanced a plate on her nose!"

They all fought to outdo each other. It be-
came an important thing to be the one who most shocked the King and
the Queen.

"I saw her hanging by her knees from the apple tree and when she saw me looking she stuck out her tongue and crossed her eyes!"

When they had all told their stories the first neighbor sighed and said "Oh, that poor child!" And pretended to wipe a tear from her eye.

"What's that about a child?" the King asked.

"Her granddaughter lives with her, your majesty. A beautiful child, poor creature. She never smiles."

"No wonder," said another, "with that crazy old woman being such a rampant fool at any hour of the day or night."

The Queen and the King, who might otherwise have left well enough alone, agreed that as a child was involved they must check the stories out.

So it was that the neighbors were satisfied in their self-righteousness and returned home to await the exciting day when soldiers in uniforms would come and take the old woman and the child away.

You can imagine their surprise when they found a large piece of familiar terrain had vanished and a yawning, gloomy valley in its place.

"How do you think she managed that?" they asked each other.

It was their practice, as it often is with stupid people, to lump all the things they didn't understand and think it was all the same thing. They didn't understand the old woman and they didn't understand the valley, so the two must be related.

Another thing they didn't at all understand or think about was that an old woman who was able to stand on her head and juggle apples with her feet and ride a goat bareback and play a fiddle, while she balanced a plate on her nose, not to mention swinging by her knees from an apple tree, might just be unusual in other ways as well.

And that *was* the case. Far from being silly and addled, the old woman was sharp as a needle and farsighted enough to anticipate just such a fool's trick as the neighbors had brought about.

She had seen them leave in a bunch, looking as false-hearted and double-dealing as she knew them to be. And she looked at them out of her window when they returned and saw that they were looking smug and triumphant.

It seemed possible that her attempts to help her granddaughter might be given a setback by the neighbors.

She wasn't particularly worried. She had abilities enough to deal with all the neighbors and the King and all his soldiers. She could have turned the whole kingdom upside down and given it a good shake if she felt there was a reason to. But she resented having to deal with her neighbor's meanness when it interrupted her hopes for her grandchild. So she decided that when the soldiers arrived, she would give her neighbors a lesson.

She had made that decision before she saw the valley.

She looked at it carefully. She was certain that it hadn't been there the last time she looked.

She walked to its edge and looked in as you might look into a cup. She put her hand out in front of her and felt the place in the air where the spell began. It felt like touching cold glass.

When she touched it the valley stirred a little and stretched just the tiniest bit, as a sleeping cat might stretch when you scratch its back.

That touch really felt good.

It was the first touch of hope the valley had had in a long time. A little shiver of pleasure rippled through it.

"I've got enough time to settle this little problem before the other one comes up," the old woman said out loud.

She went into her cottage and began to make a splendid counterspell out of good flour and sliced apples with cinnamon and brown sugar. Anyone who didn't know the difference would have thought that counterspell looked like a first-rate apple pie.

While the grandmother was involved the little granddaughter wandered into the yard and into the valley as if it was her rightful place to be. She might have been a bigger kind of toad for all the effect the spell had on her. She trailed along looking into the stagnant ponds to see her own sad little face reflected back.

The old grandmother came out of her cottage carrying the sweetest smelling, tastiest counterspell ever devised in her two hands ahead of her.

When it touched the barrier of the spell, there was a sound as if the biggest piece of glass in the world had just been smashed.

In a rush, fresh air blew down the length of the valley carrying a smell of cinnamon. The dark skies changed to pure flowing sunshine.

And the old woman heard the sound of her heart's desire, a young girl's laughter, clear as a bell.

She rushed into the valley and found her granddaughter standing by a rippling brook. The child was pointing at a tangled mass of very disgruntled toads and snakes, who were all preparing to quit this unattractive place as fast as they were able.

While she looked at the slimy, discontented beings and at her delighted granddaughter the grandmother heard a sound from beyond a nearby hill of horses riding toward her. She was reminded of her next simple chore.

In the next moment the King's soldiers came in sight over the hill.

"Begging your pardon, ma'am." A polite and handsome officer reined his horse in alongside the gentle old woman and her beautiful grandchild.

"We're looking for a madwoman who lives hereabouts. She is said to ride goats and hang from trees."

"Keep on as you are going, sir," the old woman answered politely. "You will find what you seek."

And, in fact, the soldiers found much more.

No sooner had they found one woman riding a goat and screaming at the top of her lungs, than they came on a man and his wife hanging from a tree by their knees. Only a few feet away, another woman sawed at a fiddle despite being unmusical for a couple who were jiggling and making faces at anyone who looked in their direction.

The soldiers were so confused that they ended by herding up the whole lot and taking them all back to the King.

Perhaps the experience awakened some sparks of understanding in the neighbors' minds, or perhaps they were frightened enough to be more cautious. Whichever, whatever, the fact is they behaved in an improved fashion thereafter.

And the wise old grandmother and her laughing grandchild spent many long and happy hours in the charming sunlit valley that had come to rest so near their cottage.

WALTER, THE RED-BELLIED BROWN SNAKE: HIS FLIGHT THROUGH SPACE

BY

Edward Hoagland

Y ou know how a cat puffs up its fur to look as big as possible when it is about to get in a fight. Sled dogs do the same thing. And a blowfish will bulge out its spiny skin in an emergency, not in order to fight, but to turn itself into a tough, prickly mouthful for any hungry creature that might wish to make a meal.

Our friend in this story, Walter, the Red-Bellied Brown Snake—who lived in the woodpile and swelled himself up as thick as a little cigar whenever necessary—was in his way humbler than these. He didn't know how to fight. His skin had no thorns sticking out. He was very small, less than twelve inches long. His own favorite food was only plain brown earthworms, which he swallowed without much fuss when he found one in a wet place under a log. Then he waited a day or two before he looked for another, and in cold weather he was even less active than that.

Living in the woodpile with Walter were scorpions, centipedes, beetles, and spiders. But he didn't eat any of them— just the occasional worm. Once in a while a big garter snake that had been hunting toads in the pasture would crawl through and flatten into a cranny between logs and rest. The weasels, the cats, the broad-winged hawks, the crows and ravens, the foxes and skunks and raccoons that would pick a snake apart if they caught it out in the open field couldn't reach it in such a place.

The garter snake was three times Walter's size and five times as adventurous. Indeed, the scientists who study such things say that Red-Bellied Brown Snakes (whom they call Storer's Snakes, after a man named Mr. Storer, who discovered them) once lived in the water. Their ancestors were water snakes a long while ago—maybe twenty-five million years—when North America had many more swamps than it does nowadays. And they were adventurous enough then to crawl out of the water and live more and more on the land. But they were scared of their new way of life, too. So scared that they gradually shrank in order to be able to hide under stones and inside the bark of fallen trees, as they do still, when not living under a woodpile, like Walter.

But later, after many of the swamps had dried, the Ice Age began, when the winters became very long. A snake like the Red-Bellied Brown Snake, who coiled under logs and stones, could survive the chill better than some of the snakes who were used to crawling about above ground. Also, as cities were built, the Red-Bellied Brown Snakes have lived longer in places like Central Park before being caught or killed.

These were humble qualities. But one possession Walter *did* have to be proud of—that part of him which he and his female friend admired in the spring, when they lay with their tails wrapped together—was his bright red belly. It was red like coral, and she had the same brilliant band running down the length of her stomach, edged with pearly silver. It was one of the ways they recognized each other.

After breeding in the spring, they would separate, wriggling through the wood chips and bark bits, swallowing worms, in the cool of the woodpile, during the heat of the summer. In August, she gave birth to about ten babies, each as thin as a bit of black string with a tiny white ring around its neck, who struck out in all directions as soon as they twisted free of the wet sacks they were born in. She and Walter met only accidentally, however, until the fall. Then, along with some other Red-Bellied Brown Snakes and four or five garter snakes, and a collection of toads, and a great many insects, they crawled deep down between the foundation stones of the house to sleep through the winter. The toads were too cold now to eat the insects, and the garter snakes too cold to pay any attention to the toads. One old grandmother toad over the years had grown as big as a Buddha, so that no garter snake in the state of Vermont could have gotten her into its mouth. In fact, if she had come across Walter in the course of the summer while hopping about, she might well have gobbled *him* up.

If he had lived any place less safe than the woodpile, Walter would have had lots of enemies to worry about. But he was so unobtrusive, so weak a climber and meek a crawler, that you might think that all the energy of his ancestors during the Age of the Swamps and the Age of the Glaciers had gone into brightening his gorgeous coral-colored belly stripe.

He did have one dangerous enemy—even in the woodpile. This was the Ring-Necked Snake. Blue-black, with a yellow collar, an orange belly, a tense, skinny, active body, the Ring-Necked Snake was much shorter than the big garter snake, though longer than Walter. In infancy, it had looked almost like a Red-Bellied Brown Snake, but it had kept and improved upon that collar. Otherwise, it had stayed black instead of turning brown on the back, and had developed a belly that was only pretty, not brilliant, in color.

Now, the Ring-Necked Snake also fed mostly on worms, smelling for them, winding after them under the woodpile and under the chicken coop, and around the foundations of the house and barn. But unfortunately for Walter, it had other tastes, besides. Its favorite food was not worms, but red newts and other small salamanders that crept under mossy rocks in the woods by the stream. And its *second* favorite food was Red-Bellied Brown Snakes.

The only sure way for a Red-Bellied Brown Snake to hide from the Ring-Necked Snake was by wriggling into a crevice between logs or stones that was so narrow not even the Ring-Necked Snake could squeeze through. When no hiding place was close, Walter would puff himself up as large as he could. His head lost its shape. His body swelled to four times its normal size, so that his scales no longer covered his skin and the skin showed through in pale rings around his scales. In other words, he bulged until the Ring-Necked Snake was simply not *snake* enough to be able to choke him down.

The problem was that the Ring-Necked Snake was still threatening Walter every couple of days, and Walter was getting more and more practice at blowing himself up. It stared at him as he huffed and puffed, as if it were measuring him, opening and loosening its jaws. And no matter how many worms it had eaten, it always looked hungry.

He had been bulging until he looked like a little cigar—but now he was getting as big as a sausage. Though, like other snakes, he had no proper eyelids, the scales at the top of his back were pushed out over his eyes.

Such fullness! He rather liked the feeling. He was so big he was as light as the air, and yet felt as full as after a meal. In fact, he had to twist out from under the woodpile to give himself room before he swelled up. With practice, he blew himself up even as big as a little log. But he was so light that the wind just pushed him along like a roll of birchbark.

Then one day the wind lifted him up. The Ring-Necked Snake had given up following him and eyeing him. But he was enjoying himself. He wasn't afraid. He let the wind lift him and blow him through the air for a hundred, two hundred yards, and set him down next to an entirely new woodpile. And there he lives, hoping that no Ring-Necked Snake will move nearby, and that he will never need to puff himself up again for any reason whatsoever, except maybe only for fun.

WHAT WONDERS IN THAT CIRCLE LIE, OR, THE TOAD STORY

BY
Anselm Hollo

"oh mark the beauty of his eye
what wonders in that circle lie
so clear so bright our fathers said
he wears a jewel in his head"
—the boss

we stand at the edge of a pond
under a maple brilliant with its fringes of red keys
a marshy place yellow with cowslips
& back from the water broad spreading leaves
of skunk cabbage & unrolling fronds
of cinnamon fern

when near at hand there is a sweet tremulous call
continues for several seconds then stops
abruptly

there it is again from another direction
slightly different in pitch & now
it comes in from all quarters
many voices

it is not difficult to locate the singers
they are toads

the sounds are such that they influence us to loiter

the sustained note is not only
high-pitched & tremulous
it seems to have a dual character
as though a low note were droned
while a high one was whistled

this song has been compared to the slow
opening movement of beethoven's moonlight sonata

the simplicity & quiet joyousness of it all take hold upon us

humbly & thoughtfully we continue our walk

lose tail!
leave pond!
hallelujah!

but sometimes that day
of the toads' final transformation
coincides with a day of gentle rain

a happy coincidence it seems for them
but likely to prove rather tragic instead

they cover the sidewalks & roadways
& before each individual of the migrating multitude
finds a sheltered corner he can call home

many hundreds have lost their lives
under the wheels of carriages & the feet
of hurrying pedestrians

hold the toad gently
in your hand
so that his hind feet are without support

& hear him talk

he is annoyed
he demands to be released
his tone is not irritated however
it is instead a gentle chirping sound

he twists his head about
& looks at you brightly

he pushes with his hands
he wiggles with his feet

all the time he is talking
the chirping notes
coming thick & fast

toads live to be very old

authentic record tells the story
of one that lived to be thirty-six
& was then killed
by accident

other conditions being right
the toad can live for some time without food

this may be stretched into months
possibly years
(two years in limestone)

if the temperature is continuously such that the toad
can go on hibernating

the toad does not eat lettuce
but it is not beneath his dignity
to sit & feast
on the plant lice that live on the lettuce

the toad is fitted for his place in life by what he does
as well as what he is
let an enemy seize him roughly
& he is a dead toad

playing dead saves him many a time
he will lie on his back
with scarcely any perceptible motion
for minutes at a time

even breathing
seems suspended

suddenly one leg is thrust out
then another
the eyes open wide

& in an instant more the toad has turned over
& is ready for new emergencies

a toad never has the pleasure of drinking
water in the usual way

all the water he gets is absorbed through his skin

a toad kept in a dry place grows thin & distressed
is likely to die within a few days
whereas one provided with plenty of moisture remains plump
& contented as weeks go by
even when there is little food

when drinking he sprawls in shallow water
or on a wet surface & has a blissful expression
in his marvelous eyes

in midsummer when pools & springs are dry
toads often travel long distances
to spend the night on the wet ground about a well

in their search they sometimes unwittingly fall into wells
to lead a most somber existence
feeding on the few low forms of life that live there
& on unfortunates who become prisoners the same way

release may come if the well has a bucket
but more likely their fate is a tragic one

their crushed bodies have been taken from pumps
into which they have been sucked

they have sometimes been found hibernating in old wells
where they must have been for ten or fifteen years
judging by the amount of debris under which they are buried

when cold autumn days come
he shuts the door by backing
his way farther in

& lies there with his toes drawn under him
his head bent down all secure he sleeps

the days grow colder & still he sleeps
his house yet more protected by leaves & snow

the winds blow
but he does not feel them

he is cold
we should call him frozen perhaps
he is so stiff & cold

but if the heart is not frozen
he wakes up some warm spring day
when the ferns are unrolling

& scarcely knows that he has slept more than a day

what a change

it is such a pleasure to eat
it is so delightful to move

it is such satisfaction to soak in the water of spring rains

once again he becomes a social creature
& finds himself going with many others

& now at the pond & now in the water
he can contain himself no longer
but bursts into that spring song
beautiful to himself & to his companions

CHILDHOOD

BY

David Ignatow

ILLUSTRATED BY
ROSE GRAUBART

These were among my first thoughts on earth, that I had been put here as some kind of reward, given a gift for being what I was, and I loved my bicycle as an emissary from that power to give me gifts. I talked to my bicycle, praising it for moving at the command of my pedaling and steering in the right direction at my touch. The sidewalk lying flat and still in expectation of the bicycle, also cooperated with the powers that be and no one stood in the bike's path to topple me over. The wind brushing against my face was like the hand of approval. Where then was the change hiding, the hidden change?

I never thought the bicycle betrayed me, nor the sidewalk, nor the wind, but now I see them simply as means and the betrayer is me. I could not call the bicycle an emissary. It was a tool, the sidewalk was a path, the wind a current of air. We were not talking to each other or communicating that I was aware of, but what did it matter, I told myself, as long as I was free to use them for my delight, but I was alone in my pleasure. I was not the child of anyone, for as I saw myself growing the bicycle shrank in size and the sidewalk filled with cracks and bumps, the wind on my face in cold weather chilled me and when I ate food I knew it was because of appetite. I had become something else to myself other than with the bike, the sidewalk, and the wind in one identity. I could feel cold, hunger, appetite, and the self that all this meant, because the bicycle never was hungry, nor did the sidewalk ever have to go to bed, and sometimes the wind stopped blowing and did not exist for me, which would have frightened me about myself earlier, while the wind never was frightened. I never heard it speak of itself as I was beginning to speak about myself, and I knew there was something about me very different, and sometimes I was panicky about it but more often I was glad because I had still another thing to turn to in pleasure and that was my self which always was with me, but I was alone because a tree began to look lonely to me standing by itself, whereas earlier I had thought it beautiful, expressing what I felt about myself too, that I was, that we both were. Now it looked lonely but I knew that again was my thinking and the thinking was my pleasure and my burden too. I was all alone, and so I turned to another like myself and found him happy to turn to me.

And I am growing up still more as we begin to differ about the games we should be playing or the places to visit on our bikes, or the time to go home to dinner. I become lonely again and defensive, my self needing to be defended as the only absolute friend and sharer that I have, but I know that each of us feels the same because we exchange smiles often and talk together from time to time with gentleness and kidding and wait for the voice of our parent to call us separately to dinner.

THE OLD FRIENDS

BY

John Irving

The occasion for getting together was Colin's thirteenth birthday, March 24, 1978. The Hendries were able to fly up from Mexico because Arden had found four plane tickets on the roof where his mother was sunbathing. The tickets were stuck to the sun-tan oil and plastered to Susan's back. Nathan helped Arden peel the tickets off his mother without waking her up.

"They don't look like good tickets to me," Hendrie said, and returned to reading his only copy of *The New York Times,* which was several months old.

Nathan quickly read a book about how to wash oil off airplane tickets and the tickets were soon as good as new.

"Who do you suppose these tickets really belong to?" Susan asked, when she saw the tickets drying on the clothesline.

"Doesn't matter," Arden said. "They're mine now, and we're all going to see Brendan."

And since nobody ever argued with Arden, the Hendries flew to New England and were met at the airport by John in the Old Irving Family Volvo.

"One hundred thousand fucking miles and still going!" John said, driving the Hendries north to Putney at his usual rate of 35 miles per hour.

Nathan was able to read nine books during the car ride and Arden fell asleep and woke up several times. "Aren't we there yet?" he asked.

"Soon," Susan said. An ever-cheerful person, she painted eight pictures in the course of the journey.

When the Hendries got to Vermont, they realized how different it was from Mexico. For example, there were no fruit bats hanging upside down from the telephone wires. And there was a lot of snow. Colin was still out skiing with his girlfriend, Albatross—a tall, gawky, beautiful girl who wore feathers in her ski clothes and had an unlisted phone number.

Brendan was digging in the driveway when the Old Irving Family Volvo finally got back home.

"What are you looking for, Brendan?" Arden asked him.

"Super Friends, dummy," Brendan said.

They were the Super Friends of last summer, and of the summers before that, and they were under a lot of snow.

Nathan quickly read a book about how to melt snow.

Inside the Irving house, Shyla had baked a cake made of carrots and the memories of old friends. "I don't want any," Arden said.

"Don't talk or laugh or screw around when you have food in your mouth," John told everyone.

Brendan pretended to choke, to scare his father, and Nathan read a book about choking and how to prevent it.

"I can take care of it, if it happens," Nathan told John.

"Where is my mother?" Arden asked.

"Look on the roof, dummy," Brendan said. And sure enough, there was Susan, sunning herself on the New Irving Roof, which was flat and covered with four or five feet of snow. The snow was marked with the cat tracks from the Irving cats, who tried to get into the house through the upstairs windows. The snow was also spotted with the bloody heads of decapitated birds; the cats ate everything but the heads. Susan had wrapped herself in tin foil in an effort to protect herself from the snow; she was partially frozen and partially baking in the sun when the kids found her.

John and Hendrie walked down the driveway to get the mail. The mail was a letter from Mexico, written weeks ago. It was from Hendrie. It said that they would be arriving.

"Mexico is a strange country, mail-wise," John said.

Back in the house, everyone was trying to thaw Susan.

"Bring boiling water!" Arden said.

"Give her something hot to eat," Shyla suggested.

"Kick her a few times," Brendan said.

"That's what you get for trying to enjoy yourself in a terrible place like Vermont," John said.

But Nathan read a book about how to melt people who had drifted off on snow-covered roofs, and he fixed his mother up properly.

Everybody wondered where Colin was, and John had lots to say on that subject.

"He's on the telephone talking to his girlfriend, Albatross. They're talking about the *next* time they can talk together on the phone. Or he's skiing and talking with Albatross at the same time—he's talking about when they can go skiing again, or when they can tie up the phone for hours and hours," John said. "All that kid does is ski and talk on the phone, talk on the phone and ski, ski and talk on the phone. . . ."

When the phone rang, everyone knew whom it was for, although Brendan answered it hopefully—as if it *might* be for him. "No, Colin is still out skiing," Brendan said into the phone, sadly. "And don't call him up again today, if you've got any brains, because we're having a birthday party for him—if he ever gets home—and you'd just interrupt us."

"Who was it?" John asked Brendan when Brendan hung up.

"Some *douf*," Brendan said. Sure enough, it probably was.

When Colin got home, he said hello to everyone.

"Hello, Arden—Nathan, Susan, Hendrie, Mom and Dad," he said. "Hi, *douf*," he said to Brendan. Colin and Brendan then fought for the usual amount of time, and Shyla then explained how she had arranged to have a dog delivered to the house for Colin's birthday present. It was a German Shepherd English Bulldog Mastiff sort of dog, she implied.

"What's *that* mean?" John cried. He was further upset to learn that the arrival of the dog was delayed by a "disturbance" the beast had created in downtown Putney. "And what do they mean, 'a disturbance'?" John asked, but everyone ignored him. "We don't even know what this dog *looks* like," John said, hopelessly.

"It's sort of light and dark and big and small," Brendan said. "I've seen it."

"You have not," Colin said, and they fought some more.

Nathan read a book about the breeds of dogs and John tried to explain his feelings about the kinds of dogs he didn't care for.

"Big dogs who drool," he said, "and little dogs who yip. Any dog who bites, fat dogs who fart, and scrawny dogs who slink—or look guilty. I can't stand guilty-looking dogs. And stupid dogs," he added. "*All* stupid dogs. And dogs who case other living things: cats, for instance, other dogs, and people who run. Oh, and dogs who bark," he remembered. "I don't care for any of the above-mentioned dogs."

"Dad is weird," Brendan said.

"Oh, and dogs who *shed*," John said. "And dogs with bad breath."

"Dad is *very* weird," Colin said.

"We'll get any kind of dog we want," said Shyla.

"You should try living in Mexico," the Hendries said.

"Where are my glasses?" Nathan said. "Arden took them off and Brendan hid them."

"I forget where I hid them," Brendan admitted.

"Where is my cottage cheese?" Hendrie asked. Hendrie traveled with a vat of cottage cheese, about a hundred pounds of it.

Everyone searched for the cheese and the glasses. Arden and Brendan beat up a strange kid who showed up suddenly in the driveway and tried to swipe some Super Friends.

"Douf!" Brendan cried.

"Get lost," Arden told the kid.

"Take this," Brendan said.

"And that," said Arden.

"That took care of him," they said.

Colin decided that, because of their toughness, Brendan and Arden should be renamed. Brendan should be called Ball and Arden should be called Thud, Colin thought. "Ball and Thud!" Colin teased. "Ball and Thud!"

But Nathan was upset that he could not read further books without his glasses. Colin, who now wears a stunning pair of gold wire-rimmed glasses, all the time, discovered Nathan's spectacles in the missing vat of Hendrie's cottage cheese. The vat had been temporarily concealed by the mountainous sleeping equipment with which the Hendrie Family also traveled.

"Here are your glasses, Nathan," Colin said, holding out the cheesy things with a pair of tongs.

Brendan and Arden busied themselves trying on stuff in Brendan's Costume Closet. Arden put on the antelope head and refused to take it off. Brendan disguised himself as a Foreign Exchange Student.

Shyla served an impressive flan.

"I don't have to eat any of that if I don't want to," Arden mumbled through the antelope head.

"Just don't choke, any of you," John cautioned.

Hendrie spoke to Susan about keeping a lid on the cottage cheese so that future glasses and other debris would not fall into the vat. John warned Susan about the use of the roof. He mentioned "ice slides" and "frost bite" and "spies." Susan tolerated both these men, calmly.

Shyla served a giant ravioli. It was a *single* ravioli, large enough to feed eight. Nathan read a book about Italian cooking and detailed the ingredients of the ravioli to everyone.

"I don't like it, no matter what's in it," Arden said.

"Me neither," said Brendan, who was now dressed as an electric eel.

Colin's girlfriend, Albatross, played a record in Colin's room and Colin shut himself up with her to listen to it—presumably. It was a song called "Short People," and John didn't like it.

"I'm short people," he kept saying. "What is fucking wrong with short people?"

Shyla, who is tall people, served an elaborate Irish meat pie.

"What's *in* it, Shyla?" Susan asked.

"Junk is in here," Arden said. "I can smell junk."

"Yech," said Brendan.

"No choking," John said.

But the old friends went on eating, cautiously; the younger people read comic books and watched TV.

"Do you know what my father did to a TV once?" Arden asked.

"He better not pull that around here," Brendan said.

Arden, who had surrounded himself with comic books and sat inches away from the glowing television, said: "Anybody touches this TV, I'm busting him."

From Colin's room the sounds of Albatross dancing and "Short People" went on and on. Susan's only access to the roof was through the window in Colin's room, and so she was prevented from doing herself harm.

Hendrie sat for hours by the woodstove reading through two hundred and twenty-one back issues of *The New York Times.*

"See what you've missed?" John asked.

Shyla cooked on and on.

It seemed that these people were the way they were, and nothing would ever stop them.

"Happy Birthday, Colin!" Brendan cried, throwing melted ice cream into Colin's room. Albatross shrieked, a fearsome sound which made the Irvings and the Hendries glad that they had not had *daughters*. Arden affectionately butted Colin's record player with his antelope head. Colin turned up the volume of "Short People" to drive everyone—everyone but Albatross—out of his room.

"I'm going to put you all in a story, once upon a time," said Nathan, who was so bored with all the crap there was to read that he was writing a book of his own.

A STORY BY JACK WITH INTERPOLATIONS BY JILL

BY

Jill Johnston

OTHER PARTICIPANTS: Chris, Jack's sister, aged twelve; Lynn, Jack's mother; Jamie, Jack's stepfather. Jack is eight.

I

JACK: I got this story, it's about Tommy and his friend

JILL: Who is his friend?

JACK: His friend is just some guy, I think Lee, yeah, his friend Lee

JILL: Is this a real story?

JACK: Not real no, something fake

JILL: Something you're making up, about him

JACK: Yeah, actually Tommy made it up . . . he lives right next door to Lee and he saw Lee coming home and said what are you chewing and he said oh gum, and he said, so he said, I got this little parachute, you're chewing some gum and a little thing pops out of your mouth . . .

JILL: A parachute pops out of your mouth?

JACK: No, a parachute with an army guy y'know, a guy comes out. . . .

JILL: Out of your mouth, out of the gum?

JACK: Out of the gum it pops out of your mouth, because you're chewing gum, a little liquid squirts out

JILL: Oh the guy . . . the guy falls down to the ground and a parachute like comes out of your mouth

JACK: No no no it's a little liquid it comes down on the grass and then it turns into a parachute and a guy and you can fold the thing up

JILL: Like a butterfly and a cocoon or something?

JACK: Yah

JILL: 'kay, then what?

JACK: And he says where'd you get it, at the store, he says okay I'll buy one he goes up to the store, Tommy goes up to the store to buy one, starts chewing it and all this green liquid comes out of his mouth and changes into a big green glob and it doesn't do anything it's sitting there and slowly he brings it outside it's about *this* big or so and it turns into an army tank

JILL: Yeah? Right at his feet, so to speak? Right there on the ground?

JACK: Well no it's as big as an army tank, it's a real big army tank, it's green, y'know like usually they are . . . an' he hops in it . . . then it starts shooting by itself and blowing up things . . . he's going down he goes through a bridge, he blows up the bridge behind him . . . and suddenly . . . and suddenly it blows up . . . it turns back into the glob and he just makes it through the hatch and then it turns into a glob and the police were chasing him . . .

JILL: Makes it through the *what*?

JACK: Makes it through the hatch . . . where they get out

JILL: Oh yeah, well he just gets out of the hatch of the tank and then he turns back into a glob again

JACK: No he's turning into a glob, and then he jumps out

JILL: Just before he becomes a glob himself

JACK: No just before he gets swallowed

JILL: (*laughter*) Before he gets swallowed by the glob?

JACK: Yah

JILL: By the tank which is a glob . . . by the tank which is turning into a glob

JACK: Yah

JILL: And then the police come?

JACK: No, the police were chasing him, but the police . . .

JILL: Oh because it was shooting and everything

JACK: Yah

JILL: Right

JACK: And . . . he picked up the glob and it disappeared and then he walked home and said . . . he said . . . I'll never buy one of those things again . . . cause his friend . . . just . . . spaced out

JILL: Spaced out what?

JACK: His friend that he is talking to, before, that got a little parachute?

JILL: Yah

JACK: And he was spaced out because he didn't know why

JILL: He didn't know why what?

JACK: Why that he didn't want to uh have . . .

JILL: What did he think would happen if he went and got this thing and it was gonna be a man with a parachute and it was a tank instead of a man with a parachute?

JACK: I know, but there's a whole bunch of different things

JILL: Yuh? You mean different things will come and you've got to take your chances, like a prize in a Cracker Jack box

JACK: No it's not a Cracker Jack box

JILL: I mean like one of those things that you find in a Cracker Jack box

JACK: Actually no it has to be bigger than this . . . one other kid he might probably find a tree come out or something

JILL: He didn't like it that it was a tank that went off shootin' itself

JACK: Ya-a

JILL: But he got in it to drive it . . . himself . . . I mean . . . how come he got in . . . he got in it you said

JACK: But then the hatch closed by itself and he went drivin' off

JILL: So if he didn't like the tank why did he get in it?

CHRIS: Well I would go in a tank to explore it

JACK: Man he hasn't ever been in a tank

JILL: Oh I see . . . it took off by itself . . . and he couldn't stop it. So what's the moral of this story?

JACK: What d'you mean?

JILL: Lynn, explain what a moral of a story is . . . we need a definition of a moral . . . Lynn knows one

LYNN: Well the way you take a dream and learn from it

JACK: Something you can learn from this story, right, far out, mom

CHRIS: I know, never get a tank, it might turn into a glob

JILL: (*laughter*) Very funny, I like it I like it

JACK: Never climb into a tank without someone with you

JILL: That's a good one too, okay, another one (*laughter*)

LYNN: Never try to buy magic at a store

JILL: What do *you* think?

JACK: My favorite is the one I said. My favorite is where never climb into a tank without someone with you

JILL: Yah . . . I got a question now to ask you . . . You think if someone else got in the tank with you it would save you from this tank taking off by itself and shooting everything?

JACK: Yah it could because all they had to do was bring a few hand grenades

CHRIS: So never get in a tank with a person who has some hand grenades

(*Laughter*: Jack)

JILL: Now wait a minute . . . You think anyone else got in a tank with you, why would it make a difference?

JACK: You mess me up

JILL: Why should it make a difference if someone else got in the tank with you? Why would it change things? You said something about hand grenades and I didn't understand . . . that sounds like it would make things worse

JACK: Then he could just go out of the hatch he could bust open the hatch

JILL: Oh I see . . . suppose this other guy doesn't want to get out, the other person doesn't want to leave?

JACK: He *would* want to get out because it would blow up his town

JILL: *He* would want to get out, the *other* guy would want to get out?

JACK: The guy that would be going with you, yes

JILL: So this other guy must be, what's he, the good guy or something?

JACK: Yah

JILL: The guy that got in then, Tommy, he's the bad guy

JACK: Tommy's the good guy, he couldn't help it from stopping

JILL: Oh he couldn't help it, he's the innocent guy then

JACK: Yeah

JILL: Then he needs somebody who knows better, the other guy is somebody who knows better, is that it?—this is getting complicated . . . So the moral of the story is uh that um

CHRIS: Never get in a tank without someone who knows better than you do

LYNN: Would you get in with Derek?

JACK: No

JILL: Who would you get in with personally?

JACK: I'd get in with someone walking out of the store

JILL: Anyone?

JACK: Yah

LYNN: A stranger? Just any stranger?

JACK: Actually the real thing is I wouldn't even get in the tank, I'd just let it go down by itself and go through the bridge, then I'd set a trap under the bridge, go foom and bo-oo-oommm.

JILL: Tommy was a dummy to get into the tank in the first place

JACK: Yah

JILL: So maybe the other good guy, the guy who knows better, would really be you, because you wouldn't get in at all

II

ON HEROES

LYNN: I wanna talk to you about heroes

JACK: About how I believe in them?

LYNN: Well yah, what heroes do you believe in, what are they important for, do you need heroes?

CHRIS: Heroes are totally worthless except in times of great crisis, and since I've never known a time of great crisis I don't believe in heroes at all

JILL: Did you have heroes before when you were younger?

CHRIS: I like the idea of heroes

JILL: Did you have them before, when you were younger?

CHRIS: Oh I have heroes, yes yes, except I don't believe in them . . . that sounds dumb . . . I've never known any great crisis, I like super-heroes, I like Spider Man and Howard the Duck

JILL: What would be a great crisis?

LYNN: I meant a real hero, Christine, because you obviously are beyond the age when you believe Howard the Duck is gonna make the scene and save the day, especially from boredom or whatever

JILL: What do you mean by a big crisis?

CHRIS: Well look in comic books, Tarstarkas is out

JILL: To get you

CHRIS: (*laughing*) yah, to kick ass

JILL: So then you need someone to save you you mean

CHRIS: Yah, all your superheroes save the world once or twice or so

JACK: Superman, Spider Man

LYNN: I'm talkin' about real-life heroes

CHRIS: What sort of real-life heroes?

LYNN: Oh, like your parents, when you were young didn't you sort of think they were heroes in a way?

CHRIS: They were idols, not heroes

LYNN: Same thing isn't it? Yah, idols, somebody to look up to, somebody to believe in, that they know everything

CHRIS: I still believe in my parents

LYNN: But you don't believe they know everything anymore

JILL: That's why you don't have heroes now so much because you don't think they know everything all the time now, so Jack still believes . . .

JACK: I believe in . . . heroes, like Spider Man, all those kinds.

JILL: Which other kinds?

JACK: I mean it would be really neat if there was a Spider Man

JILL: I don't know what Spider Man does

JACK: Well he was workin' in this lab and there was two ways that he got it . . .

JILL: Two ways that he got what?

CHRIS: He was a good student, a bookworm

JILL: Oh yeah and he had a laboratory accident?

JACK: No and everybody called him bookworm and they all hated him

JILL: There's a crisis, everybody hated him

CHRIS: No he was just not popular, he was not popular

JILL: That's a crisis . . . a crisis of identity

JACK: He gets bitten by a spider, a radioactive spider, and it lands on his hand and bites it 'cause it's all radioactive

JILL: So he turns into a spider

JACK: No, he doesn't . . . he goes ouch and then . . . and then . . . you see somethin' growin' on his hand . . . then when he's walkin' down this alley

JILL: Wait a minute I have to ask you something

JACK: What

JILL: Does this give him, um, certain powers, like spider . . .

LYNN: Yah spider powers

JACK: Okay now and nobody knows it yet . . .

JILL: Not even he

JACK: Not even he . . . and he's walkin' down this alley an this car starts chasin' him and he jumps on a wall and he starts stickin' to it . . . he's sayin' what in the world . . . what . . . he's stickin' to this wall . . . and he starts climbin' up this wall

JILL: To get away from this car

JACK: No he jumps really high up

LYNN: To get away from the car

CHRIS: There's this car comin' down the alley

JACK: Look at the tree way up there up there up there (*pointing*) right up there he jumped that far up

JILL: I don't think spiders can do that

JACK: Yes spiders can, they can jump you know, like how when they build a web

LYNN: It's all relative . . .

JAMIE: Like an ant is able to lift six times its own weight so he has the proportionate power of a spider

JILL: O I see . . . Do these powers come on him when he's in a crisis, when somebody's after him?

CHRIS: Whenever he wants, he's always got 'em

JILL: Yeah but he doesn't need to use 'em unless there's a crisis, right?

LYNN: And then he dresses up in a suit that he makes for himself

JACK: Now just a minute I haven't finished all of it . . . then . . . then . . . then he like . . . then he's climbin' up a wall and he grabs this pipe and he *crushes* it

JILL: A pipe?

JACK: A pipe, an' he didn't know . . . and he's grabbed it and he crushes it, an' then . . . then . . . then he goes climbs back down and just walks home . . . then he . . . he . . . he . . .

CHRIS: You're wrong

JILL: I got the idea . . . so . . . what I want to know now

LYNN: I was gonna talk about more concrete heroes . . . I mean comic book heroes don't appeal to me much at all . . . but I should've remembered that these are

JILL: That these are *his* main heroes

LYNN: Well . . . that's the heroes you can talk about although there's all the other idealism . . . he can't talk about who he idolizes . . . except

JILL: Through his comic book heroes

LYNN: Well they're so much more spectacular

JILL: Than . . . than

LYNN: Than real people

JILL: Do you have any real people heroes?

JACK: Ya-a-ss, I have some friends in my class that save me a lot—like if Greg or Alex or somebody comes up and starts beating on me . . . now he's a real strong man

JILL: And if you're in trouble he'll, uh, help you out

JACK: No no no he'll beat on me and so will Alex . . . but Nicky will come along and beat *them* up

JILL: I see . . . he is like your Spider Man

JACK: An' there's Dave and Lynn and Jamie and Susan . . .

JILL: Oh Dave and Lynn and Jamie and Susan are . . . also . . . people who will help you out when you're in trouble

JACK: Oh and Jesse, Jesse, I mean she cares about me a lot too . . . I was at this park (an amusement park) and I had somethin' in my throat and I spit it out an' I was on this little skyway thing an' it landed on someone's head

CHRIS: He couldn't help it though, he had somethin' caught in his throat, and they thought he was spitting it out on the people down below on purpose

JACK: On someone's head

JILL: So they got mad at you

JACK: So the guy got mad at me . . . an' he told me to get down . . . he said get down . . . an' so I was goin' down the thing an' I was just getting off an' was walkin' out the little walkway . . . this guy starts grabbin' me . . . pushin' me . . . grabbin' me

JILL: So who, uh, who saved you that day

CHRIS: Jesse went up and said get your hand off him

JILL: What about explaining to this guy that it was a mistake

CHRIS: Jack was trying to . . . but the uh guy just uh the guy was a dummy

JILL: Yeah, he assumed that you were bein a bad kid or something . . . misunderstandings, really

LYNN: It's nice having someone stick up for you

JILL: Yeah yeah . . . I wish I had more people . . . sticking up for me (*laughter*) . . . maybe if I was smaller . . . there's a good story . . . if I could just uh

CHRIS: Shrink a little

JILL: Is there a comic book person who gets to be a weak kid in order to be saved?

CHRIS: Howard the Duck is a duck an' he's about two feet tall but he's very strong

JILL: So who saves you, Lynn?

LYNN: Jamie (*laughter*)

JILL: So but this identification with Spider Man is how you can get to save yourself really isn't it . . . about how *you* can have special powers, right?

JACK: We'll tie you up and put you in the trunk (*laughter*)

JILL: How about saving yourself?

LYNN: Would you like to be Spider Man?

JILL: The difference is that the real people, like Dave Lynn Jamie Susan etc., that they save you but Spider Man can't save you 'cause he's not real, right? So Spider Man can't save you, but you identify with Spider Man, right? So if you were Spider Man yourself you could save yourself

JACK: I could save myself

JILL: You could save yourself . . . But you're not Spider Man, how do you get to save yourself then, cause you've got an unreal person in a comic book who can't save you and you got real people who can save you so how do you get to save yourself?

JACK: I save other people

JILL: How about savin' yourself? You don't get to save yourself?

JACK: I can save myself by blocking their punches (*laughter*)

JILL: This is obviously a joke . . . I wanna ask Jamie and Lynn, does this guy get to save himself . . . C'mon I need a little participation here . . . We got a Spider Man who can't save 'im because he's not real but we got you guys who can save him because you are real, now how does he get to save himself?

JAMIE: In about ten years

JILL: In about ten years? *Jamie*, what kind of message is that to a growing boy? Do you think that's cool? That he won't get to save himself till ten years? Can't he save himself now?

LYNN: He can

JAMIE: Sure

CHRIS: He does

JILL: Lynn, now I'm asking you

LYNN: Yeah he saves himself . . . sure

CHRIS: One day when we were in school I remember Mark . . . started picking on Jack so Jack belted him in the stomach and walked off

JILL: You saved yourself

CHRIS: I thought that was so funny . . . he's twelve years old

LYNN: You can be a hero in your dreams a lot and Jack does that; One of the first dreams that he told me about was when he was at an airport looking out and watching and the plane coming in wasn't stopping it was coming right through the window toward all the people in there so he ran out and bit the tire on the plane (*laughter*)

JACK: I ran out and I bit the wheels . . . a-a-a-a-a-a-a

JACK: I have a superhero that I made up (*shouting*) I have a superhero that I made up (*shouting louder*)

JILL: Obviously it's you (*laughter*)

JACK: Well it's me it's me it's myself; Anything man switch, and his enemy is switch anything man; Anything man means he can turn into any kind of superhero and the superhero can . . .

JILL: Turn any kind of switch

JACK: No-o-o-o (*exasperated*)

JILL: Sorry, and the superhero can, go on, back up

JACK: I can make up my own superhero and turn into that one

JILL: And turn into the anything man?

JACK: And turn into the one that I make up (*shouting*)

JILL: All right, okay, go on

JACK: All of them together y'know; Switch can turn into anything except the only superheroes he can't turn into is Hulk, Flash, and Spider Man

JILL: Christine gave an example of your saving yourself by punching some guy out, is there some other way you can save yourself?

JILL: I'm asking you a question now, sit down (*laughter*), is there some other way you can save yourself besides punching some guy out?

JACK: Yah

JILL: How?

JACK: Run (*laughter*)

LYNN: A car's coming at you you could jump out of the road before it hits you . . . like Spider Man saved himself by jumping up on a building, jumping out of the way of something that's going to uh mean your end

JILL: Do you do that a lot, jump out of the way of stuff that's comin' at you?

JACK: Yah

THERE WAS A NAUGHTY BOY

BY

John Keats

ILLUSTRATED BY
MICHELE NAPEAR

There was a naughty Boy,
  A naughty Boy was he,
He would not stop at home,
  He could not quiet be——
    He took
    In his Knapsack
    A Book
    Full of vowels
    And a shirt
    With some towels——
    A slight cap
    For night cap——
    A hair brush,
    Comb ditto,
    New Stockings
    For old ones
    Would split O!
    This Knapsack
    Tight at's back
    He rivetted close
And followed his Nose
  To the North,
  To the North,
And follow'd his nose
  To the North.

There was a naughty Boy,
    And a naughty Boy was he,
He ran away to Scotland
    The people for to see——
        Then he found
        That the ground
        Was as hard,
        That a yard
        Was as long,
        That a song
        Was as merry,
        That a cherry
        Was as red——

        That lead
        Was as weighty,
        That fourscore
        Was as eighty,
        That a door
        Was as wooden
        As in England——
So he stood in his shoes
        And he wonder'd,
        He wonder'd,
He stood in his shoes
        And he wonder'd.

A CHILD'S BOOK OF RITUAL MAGIC

BY

Robert Kelly

There are four things you must know and think about:

WANDS
CUPS
SWORDS
PENTACLES

Your mother is a cup
and your father poured you from her

Pentacles are golden
saucers with stars on them

Because the good Magician knows how to unlock a saucer
(nobody else would even notice that some saucers are
locked), Saucers have become a sign
(especially when they have
stars on them),
                        a sign of everything in
your dreams and in your secret places
that you long to open up, bring out,
set down in daylight.

What it mostly is is thinking about these things
all these things.

                    Solomon
the smart Jewish king had many
of them (saucers)
                    and walked from room to
room of his palace
                    watching his saucers
knowing
that nothing was locked up or hidden or in darkness anymore.

CUPS generally mean
you'll like it
                whatever
it is.

        It is a good thing.
Jesus (some of you will know he is the Son of God, while
others will be less certain) could think of nothing better
to leave with us than a cup filled always with good wine.

SWORDS are tongues
and often savage——
are words
when words are
bright and clear
like the sun at noontime
making crisp shadows
but very small.

WANDS are another matter.

All parts of you
that get there
before you do
are Wands
(wherever it is).

When ordinary wood
lies in fire
it takes fire into itself
it glows red,
                fire inside the wood.

Cups are water and soft bodies
Wands are fire and hard bodies
Swords are air and bright and clever
Pentacles are earth and heavy and good.

Another name for Pentacle is COIN

What do you do with Coins?
It is pleasant to touch coins
and hold them.
           But it is most
pleasant to give them away and
sometimes get something for them.
A coin rots
if you do not give it away
(Leave a bright penny in your drawer
and see what happens
             See how sleek though
an old quarter is from the thousand
hands that have used it rightly)

When you want something very much you are learning about WANDS.

When you get up early in the morning and stand at the doorway or the window breathing the fresh clean air, and you know that the day will bring happiness and sadness and that the world is very big and very many people live in it, and that you live in it, then you are learning about SWORDS.

When you are playing with your best friend or when you are lying on wet grass and feeling the earth next to your skin as almost the same as your skin, or when you are snug in bed or all alone still quiet and happy, then you are learning about CUPS.

When you are drawing a picture or writing a story or singing a song or when sometimes you learn something you didn't know before or when you are with all your friends or when you are eating or drinking alone or together, then you are learning about COINS.

These are not the only ways to learn about the Four Things but they are easy ways and ways that you are going to try anyhow, so be happy and do them and be happy with what you do because you are doing it, and because that way it gets done, and if you don't do it no one else ever will.

Wishing doesn't make things happen. Will/ing sometimes does, because when you will, when all your will is focused, it is clear and sharp and defined as a sword, deep and gentle and receptive as a cup, practical as a coin, and as intense as a wand burning in the hottest fire.

You know that you can start a fire on paper or dead leaf by focusing all the light of the sun on one spot with a magnifying glass. Your will is the sun inside you, and will/ing is making all its rays shine all at once all in the same place.

What it is is thinking about these things,

and will/ing, and doing.

LITTLE TRICKER THE SQUIRREL MEETS BIG DOUBLE THE BEAR!

BY

Ken Kesey

Don't tell me you're the only youngsters never heard tell of the time the bear come to Topple's Bottom! He was a huge high country bear and not only huge but *horrible* huge and hairy and hateful; and *hungry!?!* . . . why, he almost at up the *whole Bottom* before Tricker finally cut him down to size, just you listen and see if he didn't. . . .

It was a fine fall morning, early and cold and sweet as cider. Down in the Bottom the only one up and about was old Papa Sun and him just barely. Hanging in the low limbs of the crabapple trees was still some of those strings of daybreak fog called "haint hair" by them that believes in such. The night shifts and day shifts were shifting very slow. The crickets hadn't put away their fiddles. The spiders hadn't shook the dew out of their webs yet. The birds hadn't quite woke up and the bats hadn't quite gone to sleep. Nothing was a-move except one finger of sun slipping soft up the knobby trunk of the hazel. It was one of the prettiest times of day at one of the prettiest times of year and all the Bottom folk were content to let it come about quiet and slow and savory.

Tricker the Squirrel was awake but he wasn't about. He was lazying in the highest hole in his cottonwood highrise with just his nose poking from his pillow of a tail, dreaming about flying. Every now and again he would twinkle one bright eye out through his dream and his puffy pillowhair to check the hazel tree way down below to see if any of the nuts was ready for reaping. He had to admit they were all pretty near prime. Yesterday he had watched them all day long turning softly browner and browner and had judged them just one day short of perfect.

"That means if I don't get them today, to-*morrow* they are *very apt* to be just one day past perfect."

So he was promising himself, "Just as quick as that sunbeam touches the first hazelnut I get right on the job." Then, after a couple winks, "Just as quick as that sunbeam touches the *second* hazelnut I'll zip right down with my tote sack"—and so forth, dozing and dallying, savoring the still, sweet air. The hazelnuts get browner. The sunbeam inches silently on—the fif*teenth!* the *twentieth!*—but the morning was simply *so* still and the air hanging *so* sweet he hated to break the peace.

Well then, the finger touches the *thir*tieth hazelnut . . . then the *for*tieth . . . the *fif*—when a holy goshamighty roar came kabooming through the Bottom like a freight druv by the Devil himself, or at least his next hottest hollerer!

Oh, what a roar! Oh oh oh! Not just loud, and long, but high and low and chilling and fiery all to once! The haint hair and the spider webs all froze stiff—it was *that chilling!*—while the springs boiled dry and the crabapples burned black from the hellheat of it! Even way up in Tricker's tall, tall cottonwood the leaves turned red and looked ready to fall still *weeks* before their time. Tricker was startled out of his snooze so sudden that he *stuck startled,* halfway between the ceiling and floor. And hung there, petrified, spraddle-eagled spellbound stiff in midair, with eyes big as biscuits and every hair stabbing straight out from him like quills on a puffed-up porcupine.

"*What* in the name of *sixty cyclones* was *that?*" he asks himself in a quakering voice; "a dream gone nightmare?"

He pinches his nose to see. The spellbind busts and Tricker drops hard to the floor: Thump!

"Huh," he puzzles, rubbing his nose and his knees; "it's like a dream with a little nightmare noise thrown in—like a plain old floating and flopping *dream* dream . . . except when you get real bumps it must be a real floor."

And right then it cut loose again: "ROAWRRR!" shaking the cottonwood from root to crown till a critter couldn't hardly stand. Tricker crawls cautious across the floor on his sore knees, and very cautious sticks his sore nose out, and very *very* cautious cranes over to look down into the clearing below. . . .

"Again I say ROOOAWRRR!"

The sound made Tricker's ears ring and his blood curdle, and the sight he saw made him wonder if he wasn't still dreaming, bumps or no.

"I'm BIG DOUBLE from the high wild ridges and I'm DOUBLE BIG and DOUBLE BAD and DOUBLE DOUBLE HONGRY AROARRR!"

It was a bear, a grizzly bear, so big and hairy and horrible it looked like the two biggest baddest bears in the Ozarks had teamed up to make one.

"Again I say HONGRY! And I don't mean lunchtime snacktime little hongry, I mean grumpy grouchy bedtime *big*-time hongry. I live big and I sleep big. When I hit the hay tonight I got six months before breakfast, so I need a supper the size of my sleep. I need a *big* bellyful of fuel and layby of fat to fire my fulltime furnace and stoke my six months snore a-roOOARRRR!"

When the bear opened his mouth, his teeth looked like stalactites in a cavern. When he swung his head around, his eyes looked like a doublebarrel shotgun going off at you.

"I ate the high hills bare as a bone and the foothills raw as a rock and now I'm going to eat the WHOLE! BOTTOM! and everybody in it ALL! UP!"

And with that gives another awful roar, and raises his paws high above his head, stretching till his toenails strain out like so many shiny sharp hayhooks, then rams down! sinking them claws clean outta sight into the ground. And with a evil snarl tears the very earth wide open like it was so much wrapping paper on his birthday present.

In the sundered earth, there was Charlie Charles the Woodchuck, his bedroom split half in two, his bedstead busted beneath him, and his bedspread pulled up to his quivering chin.

"Hey you," Charlie demands, in the bravest of voices the little fella can muster; "This is *my* hole. What are you doing breaking into my home and hole!"

"I'm BIG DOUBLE from the HIGH WILD HOLLERS and I'm loading the old larder up for one of my DOUBLE LONG WINTER NAPS," the bear snarls.

"Well just you go larding up someplace else, you high hills hollerer," Charlie snarls back. "This ain't *your* neck of the woods. . . ."

"When I'm hungry, it's ALLLL Big Double's neck of the woods!" says the bear. "And I AM HONNNGRY. I ate the HIGH

HILLS RAW and the FOOTHILLS BARE, and now I'm going to EAT! YOU! UP!"

"I'll run," says the woodchuck, glaring his most glittering glare.

"I can run *too*-oo," says the bear, glaring back, and with a blast turns poor Charlie's glitter to gloom. Charlie meets the bear's blistering stare a couple ticks more, then *out* from under the covers he springs and *out* across the Bottom he tears, ears laid low and tail heisted high and little feet hitting the ground sixty-six steps a second . . . *fast!*

But the big old bear with his big old feet merely takes one! two! three double big steps, takes Charlie over, snags him up, and swallers him down, hair hide and all!

High up in his hole Tricker blinks his eyes in amazement. "Yep!" He has to allow; "That booger truly *can* run. . . ."

The bear then walks down the hill to the big granite boulder by the creek where Longrellers the Rabbit lived. He listens a moment, his ear to the stone, then lifts one of those size fifty feet as high as his double big legs can hoist it, lifted like a huge hairy pile driver, and with one stomp turns poor Longrellers's granite fortress into a sandpile all over the rabbit's breakfast table.

"You Ozark clodhopper!" Longrellers squeals, trying to dig the sand out of one of his long ears with a wild parsnip; "This is *my* breakfast not yours. You got a nerve, come stomping down here into our Bottom, busting up our property and privacy. This ain't even your stomping grounds . . . !"

"I'm BIG DOUBLE and ALLLL the ground I stomp is mine. I ate the HIGH HILLS BARE and the FOOTHILLS CLEAN. I ate the woodchuck that run and now I'm going to EAT! YOU! UP!"

"I'll run," says the rabbit.

"I can run, *too*-oo," says the bear.

"I'll jump," says the rabbit.

"I can jump, *too*-oo," says the bear, grinning and glaring and wiggling his whiskers wickedly at the rabbit. Longrellers wiggles his whiskers back a couple of ticks, then *out* across the territory rips the rabbit, a cloud of sand boiling up from his heels like dust from a motorscooter scooting *up* a *steep dirt road.* But right after him comes the bear like a loaded logtruck coming down a steeper one. Longrellers is almost to the hedge at the edge of the Topple pasture when he gathers his long ears and elbows under him and leaps for the brambles, springing up into the air quick as a covey of quail flushing . . . fast and *high!*

But the big old bear with his big old legs springs after him like a flock of rocketships roaring, and takes the rabbit over in midair, and snaps him up, and swallers him down, ears elbows and everything.

"Good as his word, the big bum *can* certainly *jump*," admits Tricker, watching bug-eyed from his high bedroom window.

Next, the bear goes down to where Whittier Crick is dribbling drowsy by. He grabs the crick by its bank and with one wicked snap, snaps it like a bedspread and shakes Sally Snipsister the Martin clear out of her mud-burrow boudoir and her toenail polish, landing her hard in the emptied creekbed along with stunned mudpuppies and minnows.

"You backwoods bully!" Sally hisses; "You ridgerunning rowdy! What are you doing down out of your ridges ripping up our rivers? This ain't your play puddle———"

"I'm BIG DOUBLE and ANY puddle I please to play in is mine. I ate the RIDGES RAW and the BACK WOODS BALD. I ate the woodchuck and I ate the rabbit. And now I'm going to EAT! YOU! UP!"

"I'll run," says the martin.

"I can run, *too*-ooo," says the bear.

"I'll jump," says the martin.

"I can jump, *too*-ooo," says the bear.

"I'll climb," says the martin.

"I can climb, *too*-ooo," says the bear, and champs his big yellow choppers in a challenging chomp. Sally clicks back at him with her sharp little molars for a tick or two, then *off!* she shoots like the bullet out of a pistol. But right after her booms the bear like a meteor out of a cannon. Sally springs out of the creekbed like a silver salmon jumping, but the bear jumps after her like a flying shark. She catches the trunk of the cottonwood and climbs like a electric yo-yo whizzing up a wire. But the bear climbs after her like a jet-propelled elevator up a greasy groove, and takes her over, and snags her up, and swallers her down, teeth toenails and teetotal.

And then, it so happens, while the big bear is hugging to the trunk and licking his lips, he sees! that he is eye-to-eye with a little hole that is none other than the door of the bedroom of Tricker the Squirrel!

"Yessiree bob," Tricker has to concede. "You also can sure as shooting *climb*."

"WHO are YOU?" roars the bear.

"I'm Tricker the Squirrel, and saw it all. And there's just no two ways about it: I'm impressed. You may have been a little short-changed in the thinking department, but when it comes to running, jump-ing, and climbing you got double portions."

"And EAT!" roars the bear into the hole. "I'm BIG DOUBLE and I ate———"

"I know, I know," says Tricker, his fingers in his ears. "The ridges raw and the hills whole. I *heard* it all, too."

"NOW I'm going to EAT! YOU———"

"Gonna eat me up. I know," groans Tricker. "But first I'm gonna *run,* right?"

"And I'm gonna run, too," says the bear.

"Then I'm gonna *jump,*" says Tricker.

"And I'm gonna jump, too," says the bear.

"Then I'm gonna *drink some buttermilk,*" says Tricker.

"And I'm gonna drink buttermilk, too," says the bear.

"Then I'm gonna *climb,*" says Tricker.

"And I'm gonna climb, too," says the bear.

"And *then,*" says Tricker, smiling and winking and plucking at one of his longest whiskers dainty as a riverboat gambler with a sleeve full of secrets, "I am going to *fly!*"

This bamboozles the bear, and for a second he furrows his big brow. But everybody—even short-changed bears named Big Double—knows red squirrels can't fly, not even red squirrels named Tricker. "Well, then," says the bear, grinning and winking and plucking at one of his own longest, whitest whiskers with a big clumsy claw, "when *you* fly, I'll fly *too*-ooo."

"We'll *see*-eee about that," says Tricker, and without a word or wink more, reaches over to jerk the bear's whisker *clear out.* UhROAWRRR! roars the bear and makes a nab, but Tricker is *out* the hole and streaking down the treetrunk like a bolt of greased lightning with the bear thundering behind him, meaner and madder than ever. Tricker streaks across the Bottom toward the Topple farm with the bear storming right on his tail. When he reaches the milkhouse where Farmer Topple cooled his dairy products, Tricker jumps right through the win-dow. The bear jumps right through after him. Tricker hops up on the edge of a *gallon crock* and starts to guzzle up the cool, thick buttermilk like he hadn't had a sip of liquid for a month, but the bear knocks him aside and picks up the whole crock and sucks it down like he was a seven-year drought. Tricker then hops up to the brim of the *five-gallon* crock and starts to lap up the buttermilk. But the bear knocks him aside again, and hefts up the crock and guzzles it down. Tricker doesn't even bother hopping to the brim of the last crock, a *ten*-galloner. He just stands back dodging the drops while the bear heaves the vessel high, tips it up, and gradually guzzles it empty.

The bear finally plunks down the last crock; he wipes his chops and roars, "I'm BIG DOUBLE and I ate the HIGH HILLS———"

"I know; I know," says Tricker, wincing. "Let's skip the roaring and get right on to the last part. After I run, and jump, and drink buttermilk, then I *climb*."

"I climb, *too*," says the bear, belching.

"And I fly," says Tricker.

"I fly, t———*oo*," says the bear, hiccupping. So *back* out of the milkhouse jumps Tricker and off he goes, scorching back toward his cottonwood like a house afire, with the bear huffing behind him like a volcano. And *up* the tree he zooms with the bear's hot breath huffing closer and closer. Higher and higher and closer and closer till there's barely any tree left, then *out* into the fine fall air Tricker springs, like a little red leaf light on the wind. And—before the bear thinks better of it—*out* he springs hisself, like a ten-ton milk tanker over the edge of a sheer cliff.

"I forgot to mention," Tricker sings out as he grabs the leafy top of that first sun-touched hazelnut tree and hangs there, swinging and swaying: "I can also *trick*."

"ARGH!" his pursuer answers, plummeting past: "AAARRG———" till he splatters on the hillside like a ripe melon.

When the dust and debris clear back, Sally Snipsister wriggles up from the wrecked remains and says, "I'm out!"

Then Longrellers the Rabbit jumps up and says, "I'm out!"

Then Charlie Charles the Woodchuck pops up and says, "I'm out!"

"I," says Tricker, swinging high in the sunny branches where the hazelnuts are just about perfect, "was never in to *get* out."

And everybody laughed and the hazelnuts got more and more perfect and the buttermilk just rolled . . . down . . . the hill.

CHILDREN

BY

Jamaica Kincaid

ILLUSTRATED BY
ALLEN SHAWN

We are walking down the street without any shoes, picking up worms through the soles of our feet on purpose. We are walking down the street without any clothes, our hair done up in corkscrews. The sun is so hot on our bare skin, behind our ears we smell sour. As we go down the street, we pass many flowering flamboyant trees, their branches not swaying in the loud wind. As we go down the street, we pass many houses, some with the head of a bird nailed to the door, some with the foot of a bird nailed to the corner, some with people inside washing their hands in a calabash. We go down the street eating the remains of tamarind stew out of our hands. Our tongues make

a soft sound as they touch our brown palms. We are very happy. We go down the street and pass through some bramble bushes, which have prickles. We say, "Ouch!" and "Ouch!" and "Oh-oh." We emerge from the bramble bushes with the prickles onto the sand. We look at the blue sea, the blue sky, and the line where they meet, like the rim of a plate.

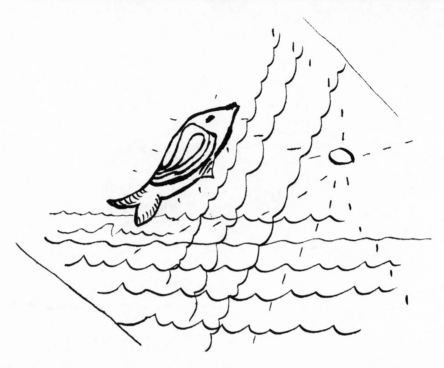

We climb into a navy blue boat named Pam. We are even more happy. To ourselves we sing different songs, songs that we have never heard or sung before. To ourselves we sing so hard, so hard, a tee la la, tee tee, tee la la, the roofs of our mouths tremble and hurt and turn red. We are so happy. We whisper sea greetings to each other, but because of the wind and the sound of the waves, what we say is lost.

We sail out on the water, far out on the water, to the plate rim to watch the flying fish. We watch them from a great distance, and from a great distance they look like blanks in sentences we have written in our school books. "Under the ——— ——— tree, the Village Smithy stands." Silver blanks on blue school-book paper. The flying fish fly back and forth, back and forth. They never do somersaults. They never take dives. They believe in the sun and deep water, floating weeds and living turtles, rocks that slide east on the floor of the sea, and yellow stripes, small spots, and the sound of a big steamer passing, but they do not believe in half moons. They are very beautiful and taste quite

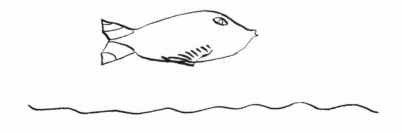

sweet, especially the roe. We love them and call out to them. We say, "Dear flying fish—love." But because of the wind and the sound of the waves, what we call out is lost.

Now the flying fish are swimming away. Now they are swimming away to the west. They swim away together in a wrinkled path. They never wave good-bye. We are sticky and cool. We put our arms around each other's necks, our cheeks on each other's cheeks. Our bodies bend with the movement of our navy blue boat named Pam, now this way, now that way, now that way, now this way. Now we are like sugar cane growing in a big cane field. Now we are like children. We are going back. We pass a crooked island. We pass an island and can smell molasses boiling. We pass an island where only black and horned pigs live. The black and horned pigs are playing, the black and horned pigs are happy, the black and horned pigs have never tasted an apple. We wave to the black and horned pigs, but they only look at us out of the

corners of their eyes. We pass a starfish—so pink, so pink. We pass many things whose names we do not know, and we think, "Look at that, just look at that." Not far from the shore we pass cockles. Their mouths are open and they are laughing—laughing and laughing. Soon they will look just as pretty on a bed of rice. On the shore, our heels leave cups in the sand. We lick the salt from each other's lips. We are smiling. We are walking home without any shoes, picking up worms through the soles of our feet on purpose.

SMALL KID TIME

BY
Maxine Hong Kingston

Ways to fly:

bad methods:

Pretty good methods:

no more than 10 ft.

watch for frays

pulley

Coincidences not to worry about:

Fly high sky I

I & English for 'me'

I Chinese for 'work'

How to make knives out of nails:

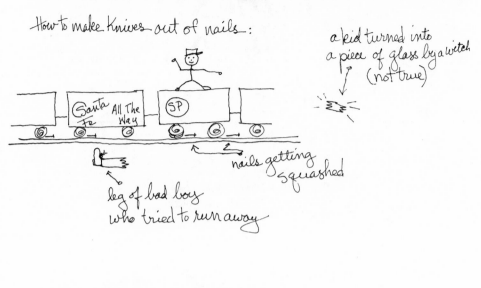

a kid turned into
a piece of glass by a witch
(not true)

nails getting
squashed

leg of bad boy
who tried to run away

People you don't see so much
when you grow up:

man with turtle
growing on his
back (not true)

Harry the Half-Man
Half-Woman
Handyman

bucket

spastic man
walking his
cat

michele

witch
ladies

a kid captured in
a bottle after
uncorking
an imp.
(not true)

Guarantee: I have been a
kid, and I have been a
grown up. Grown up
is better. (signed)
Maxine Hong Kingston

CHUCK CHUCK

BY

Galway Kinnell

Dug, dug,
Jug, jug,
Good yere and good luk,
With chuk, chuk, chuk, chuk!
— John Skelton

Back when the dairy business first started to fail in Caledonia County, which is located in the impoverished part of Vermont known as the Northeast Kingdom—why it's called that I'll get to later—the farmers on those remote and abruptly milkless farms did some experimenting with hybrids, trying to get a crop that could replace the cows. They took chaff of wheat and mixed it with shucks of corn, and they found the stuff crossfertilized and actually grew. What would they call it? The motel between Lyndonville and Burke is called the Lynburke Motel, and the one between Plainfield and Marshfield is called the Plainmarsh, or the Marshplain—I forget which, though I stayed there once. Using the same principles, the local nomenclators, which were just about everyone, combined chaff and shucks and came up with chuck. Before long a splendid crop of chuck was blooming all over Caledonia County.

But one day, alas, the woodchucks decided they liked chuck. They liked it so much, in fact, that they stopped chucking wood and devoted themselves entirely to chucking chuck. Children looked out their windows at the woodchucks—now called chuckchucks, of course —and said to their parents in worried voices, "How much chuck do you think a chuckchuck will chuck when a chuckchuck chucks chuck?" Their parents answered, "Children, I'm afraid he'll chuck all the chuck a chuckchuck chucks when a chuckchuck chucks chuck." That is exactly what happened. The chuckchucks reduced the fields recently blooming to stubble and Caledonia County reverted to its regular poverty.

But one day the county agent—whose name happened to be Chuck—came along carrying bags of seed. By imbalancing the hormones, he had managed to produce a kind of chuck which grew considerably faster than chuckchucks chuck. Now, up in this part of the world hormones were a new thing, but no one cared, for once again the fields were blooming. What did they call the new chuck? Using the linguistic precedents of beri-beri (from *beri*: weakness, the reduplication being intensive) and Baden-Baden (the reduplication giving you an idea of the low morals at the health spas of Europe), they called it chuckchuck—well, *Chuck's* chuckchuck, after the county agent who invented it. When parents tucked their little ones into bed they would chuck them—punningly—under the chin and tell them in satisfied voices, "He'll only chuck the bit of Chuck's chuckchuck a chuckchuck chucks when a chuckchuck chucks *Chuck's* chuckchuck."

All went well, until one day a chuckchuck was seen chucking its way with unusual swiftness through a field of Chuck's chuckchuck. He wasn't just chucking, he was superchucking. For, due to eating all those imbalanced hormones, a mutation had occurred in the chuckchucks' chucking mechanism. They now could chuck many times faster than previously. What to call this new chucking action? When children micturate a full stream they call it pee-pee, and when they want to emphasize the expulsive power of the verb *to do,* they call it doo-doo. Accordingly, it was said of these new chuckchucks that they chuckchucked. Families looked out and said, "How much of Chuck's chuckchuck will the chuckchucks chuckchuck when the chuckchucks *chuckchuck* Chuck's chuckchuck?" and they answered glumly, "Chuckchucks will chuckchuck all of Chuck's chuckchuck chuckchucks chuckchuck when chuckchucks chuckchuck Chuck's chuckchuck." Which was correct. Which was all of it. Caledonia County reverted to stubbly hay field and bare pasture, as it once had been and as it remains to this day, up in the back hills of the Northeast Kingdom.

I was going to say why it's called that. It *is* located in the northeast part of the state, and comparatively speaking, it *is,* or at least was, and certainly will not be, a kingdom. But that's not the reason. It's called that because, due to the failure of Chuck's chuckchuck, or looking at it positively, due to the success of the chuckchucks—now called woodchucks again, of course—an important name was required to raise the spirits of the men and women still living on those remote and milkless farms; a practice authorized by widespread linguistic precedent.

"ONCE UPON A TIME"

BY

Christopher Knowles

Once upon a time. There's something about typewriters. So when you tape on the tape recorder. You say Hello, how are you? And you tape records. So you record records. So you could record music. And you could record buy the Beatles. So than you have about horses to ride. So you have like radios televisions. So here's about to fly in the sky, Lucy In the Sky with diamonds. But dimes and diamonds. So here's Lucy In The Sky With Diamonds. So here's diamonds and dimes. So there's money to spend about food. 1 dollar, 5 dollars, 10 dollars, and 20 dollars. So there's quarters, dimes, need nickles, and pennies. So there's about the sun was hot, and the moon was cold. So there was the earth. So there was the universe. So here was about clocks. And it has 24 hours around the earth. So here's about the sun, moon, earth, universe, and clocks. So here's about the primary colors, red, yellow, and blue. So here's about the secondary colors. orange, green, and violet. So these cards to play with 52 cards. So the 13 hearts, 13 diamonds, 13 clubs, and 13 spades. So the 52 cards is to play cards. So you have

52 cards. So than it should be 52 cards to get the same number. So there's about them to play 13+13+13+13=52, So here is 13+13+13+13=52,. So here was about signals where the real fires were. So here's a signal on a map. So here was a signal where the real fire was. So there was about the speeds. So there was 10 miles per hour. So here's about where cars goes for 55 miles per hour. So than it should to be ware of animals. So here was about Allaigator, Bear, Camel, Dinosaur, Ellephant, and something like that. So than there's like something to do thing to feed the dogs. So to feed the cats. So there was to do like to feed cats and dogs. So here in Laundry Mats. So to do all sorts of clothes. So here we do to get where all the light clothes together, and to get the dark clothes together, So where to get where the clothes go into the washing machines, and so to put into the driers. So there would be some of the white clothes. And than will have 6 colors. So here's red, orange, yellow, green, blue, and violet. So here's a rainbow. So there's like to have about for beds to make with sheets, blankets, and spreads, ②

And then I aneve. So then I and eye have let the I an eye. But all of the eyes and I were beautiful. So than when have something to do like than. So here is something to do about paintings. When painters paints the walls white. So than it should have be clean. So than it should be sure to know to be clean. So the toaster to heat up the toast. So there would be some where to have english muffins to say where could it be some where to be where of the rainbow. It has red, orange, yellow, green, blue, and violet. So there the universe and the sun and the moon and the earth. Than it should have something to do to be the delicous cake to have. So than it should have like salad vegetable and chicken. So here we go to do about them, so here's meat, So ever since it should be ware of animals. Happy Ever After The End. ③

THE FIRST BEST FRIENDS

BY

John Knowles

Long ago a man was alone in the wilderness. Wild beasts were all around him, thick forests, black night, and from time to time howling storms. He felt very strange and very alone.

Out of the thick woods toward his firelight came something with shining dark eyes and ears up at the alert.

Another wild beast, he thought, and reached for his spear. The beast stopped, but kept on staring at him with those shining eyes, ears rigid.

The man thought: Maybe that wild beast is not going to attack me after all. What shall I do?

He lowered his spear and waited.

So did the beast. And then the alert ears slowly sank back onto the sleek head, and the beast, step by slow step, came into the circle of firelight.

From a safe distance, about five feet, he began to sniff in the direction of the man.

He's asking a question, the man thought. "Come here," he then said, surprised at himself.

The beast stood there, eyes shining, ears laid back against his head, sniffing eagerly.

"Come here," the man repeated.

Very slowly and deliberately, the first dog came forward to join the man.

And then the man no longer felt strange and no longer was alone.

LULLABYE

BY
Ruth Krauss

speak to me your darkness
tell me your memory and storms
tell me your darkness and storms
your rivers that are bad and red tell me

sleep little one sleep

a flight of white buildings (they happen)
the green hills the poppies (they happen)
and one black cat wandering
your darkness your rivers

sleep little one sleep

PLACE OF HIGH MOUNTAINS

BY

Julius Lester

Long ago and far away, there was a land where the leaves on trees shimmered like iridescent green whispers, the blue of the sky trembled like hummingbird wings, and, like billows of cumulus clouds measuring infinity, mountains stood in every direction.

The land was called Place of High Mountains, and none who lived there ever thought of leaving. If anyone knew of a world beyond, he did not say and no one thought to ask.

There was one, however, who wondered. On green sky evenings a boy named Radhikhi would stop in the midst of playing with the other children and stare into the mountains.

"What's the matter, Radhikhi?" someone would ask.

"Huh?" he'd reply distractedly. "Oh, nothing. Go on and play without me."

Radhikhi's parents saw and, with distress, remembered the prophecy of the Old One: "A child will be born whose stares at the mountains will be so intense and serious it will seem that he or she is trying to see through to the other side. Such a child is to be watched closely. That child will be the Wise One." But the prophecy concluded with chilling words. "And wisdom often brings danger."

Radhikhi's mother, Carsama, did not understand how wisdom could be dangerous. She imagined wisdom to be like the giant trees of the forests, which were as mountains unto themselves, silent with the knowledge of ancient silence.

But why think of such things? Her son couldn't be the one of the prophecy. Probably working in the fields tired him more than it did other children and that was why he withdrew. One day soon she would hear him laugh and see his eyes bright like the streams when they at last broke free from white sky ice.

Carsama and her husband, Barindi, watched as their son ceased playing altogether, and in the late afternoon, when the last meal had been eaten and people visited with each other around the meadowed forest clearing where they lived, Radhikhi would slip into the forest as quickly and silently as the sun vanished from the sky at day's end. The disquietude of his wondering was like gnats biting the soft flesh of the peace everyone had known.

Barindi wondered why it should be his son. Obviously some flaw in his wife had produced this child. After all, she had had moonshine hair when she gave birth, and who'd ever heard of such a thing. It was unnatural as with this child.

One evening during the days of parti-colored sky, while green sky lingered on the mountains like a soft kiss, Barindi and Carsama sat around the fire before their pine-boughed sleeping hut. Dotted around the clearing like flowers were the fires of the others in the community. Radhikhi came out of the forest, crossed the clearing slowly, and sat before his parent's fire.

"Do the mountains go on forever?" he asked with twelve-year-old abruptness.

The moment had come, and Barindi and Carsama, hoping that it would not, had lulled themselves into being unprepared. Carsama waited for her husband to speak and when it was clear that he would not, she answered, without knowing what she would say. "No, Radhikhi." And as she spoke, she knew: Prophecies would be fulfilled. It did not matter who was chosen to fulfill them.

"And what is beyond the mountains?" Radhikhi wanted to know, as if the answer to his first question was obvious.

"Why all these questions?" came Barindi's voice, hot and burning like the fires that sometimes went through the forests.

"No, Barindi!" Carsama was shocked that she had spoken so forcefully. "No!" she repeated. "It is out of our hands now. You must tell him what he needs to know. The moment was prepared long before."

The man sighed, gazing into the fire. At length, he nodded and said in a voice as limp as rain-soaked grass, "Beyond the mountains is the World Below."

Radhikhi felt the pain-infused words, but persisted. "Is it as wonderful there as it is here?"

Carsama spoke. "We don't know. It wasn't when we left."

"What do you mean?" Radhikhi asked excitedly. "You used to live in the World Below? Tell me about it. What is it like?"

"It is a place where people hate each other," Barindi said, "and especially people who look like us."

Radhikhi laughed. "What kind of a place is that? Why would people want to live in a place where they hated each other? That doesn't make sense, father."

Barindi slammed a stick into the fire, causing sparks to jump dangerously. Radhikhi moved back, afraid, and shivered beneath the coldness in his father's voice: "Who said the answers to your foolish questions were going to make sense? Your laughter is a sign of your ignorance. The first sign of knowledge is knowing one's ignorance."

Radhikhi accepted the rebuke. "You are right, father. I am ashamed."

Barindi grunted and then continued. "The World Below is a place of great and continual suffering, a suffering which has so distorted those who live there that they would destroy Place of High Mountains, if they knew of it. Fortunately, we are safe.

"Listen, child. I will tell you one of the ancient stories."

Radhikhi smiled and moved closer to the fire. He loved the ancient stories, especially the words with which they all began.

"In the beginning," Barindi intoned, "the blackness. The blackness was Wawara. Our people were created in the color of Wawara.

"For many, many years there was one world and that was the World Below. We were at peace with ourselves and each other, for we were the color of the darkness, the color of Wawara.

"Then, there came a new people, a people who were not the color of Wawara. These people were of no color and hideous they were to look upon."

Radhikhi shuddered, trying to imagine them.

"Our ancestors felt sorry for them. How awful to be without the color of Wawara, they thought. Surely, Wawara had sent these people to be taken care of, to be taught the mystery of the blackness which is Wawara.

"But the people-of-no-color mistook their ignorance for knowledge. They laughed at our people for being black like Wawara. They laughed at mystery. They warred upon our people, killing many and forcing the rest to work for them.

"Slowly, as time passed, many of our people forgot that they were the color of Wawara and they ceased living in the darkness where nothing is known and nothing is made known. They carried Wawara's color only in their flesh.

"A few, however, remembered and they had the gift of seeing. They could see who were only skin of Wawara's color and who was marked within by Wawara's color. When they saw one of the latter, they took him into the darkness and instructed him or her in the ancient ways. So it was with your mother and me. When the instruction was finished, the person was sent here, to Place of High Mountains.

"Once in each generation, a person from here is chosen to return to the World Below to seek new ones to instruct. It has been some time since anyone has come to us from the World Below. I fear that there are no longer any people remaining there who are of the color of Wawara."

Radhikhi did not know how to hear all he had heard, but he longed to be the next one selected to go to the World Below.

"No," Barindi said when he was asked. "The one selected never asks. He or she is chosen, either by Wawara or The Circle. We do not know. We awake one morning and someone is not here. Then we know. By the fact that you have asked, you will not be chosen."

Radhikhi could not hide his disappointment. "That's not fair," he pouted.

"Only Wawara knows what is fair and not fair. What happens in the World Below is not your concern or mine. It is enough to know that the people-of-no-color cannot harm us here."

"But why not?" Radhikhi wanted to know. "Can't they look up and see Place of High Mountains and come kill us?"

Barindi shook his head. "Place of High Mountains can be seen only by those who know blackness as Wawara. In the World Below, people look up here and see only the sky."

"I don't understand."

"Place of High Mountains cannot be seen by looking. It can only be lived in and it exists only to us who live here. There are many living throughout these mountains in the same way that we do. All of us create Place of High Mountains by our living."

Radhikhi laughed nervously. "I still do not understand."

"Good. Understanding was a disease of the people-of-no-color. We do not need it here, especially when there is so little to understand. When you make your journey into the darkness, then you will know that which is to be known and can never be understood."

"What do you mean?"

"You were born here. Those born here acquire knowledge of Wawara's blackness in the Twelve Rituals when they are sixteen. Some complete the rituals, however, with no greater knowledge of darkness than before. They disappear before our eyes and suddenly find themselves in the World Below with no memory of Place of High Mountains. Those who make their journey well join the rest of us who daily create Place of High Mountains."

"That means I must wait four years."

Carsama shook her head. "No, Radhikhi. I think your journey has already begun. Tomorrow we will report what has happened tonight to The Circle."

"The Circle?" he said, awed. "But why? All I did was ask a few questions."

"Questions no child ever asked before. It must be reported."

2

Place of High Mountains was divided into twelve regions of four mountains each. Over the life of each region presided a member of The Circle. They were the guardians of the ancient ways and the interpreters of the sayings of the Old One. They also performed the planting and harvesting rituals and others so secret that they were known to none outside The Circle. How you became one of The Twelve was not known to Barindi and Carsama, but who would want to join? How could one have joy in his or her life if they were the guardian of the ancient ways?

The following morning Carsama took her son across the clearing and through the woods until they came to a small hut. His mother made him wait outside while she went in.

Some time passed before she emerged and with her, to Radhikhi's surprise, was Lutici. She was one of The Twelve! But he had worked beside her in the fields and she'd even taught him a game once. He wished he could go back and tell his friends. Wouldn't they be surprised? They'd often tried to guess who among the adults belonged to The Twelve, as that knowledge was kept secret from the children. No one had ever thought of Lutici. She was not much older than they, or so she looked.

His amazement left him momentarily unaware of his mother standing over him.

"Radhikhi?" It was his mother.

"What is it, mother? What's wrong?"

"Lutici will decide what you are to do from now on."

"I don't understand." He knew, however, that it would be a long while before he saw his mother again, and he started to cry.

"The gift of crying is a precious one," came a voice with a strength so soft that it comforted him even as it quieted his fear. Lutici stretched out her hand and he took it.

Carsama saw and knew that he was no longer hers. But had he ever been, she wondered, walking away.

Radhikhi turned to watch his mother, but Lutici gave him a gentle pull and he turned. She dropped his hand and walked swiftly into the forest.

"Where're we going?"

Lutici did not answer or acknowledge that she had heard, but quickened her pace. They walked through the day, down one mountain and up another. Very quickly, he lost any idea of where his home was. Finally, toward evening, they climbed another mountain and Lutici stopped in a clearing just below the summit. "You will stay the night here. Gather wood for the evening fire."

When he'd finished, she asked, "You know how to make a fire, of course?"

Radhikhi nodded.

"Make one. Then sleep. I will return in the morning by the time you awake. And don't be afraid. You are safe here. This is a very special place. Sleep well." Without waiting for a response, she merged with the darkness and was gone.

The next morning when he awoke, he was startled to see twelve people staring at him. The Circle! There were eight women and four men, he noted as he sat up and looked around. They looked so ordinary. He had always imagined The Twelve to look special. These people didn't. Some were young, like Lutici, and others were old. But none of them looked like they could make trees fly through the air, as one of his friends had said a member of The Circle could.

"Sit up straight," a voice came from behind him.

Radhikhi started and sat erect.

"Now, what is it you wish to know?"

He wanted to turn and see who spoke, but her voice held him as firmly as a strong hand on his neck. "I don't want to know any-thing."

"Quickly, please. You asked questions. What were they?"

"Oh, those. They were nothing. Just as if there was anything beyond Place of High Mountains, and what it was. That's all. And anyway, my parents answered those for me."

"That is unimportant," came a man's voice from his right.

"The question is always its own answer," said a young man in front of him.

"Were you satisfied with your parent's answers?" He recognized Lutici's voice.

"Well," he began slowly, "not really. They told me about the World Below." He laughed. "I just can't believe that there's a world where people hate each other. That doesn't make sense."

No one spoke. Radhikhi wondered if he'd said something wrong. So he sat and waited. The sun climbed the side of the mountain and on to the sky. Still no one spoke. The sun reached the top of the sky and began its slow fall toward the bottom and still no one spoke.

Radhikhi could not know it, but The Circle conversed in the ancient way—in silence and without words. His simplicity, his naiveté in not knowing how extraordinary his questions were, his possession of the gift of crying were all signs. But what were they to do with him? There was nothing in the sayings of the Old One to guide them. They couldn't know how to prepare the child, because they didn't know what to prepare him for.

Because they didn't know, they decided that they must teach him everything they knew. What he needed to know would be decided in the Darkness when it came time for him to take his measure of it.

Throughout the day of parti-colored sky, from dawn until dusk, The Twelve taught Radhikhi. He not only learned all the sayings and prophecies of the Old One and the many rituals, but even the secret learning known only to The Circle. He learned the stars and the phases of the moon. He learned the names and uses of everything that grew. He learned how to make rain, ride a wisp of wind, catch a thunderbolt, and how to hold thunder in his belly. (He loved learning that.) Finally, nothing remained for him to learn except Darkness, and Darkness taught itself.

"It is time," Lutici announced one evening. They were seated around the evening fire. Radhikhi sat in the center. Lutici stood behind him, holding a torch over his head. She snapped her fingers and the evening fire was extinguished. "You must go now. There is no place for you among us. You know all that we know, but there is something Darkness will teach you that we are not to learn. There is no place for such a one as you among us. We know the ancient ways. Perhaps the time has come when the ancient ways will not suffice. Maybe that is why you have come. Darkness will teach you."

Tiny pieces of white sky began falling, fragile and cold. "Will you leave me the torch?" Radhikhi asked.

"No! The way cannot be found if we can see it. You must go. Go!" She swung the torch around his head four times and then flung it high into the falling white sky where it suddenly went out. Before Radhikhi could cry aloud at being dropped into darkness, he heard footsteps moving away.

He sat where he was, enclosed by the hard darkness. Though he knew how to make fire now by clapping his hands, how to ride the wind and hold a mountain in his hand, he was wise enough to cry when he was afraid. Ashamed, he cried and cried, hoping his tears would mollify the darkness and it would pity him and speak its truth. The darkness would not yield. Radhikhi plunged into it, cursing it for being; he tripped over logs, stumbled into trees, and fell in the new snow. The darkness was implacable and Radhikhi screamed into its throat and the darkness spat his screams back into his own ears, for the darkness was deaf. Finally, the sun, with its pale white-sky light, broke free from Darkness's grasp and Radhikhi could dimly see a cave a short distance away. He stumbled into it and trembled into sleep.

The sun was climbing down the farther side of the sky when he awoke, but the darkness had invaded the day. As he stood in the mouth of the cave staring at the sun, staring at the snow glistening in the light, he knew that it was a day which he would have called bright at an earlier time. How could the darkness overwhelm the bright? Then, looking at the trees, at the rise and fall of the land, listening to a silence so deep that it hurt his ears, he called the darkness by name—Loneliness.

He smiled and the darkness softened, warming him. He stood, savoring himself, and then, noticing the claw of night closer to grabbing the sun, he gathered wood for his evening fire and clapping his hands, watched it flame into warmth and light. He walked outside the cave and, holding his arm high above his head, swung it around four times and before his arm dropped to his side, a large hawk with wings like storm clouds came out of the forest and landed at his feet. He locked the hawk's eyes with his and fixed the image of a rabbit in its mind. The huge bird ruffled its feathers as if it were resisting or preparing to take flight, but Radhikhi's gaze on the hawk was like that bird's own talons on the rabbit it now spread its wings to seek and kill. Radhikhi watched the bird quickly become smaller than a star against the sky, but having given the bird his own will he was surprised to find himself staring down on the mountains from Place Where Clouds Are Born. He felt the upper currents of air holding him with the strength of a log. Then he saw—brown against the snow, as still as a fallen pine cone—and he plunged like a bolt of lightning from a cloudless sky. His talons sank deep through the rabbit's fur and flesh and into its heart even as he began beating his great wings toward the sky and back to the cave. Radhikhi watched the sky for the bird's return even as he looked down from the sky at himself squatting at the mouth of the cave.

The hawk laid the killed rabbit before Radhikhi. Radhikhi waited a moment until he saw only the bird and not also himself through the bird. "Thank you," he greeted the hawk. "You served me well. Your name from now on is Jopha. We will journey together."

The hawk blinked its lidless eyes, flew to a high limb of a nearby tree, and settled itself.

The days came and went and Radhikhi sat in loneliness until it was separate from the darkness. He was surprised that loneliness did not become bright when it ceased being confused with darkness. But it was the color of stone and just as hard. There was no joy in it, but neither was there sadness or fear now. Perhaps it was this he had been sent to learn.

More days passed without event, and he concluded that, indeed, this was his learning. He decided to return to the mountain where he'd lived, if he could find it. He was disappointed, though. Certainly something more momentous was to have happened.

The following morning he awoke, and though he told himself to return, he could not. What was there to return to? Being the son of Barindi and Carsama? That wasn't possible now. He knew more than any twelve-year-old and adult, too. He knew as much as The Twelve, and yet, he couldn't be with them. Lutici had been right. There was no place for him. It was then he looked up to see Darkness walling the mouth of the cave and he knew a loneliness more wide than a starless sky.

He shuddered violently, uncontrollably. He shuddered as if his body were being assailed by the Four Brother Winds. Jopha sensed danger and his opportunity and took flight. Radhikhi tried to call the hawk back, but Darkness filled his mouth with sand and he fell back into the cave.

He lay on the floor of the cave and stared at Darkness. Time passed. He did not sleep. He stared at Darkness and the longer he stared the less his body shuddered until finally, it was still. Radhikhi lay with the quietness, his eyes on Darkness, neither challenging or questioning it, never beseeching or cursing it. He stared (days? months? years?) until Darkness parted the folds of its robe and Radhikhi stood and walked into It.

Darkness was not before him now but all around and he turned slowly, around and around, rubbing the blackness over his own. In the beginning, blackness, he remembered. And he dove—arrow-swift, arrow-silent—into It. Darkness rippled along his body as tender as water. It lapped at his lips and tickled his thighs. He swam deeper and further and Darkness was as smooth as flower petals on his cheeks. He laughed and Darkness laughed; he shouted; Darkness shouted. Crying with joy, Radhikhi flung his body into Darkness and Darkness held and caressed him.

Time passed. Radhikhi sat with Darkness and watched the white sky drain away as the sun gathered strength. The snow melted. The rains came. Radhikhi sat with Darkness. Green sky looked down upon him and from it, one afternoon, Radhikhi watched a speck moving toward him. Closer and closer it came until it was before him, laying a rabbit at his feet.

Then Darkness spoke: "It is time."

Radhikhi nodded. "Yes. It is time." He stood and walked away.

3

Time passed. Radhikhi did not count the seasons of white sky which came and went. They were many. He and Jopha traveled the mountains when they chose or stayed at one place. It did not matter. He accepted that there was only the Unknown and it must be followed. In the beginning, blackness. And was there ever a time which was not the beginning? He had found what he had been expelled to learn, but having learned it, it was unteachable. That was part of Darkness, too—knowing that which only you can know. Even The Circle could not understand. Their duty was to tend the known. His was to suckle the Unknown.

He was not surprised, therefore, when he saw her that day. Sitting beside a stream, Jopha on the limb of a nearby tree, he looked up to see her walk out of the forest on the other side. Her skin was the color of white sky.

She saw him and stopped, not knowing what to do. He wanted to wait and see what she would do. But he didn't need to do that. Neither did he need to speak to her. Therefore he chose.

"Are you hungry?" he asked.

She nodded, afraid.

"Join me. The water isn't deep."

She hesitated for a long while, but Radhikhi's attention was on the stream. It was not his to care if she crossed over. Seeing that he left her alone, she waded the stream and sat down near him. He took no notice, concentrating on the stream still, peering deeply into it until he fixed a fish with his eyes. Then, slipping his hand into the water and grasping the fish, he pulled it out slowly.

"How did you do that?" the girl asked.

Radhikhi shrugged. "It is nothing to take notice of."

She ate and was quickly asleep. Radhikhi stared at her. So. A person-of-no-color has come to Place of High Mountains. What does that mean?

It was the following afternoon when she awoke and after she'd eaten the rabbit he'd cooked for her, she asked, "Where am I?"

"You don't know?" He was surprised.

She shook her head.

"How did you come here?"

She shook her head again in confusion. "I don't know. I went to sleep one night and the next thing I knew I was walking out of those trees and saw you."

"You know more," he said simply. "Perhaps you are here because you wanted to be."

"What do you mean? How could I be somewhere and not know where I am?"

He laughed softly. "Ah, that is easy."

She thought for a moment, then laughed, too.

"What have you wanted more than anything else?" he asked.

She looked at him seriously. "Why do you ask?" she hedged.

"So you can hear yourself say it."

His words stilled her and she lowered her eyes. "Why do I feel shame?"

He did not answer, but allowed the silence to hold them as if they were just born children. She did not dare look at him or even wonder why she cried. It was enough to feel the emptiness filling her.

Now that it was time to return, Radhikhi knew the way. The girl walked beside him and many days passed before he stopped at the edge of the familiar clearing. He did not pause long, as he was eager to give the girl to Lutici and be on his way.

They stepped into the clearing and immediately the silence sharpened. Radhikhi stopped. Everyone was staring at the girl. He felt his powers surging through him and wanted to wave his arm and set the forest ablaze around them. He wanted to clench his fist and have the sky throw down stones. But he calmed himself, because he could not use his powers against people. If he did, Place of High Mountains would be destroyed.

"Where is Lutici?" he asked, breaking the stillness.

Even as he spoke, he saw her moving toward him from the far side of the clearing. "What is this?" she asked sharply.

"I have brought her to you for instruction."

"But she is a person-of-no-color."

He nodded. "I have brought her to you for instruction."

Lutici stared at Radhikhi, but he did not fall to his knees as others did from that stare. Instead, she found herself unsteady because he did not even need to resist her. "No one can come here who has not already been instructed." Her voice was loud and angry and it became even louder as she thought she understood. "You have been to the World Below and have somehow managed to bring her back."

Her words released everyone from silence and the sound of their anger was like the rumble of distant thunder. The girl moved closer to Radhikhi and he reached for her hand, holding it firmly.

"No, Lutici. I have not been to the World Below."

Lutici laughed harshly. "Then how did she get here? Can you explain that?"

Radhikhi could not, because he knew the grace of the Unknown. It was then that he understood the prophecy of the Old One and what it was that he, Radhikhi, had been chosen to do. Tears glazed his eyes.

"Well, say something, Radhikhi," Lutici prodded him.

"I have brought her to you for instruction."

"It cannot be done. There is nothing in the ancient teachings about instructing a person-of-no-color. Persons-of-no-color are not allowed in Place of High Mountains. That is the ancient teaching! She must be destroyed. You have betrayed the teaching and the prophecy. Your journey into darkness was abortive. Unfortunately, I cannot destroy you, for your power is equal to mine. However, I will call The Circle together as soon as I am done with the girl. Your power is not equal to the power of twelve." Lutici turned away and called out, "Take the girl! Bind her! Who has the sharpest cutting stone?"

Radhikhi was not surprised when he heard his father's voice shout, "I!" He heard screams and sobbing and recognized his mother. Then came another scream from the girl as people pulled her away from him. She struggled, reaching out for Radhikhi. He gazed at her and Darkness rushed into him. He spread Darkness over her like a cloak and nodded to her to take it around her shoulders. She did so and was quiet.

Radhikhi watched as the girl was bound and left alone at the center of the clearing. She looked at him and he at her. He went deeper into Darkness and stilled his desire to save her, even as his father stepped forward and hammered the cutting stone into the girl's heart.

There was only the sound of Carsama crying as Radhikhi walked forward, untied the girl, and picked up her body. Holding her in his arms, he looked around and said simply, "It is done." One by one, as if they were flames on candles being snuffed out, the people began disappearing. He knew that on each of the forty-eight mountains at that moment, people were being returned to the World Below, including The Twelve of The Circle.

Lutici looked around and, too late, understood. " 'And wisdom often brings danger,' " she said, repeating the ancient words of the prophecy. "But it did not say to whom or in what form. There is nothing in the ancient teachings about instructing persons-of-no-color, because that was the teaching you were to bring from Darkness." And with tears on her face, she vanished, too.

Radhikhi stood in the clearing, the body of the girl resting easy in his arms. Only his mother remained. That helped. He turned away from her, however, and stared at Darkness. Darkness, tears on Its face, smiled, and Radhikhi walked in and lay the girl down.

He would stay there for a while with his sorrow, as deep and penetrating as Darkness. Then one day he would leave and there would be an afternoon when he sat beside a stream, Jopha high in a tree nearby, and out of the woods someone would come. He would bid them to cross over and, taking no further notice, would peer deeply into the stream until he fixed a fish with his eyes.

WINTERPIG

BY
Denise Levertov

At the quick of winter
moonbrightest
snowdeepest

we would set out.
I'd run up my ramp
into the pickup,

we'd rattle and shake
two midnight miles
to the right hill.

Then on foot,
slither and struggle
up it—

they'd
ready their sled
and toboggan down

and I'd
put down my nose and
spread my ears and

tear down beside them,
fountains of snow
spurting around me:

I and my Humans
shouting, grunting,
the three of us

wild with joy,
just missing
the huge maples.

Yes, over and over
up to the top of the
diamond hill—

the leanest, the fastest,
most snow-and-moon-and-midnight-bewitched
pig in the world!

AUTHOR'S NOTE: *This poem is from a series about a real pig, Sylvia, who is still alive and well in western Massachusetts where she owns her own apple tree. She is house-trained and used to spend a lot of time indoors with her Humans when she was young and small.*

STARTING YOUR OWN *MAGAZINE*

BY

Denise Levertov

When I was a child my family formed a "Fellowship of Goodwill." We used to meet about four times a year—spring, summer, autumn, winter—and each of us would tell something of what he or she had experienced and accomplished in the months since the last meeting, and what we hoped to do in the immediate future. My mother or my oldest sister would be Secretary for the meeting, and "keep minutes"—do you know what that means? It's nothing to do with seconds and hours, the measurement of time. It means writing down what is said at a meeting, and what is voted on, and how the vote goes. Then, at the next meeting these "minutes" are read aloud (or copies of them are handed out to everyone) to remind people of decisions and promises they made, as a group, last time.

We used to discuss problems—like, where should we try to go for the summer vacation, inland where we could take long country walks, or to the seaside where we could bathe and make sandcastles? Or, should my sister go on taking violin as well as piano lessons, or was it too expensive? Did she really want to play the violin as much as she wanted to play the piano? Or, was I old and sensible enough to go up to town by myself (we lived just outside London, England)? My mother thought yes, my father was nervous about it. So we all discussed the pros and cons—and it was decided that I could do it.

Then, part of each meeting was a kind of "show and tell" time. Each person would tell a story, or read a poem they'd either found or written. We really had a lot of fun, and it put everybody—grown-ups and children—on an equal basis. Sometimes we would have a guest, some special friend, from outside the family. Out of this grew the idea for a Family Magazine, of which I became the editor.

What I used to do was to ask each person in the family, and any friends who seemed to be a good bet, for a contribution—a story, a poem, an article, or a drawing. I tried to think of subjects they knew about. For instance, my father knew lots of little anecdotes and fables about the Jewish mystics of the eighteenth and nineteenth centuries, which he used to tell sometimes—so I got him to write some of them down. My mother knew long tales about the people of the little towns in Wales where she grew up; those were ideal! Someone we knew had a pet parrot—it would be interesting to have an article on Polly, and parrots in general. My sister was good at music—she could contribute a song, or something about the life of a composer, for instance. I don't remember what I contributed myself—I was shy about my poems, so I think I must have supplied colored drawings. I also used to find curious items in old books, and copy them out.

All this was before xerox machines were invented, so this magazine appeared in an edition of one! Some of it was read aloud at the meeting, and it was also passed around for people to read to themselves at leisure, and see the pictures.

Maybe some of you would enjoy adapting the idea. You could get contributors to make carbon copies or xeroxes of their writings. Colored pictures present a problem; there are special xerox machines now that do reproduce colors, but they are expensive to use. But perhaps you could ask for line drawings that would be easy to xerox.

For contributions, you might reach out further than I used to: For instance, instead of making it basically a family magazine, you could make it a *block* magazine if you live in the city. Let's suppose you have a few stores on your block—a newspaper store, a grocery, and a tailor and cleaner's. How about doing interviews with the people who run them (or asking them to write down something about how they became tailors or grocers or whatever)? Let's say the lady next door has beautiful window boxes—okay, how about an article on window gardening? Do you have a hobby, or a sport you especially like? And what about the young man four doors down who practices the trumpet? Where did your father and mother live when they were children, and what kind of fun did they have? And your uncle who went to India with the Peace Corps—what was that like? The point is, everyone has *something* interesting to tell about if you can get them to—and those who refuse to *write* their ideas or experiences down might be persuaded to let you interview them. (Maybe you could borrow a tape recorder for the interviews.)

Stories, poems, riddles, jokes—oh, and dreams! Do you remember yours? Write them down as soon as you wake up, and you'll find you remember more and more. Some dreams don't seem very interesting to anyone but the dreamer, but some are like wonderful fairy tales.

If the idea of starting your own magazine, by and for the people you live among, appeals to you, I'm sure you will get lots of ideas of your own about how to do it and make it interesting. I'll just make two more suggestions: (1) If you are not going to produce a large number of copies, but just, say, five or ten, it would be possible to stick photos into them, i.e., to ask someone who's taken a good photo to have five or ten prints made of it. And (2) Do you know much about the history of the place where you live—a little town in the country, perhaps, or a city neighborhood? There are two good ways to find out more. One is to ask the librarian at your public library to help you find material on this. When I was about twelve years old, I managed to get permission to go into the Archives in the basement of our public library, and look at old maps and documents. It was exciting! The other way—though it doesn't take you as far back in history—is to find some old people who have lived in the same place all of their lives, and ask them what it was like when they were young. If they have good memories and can describe things well, this can be fascinating. You can begin to imagine trees and grass where now there are tall buildings, and horse-drawn buses and milk wagons where now the cars zoom along the freeway. Quite a trip!

I hope you have a good time editing your magazines. Good Luck!

COYOTE SHOWS HOW HE CAN LIE

BY

Barry Lopez

Coyote came into a group of camps. The men were all sitting around. They knew Coyote was always telling lies.

The men called Coyote over. "Coyote," they said, "you are the biggest liar we've ever known."

"How do you know I lie?"

"Oh, you always make trouble and then you lie. You get away with things like that. You are very good at it. Why don't you teach us how to lie so we can lie successfully too?"

"Well," said Coyote, "I had to pay a big price for that power. I learned it from my enemy."

"What did you pay?"

"One horse. But it was my best buffalo horse, with a fine bridle."

"Is that all?"

"Yes."

They did not think that was much, for in those days there were plenty of horses. One man brought out a fine white buffalo horse, his best.

"Yes," said Coyote. "This is a good-looking horse. This is the kind I mean. It was with a horse like this that I paid for my power."

Then Coyote said, "Let me try the horse. If he doesn't buck, I'll explain my power."

They agreed and Coyote got up on the horse. Coyote had never been on a horse before and he dug in with his claws to hold on. The horse began to buck.

"Oh! This horse needs a blanket, that is the trouble," said Coyote.

They put a blanket on the horse.

But Coyote's claws were sharp and they went through the blanket and the horse jumped again.

"Oh! He wants something more over his back. He wants a good saddle on."

So they got a good saddle and helped Coyote put it on the horse. Coyote got on again and then turned his head as though he were listening for something.

"That is my power speaking," he said. "That voice tells me he wants a whip, too."

They gave him one.

He said, "I'm going around now and try this horse to see if he still bucks. I'll come right back and tell you about it."

He rode off a little way and then turned around and shouted back, "This is the way I lie. I get people to give me horses and blankets and saddles and other fine things." Then he rode away.

The people couldn't do anything about it. Coyote went home and showed his wife what he had.

"Look at my fine horse," he said. "I took it away from an enemy out on the plains. It was some fight."

But Coyote did not know how to take care of the horse. When he got off, the horse walked away, back to its owner.

WHIRLWIND WOMAN

BY

Barry Lopez

Coyote was traveling. He met Whirlwind Woman, who sometimes crawled along in the shape of a caterpillar. "Get out of my way," said Coyote. Whirlwind Woman went away and the dust spun around in a circle. Soon Coyote came on her again. "I don't want you, Whirlwind Woman, go away!" She whirled off. Again he came on her and he said, "There are some people I like to have near me, but I do not like you." She flew off but she came back in his path as he went along the river.

By now Coyote was beginning to like her. "I want you for my sweetheart," he said to her.

"No," she answered. "I am used to moving all the time. I do not like to stay in one place. I travel. I would not be the wife for you."

"You are just like me!" insisted Coyote. "I am always traveling. I even have the same power you do." Coyote began to run and turn and spin around, throwing dirt up in the air with his feet and trying to raise a lot of dust. Whirlwind Woman refused to look over where he was. Coyote began spinning around again. He spun and kicked up the dirt and jumped up and down stirring up more dust and kicking it up higher.

"There, you can see I have the same power. You're the wife for me. I'll take you now." He grabbed her and tried to lie down on top of her.

Whirlwind Woman began spinning and she caught Coyote and threw him headfirst into the river bank. Then she blew him into the water so he stuck there in the mud.

"I was only joking. I was not intending to do anything," called Coyote.

But Whirlwind Woman was already far away. "Such is my power," she called back at him.

BE POLITE TO THE GRASS
(selections)

BY

Walter Lowenfels

Don't cheat the linen closet
Don't lie to the dishwasher
Don't swear at face towels
Always tell the hot water faucet the truth
Remember it's simpler to begin at the end
Acknowledge that the toaster is supreme
Above all, don't poke fun at the refrigerator
Pray for the curtains that they may survive in the hereafter
And you will live happily until all the tablespoons unite.

In the beginning was Africa
And then came the word.

A whale fell in love with a goldfish. "Be my wife,"
the whale proposed. "Oh no," the goldfish replied,
"there isn't enough room in my kitchen for you."
"I can't live without you," the whale sobbed and
swallowed the goldfish. And the whale lived happily
forever after.

When the windows start opening by themselves and the doors refuse to
shut, don't call the police, just remember the revolution is spreading.

A little pebble started rolling down the mountain. He passed another pebble and told him: "I'm lonesome, come on along." The two pebbles kept rolling down the mountain, when a third pebble asked: "Can I come along?" "Sure," the two pebbles cried. And that's how the great mountain slide began.

"Let's have a long life together," said the buttonhole to the button. "I can't," said the button. "Why?" "I'm losing my balance, my thread is tearing." Then the thread broke and the button fell and was never found. The buttonhole cried forever after.

I was walking along the street when suddenly the sidewalk collapsed. I fell straight down for fifteen hours. Then I hit bottom. Strange faces peered at me.

"Who are you?" one asked.

"I forget."

"How did you get here?"

"I was walking along when the sidewalk collapsed."

"Well, we don't want you here. Go back where you came from."

"How can I climb up that hole? It took me fifteen hours to get here."

"No trouble," one of the strangers said. He tied some firecrackers on my backside, lit them, and off I went up the big hole.

But when I reached the sidewalk, I couldn't stop. I kept going higher and higher. And I am still going up. I expect to reach the moon very soon.

Once upon a time nothing happened. There was no light, no clocks. Everything was empty, even the schools.

Then a door opened.

And He appeared.

It was Grandpa, dressed in a snow suit.

"Why do you wear a snow suit? It's not snowing," the kids asked.

"Not now, but it will. Just wait."

All this took place in the Sahara Desert.

And everybody is still waiting for the snow.

Grandpa was flying to Heaven. He passed by a dozen angels. Their wings were flapping. Their mouths were opening and shutting.

"I can't hear a sound," Grandpa said. "I forgot my hearing aid. I better go back."

"No use," a loud voice whispered. "It's already given away."

"What's the use of my going to Heaven if I can't hear the angels sing!"

"Okay. Then go to Hell."

And he did.

One day Johnny turned into a rock, but he walked around as usual. So nobody knew the difference.

"I'm going after the simpler things in life," said the camel with the two humps.

"Such as?" asked the other camel.

"One hump."

Billie started to bump his head against the wooden wall of the dining room.

"Ouch!" cried the wall. "Why are you bumping me?"

"I'm trying to pound some sense into my head," Billie answered.

Just then Billie bumped a hole into the wall. "I'm all broken up," said the wall. "Are you any more sensible than you were?"

"No, not yet. But by the time I have pounded you all up with my head, I hope to have more sense than anybody else in the world."

Just then the wall gave way. Billie fell through the wall. "Doesn't your head hurt?" asked the broken wall.

"Oh, no. I have an iron head. That's why all I have in my head is nonsense."

"Aren't you ever going to have any sense?" asked the wall.

"Not until I break you all up into little pieces."

Billie kept on bumping and the whole house fell down. "Now that makes sense," said Billie. "The house was no good anyhow."

"Billie, wake up," his mother called.
"I can't," said Billie, "I lost my head."
"Well, go find it."
Billie is still looking.

MOLLY WHUPPIE

BY

Alison Lurie

Once upon a time there was a man and his wife who had so many children that they could not feed them all. So they took their three youngest daughters into the forest, and left them there. The girls walked and walked for hours; it began to be dark, and they were hungry. At last they saw the lights of a house and made their way toward it. They knocked at the door, and a woman opened it and asked what they wanted.

"Oh, please," said they. "Could we come in and have a bit to eat?"

No, said the woman, they could not do that; for her husband was a giant, and he would kill them if he found them there.

"Please, ma'am," said the girls. "We'll just stay a little while, and be gone before he comes home."

So she let them in, and sat them down before the fire, and gave them some bread and milk. But just as they had begun to eat there was a great knock at the door, and a dreadful voice cried:

"Fee, fie, fo, fum,
I smell the blood of some earthly one.

Who have you there, wife?"

"Oh," said his wife, "it's just three poor lassies who were cold and hungry, and they'll be going soon. Let them be."

The giant said nothing, but gobbled up a huge supper; then he ordered them to spend the night.

Now this ogre had three daughters of his own, and they were going to share their bed with the three strangers, the youngest of whom was called Molly Whuppie. Molly was a very clever girl, and she noticed that before they all went to bed the giant put straw ropes around her neck and her sisters' and gold chains around the necks of his own daughters. So Molly stayed awake, and when the rest were sleeping sound she slipped out of bed, and took the straw ropes off her own and her sisters' necks, and the gold chains off those of the giant's daughters. Then she put the straw ropes on the giant's daughters and the gold chains on herself and her sisters, and lay down again.

In the middle of the night, up rose the giant armed with a great club. He came over to the bed and felt for the necks circled with the straw, for it was too dark to see. When he found them, he took his own three daughters out of bed and beat them with the club until they were dead. Then he lay down again, thinking he had managed fine.

Molly thought it was time she and her sisters were out of that, so she woke them and told them to be quiet, and they slipped out of the house. They ran and they never stopped until morning, when they saw a grand house before them. It was the king's palace. So Molly went in, and told her story to the king.

"Well, Molly," said he, "you are a clever girl, and you have managed well. But if you would go back to the giant's house and bring me the magic sword that hangs on his bedpost, I would marry your oldest sister to my oldest son."

"I will try," said Molly.

So she went back, and slipped into the giant's house, and crept under his bed. Presently the giant came home, gobbled up a big supper, and went to bed. Molly waited until he was snoring, and then she crept out and reached up over the sleeping giant and got down the sword, but just then he woke. She ran out of the door, and the giant ran after her. And she ran, and he ran, till they reached the Bridge of One Hair. And she ran over it, but he could not, and he said:

> *"Woe to ye, Molly Whuppie!*
> *Never ye come again."*

And she said:

> *"Twice more, churl,*
> *I'll come to Spain."*

Then Molly took the giant's sword to the king, and her oldest sister was married to his oldest son.

"Well, Molly," said the king. "You are a clever girl. But if you would go back to the giant's house and bring me the magic purse of gold that he keeps under his pillow, I would marry your second sister to my second son."

"I will try," said Molly.

So she went back, and slipped into the giant's house, and crept under his bed, and waited till he had eaten his supper and was fast asleep. As soon as she heard him snoring she crept out, slipped her hand under the pillow, and drew out the purse, but just then he woke. Molly ran out of the door, and the giant ran after her. And she ran, and he ran, till they reached the Bridge of One Hair. And she ran over it, but he could not, and he said:

> *"Woe to ye, Molly Whuppie!*
> *Never ye come again."*

And she said:

> *"Once more, churl,*
> *I'll come to Spain."*

Then Molly took the purse to the king, and her second sister was married to his second son.

"Well, Molly," said the king. "You are a very clever girl. But if you would go back once more to the giant's house and bring me the ring of invisibility he wears on his finger, I would marry you to my youngest son."

"I will try," said Molly.

So off she went to the giant's house, and hid herself under his bed. As soon as she heard him snoring loud she crept out, and reached across the bed, and took hold of his hand. She pulled and she pulled until she got off the ring; but just then the giant woke, and caught her fast by the hand.

"Now I've got you, Molly Whuppie," said the giant. "And as you're so clever, answer me this: If I had served you as you've served me, what would you do with me?"

Molly considered how she might escape, and then she said, "Why, I would put you into a sack, and I would put the cat and the dog in with you. Then I would hang the sack on the wall and go into the woods, and bring home the biggest and thickest stick I could find, and beat the sack till you were dead."

"Well, Molly," said the giant, "I'll just do that to you."

So he got a sack and put Molly into it, and the cat and the dog with her, and he hung it up on the wall, and went off to the woods to choose a stick.

As soon as he was gone, Molly began to sing, "Oh, if you could only see what I see!"

"Oh," says the giant's wife. "What do you see, Molly?"

But Molly never answered a word but "Oh, if you could see what I see!" The giant's wife pleaded with Molly to take her into the sack so that she could see what Molly saw. So at last Molly agreed, and the giant's wife cut a hole in the sack with a pair of scissors, and Molly jumped down. Then she helped the giant's wife up into the sack and sewed up the hole.

The giant's wife saw nothing in the sack, and began to ask to get down again; but Molly never answered her, only hid herself behind the door. Presently home came the giant, with a great big tree in his hand, and he took down the sack and began to beat it.

"It's me, man!" cried the giant's wife, but what with the dog's barking and the cat's meowing he did not know her voice. Molly did not want her to be killed, so she came out from behind the door. The giant saw her, and ran after her. And she ran, and he ran, till they reached the Bridge of One Hair. And she ran over it, but he could not, and he said:

> *"Woe to ye, Molly Whuppie!*
> *Never ye come again."*

And she said:

> *"Never more, churl,*
> *I'll come to Spain."*

Then Molly took the ring to the king and was married to his youngest son; and she never saw the giant again.

AUTHOR'S NOTE: This female version of "Jack and the Beanstalk" comes from Aberdeen, Scotland, not Spain: the rhyme with which Molly taunts the giant is probably the tag from an old children's game, the Scottish equivalent of

> *Rover, red rover,*
> *Once more I'll come over.**

* *Folk-Lore Journal,* Vol. II, "Molly Whuppie."

WILLIS LEE
AND THE DREAM
OF THE DRAGON

BY

Lewis MacAdams

O nce upon a time there was a little boy and his name was Willis Lee. He lived in a small house next to the seashore with his mother and father. Willis Lee loved his house and he loved living next door to the Ocean, and he loved the games that most six- or seven-year-old boys do. He was learning how to ride a bike really well. He knew how to stand up on a skateboard, but he was still a little afraid to ride down hills. He liked to do puzzles, and play Monopoly; but his favorite game was Clue. He played Clue with his mommy and daddy in front of the fire almost every night. The hour before bedtime was always Willis Lee's favorite time. His daddy had finished doing the dishes. His mommy was feeling happy and wide awake after a short nap, and the three of them sat together around the Clue board. "I think that it is Colonel Mustard." Willis looked down at his Clue cards. "In the kitchen." Willis looked at his cards again and shuffled them nervously. "With a KNIFE!" He shouted. His mommy and daddy looked at their cards, and then at each other. "AAARRRGGHH," groaned Willis's daddy, "you got me." And Willis's dad stuck out his hands palm upward. "You win. Gimmee five. No, gimmee ten." And Willis proudly pulled his hands back and slapped his daddy ten.

"Okay, Willis," said his mom. "Bedtime."

"Just one more game."

"No more games. Into bed."

"Right kiddo," said his dad. "You heard your mom. Into bed. But I'll bring you some milk and a cookie. And then I'll tell you a story."

"You mean *read* me a story."

"No. I think tonight I'll *tell* you a story."

A few minutes later, Willis's daddy came in with the milk and cookies and sat on the edge of Willis's bed.

After he handed the boy the bedtime snack, the daddy sat there for a few seconds watching his son eat. How much he looked like the boys' mother, he thought, with his deep-set, dark eyes and wild, flashing grin.

The boy finished his cookie and took a sip of the milk. "Tell me the story now, okay?"

His dad took a deep breath and blew it out like he always did when he was nervous. The man rubbed his eyes and forehead with his fingers while the boy waited, looking up at him.

"Okay," his daddy said, and he started telling the story:

Once upon a time there was a little boy and he lived with his mommy and daddy in a castle on the edge of the sea. They had a warm, beautiful castle with five sides. And, as the sun crossed the sky by day the house was filled with light; and as the moon moved across the sky by night, it bathed the castle in its own milky glow. The little boy and his mommy and daddy were happy in the castle; but one day a messenger came for the boy's daddy, and said that the king of the country was calling a meeting of all the knights, and that the boy's daddy, as one of the great knights of the land, was to report to the king's castle in two days' time. The little boy was proud when he heard that his daddy was going off to talk to the king. The boy too wanted to grow up to be a knight, and his daddy had promised him that when he was a little older, the boy could go with his daddy to the king's palace and meet the king, and watch one of the king's great parades. The little boy was very proud as he watched his daddy saddle up his horse and mount and ride away.

Two days later the little boy's daddy was back, but he had a very worried look on his face. When the little boy's daddy bent over to pick him up and kiss him, it seemed to the little boy that his daddy held him and looked at him for a very long time before he put him back down. The little boy watched his mommy and daddy kiss, too. They held each other tight for a long time; and when his daddy looked at his mommy, his dad would smile. But as soon as she buried her head in his shoulder, the same worried look would come over his daddy's face, and his daddy's eyes would look far away.

When his daddy came in that night to kiss the

little boy, he still looked worried. And, after he kissed him good night, his daddy told the little boy that he had something very important to tell him, and to listen very carefully.

His dad said, "Tomorrow I have to go very far away, and I won't see you for a very long time. The king has an important job for me to do, and I must go."

The little boy looked worried now, too.

"Tell him you can't go," the little boy said sharply, trying to sound brave and certain.

"I can't do that," said his daddy. "When a knight has chosen his life, when any man has chosen his life, he must follow it through. That's what a man has to do. That's what I have to do, and that's what you'll have to do, too."

The little boy understood, more from just the tone of his daddy's words than from the words his daddy actually said; and somehow he felt reassured, and the little boy fell asleep.

Almost as soon as the little boy fell asleep, he began to dream. In his dream, the little boy was grown into a great knight, and he was sent out on a shining afternoon to do battle for his king against a dragon that had been terrorizing the neighborhood for days. How fine the little boy looked with the sign of the lightning bolts embroidered across the chest of his shirt. He carried a sword in one hand, and in the other he held his horse's reins. Hanging down behind his helmet were the feathers of hawks and owls; and, as the little boy galloped across the prairie toward the dragon, it seemed to the little boy that his horse could fly.

As the boy knight passed through the neighborhood, all the people came out into the sunlight to cheer him on; but after the boy and his horse had left the people far behind, and the pony had slowed for the long climb into the foothills, the boy began to feel a little bored with his journey. There weren't any farms along the road now, and as the boy's horse carried him into the pine forest, and the late afternoon sun began to sink, the boy knight actually began to feel even a little bit scared. But the boy remembered what his daddy had said, and the boy knew that he must carry his journey through.

The boy began looking for a place to camp for the night, and he stopped by a stream. He took off his horse's saddle, watered her, and tethered her at the edge of a clearing so that she could graze. Then he built a fire from matches and twigs and shavings, heated up some of the stew that his mommy had made for him, crawled into his sleeping bag and, using his saddle as a pillow, went to sleep.

But before the little boy could begin to dream, the boy heard a tremendous roar moving toward him through the forest. He sat up in time to see trees crashing to the forest floor in all directions, and then a huge dragon, who must have been forty feet tall with green and red scales like a snake or a fish or some kind of prehistoric bird, standing over him with his arms raised over his head and his fists balled like he was about to smash the little boy into oatmeal.

"Hey," yelled the little boy, too surprised to be frightened, "who the hell do you think you are?"

"Who do I think I am?" screamed the dragon. "WHO THE HELL DO I THINK I AM?" The dragon's voice was like a hundred freight trains roaring through a railroad yard. "I am Felix the Dragon!" He paused to blow a cloud of awful-smelling steam from his nose into the little boy's face, making him cough. "And you better believe it. Whaddarya doing in my FOREST, chump?"

The way the dragon sneered out the word *chump* made the little boy mad. For a second his knees trembled, but then he yelled up at the monster in his bravest, deepest voice, "Hey, don't call me a chump."

Then the dragon leaned over and stuck his huge face right into the little boy's face so close that the little boy could see only the dragon's whiskery chin and jaggedy crooked teeth and over the top of the dragon's blue-purple upper lip, part of one bloodshot, yellowish eyeball.

"Chump," the dragon repeated in a thunderous whisper. And then, once again, just to make his point, the dragon repeated it, "Chump."

This time the little boy didn't say anything. He just stared fiercely into the dragon's bloodshot eye. But inside his head, the little boy was thinking as fast as he could what he should do. "If I pick up my sword right now," the little boy thought, "the dragon'll just smash me to pieces. But if I wait for the right second, maybe I——"

The rest of his thought was interrupted by the dragon's roar. The dragon whirled around and uprooted a pine tree from the ground, just pulled it up roots and all so fast that the condors who had been sleeping in the upper branches barely had time to fly away before the dragon cracked the tree in two over one of his mountainous knees. The dragon was so mad he could barely see the boy for all his anger, and dragon smoke, and for all the branches that were crashing to the floor of the forest. In fact, at this point the little boy was more scared of being hit by a falling branch, or having the dragon accidentally *step* on him than he was of the dragon's actually killing him on purpose. So while the dragon leaped about in his rage, the little boy ran between the dragon's legs and hid behind a boulder on the edge of the forest, next to where his pony was still tethered. The horse's eyeballs were practically rolling back into his head in fright, and the little boy knew he had to calm his pony down. So the little boy talked to his pony in a low, calm, steady voice, stroking his long neck and shoulders until the pony was soothed. And in quieting the pony, the boy calmed himself down, too.

The dragon calmed down a little, too. He stood up straight and his head and shoulders reached above the forest's tallest trees. His eyes darted around, but the pine tree branches now shielded the boy and his pony from the dragon's eyes.

"Little BOY, little BOY," howled the dragon, but to no avail. And then, more quietly, pleadingly, the dragon called again, "Little boy, little boy." But the little boy knight still wouldn't answer. The boy was wondering how he could get back to his campsite and retrieve his sword. "Little boy. Oh little boy," the dragon hissed in an almost-whisper. Finally the boy decided to answer: "What do you want?"

The boy's answer surprised the dragon, who jumped backward at the sound of the little boy's voice. The dragon replied in a kind of fake-friendly voice, "Oh, I was just wondering where you were, that's all."

"Well, I'm not telling you where I am."

"Well," the dragon paused, trying to phrase his next question carefully, "could you at least tell me why you came here?"

It was the little boy's turn to answer carefully. "There's been some complaints about a dragon in the neighborhood, and I came out here to check 'em out."

"Really?" replied the dragon, thoughtfully. "There've been complaints. What sort of complaints?"

"YOU ought to know what kind of complaints. YOU'RE the one who's been terrorizing the neighborhood. It was you that pulled up Mrs. Johnson's tomato plants. It was YOU that stomped on

Jackie Murphy's cat and stole his sister's bicycle and ran off with Sean Mendelssohn's skateboard."

"I did not," answered the dragon, with an insulted expression in his voice.

"Well then, who did?" yelled the little boy, scornfully. "And who broke Sarah Allston's greenhouse windows, and broke all the limbs off of Orville's baby apple trees?"

"It could have been deer," offered the dragon, helpfully.

"Deer!" screamed the little boy self-righteously. "Deer don't know how to ride skateboards or bicycles."

"You're right," the dragon agreed, "that couldn't have been deer."

"It was you!" the little boy screamed, so loud that it was his turn to frighten the horse.

"It was *not* me," the dragon roared back so loudly that the whole forest shook. The roar echoed off into the silence while the little boy thought of what else to say. He still couldn't figure out a way to get to his sword.

"Assuming," said the dragon, staring off into the night sky, "I could tell you who did all that stuff, what would you do for me?"

"Well," the little boy hesitated, thinking of his sword lying next to his sleeping bag on the other side of the dragon's mammoth feet, "well, in that case I might let you go free."

The dragon paused. "Hmmmmmm," thought the dragon, "hmmmmmmm."

The boy waited.

Finally, the dragon answered, "That seems fair."

"Okay," said the little boy, "who did it?"

"Actually," replied the dragon, "it was you."

The little boy felt like somebody had slugged him in the face with a fistful of dynamite and his head had just exploded. Instantly the dragon disappeared into a yellow cloud of its own smoke, and in the dragon's place the boy knight found himself face to face with another little boy.

And this little boy even looked like Willis, except where Willis had curly blond hair and deep blue-black eyes, this new little boy had green hair, and a bright red face with red cheeks that had steam and sweat pouring off of them. And where Willis was dressed in his knight's clothes with the lightning bolts across his chest, and a silver helmet with hawk and owl feathers streaming down the back, this new little boy's outfit was dragon green, and the new little boy had claws sticking out from the legs of his pants, cruel talons; and the new boy wore no helmet. His hair was jet-black like a crow.

Willis jumped back and kind of hunched forward with his hands loose at his sides like he was ready to fight. The new kid with the talons looked like a tough kid to beat, but he was just Willis's size.

The new kid pointed a long, yellow-fanged finger at Willis. "You are guilty," he howled slowly at the little boy.

Willis blinked. "What do you mean, 'guilty'?"

"You did it. You broke into those gardens and broke those greenhouse windows and tore the limbs off of those apple trees. It was YOU that took that bicycle and rode it around all day and left it in the bushes. It was *you* that took Jackie's sister's bike."

Willis's eyes screwed up tight and he bunched his fists and his face turned red. "I did not."

"Yes you did. 'Cause I saw you."

Willis got madder. "You did NOT."

"Yes I did."

"No you didn't."

"Yes I did," the new kid insisted; and with that Willis jumped for him and they wrestled each other to the ground. First Willis was on the ground, and the other kid would hold Willis down and pin his arms and legs and scream in his face "You did it!" And that would make Willis even madder, and he would turn on his super *super* strength and spin out of the holds, and then Willis would pin the red-faced little boy down and try to punch his face to get him to shut up, but then the new kid would bend his legs and use his talons to pry Willis's hands loose from the new kid's arms. And then they would wrestle some more. And every time Willis would get the new boy down, he'd punch at his face, and he punched at the new kid's face until he felt like his arms were going to fall off; but somehow the new kid rolled away every time, and the fight swirled on and Willis was getting tireder and tireder. He was getting so tired that the other little boy was starting to whirl in front of his eyes, and the new little boy's face and arms and skin started to melt into each other and Willis started getting dizzier and dizzier, and Willis started rolling over in space as the other little boy disappeared. The words "You did it" flashed on and off like a neon sign in the void between the stars as Willis fell. And fell. And fell. And then he woke up and he was back in the castle with his daddy, the great white knight. And the knight was sitting on Willis's bed. And there was a light behind the boy's daddy that poured over his daddy like light from the sun.

"You came back from the battle," the boy said, surprised, trying to rub the sleep from his eyes.

"Well I had to, for a second, because you called me."

"I did?"

"Sure. Now, what did you want?" The knight smiled at his little boy, and there was light in the father's eyes.

"I—" Willis hesitated—"I . . . did break those greenhouse windows. And I did take that bike and ride it around and leave it in the bushes. And I did borrow Sean's skateboard. But I didn't mean to. I mean . . . And I only took the bike because . . ." The little boy stopped, and looked away for a second. But then he finished, ". . . because I was lonely for you. And you're never around. And there's nothing to do."

Now there was a sad look in the knight's eyes and it was his turn to look away. "Yeah," he sighed, "I know." Then he looked into his son's eyes, and between the father's and the son's eyes it was like a pair of rivers flowing back and forth between them, carrying the father and son into each other until it was impossible to tell who was the man for a second and who was the boy. Finally the knight spoke: "Willis, there are times in a man's life when he *has* to know how he feels. And when he knows how he feels, he has to act on that knowledge, and on those feelings. If he doesn't, he'll be doomed by his knowledge and he'll no longer be a man. That's what being a man is. That's what it means to be responsible for what you do. You *have* to be responsible for what you do."

The father had said what he had to, and he stretched out beside Willis on Willis's bed. "Now you have to get some sleep," he said in a low, soft voice into Willis's ear. "But don't you worry, son, I'll be coming back. Everything'll be different. It always is. And we won't be living in the same house, but I'll be near. . . ." His voice trailed off as he realized that Willis had gone to sleep. "I wonder if I'm just talking to make myself feel better," the man thought to himself. But he looked down at the little boy who was breathing easily, steadily, sleeping quietly with a slight smile on his lips; and somehow, the father's fears and loneliness were eased. And as the father got up from the bed and left the room and the house, the knight faded from Willis's dream, and the next thing that Willis knew was his mommy in her blue bathrobe shaking him gently by the shoulder the next morning to tell him it was time for breakfast, and to get a move on or he'd be late for school.

COUSINS

BY

Norman Mailer

ILLUSTRATED BY
NORRIS CHURCH

What's your name, man?

            Well, my name is McBoing-boing.

I know your name, but
   what's your shame?

            My shame is that my name
               is McBoing-boing

Poor McBoing-boing. Where
   do you live?

            East Haaaaaartford!

A sneezy place,

            Poo-poo, it's better than
               Kalamazoo

I'd rather be the sheik
   of Battle Creek.

            The sheik?
            When you came in,
               I thought you was Flynn.

You talk like a twit
   who's having a fit
I, Boing-boing, am McBingo.

            Bingo, I will ring your bell
            Boing McBoing can duke it like
               hell.
      It was a donny bing dinger
        Before they were done
        They sang as one:
His shame is that his name is McBoing-boing.
    John Buffalo McBoing-boing.
John Buffalo McBingo McBoing-boing,
     East Haaartford!   Boing!
       Kalamazoo!

THE GIANT SPIDERWEB

BY

Harry Mathews

for Léonore

There once was a spider who was very good at spinning spiderwebs and who decided one day that he would spin the biggest spiderweb in the world. He was a happy spider who had done everything spiders are supposed to do in life. He had learned how to protect himself. He knew how to catch insects for food. He had raised several families of young spiders, all of whom had grown up and no longer needed to be protected or fed. All he had to do now was to take care of himself and his wife, and this was something he could manage easily. He had lots of spare time on his hands. It was on a day when he found himself with even less to do than usual that the idea came to him of spinning the world's biggest spiderweb.

There was no particular *reason* in his wanting to do this. The web that he dreamed of spinning wasn't meant to catch more insects, or bigger insects, for him and his wife to eat. It wasn't meant to catch anything at all. It was just going to be the biggest spiderweb in the world. Spinning it would allow him to have fun doing something he did very well. And perhaps he felt like showing the world what a great spinner of webs he was.

The spider lived in the woods. In the middle of the woods there was a clearing about a hundred yards wide. This seemed a natural place for the spider to set his giant web. The web would be easy to see because of the empty space around it, and at the same time the trees that grew around the clearing would shelter it from the wind. It is true that, out in the open, rain would fall on the web, but this didn't worry the spider, since his web would stretch straight up and down, and no more than a few drops of rain were likely to touch it.

So the spider and his wife moved their belongings to the edge of the clearing, and he went to work. His wife, by the way, when he told her what he was planning to do, had decided he had gone crazy. Why should he want to take the trouble of spinning a huge web that wasn't any use to anybody? But she also decided that it wouldn't do anybody any harm. And it would certainly keep her husband occupied, which was something that appealed to her. Lately he had been hanging around all day and getting on her nerves; she enjoyed the idea of having a little time to herself. She agreed to move to the clearing with her husband and promised to take care of the insect catching while he worked on his crazy project.

The spider began spinning his giant web. He started at the edge of the clearing, on the side from which the wind generally blew. The spider hoped that as the web started growing, the wind— in the middle of the woods it was only a mild breeze—would lift it out into the clearing so that he could go on working at it while it floated in the air. Then he could gradually extend it until it reached the trees on the far side. A safer way of making the web would have been to stretch it along one side of the clearing, where there were branches every few feet to drape it on; but the spider thought the web would look better if it hung straight across the open space.

So the spider strung strand after strand of silk up through the branches of a pine tree, to a height of about fifteen feet. When he was sure that the strands were strong enough to support the weight of the great web he was going to make, he started working out toward the middle of the clearing. He soon found that he had guessed right. The steady breeze blew the sideways strands of the web out straight, like a flag that flew but didn't flap, and the spider was able to keep working on his web as it hung in midair, gently swaying.

At first the spider had planned to work only during the day, while there was light out. It was midsummer, the days were long, and he figured that he would have enough time to finish the web before the end of October, when frosts started and the cold winds came. The spider could spin a web the size of a large handkerchief in about twenty minutes, which meant that in an hour he could make almost a whole square yard. He knew that by working every day he could finish his web in two months' time.

But the more the spider worked, the more excited he became at the thought of seeing his giant web completed. He also started to worry. He was longing to see the web himself, and to have the whole world see it. But what if some accident ruined his work before it was finished? He thought of forest fires, and late summer storms, and hungry birds who might spot him out on the web, where he had no place to hide, and gobble him up. At other times the spider felt a little frightened, when the wind was rising and he found himself bobbing up and down in the air, three or four or five yards off the ground. So he decided to finish his web as fast as he could.

The spider began working later and later. He worked after dark, then halfway into the night, then the whole night through. He knew that he could work just as well in the dark; and spiders never sleep—so that was no problem. He found that he didn't have to go home to eat the insects that his wife had been catching. So many insects flew into his own web that there was enough food for hundreds of spiders. In fact, he had to spend more and more time getting rid of all these insects that were messing up his giant web, which he wanted to keep perfectly clean.

After a while the spider was working all day and all night. He was too excited by now ever to stop and rest. Three weeks after he had started, near the end of August, the great silken banner stretched halfway across the clearing. And one bright September afternoon, two weeks after that, it was almost touching the trees on the far side.

The spider was sailing high up on the edge of his web, waiting for the wind to carry him right next to a big fir tree. This was the tree he had been aiming for ever since he had begun working. When he came close enough to the tree, he took a big jump, spinning as he went, and landed on one of its branches. He ran up and down the edge of the web, looping and winding its fringe among the prickly fir twigs. Finally he knotted the entire side with strong silk strands to the branches of the tree.

Now long before this—weeks before this—the other creatures in the woods had noticed what the spider was doing. At first some were frightened; some thought he was crazy (just like his wife); and some watched him without thinking or feeling anything at all. But when the spider had finished his work, and the giant spiderweb hung across the clearing shimmering and rippling in the sunlight, every single animal was filled with astonishment. Rabbits came out of their burrows, squirrels came down from their trees, and birds flew down onto the tips of branches to look in wonder at the extraordinary thing this tiny being had created. None of them had seen anything like it. And none of them had *done* anything like it, since it had never occurred to any of them to take the trouble of doing something that was of no use to them in their ordinary, everyday lives.

One by one the animals came out of the woods into the clearing and gathered in front of the giant spiderweb. And one by one they began experiencing a particular feeling about it. It was a new feeling for them, just as the giant web was a new thing for them. It took them some time before they realized just what the new feeling was. It was a feeling of gratitude. All the animals, one after the other, felt compelled to respond to the astonishment that this glistening new thing aroused in them by showing their thanks. They felt a need to acknowledge what had happened, to acknowledge the spider for being crazy enough to make this newness happen in their lives.

Of course the animals and birds and other creatures didn't tell each other in words how they felt. None of them knew how to talk. But they didn't have to talk. They just knew. They also knew that they must find some way to show their thankfulness to the spider.

(The spider, by the way, after finishing his web, went right on working. He was busy cleaning off the thousands of insects that kept getting caught in the web. In fact, he had been so taken up with his web cleaning that he hadn't even noticed the animals and birds that had gathered around him.)

But the animals and birds could not think of a way of showing their thanks to the spider. They couldn't talk to him. They couldn't sing to him. (Any noise they made wouldn't mean anything to him, even if he could hear it, which he couldn't.) If they danced for him he might not see them, and if they danced too close, or if they tried to caress him, he would certainly be terrified and run away. In any case, singing and dancing were all very well, but once they were over there was nothing to show they had ever happened. And the animals and birds wanted to express their thanks in some lasting way. They wanted to make their thanks last at least as long as the web itself.

Finally the animals, the birds, and the other creatures agreed that they could not do anything appropriate or right by themselves. And so they decided to ask a man to help them. The thought was not one that appealed to them, quite the contrary. Men were creatures they liked to have as few dealings with as possible. But they now found themselves in an unusual situation; and they knew that even if men were thoughtless and cruel, they could do things that animals and birds could not do. They could change the face of the earth in lasting ways. They might be able to help them show their thanks in a way that would be solid and lasting and plain for everyone to see—plain enough even for the spider, who was still scurrying around his web picking off insects, dirt, and leaves. (A few leaves were starting to fall.)

So that very night, after the animals had all agreed to ask some man to help them, a fox went trotting off to the edge of the woods. He waited there until his friend the cat appeared. The cat lived in the town nearby, and each night he came out to the woods to hunt. When the cat arrived, the fox told him what had happened. He did not tell his story in words, but the cat understood him all the same, and he promised to help. He went back to the town nearby and paid a visit to his friend the dog—well, he wasn't exactly a friend, but he was someone the cat knew well enough to consult about important business. The dog saw exactly what the problem was. He promised to take care of it next day, as soon as the sun was up. He knew a man who might be able to help the animals. This man lived among the other people in the town, but he was not quite like them. He looked and smelled and spoke differently from the others, and because of this the dog thought he could understand the animals in the woods and help them with their unusual problem.

Early next morning the dog went out looking for this man. When he found him, he went up to him in his usual friendly way and then bit him—not hard enough to make him bleed, but hard enough to hurt him a little and make him angry. The man was angry, all right. He was so angry with this dog whom he thought was his friend that he started chasing him. The dog ran, and the man ran after him. The dog was careful not to run so fast that the man would decide to stop chasing him. And little by little he led the man out of town, down a lane between some fields, out to the edge of the woods, and then into the woods, right to the edge of the clearing.

At this point the dog somehow managed to disappear into the bushes; but he needn't have bothered. The man had forgotten all about the dog. He was looking at the incredible giant spiderweb.

He had never seen anything so amazing. As it hung in front of him, sparkling faintly with dew and sunlight, it seemed like something in a dream. At first he looked at it from the edge of the clearing where he had stopped running. Then he walked up to it for a closer look. He touched it, as if to make sure it was real.

(When he saw the man suddenly standing next to him, the spider stopped cleaning his web and stayed absolutely still. He was not so much frightened as furious. How could he ever get his work done with this monster looming over him?)

The man stepped back a little way and sat down on the ground. He sat there for a long time, never taking his eyes off the giant web.

When the man appeared at the edge of the clearing, the animals had gone running into the woods to hide, and the birds had flown away. But after the man had sat still for a while, one by one they came back, creeping, hopping, and fluttering. There were rabbits, chipmunks, squirrels, and skunks; crows, robins, sparrows, and starlings; and many others whose names are harder to remember. They gathered behind the sitting man—not too close—and waited.

Finally the man got up. He looked around. Then he sat right down again.

He was even more amazed than when he first saw the giant spiderweb. He immediately knew that something absolutely extraordinary was happening. He knew that not he or anyone else probably had ever seen such a thing—hundreds of animals and birds quietly gathered around a human being in the middle of the woods. It was a kind of miracle.

For a while the man only looked at the animals. Then he began speaking to them. He spoke in a low, sweet voice. The animals and birds did not understand what he said, but they could tell by his voice that he meant them no harm and that he wanted them to know this. After speaking to them for a few minutes, the man again sat and looked at the animals without saying anything. He looked at the animals and birds, and the animals and birds looked at him. Some looked past him at the giant spiderweb, which was shining more and more brightly as the sun rose in the sky. The man looked at the animals and birds and wished he could understand what was happening. The animals and birds looked at him and waited for him to understand.

No one knows if the man ever did understand what the animals wanted. But as things turned out, it made no difference if he did or didn't.

The man turned to look again at the fantastic spiderweb, which was shining in sunlight and trembling faintly in the breeze. It was so beautiful he wished that he could stand there and look at it for the rest of his life. It was as though he had fallen in love with it. He wanted to become a part of it, he wanted to disappear and just be a part of the magical thing in front of him. The animals watched him standing there. The longer he stood there gazing at the web, the surer they felt that sooner or later he would do whatever it was that had to be done. He would show the world how thankful they were for the wonderful work the little spider had created.

The man spent the rest of that day gazing at the giant web. When night came, he went back to the town nearby where he lived. He was hungry and tired, but he was happy.

When the sun rose next morning, he came back to the clearing and again spent the day gazing at the miraculous web. He came back the next day as well, and the day after that.

On the morning of the fifth day, he arrived later than usual. Each day after his first visit to the clearing, he had brought with him a little bag, which he wore over his shoulder. In the bag was a bottle to drink from and a little food. Usually the man left this bag in the shade of the trees when he arrived; but on the fifth day, he took the bag with him to the middle of the clearing. He set it down in front of the giant spiderweb and opened it. The animals and birds, who always gathered around him as soon as he appeared, came closer to see what he was doing.

The man was spreading on the ground a bright assortment of spools of thread and balls of yarn. Red, blue, purple, yellow, green, gold, black: There seemed to be every possible color of thread and wool. When all the spools and balls of yarn were spread out, the rich display made the animals wriggle and hop with pleasure, and the birds circled and swooped to show their delight.

The man had brought something else with him that morning: a huge stepladder. He had had a hard time carrying it from the town nearby, and all the way he had kept shifting it from one shoulder to the other. Now he set up the stepladder next to the giant spiderweb. He climbed the ladder as high as he could. When he was standing on the last step before the top and lifted his hands as high as they would reach, he could just touch the top of the web. He climbed down and folded up the ladder. He carried it to the lefthand side of the web and set it up again. He went back to his spools and balls of yarn and picked out some black thread and some green wool. He took the wool and thread over to the ladder, climbed up it, laid the spool and the ball of yarn on a little platform near the top of the ladder, and set to work.

He started looping little pieces of wool and thread through the holes in the spiderweb, slipping them gently through the silk so as not to break it; then when the wool and thread were where he wanted them, he would pull them straight and knot them into place. He worked carefully and slowly and steadily. He went on working all the rest of that day, except when he came down from the ladder to eat his lunch.

The animals watched to see what he was doing with the thread and wool. At first they could only recognize different bits of color arranged in particular ways. But after a while they were able to see what the man was really up to. The bits of color turned into shapes, then the shapes turned into pictures, and they knew that the man was weaving the thread and wool into the giant spiderweb to tell a story. It was a story that was being told in colored pictures instead of words. It was a story that pleased the animals, because it seemed to be the right kind of story to show how thankful they felt toward the little spider and the wonderful work he had created.

The little spider himself was not all that pleased. He and his wife were frightened by the man on the ladder, and bothered, too. They wondered how they would ever catch up with their work of cleaning the web.

(The spider's wife had joined her husband on the giant spiderweb because she had become restless waiting for him to come home. He was happy to see her again, not only because he was lonely—he was so busy he hardly had time to feel lonely—but because he was finding it hard all alone to deal with the tremendous amount of insects, dirt, and leaves that kept getting stuck on the web. And more leaves were falling every day.)

But as time went by, the spiders started getting used to the man and his ladder. After all, he left them alone. The spider couldn't tell exactly what he was doing. It seemed a shame to clutter up the web with all that junk, but the man wasn't actually doing any damage. More important, he cleaned all the insects and dirt and leaves from whatever part of the web he was working on. So the spiders stopped worrying about the man on the ladder. They just were careful not to go too near him, and they went on with their own web cleaning at a safe distance.

Each day the man came back with more wool and thread and went on with his work. From time to time, when he finished one part of the web, he would shift the stepladder a few feet to the right. Each day the animals came back to see what he had done. They followed the story of brightly colored pictures as it spread across the clearing in the middle of the woods.

The day came when the man moved his ladder all the way to the far side of the clearing. The story had come to an end.

The man tucked a few last bits of black and green into the giant spiderweb. He put the rest of the wool and thread into his bag. He closed the bag, folded up the stepladder, then walked away from the web to the edge of the clearing. There he turned around and took a long look at the story he had told. He smiled. When he went home that night to the town nearby, even though he was more tired than he had ever been in his life, he was happier, too.

The animals were as happy as he was. The man had done what they could not do all by themselves. They looked at the story of brightly colored pictures that covered the giant spiderweb, and they knew that their astonishment and thankfulness had been made plain for all to see. They felt satisfied. They had done what they could. They had done the right thing. Soon they turned back into the woods, to their burrows and nests. They began leading their ordinary, everyday lives again, the way they always had.

No one knows if the little spider ever saw the story on his web. If he did, he must have liked it. He must have felt proud of the acknowledgement he had been given. Probably, though, he was too busy cleaning his web to realize what had happened. He had so much to do—rooting out insects, and dirt, and the leaves that were now falling by the dozen from the trees that grew around the clearing in the woods.

The day after he had finished his work, the man came back to look again at the story of brightly colored pictures that he had woven. He came back the next day, too. Then three days passed without his coming; then five days; then a whole week. He never came back after that.

The giant spiderweb and its story of colored thread and wool hung in the clearing till the end of October. Then the first frost came, and after the frost came cold winds that lashed at the silken web, lashed at it until they tore it loose. The giant spiderweb broke away one windy morning and floated up into the air, over the woods, out of sight. The animals in the woods never saw it again. The spider and his wife were gone, too. Some birds saw the web when the wind carried it off. They saw that the two spiders were still hanging onto the web—they were curled up into specks, under some pieces of brown wool. They looked as though they were asleep. The birds watched the web as it drifted away into the cold blue sky.

What was the story that the man told on the giant spiderweb with his thread and wool?

At first he had not planned to tell a story at all. He had changed his mind many times about what he should do. He had thought of painting a spectacular sunset, full of red, orange, and gold, the kind of sunset that makes you feel both happy and sad. He had thought of covering the web with a wild display of colors—colors that would be mixed up in crazy ways without meaning anything at all. He thought of making a picture of the animals and birds that had gathered around him in the clearing. But in the end he decided to tell a story. And the man knew right away which story to tell. It was the only story that was as wonderful as the wonderful things that had happened to him. And telling that story was what he finally did.

He told the story of a little spider who lived in the woods. This spider was very good at spinning webs; and one day he decided to spin the biggest spiderweb in the world. . . .

TUKUM
THE
SWINEHERD

BY

Peter Matthiessen

The peaks of the Snow Mountains, on bright mornings, part the dense clouds and soar into the skies of Oceania. Beneath the clouds, like a world submerged, lie the dark rocks which form the great island of New Guinea; climbing abruptly from the Dampier Strait in the East Indies, the range extends eastward fifteen hundred miles until, at land's end in Papua, it sinks once more beneath the ocean.

The Snow Mountains are the summit of western New Guinea. On a high flank in the central highlands lies a sudden valley: Here the Baliem River, which had vanished underground some twenty miles upstream, bursts from the mountain wall onto a great green plain. The plain itself, ten miles across, is a mile above the sea. Fifty miles southeast of the valley's head, the river drops into a gorge and passes from the mountains, to subside at last in the vast marshes of sun and mud and sago palms stretching southward to the Arafura Sea. The last large blank on the most recent maps is the land of the Kurelu, one of the last people on earth who are still living in the Stone Age; although they have dogs and pigs, and grow sweet potatoes and taro, their tools and weapons are still made of wood and stone. They are surrounded on all sides by enemy people, and never travel more than a few miles from where they were born.

Early in the morning when the pigs of U-mue's village are herded out into the fields, they are apt to consort briefly with a herd from the village adjoining. The animals of U-mue's village are tended in rotation by the numerous children, while those of the village of Asokmeke are tended invariably by Asokmeke's stepson, Tukum.

Like all the swineherds in the Kurelu, Tukum conducts his pigs each morning to a predetermined pasture, usually a sweet-potato field gone fallow. Here the pigs eat greens and the stray vegetables which have escaped the harvest, and root for grubs and mice and frogs and the small lizards along old ditches. In the afternoon he escorts them back to village pens, where they are fed sweet-potato skins and other offal from the fires. Each pig is marked almost from birth for a certain fate—a ceremony, a marriage gift, the payment of a debt—but until the day of its demise it leads an orderly and pleasant life, prized and honored on all sides.

• Despite the great worth of the pigs and the prestige they bear, little husbandry is practiced, though piglets, very small or ailing, are usually carried in the women's nets and receive special attention. Should a sow reach breeding age, she may be escorted to a noted boar, lest one of her scraggy kin should work his way with her. The daytime haunts of these illustrious boars, like the haunts of every animal in the villages, are common knowledge, and, while permission may sometimes be asked of the boar's owner, the decision is more often left to the stern animal itself.

As Tukum is thought of as incompetent, even for a child of seven, such a delicate matter as sow-breeding would probably be left to his mother. Tukum's mother is a shrill, cheerful woman, the gat-toothed bane of her young son's existence, who with her infernal pigs and her incessant shouting, reduces Tukum almost daily to bitter tears. Not only is Tukum smaller than the children of U-mue's village but her pigs are larger. The pigs take advantage of Tukum's forgetful nature by losing themselves in the low wood or barging into gardens where they do not belong, and as they are far stronger, better coordinated, more numerous, and more intent than he, they make of his days a series of small emergencies. His only weapon is an extraordinary voice, both loud and gruff, and hoarse with use, which signals the presence of Tukum and his charges from great distances away.

Elf-faced and potbellied, Tukum shouts gruffly at his pigs while his mother shouts at him. He is followed on his way not only by pigs but by small girls and women; they go along through the low wood to the fields in front of Homuak. There is straw in Tukum's hair and gray dust on his skin. He marches along, a half sweet potato in his hand, and now and again he stifles his own growling by plunging his round face into it.

Tukum hates pigs, and though he tends them nearly every day, the very idea makes his huge eyes overflow. At these moments he looks more like an elf than ever. Tukum is nearly four feet tall and looks not full grown, but complete. In his way, Tukum is spiritual; his natural haunt is not the pigsty but the toadstool. Tukum, with his wild brown eyes and portly evanescence, does not belong among the flies and swine, nor even in the sun, but in the ferny glades of distant woods.

High in the dark cloud forests of the upper Elokera stands a huge beech, and high in this tree hangs a ponderous nest of the great black hawk. The war chief, Weaklekek, wished to obtain this hawk, the feathers of which are valuable, and he set off with his bow and arrow to investigate the nest, the news of which had spread down to the valley. With him he took Asukwan, the young warrior of his men's house, who is credited with a sense of birds and a keen eye. They were accompanied by Tukum, who is credited with almost nothing.

The three went up the valley along the stream bed of a tributary, wading the quiet pools under the banks and leaping from rock to mossy rock; honey eaters and birds of paradise shrieked at their passing, and mountain pigeons, veering off, broke the humid airs with the sharp clap of pigeon wings. Farther on, they took to high ground, crossing abandoned fields; in the hillside woods small flocks of parakeets, red under wing, crisscrossed the treetops in loud senseless consternation.

In the forest of the upper slopes, with its black mud and thorned rattan, its hanging shapes and gloom, the pale clear boles of the canopy trees soared to crests which closed away the sky; the trail crossed sagging pig fences, and hidden animals grunted hollowly from the shadows of these dark pastures. The trail skirted dismal wells where the limestone had caved in; one well was a hundred feet or more in depth, and strongly fenced around, though the fence was water-logged and rotten. Asukwan tossed a stone into the well, and the three exclaimed at the time which passed before the splash resounded. Lagging behind, Tukum tossed another stone, but this time a sound came back immediately, for Tukum's stone, barely clearing the edge, had fallen on a ledge inside the rim. Tukum glared balefully at the well and trotted onward.

Farther still, in a steep clearing, lay a new pig village, perched on a ledge of mud. Here miniature blue butterflies fluttered like gentian petals, alighting as one on the mud's black gleam and all but vanishing, for with closed wings they were nothing more than small scraps of drab gray. Then the blue color would explode again as the butterflies danced in their odd motion. Tukum laughed, pronouncing their apt name—*sigisigit.*

One morning, Tukum found a bird's nest in a pink-flowered myrtle tree. The nest was a miniature cup of soft grass, circled around with bright green sphagnum moss. There were two tiny birds in it, olive and yellow, and, though they had never done so before Tukum found them, they could be made to flutter for short distances. Tukum carried the nest about all morning, making the little birds fly; they would buzz along on a downward angle, careening inevitably into the ground. The birds delighted Tukum, who talked to them and encouraged them, but he had no recognition of his feeling, and late in the day he would take them home and eat them.

Running home by way of Homuak, Tukum stubbed his toe upon a root. Tukum is at odds with his own reflexes and is constantly stubbing his toe or stepping on bees; when he shows someone something he has found, he is apt to open the wrong hand in his excitement, permitting the escape of a huge cicada, or a beautiful hesperid moth with a scarlet silken head, or one of the lovely tropic butterflies with bright metallic wings, or some other, earlier prize he had forgotten that he had.

Discomfited, Tukum growls in his deep voice, talking fiercely in a series of sharp breaths, his large eyes flashing. He lives in a state of perpetual astonishment, and his words come in gasps, so that, when excited, he sounds like a small bellows.

"*Mel . . . mel . . . mel,*" he stammers. *Mel* is an interjection, uttered as a stopgap, while the correct answer to a question is being considered. Tukum rarely arrives at the right answer, and at the end of a long series of *mel*s, he usually says his favorite word, *welegat*. *Welegat* means "any old thing," or "just for the hell of it," or "how should I know?"

When his injured toe permitted him to walk, Tukum marched straight out to the fields and plucked a long blade of grass; bringing it back to the offending root, he tied it in a sort of forlorn bow, to indicate to other passers-by that a dangerous root existed.

Kabilek, son of Ekali, who may be twelve, wishes now to be known to his people as Lokopma. The latter name will commemorate the death of Kabilek's uncle, who was killed in a Wittaia raid near a stand of *lokop* cane, or "place of cane"—*lokop-ma*. Kabilek sees no reason to retain his present name, Kabi-lek, which means "sharp not," or "dull." While the people try as best they can to adapt to the frequent name changes, the chances are that Kabilek will henceforth go by two names rather than one. This is common enough: Asikanalek is also known as Walilo, U-mue as Wali, Polik as Mokat.

Yeke Asuk too is in the process of a name change, though his reasons are quite different. Having been wounded twice in recent months, he has decided that Yeke Asuk is an unlucky person and that he will fare better under the name of Iki, which means "finger."

A few days after Kabilek and Yeke Asuk decided to change their names, Tukum announced that he was henceforth to be dealt with under the name of Pua. *"Tukum* No!" he growled at everyone. *"An etara Pua.* I am called Pua." When asked the reason for the change, he said, *"Mel . . . mel . . . welegat."* Unlike all other name words among the Akuni, the word *Pua* means absolutely nothing, though Tukum himself insists that it means "mud."

Some time afterward, Tukum admitted that he named himself in memory of his friend Weake; Pua was short for Pua-kaloba, the sentry tower near which Weake had been killed by enemy raiders.

Tukum and his friends went on a crayfish hunt in a grassy little stream which trickles down past the salt-burning rocks and around the fences of Wuperainma, through the grove and down into the gardens. They arrived at the brook on the run and leapt into it with a great shout, though the stream, even in time of flood, is rarely more than two feet wide and one foot deep. Coming down off the steep bank, Tukum misjudged the opening and hurt his leg; he sat dolefully in the grass, feet in the water, consoling himself, uncertain about crying.

The boys moved quickly up the stream, extravagant and inefficient in their power; they felt in the mud with their swift feet, darted their hands under the grassy banks, and flew ahead. Soon Kabilek came and joined them, leaving his pigs to fend for themselves. *"Kok-meke! Kok-meke!"* they cried out—"Big one! Big one!"—and in a file, Tukum zigzagging in the rear, they would crowd and pummel into one stream behind them. In the shadows of the grass, facing each other as they probed, the tops of two heads would press together in concentration.

Weneluke found a first small crayfish, and because Weneluke is a sissy his feat irritated Uwar; he hurled grass spears at Weneluke in false playfulness, while Weneluke, backing off, smiled miserably. *"Kok-meke! Kok-meke!"* Tukum cried for no reason at all, and the boys rushed ahead, darting upstream through grass and sedge and the wild sugar cane.

In the fields above Homaklep, with Kabilek and Uwar, Tukum played a game of whirligig: the point of the game was to whirl, arms outstretched like wings, over and down a steep bank of grass, and to land gracefully on one's feet at the bottom. Since Tukum landed regularly on his back, in a stunned, crucified position, the point of the game was lost on him, and after a while he trudged away.

Down in the little stream which flows past Wuperainma, some children much smaller than himself, mostly small girls like Namilike and U-mue's daughter Nylare, were throwing twigs at dragonflies; they threw delicately, from ambush, as the dragonflies zipped past. Tukum took charge of this game, barking orders in his commanding voice, but as he was no more successful than themselves at downing dragonflies, and as his frontal assault drove all the dragonflies away, the game soon ended.

Left to himself, he dug a long, deep burrow in a bank. Into this he placed an ear-shaped fungus he had found nearby. He packed it in with earth, then sweet-potato leaves and grass, then more earth, then more leaves, and so on, until the burrow was full. The fungus he called *mokat-asuk,* or ghost-ear, and his idea was that the mokat-asuk would listen for the return of his father, who is dead. Since Tukum is beset by his mother and stepfather over the matter of his pigs, he misses his father very much and would like to have him back. But, so far as is known, the ceremony of mokat-asuk is not an effective one, and is in fact unknown to any of the people except for Tukum.

The mother of Tukum has been having trouble with Asokmeke, her husband, and has gone away to her own people at Lukigin, on the far side of the Elokera River. Tukum remained behind in Wuperainma, but yesterday he was reprimanded by Asokmeke for permitting one of their pigs to wander away toward the frontier. Tukum is at times forgetful about his pigs, being readily distracted by the other children, dragonflies, puddles of water, and wild foods, and the chances are that Asokmeke was in the right.

Nevertheless, Tukum is a very proud little boy, and since his uncle lives in Lukigin, where his mother has already gone, he has decided to go away for good. This morning he put on his thin neck the cowrie collar with its brief string of shells which is his sole belonging;

he smeared his body with pig grease until it shone, in order to make a fine impression at Lukigin. There, perhaps, he will be known as Pua. Then he set off alone on the long journey in the sun across the woods and fields, a small brown figure with a flat head and potbelly. His back was turned on Wuperainma, his pigs and his friends, his childhood, and he clutched a frail stick in his hand.

Stanzas from FLEAS

BY

Michael McClure

Fleas *is biological proof that childhood is a vision. One childhood memory lights up another—that one lights up two more that were almost hidden—those two set off several more....*

There are 250 stanzas in Fleas. *They are rhymed and spontaneous and written as fast as I could type them on an electric typewriter.* Fleas *is a Sistine doodle—a cross between the worst of Lord Byron and the best of Terry Toons.* Fleas *is an obsession like Billy the Kid and Jean Harlow were when I was writing* The Beard.

Fleas *is for my daughter Jane.*

We're angels DREAMING IN OUR HOLLOW LOGS
AND HOLES IN SNOW
the henny chicken picks and pecks
without about
&
leaving tracks.
(WE LAUGH AND GLOW)
WHAT IS THE WAY TO DREAM HELLO?
THE LEAVES HAVE LITTLE STREAMS
called veins
and dreams
of photosynthesis.
TOILET PIPES IN SCHOOLYARDS
scratched with sticks
—capturing the turds.
Frantic. Speeding. Spinning.

Henny Penny singing.
BIRDS
&
shoveler ducks with flattened beaks
and Lee and whatsisname
with sexy dirty stories.
Coronets with pink and naked chicks

ROBERT MCBURNEY
A HURDY GURNEY
His mother hired Bill Driver
(I thought)
to hold me while he kicked me.
POOR DUMB BOBBIE
who played with dolls
(boy dolls)
and tweedled little sticks
one at a time
between his fingers.
Hills Bros. coffee
and Big Chief chewing
licorice and but-
terballs and licorice root
ICE
CREAM
CONES
DOUBLE DIP
for a nickel
A big fat depression dill pickle
Bobbie's sister had birds
come and sit on her arms.
I think I saw her call them.
Magic concrete goldfish pond and evergreen cave
behind it.
Poor Toby Tortoise—it's a long ways
from Lincoln.

LADY ON THE TRAIN FROM LINCOLN
WHO WERE YOU? AM I
THE DISPOSSESSED?
Arunning down the path
through big madrones the dusty path
downhill to meet my
mother. Like a train
my frozen brain
takes shape of that lane
and then the asphalt steep.
I'd leap adashing
down
a mountain goat
a kid
Tarzan
without a plan
(not even heard of Batman)

And admirable older kids
aclicking spoons and sticks
on schoolbus
singing:
K-K-K Katie . . . Beautiful Katie
When the M-Moon shines
On the train from Lincoln were you my Muse?

WHAT DID I SEE
WHEN I TOOK A PEE
I saw myself dreaming of me
not imagining what I'd be
((((I SAW THE GIANT SPOOKY TREES
OF NEVER AND THE HEATHER OF THE FLEES
AND JASON CATCHING FLEECE
UPON THE ARGOS
AND MYSELF IN ARMIES OF THE NIGHT
A-MAKING FLIGHT
TO BE A THING OF NETHER BRIGHTENING
IN THE LIGHTNING
of a grown man
who would understand

LIKE AN INITIATE
what the shot's about
I'd set the world
to rout like Tarzan
Prince Val
& Little Nemo
in the dreamoh
of Winken, Blinkin & Nod
I imagined
I was God . . .)))
Leaning o'er the pot . . .

I LIKED PEBBLE CANDY
SHAPED AND COLORED LIKE THE ROCKS
Mother brought me some in a box
from somewhere . . .
Or was it some old lady brought
me some in a bag. . . ?
I remember running down the slope
and a dusty path past tall madrones
No bones there
no graveyard but a shortcut
to Greenwood
Mama, Mama ringing in my head . . .
And all those dreary waits
for mama—late . . .
Thirty seconds late to me
was the age of a Sequoia Tree
—And I imagined
cars driving
through
them.
I liked the rain
I'm glad I wasn't born in Spain . . .
Pretty soon I'd better
make an image
or a train . . .

LET ME PLOP DOWN SOME ANCIENT SUBTERRANEAN
EXTERIOR VISION
THAT I MIGHT HAVE HAD
of a collision
SCREEEEEEEEEEEEEEECH
eeeeeeeeeeeeek!
Batman swinging through
the window to save the chick
I could lick
those crooks myself
and save the pelf
and treasure
to return it at my leisure
secretly.
ANCIENT ELDER AARDVARKS TROMPLING BABY CITIES
Schlupping up little people
with their sticky tongues
BOOM BOOM BOOM
CRASH CRASH
TINKER TOYS AND LINCOLN LOGS
How I loved them!
I never had enough to build
a cabin.
Later I even had a little erector set!
With tinker toys I made
the weirdest creatures
and machines . . .

THE LITTLE BALLS AND JACKS GAVE ME THE CREEPS
BUT I MADE LEAPS
to learn pick-up-sticks
in Portland, and I loved
the nervous tension of the game
It was all the same
if it was a substitute for adventure
Dominoes were fun
I loved to make the little walls
and watch them run
one another down like a riffling
book—ooking like a skook . . .

And flipper movies on the corners
of big-little books
—and Chinese checkers
gave me the jitters
but I played them . . .
Hop Hop Hop
Hop Tic Tic
And legs going to sleep
in movies
and the peep
of an awakening brain
goes the woody woodpecker song
CARMEN MIRANDA

I IMAGINED I DWELT IN A SWAMP
I PLAYED IN THE SHADOW OF THE LAMP
and knew the onyx
ink holder
and the feder
pen
I was Lincoln and Jefferson
till Jimmy Martinson
stole my rubber eraser
with the picture of an ape
engraved
upon it. Then I knew
even if the sky was blue
the meaning of an evil
conning THEFT.
I left
to go home and think
and never was the same again!
APE ANGEL! APE ANGEL!
Go, Ape,
a theft is a rape
on the shape
of the spirit.

What a tiny thing to hold within
my brain
like a refrain
distaffed on reality
Descant on an old beauty . . . dreams of duty

I WANT TO GO WHERE
I WAS SO RARE
before
Aunt Jemima looked so pretty
and the man on Quaker Oats
was fat and Log Cabin
came in little tins
with chimneys for a spout . . .
BLASS GLASS SCOTTY CREAM PITCHER
I din't know what a baseball mitt
was all about . . .
((((There are seven hundred glass million
cut glass scotty cream pits in pits
screaming dreams of Arabia to lion
faced mutant men . . . Mutando mutatis . . .
Epiglottis . . . And the girl next door . . .))))
We had a bunny
I thought he was funny
but he was Satan
& silk and lace
his face
changed one day
to evil
and I coughed and coughed
and my ear
dripped out . . .
I'll remember it all
ONE DAY
&
I'll
be o.k.
and smart and pretty.

NOT DREAMING

BY

David Meltzer

Not dreaming I open the door and more flags than you can imagine fill up my room like sails.

Not dreaming I close the door and feel my toes leave the ground and my hands out of old knowledge grab for the trapeze bar and as I soar the earth below is more beautiful than fantastic photographs taken by space satellites.

Not dreaming I give up my hold on the bar and float as I've always known I could, up and down or sideways or backward, like a wheel in space I tumble through clouds which do not taste like cotton candy.

Not dreaming I am afraid of nothing at all and the earth grows green and blue, it glows with sunset gold, the electric awakening of city lights.

Not dreaming I know as I've always known that anything at all is possible and that big is small and up is down and I am a clown who is easily a butterfly who is an eye which lets light in and out of its center and I am a mouth opening to make sounds and songs and loud pleasure of laughing.

Not dreaming I land on my toes with incredible grace and face the door to my bedroom again and open it and the flags are gone and it's night outside the window and the stars are bright because I live in the country where they can be seen with great clarity.

Not dreaming I get into bed and am delighted by the cool new sheets which crinkle like paper and a feather-filled quilt warms me instantly and not dreaming I go to sleep and you can not imagine how terrific my dreams are.

MOE

BY
Leonard Michaels

ILLUSTRATED BY
ETHAN MICHAELS

Moe had a black dog, a bike, and four hundred marbles, but he was unhappy because his mother and father argued so much he couldn't ever practice his trumpet. They argued about what one of them said to the other about what the other said. Moe couldn't even hear himself play "Yankee Doodle."

So one day Moe took his bike, black dog, marbles, and trumpet and he wrote a note for his mother and father. He pinned it to the door.

> Dear Mom and Dad,
>   I'm running away for a while.
> Don't worry about it. Your son,
>   Moe

But Moe was carrying too much to run and you can't really run if you don't know where you're going. So he walked to a highway where cars and trucks were going someplace. He figured he would be someplace, too, in a little while, but the highway went through cities and over mountains to no particular place and the day became windy and cold. Moe felt tired and sat down on a grassy hill. The sun was low. There were few birds in the sky. The black dog curled up beside Moe and fell asleep. Moe then fell asleep, too.

He dreamed he was running away but carrying his trumpet and so many marbles that he had to walk, and in his dream he came to a highway and then to a hill. He sat on the hill. The moon and stars appeared as if to look at Moe. Other hills came closer and the trees gathered about him, close enough to hear if he played his trumpet. So he stood up and played all the songs he knew. Then he bowed and the trees began clapping their leaves and the hills murmured with pleasure. When he looked up for the opinion of the moon and stars, they gleamed at him. So he played his songs again and he could hear the trees whispering and the moon whispering back to them, and soon the hills began to moan and the whole world seemed very noisy. Moe cried out, "Oi, another argument," and he woke up. The sun was in the sky again. Birds were flying everywhere. Moe figured he had run away long enough. Furthermore, he felt very hungry.

So he gathered up his marbles and his bike. His black dog picked up the trumpet, and they walked back home. His mother and father were so happy to see him they stopped arguing and laughed and hugged each other. From that day on, whenever Moe was practicing his trumpet, they would become quiet and listen.

I WANT
TO HOLD
YOUR SCALPEL

BY

Marilyn Suzanne Miller

AUTHOR'S NOTE: *When I was in ninth grade, I wrote this story and sent it to a magazine. The magazine said they would print it, but only if I would change some of it. I wouldn't and they didn't. Now it is fifteen years later and the story is getting printed with no changes. The moral of this is: You may have to wait fifteen years for certain things, so try to keep busy.*

Sandy poised the scalpel over her dissecting tray, bit her lip, and lowered the scalpel into her specimen. She cut as she might a piece of juicy steak, but she hardly felt like having steak at the moment. The freshly caught lizard was easy to cut; the sight of blood made her feel faint. . . .

"No! No!" Sandy tussled with her covers in an effort to wake from the dream. Her room was drenched in pastel light and she had to blink before she could see.

"Today's D-Day," she thought, not in the least amused by Mr. Stephenson's abbreviation for Dissection Day. "Today's the day I'm going to have to cut up a dead frog, whether I want to or not."

She rolled over and stared for a moment at her hands. They were soft, small hands meant for "sonatas not soapsuds," as the detergent commercial put it. "And," she concluded sleepily, "they're not meant for chopping up dead frogs either."

The pink and orange glow that had radiated into her room at sunrise was rapidly fading now; day was approaching. She thrust one foot from between the covers. It was getting late. What was she going to wear today?

"It'll have to be the red skirt and blouse," she contemplated groggily. "That's the only thing blood stains won't show up on."

With irritation she felt herself drifting back to sleep. Realizing that she had to be up and off, she made a terrific lunge forward, succeeding only in sending the sheet flying.

The clock in the biology lab ticked loudly and buzzed ominously, signifying the beginning of fourth-period biology class. Sandy fidgeted in her seat; the dreaded hour had arrived.

"Well, now." Mr. Stephenson cleared his throat as he slammed the door. The class quieted. "I know you'll all be pleased to recall that today is January twelfth." He pointed to a red circle on the calendar behind him, his worn tweed coat sleeves brushing against the blackboard. The twinkle in his eye was unmistakable.

"As if any of us could forget," Sandy reflected grimly to herself. The red circle had been etched in her mind like acid on soft wood.

". . . meaning," Mr. Stephenson was still talking, "that today is D-Day." His voice rose in joyful anticipation. The girls moaned. "And so I suggest that you all go over to the sink and get your frogs and dissecting kits. You have one minute."

During the flurry that followed, Sandy had little time to reflect on her misfortune of having an absent lab partner. She gingerly carried her frog and dissecting implements to her seat and sat down. She set the things on her desk and stared distastefully at her frog. Its bulging eyes offered no comfort. They looked as if they might be enjoying her mental agony. They followed her every move.

Mr. Stephenson was striding toward the blackboard again, evidently preparing to lecture. As Mr. Stephenson cleared his throat to speak, Rory Davis leaned over from the desk behind Sandy's to whisper, "I hope you have fun chopping up Prince Charming!"

"Hah!" Sandy grimaced. "As far as I'm concerned, Prince Charming can climb back on his charger and clear out!"

"Now," Mr. Stephenson was saying, "considering that we probably have a few cowards in here, especially among the girls, suppose we all pet our frogs."

With a trembling hand, Sandy reached out and touched the frog's stomach. The instant her fingers made contact, she heard the frog croak.

"Chuggarrumph!"

"Eeek!" Sandy screamed. Her chair shot backward as she bolted to her feet. All talking ceased, and all eyes were upon her.

Mr. Stephenson glared at her. "Something *wrong*, Miss Turner?"

"N-n-n-o, n-n-othing," she stammered, trying to smile.

Mr. Stephenson sighed, then continued. "Now, everyone, take your probes and pull them across your frog's back a few times, sort of like back scratchers."

Sandy sat down again. Hesitantly, she picked up her probe and rubbed the frog's skin. All of a sudden, she heard a voice.

"If you kiss me," the almost inaudible baritone said, "I'll turn into Paul McCartney."

She looked furtively about. Everyone around her seemed lost in frog back-scratching. Who said that, she thought.

Dumbfoundedly she stared at the frog, realizing that *it* had spoken. It seemed to her that she recalled reading something of this sort in a fairytale somewhere. But, no, this was ridiculous. Here she sat, a perfectly normal student with a perfectly normal frog. . . .

"Kiss me," the voice whispered. This time she had no doubt that it was the frog talking. "Kiss me," it pleaded.

Suddenly, feeling a brave "it-never-hurts-to-try" streak, she leaned over and pushed its clammy face toward her lips.

"Miss Turner!" Mr. Stephenson's voice directly behind her made her jump. "May I ask what you are doing? I realize that we are all trying to establish a friendly rapport with our frogs, but wouldn't you say that this is going to an extreme?"

Turning many shades of red with embarrassment, she smiled meekly up at him.

"Well. . . ."

"Never mind. I understand. We all have our little idiosyncrasies." He gave her a condescending smile and walked to the front of the room.

Sandy touched the frog again.

"Kiss me!" it hissed.

Swiftly she leaned down and planted a kiss on

its moist forehead. Fairy tales could come true. She sat up quickly. Nothing happened.

In the front of the room, Mr. Stephenson continued his lecture. The students were calmly taking notes, unaware of all that had just happened.

In a panic she thought, "Maybe it has to be more potent." She leaned over and zeroed in on the frog's forehead again, implanting a firm kiss. Nothing happened.

"What could I be doing wrong?" Frantically she searched her mind for possible slip-ups. Suddenly it occurred to her that perhaps the frog wanted to be lifted up. But, no; how embarrassing, to kiss the frog in front of Mr. Stephenson like that—in front of the whole class.

"Wait, wait," one side of her consciousness cried. "This is for Paul! For Paul, anything!"

After a hasty glance around the room, she picked up the frog. She kissed it once. Nothing. She kissed it again. Nothing. She kissed it a third, fourth, and fifth time. Frantically, in a hysterical frenzy, she planted kiss after kiss on its forehead, adding an occasional "M'wah, m'wah!" for effect. Suddenly she realized that Mr. Stephenson had stopped talking. Face flaming, she looked up at him.

"Miss Turner, are you quite sure that you wouldn't like to see the nurse?"

"Oh, no, sir," she said hesitantly, and then rushed on. "It's just that the frog told me. . . ." Realizing her error, she bit her lip.

"And what did the frog tell you?" he asked in a sarcastically soothing tone.

"Never mind," her voice cracked with embarrassment. "Never mind."

Behind her, Rory Davis was doubled up with laughter.

"What's so funny?" she lashed out angrily under her breath, turning to him.

All of a sudden, it was as though the frog spoke again, only this time Rory was moving his lips.

"If you kiss me, I'll turn into Prince Charming."

"Oh, you!" Too furious to trust her own voice, she swiveled back in her seat.

Then, suddenly, the frog moved. It hopped off the table, jumped around, and began to grow. It grew and grew, shedding its green skin and bulging eyes—three feet, four feet, five feet tall. It grew up and up. All at once, there stood Paul.

"Paul!" she gasped. Then, regaining her composure, she smiled sweetly. "Hello, Paul."

He grinned back at her. "Chuggarrumph!"

SHARE THE CHAIR, CHEW THE SHOE

BY
Frank Modell

AND SING THIS CRAZY SONG FOR YOU

SHARE THE CHAIR
CHEW THE SHOE
AND
SING THIS CRAZY
SONG FOR YOU

CHOMP, CHOMP, CHOMP,
CHOMP CHOMP,

OH, WE, SHARE, THE CHAIR

WE, CHEW, THE SHOE, (repeat)

AND SING — THIS CRAZY SONG FOR YOU

CHOMP, CHOMP, CHOMP
CHOMP, CHOMP.

THE MEADOWS OF UELEN

BY

N. Scott Momaday

ILLUSTRATED BY
N. SCOTT MOMADAY

The boy Pai-talee dreamed. In his dream he journeyed to the very edge of the earth, where there is frost on the sun. He stood for a long time on the edge, looking out across the dark distance. After a time he could see the meadows of Uelen on the other side. There was a field of bright light and in it were wildflowers of many colors. Horses pranced in the meadows. The young man Pai-talee saw that the horses had horns. He had never seen such a sight, and he knew that he must make a powerful song.

> *I have seen*
> *the horses with horns*
> *the horses with horns*
> *they roam in the meadows*
> *the meadows of Uelen*
> *their horns catch the light*
> *their hooves catch the light*
> *the horses with horns*
> *I have seen*

This song Pai-talee brought back from his dream. This song the old man Pai-talee brought back from the edge of the earth, and he kept it in his heart all the days of his life.

THE CHINESE HONEY-SELLER'S JOURNEY

BY

Jan Morris

Long ago in China a honey-seller set out on a journey. In those days China was divided into many little states, and he had to walk right across one of them, on his way from Ping-Ting, the next state to the south, to Ho-Yun, the next state to the north, where a customer awaited him. He carried his honey in a big vat on his back, and as he passed through the village of Lo-ping a drop fell out of it to the ground: but he did not notice it, of course, and walked cheerfully on to his destination.

Behind him, though, a cat emerged from a doorway to lick up that drop of honey. A dog attacked the cat, snarling and biting. The cat's owner threw a hammer at the dog's owner. The dog owner's family, seizing their swords, fell upon the cat owner's family. The neighbors of each ran to their support. The village was divided, and presently the country neighborhoods took up arms as well. District fought against district, province against province, until the two supreme war lords of the state summoned their battalions and spike-wheeled chariots, and marched upon each other. For several weeks the whole state was plunged in civil war. Cities were wrecked, the countryside was devastated, and whole communities were put to the sword.

The honey-seller did not dare return home until the fighting had ended, so he stayed with cousins of his in Ho-Yun. When all was quiet, he walked back to Ping-Ting. He was very sorry to see the destruction around his path, and surprised to find that the village of Lo-ping seemed to have disappeared altogether: but he had got a good price for his honey, and had quite enjoyed himself in Ho-Yun, so all in all he was not dissatisfied with his journey.

MORAL: Feed your cat twice daily.

THE DAY I FOLLOWED THE MAYOR AROUND TOWN

BY

Willie Morris

To Marina, a little girl who has a lot of big dogs

I am acquainted with dogs. In Mississippi when I was a boy I grew up with dogs. First there were the tall, slender bird dogs my father and I took hunting in the delta swamps. They helped us hunt quail and squirrels and they shared in the feasts my mother made from these delicacies of the forest. Their names were Tony, Sam, and Jimbo, and on those long-ago winter nights down in Yazoo when I was growing so fast that my knees and elbows hurt, Tony, Sam, and Jimbo slept in my bed with me, wrapping themselves around me soft as ermine, waking me every morning at two A.M. with their sudden howls as the Memphis-to-New Orleans train roared through the drowsing town. As the years passed, one by one my bird dogs died. I prayed they had all gone up to the Methodist dog-heaven.

Then there was a succession of English smooth-haired fox terriers. Their names were Sonny, Duke, and finally Old Skip, shipped down to us all the way from a kennel in Missouri. Old Skip was the smartest dog in the state of Mississippi. I got him in the fourth grade and he went right through high school with me. He was black and white and had a sturdy body, and with the exception of Ichabod Crane, a dog of my adulthood, he was the most athletic of all my dogs. He could play football with the boys, or catch a tennis ball thrown forty feet up on the fly. Every morning for years he walked the eight blocks to school with me, then went back home and lounged under an elm tree all day until I returned. He loved listening to the radio, especially country music, and he went to Mr. Buddy Reeves's grocery store every morning to fetch the Memphis *Commercial Appeal* for us, returning with it rolled up in his mouth. We were inseparable in the summers of my youth, in that isolated Southern hamlet before the expressways and television, and I can see his funny black face as if the years had stood still for me.

I taught Old Skip how to drive a car. I would prop him on the steering wheel of my father's green DeSoto and duck my head under the dashboard. We would drive by the Dew Drop Inn where the old Negro men sat on their haunches in front chewing tobacco and whittling on wood amid the dusty facades, and with my foot on the accelerator I would slow the car to ten or twelve miles an hour and guide the steering wheel with a couple of fingers. Old Skip would have the steering wheel in his paws, his long black head peering through the windshield at the dirt road ahead. The men would shout: "Look at that old dog drivin' a car!" Old Skip, the comrade of my adolescence, died when I was far away in college, trying to outflank a flea which had plagued him for most of a decade. My father buried him in the backyard not far from Tony, Sam, Jimbo, Sonny, and Duke.

2 Years later, when I was a grown man living in New York, I got my little boy David a fox terrier like Old Skip. She was a girl and we named her Harper. One night David saw her killed by a car in front of our farmhouse. He grieved only as little boys can grieve. He vowed he would never again have another dog.

The days passed. On misty evenings I read to the little boy from Washington Irving, a writer of brooding and scary tales who had lived not far from us many years before. I especially read to him *The Legend of Sleepy Hollow,* and his eyes grew wide as he heard about the Dutch schoolteacher frightened away by the Headless Horseman. Slow as could be, in that strange chemistry of diminishing hurt, he began to change his mind. All of a sudden one day he said that he wanted a big dog who would fit the name Ichabod Crane.

He and I searched many counties in the Hudson River Valley. This quest lasted for weeks. We followed the classified advertisements in the newspapers. We visited kennels and looked at German shepherds, Dalmatians, collies, Irish setters, sheepdogs, bulldogs, and various other kinds of outstanding puppies. But the little boy always looked at them and shook his head. They failed to fit the name.

We had almost given up. Then one luminous autumn afternoon, the fields of the Hudson Valley lush with corn, and pumpkins sometimes far as the eye could see, we drove a long way to look at some black labrador retrievers. The owner of the kennel opened the gate to a fence and six shiny black puppies came out, wobbling back and forth on their new legs. One of them circled around for a while, investigated a shrub with much curiosity, and then came to David, nuzzling his hand with a cold wet nose. David sat down to touch him. Then he looked up at me. "That's him," he said. "That's Ichabod Crane."

We wrapped him in a blanket and took him home, and he was with us for seven years, our Ichabod Crane. He grew so fast he almost buzzed like a bee, and when he reached his full size he was coal-black and strong, with floppy ears and web-feet and liquid brown eyes full of comprehension. He was a fount of delight and unfailing mischief, a devilish intellect, a retriever of sticks, balls, and all other flying objects, a loyal friend of tenderness and love. He slept in the bed with David as my old bird dogs had done, but he never once howled at the trains. When we moved to a small village on Long Island called Bridgehampton we found him to be an ocean swimmer, too, and we would watch his head bobbing above the Atlantic waves on many afternoons of summer.

We were planning a beach cookout for Ichabod Crane on his seventh birthday. But that day he did not come home. David and I got in the car and drove around the countryside for hours. On a road near the ocean I saw a black speck far in the distance, and as we drove closer it was the unfolding of my deepest premonitions. It was Ichabod Crane, struck dead by a car. David and I put him gently in the back seat and went home and cried. Later we buried him in one of his favorite places, under some shade trees by a cool inland pond.

The little boy was no longer so little, and the father was no longer so young. It was the father this time who vowed never to have another dog.

3

The island seasons changed, and changed again. The years passed, and the little boy went away to college.

There was a dog I had begun to notice casually in the village, a black labrador almost the replica of Ichabod Crane, about the same age and with the same floppy ears and black mane and liquid brown eyes, yet more pensive in his demeanor—a pedigreed individual, for sure, with good blood flowing in his veins, yet with scars here and there on his body from his wanderings of the earth. He had come to the village from Lord knows where, and he more or less lived with the men who ran the service station on main street. Had he run away from some cruel

master somewhere? Or had he simply sought out our village as a fine
place to settle down? No one knew, but after a time the questions which
at first intrigued everyone did not matter at all. Since I would stop at the
service station for gasoline, I got to know this most distinguished vaga-
bond, whose name was Pete. Sometimes I would bring bits of candy to
him, and he grew to recognize my car and would hail me down on
main street and ask to ride around with me for a while. He would get in
the back seat and stick his head out the window to let the breeze rustle his
big old ears. Or he would sit up front with me to let me know he liked
me. When he took a nap in the village, it was in the shade of the war
memorial with the names on it of the village boys killed in all the wars.
He got to know everyone in town, and would wander up and down main
street all day greeting the people. It was for just such as this that Pete
came to be known as "The Mayor of Bridgehampton." Once David, back
home on a vacation, took a photograph of Pete at the war memorial and
had it published in the local newspaper, which ran it with the caption:
"His Honor the Mayor."

Then an unexpected thing happened. One after-
noon I heard a loud scratching at my back door and went to see who
it was. It was Pete, asking to be let inside. I opened the door and he came
right in and flopped down next to a sofa, as if he owned the place. He
stayed there most of the day. Around sunset I told him to get back to the
service station before it closed. He refused to leave.

I had often talked to the dogs I knew, partic-
ularly when they were being unreasonable, so I said: "Look, Mr. Mayor,
I promised myself I wouldn't ever have another dog." When he looked up
at me, I was certain he understood. But he did not budge.

Pete had come to live with me. I was convinced,
in fact, that for the past several weeks he had been looking me over with
just that aim in mind. Had he been a human, he would have brought
along a toothbrush and a suitcase; it was that kind of decision.

So now I have another dog, and a most unlikely
one he is. Unlike Ichabod Crane, he refuses to chase sticks or balls. When
I throw something for him, he simply gazes at me as if such diversions
are beneath his official station. Furthermore, he is the only labrador I
ever saw who does not like the water. He will go to the beach and stroll
down to the ocean and put his paw in it, and then grimace with distaste.
As with Old Skip, I tried to teach him to drive a car, but he spurned that
also. I am not suggesting that he is lazy; it is merely that he has certain
priorities. He moves slowly, with a studied calm that borders on a royal
dignity. He is not young—Doctor Gould, the veterinarian, once looked

down in his mouth and ears and pronounced him to be eight years old—
but his age has nothing to do with these circumscriptions. It finally
dawned on me that Pete knows he is the Mayor.

It is for this reason, among others, that he is the
most fiercely independent dog I ever knew, zealously aware of his own
prerogatives, a living symbol of Jeffersonian democracy. He goes his own
way whenever he wishes; most of the day he is in the village among his
constituents.

Sometimes I believe he considers me slightly
insane. He sleeps under the worktable where I write, and occasionally he
wakes up and looks at me at work on my typewriter, as if to say: "Why do
you pound on that little box all day, you crazy fool?" In retaliation, occasionally I pick the ticks off him one by one.

Yet, since I am acquainted with dogs, I know
that beneath our alliance lies an ineffable friendship. The gestures of it
are not idle. When he sights me in the village in his eternal peregrina-
tions, he rushes up to me with his eyes ablaze and embraces me with his
paws. When I talk to him as he lies on the floor of our house, his tail
thuds vigorously on the floor with the sound of each word. Sometimes he
nuzzles my hand with his nose, just as Ichabod Crane did many years ago
when David discovered him at the kennel in the Hudson Valley, and he
says to me with his eyes: "Good ol' buddy."

4 One morning quite recently I de-
cided to follow him into the village without his knowing it, merely to see
what he does with his rugged independence. He breakfasted on half a
can of dog food, then left the house at ten A.M. as he always does and
strolled down the broad boulevard dappled in the shade of enormous oak
trees toward main street. I gave him a decent start, then trailed surrepti-
tiously fifty yards behind him.

His first stop was in front of the Polish grocery,
where he greeted the old men who loiter there at all hours. "There's the
Mayor!" one of them shouted, and the others swiftly joined in the chorus.
Pete made his salutations to each of them, then sat among them for a while
watching the cars go by. A large dog named Cato, known in the village
as Pete's police commissioner, appeared from around a corner and sat next
to Pete scanning the morning scene—a kind of informal policy confer-

ence, perhaps. I was hiding behind the war memorial and watched Pete as he got up and crossed the street to the drugstore, pushed open the door with his nose, and walked inside to see Emil, the proprietor. "Good morning, Your Honor," I heard Emil say, and Pete sniffed among the cosmetics and waited around tactfully until Emil gave him a lifesaver mint.

After a few minutes he strolled outside again and went next door to the library. He sat on the front lawn as the people he knew came by, each one calling him by name, paying their deferences to the dignity of his office. Next he ambled down to the Village Restaurant, opened the door again with his nose, and went in to mingle with the potato farmers having their morning coffee. "Hello, Mr. Mayor!" I heard a shout from inside. "How's politics today?"

After ten minutes or so with the potato farmers, he emerged once more. I trailed at a discreet distance as he paused near the hardware store and played a while with some small children, then said hello to the people waiting in line at the welfare office. Momentarily he pushed his way into the Vogue Beauty Salon and dallied for an interval with the ladies reading Hollywood magazines under the hairdriers. Next he went to the bank to see the tellers and the people he knew cashing checks. After that he walked down to the Post Office and tarried among the activity there, then he went to each of the three bars in the village to give his respects to the morning beerdrinkers. In the bars there was much amiable banter directed his way, and one solicitation in particular: "Here's our Mayor! How about a Budweiser, Your Honor?" Next, as I hid behind a tree near the Community House, he stopped at the Candy Kitchen to welcome the high school students at their noontime break; one of them rubbed his back and presented him the remnants of an ice cream cone. Then on to the jailhouse, where he poised beneath a cell window and a prisoner he had gotten to know threw him a piece of bread. His stop after this was the train station to see who might step off the 12:15 from Penn Station. He only recognized one person here, an elderly gentleman named Halsey who paused to give his ears a friendly tug.

Then he retraced his steps back up main street, moving ever so slowly, stopping to exchange salutations with his constituents on the sidewalk. Sometimes he wandered onto the porches of the houses lining the street to pass a little time with the women sweeping, or snapping string beans. Near the church with its tall spire gleaming in the sunshine he loitered with some construction workers who were putting in a new sewer; he stood at the edge of the hole in the street and gazed into it with official curiosity. He glowered at a pair of frolicsome cats—a stare of cold political hostility. Briefly he retreated into the shade of the graveyard, and as I spied on him from behind a large gravestone he lay down with all four feet sticking up and scratched his back vigorously on the grass. Occasionally someone in a passing car would see him and yell: "Hi there, Pete! How's His Honor today?"

Fully rested after a few minutes, he got up, stretched and yawned, and looked up and down main street again. Since nothing unusual caught his attention, he took a shortcut through the graveyard and several backyards to our house. Knowing him as I did, he would now have an afternoon siesta and then, regular as a metronome, repeat his morning ritual later in the day, stopping at the places he had not had the inclination to visit on his earlier rounds.

He is sleeping now under my worktable. I look down at him, awash in his labrador dreams. Once I thought he might be Ichabod Crane, returned from the grave to watch out for me. No—he is too much his own character for such as that. He is Pete and nobody else. Yet he brings back to me my boyhood, all the long-ago things I miss— my father's footsteps on the porch, my mother playing a hymn on the piano, all the boys and girls I once knew, the smells of a new spring morning in Mississippi—and in him for me are the vanished spirits of Tony, Sam, Jimbo, Sonny, Duke, and Old Skip, especially good Old Skip dead these years. Dogs give continuity to a man's life; they help hold the fractured pieces of it together. When Pete the Mayor came to live with me, he reaffirmed the contours of my own existence.

M'HEND
AND THE
MONSTERS

BY

Mohammed Mrabet

M'hend lived with his mother and grandmother at the edge of a little village high in the mountains. Very early each morning he got up and drank a big wooden bowl full of milk. Then he would take up his staff of olive wood and lead all the sheep and goats out into the valley so they could graze. There he would meet the other boys of the village with their flocks, and all day they wrestled and fenced with their staffs, pretending the sticks were swords. When the sun went down each boy would get his animals together and drive them back home. Even when he was very young, M'hend was the best fencer in the village. He could always knock the staff from the hand of the other boy.

For some time his grandmother had noticed that their sheep and goats were fatter than the others in the village. One day she asked M'hend about it.

"I take them to a different place, farther away," he told her.

"Take them where you like, but don't go into the forest. It's a bad place," she said.

"I'll be all right," M'hend assured her.

"No!" she said. "You stay away from the forest."

"But that's where I've been taking them all this time," he said. "And nothing has ever happened."

Then his mother spoke up. "Listen to me," she said. "I'm going to tell you something you don't know. It happened only a few months before you were born. One day your father went up into the forest to get some wood. The monster that lives there saw him and killed him. The other men didn't find him for three days. That's why you have no father. And you go up there with the goats and sheep? Have you ever seen anybody else take his animals there?"

"No," said M'hend. "I'm the only one."

"So don't go there again."

After that M'hend let the flocks graze in the valley with the others. The years went by.

When M'hend was sixteen he began, like most boys of that age, to dream of having adventures. One day he went to his grandmother and asked her to show him his father's sword.

"Very well, son," she said. She opened a big chest at the end of the room. Then she pulled out the sword and handed it to M'hend, who looked at it with love.

His grandmother went on taking things out of the chest. She showed M'hend some heavy woolen capes that his father had worn, and the saddle and stirrups he had used.

"Tomorrow I'm going to market," M'hend told her. "I want to look for a horse."

"You needn't do that," she said. "Your uncle has a horse he'll let you use. Ask him."

The next morning M'hend went to see his uncle. He looked at all the horses and picked out the one he liked best. After kissing his uncle's hand, he led the horse to his house and fitted his father's saddle over its back. Then across his own shoulders he threw one of his father's capes, took the sword in his hand, and led the flocks out to pasture on horseback.

This time he went straight to the forest. He kept watch over the animals from where he sat astride his horse. It was not long before he saw that a storm was coming. A wind had sprung up, dark clouds rolled overhead, and the sound of thunder grew louder. When the rain began to fall, the sheep and goats went deeper into the forest for shelter. And as M'hend sat there on the horse, staring after them, he saw a huge animal shaped like a man coming toward him between the trees.

It came nearer, and then it spoke. "What are you doing here, son of Adam?"

"Waiting for you," said M'hend. "You killed my father, and I'm waiting for you."

The animal grinned. "You want to kill me? Is that it?"

"That's right, and I'm going to."

The animal bounded at him, but failed to reach him. Then, still astride his horse, M'hend brought his sword down on the monster's arm. At this, it turned and ran into the forest, while M'hend rode after it.

In a dark part of the forest there was a great well. When the animal came to this, it disappeared over the side, down into the hole. M'hend rode up, jumped to the ground, and uprooted small trees and bushes, which he threw down the wall, packing them in tightly.

It took him a long time to get his flocks together and drive them back to the village in the rain.

The next day M'hend returned to the well in the forest, taking with him another young man from the village, named Mlaqine. Together they pulled the trees and bushes out of the well, and looked down into the darkness.

"There's no monster down there," said Mlaqine.

"Let's go down and see," said M'hend.

"No, no. You go if you want," Mlaqine told him.

"All right," said M'hend. "I'll go down. But you stand guard up here. If I tug on the rope, you pull it up."

He fastened a stout rope around his waist, and slowly Mlaqine lowered him into the well. At the bottom he found no water, but at one side there was a recess in the rocks where a dim light flickered. Then he saw that the light came from a small oil lamp hung on the wall beside a door. He pushed the door open and walked into a cave. A very beautiful girl in a yellow and gold caftan stood there, staring at him in surprise.

"What are you doing here?" she cried.

"I'm looking for a monster that came down here," M'hend told her.

"He's had an accident," she said. "He's my father."

"I want to see him."

"What for?"

"Because I'm the one who wounded him," said M'hend.

The girl shook her head. "I can't bear to see a nice young man like you killed in front of my eyes," she told him.

"But I still want to see your father," M'hend insisted. "Just show me where he is."

The girl sighed. "All right. Come with me."

She opened a door into an inner room, where a girl was sitting. "This is my sister," she said. "I have six." Then they continued into a farther room. One of her sisters was in here. Each room opened into another room, deeper inside the cave, and there was a girl in each one, until they came to the sixth room, which was empty. The girl who was leading M'hend pointed to a door beyond.

"That's my father's room. My oldest sister is in there, taking care of him."

When she opened the door, M'hend saw the monster lying on the floor. The monster looked up, saw M'hend, and began to laugh. "So you managed to get all the way down here," it said.

"Even if you were in the seventh hell I'd find you!" M'hend cried. "You killed my father, and I've got to kill you."

The monster laughed again. "When I get well, I'm at your service," it said. "My daughters can look after you while you wait."

"The only one I want is this one here, the one who brought me to this room," said M'hend. "And I'm not going to wait!"

As he said this he raised his sword high in the air and came down with it on the monster's neck. The oldest and the youngest daughters merely watched.

Then, carrying the head in his hands, he went back through the seven rooms and out into the well. He tied the head to the rope and tugged on the rope. Mlaqine pulled it up.

When the daughters saw that their father was really dead, they asked to be pulled up out of the well. So, one by one, M'hend tied them to the rope, and Mlaqine pulled them up. When M'hend himself appeared from below, they all set out for the village. The people came out of their houses at the sight of the seven beautiful girls in their fine caftans of silk.

They went to M'hend's house, where his mother and grandmother prepared a big dinner for them. Meanwhile the news spread that M'hend had killed the monster, and everyone in the village came to thank him.

M'hend's mother saw that M'hend paid attention only to the youngest girl, and after they had eaten she asked him if he was thinking of marrying her. Before he could reply, the girl spoke.

"There's no use in even thinking about such a thing as long as my cousin is alive. He's a monster, too, and we're going to be married this year. If you and I got married, he'd come and kill us all. It's impossible."

The six girls nodded their heads. "Yes, it's impossible," they agreed.

M'hend said nothing, but later he got the youngest girl by herself for a moment and began to ask her questions about her cousin.

"He lives beyond the Hundred and One Mountains," she told him. "There's a high peak with a round lake at the top, full of hot water. He lives there by himself on an island in the middle of the lake. He's famous all through the Hundred and One Mountains as a great swordsman. But this is only because he has an ancient sword with special power in it. When he strikes at a tree with it, the blade goes straight through to the other side of the trunk."

"Just tell me how to get there," said M'hend. "And tell me what you want me to bring back for you. His clothes, or some part of his body?"

"No. Just his sword. I'd like to see you wearing it," said the girl. And she went on to tell M'hend how to get to the Hundred and One Mountains and which paths to take in order to cross them.

"There's one more thing," she said. "If you go, you must take all six of my sisters with you. They want to go and live there on the island. They'll go with you and stay there, and if you can kill him, you'll come back."

M'hend spent three days preparing for his journey. Then, leaving the youngest sister in the house with his mother and grandmother, he set out with the other six girls for the Hundred and One Mountains. They walked for several weeks, until ahead of them they could see a high peak with a great cloud of steam rising from it.

"That's the place!" the girls cried. "Our father told us about it many times, and it looks just as he said it did."

They spent two days climbing the mountain. When they got to the top, they looked down from a rocky ledge at a circular lake with a small island in the center. The steam blew into their faces, and M'hend could feel the heat that rose from the bubbling water below. Then they began to make their way over the rocks, down toward the edge of the water. At each step it grew hotter. M'hend found it hard to breathe, but the girls did not seem to notice the heat. When they reached the shore, M'hend stood still, looking across the water at the island. Three of the girls went to the left along the edge of the water, and the other three went to the right.

Soon they began to call out: "Sayid! Sayid! Sayid!" The echoes bounced from rock to rock around the lake. And a moment later a wind came up, driving the steam toward them in even heavier clouds, and M'hend saw the monster opposite him on the island. It was huge and held a sword in one hand.

"Cousins! Daughters of my uncle!" it bellowed. "Have you come bringing good news, and with a friend?"

"No! No!" they cried. "He's an enemy, and we have bad news for you."

The monster snorted and dived into the water, making a great churning and bubbling. In no time at all it had swum ashore and was advancing upon M'hend with its sword.

Each time the monster dealt a blow it shut its eyes for an instant. M'hend, who was an expert at dodging, kept out of its way with ease, so that the monster's blade merely split the rocks around them. Finally M'hend managed to thrust the point of his sword into the other's eye. The monster roared, dropped its sword, and put its hand over its eye. Swiftly M'hend buried his sword in the monster's belly, and picking up the other sword, brought it down with all his might on its huge head. When the girls saw this, they jumped into the lake and disappeared.

Using the monster's sword, M'hend chopped its body into small pieces and left them to dry in the sun. Then he started to climb up over the rocks, to get away as fast as possible from the terrible heat.

He had not climbed more than halfway to the top before he heard the girls screaming. He stopped and listened. "Save us, or we'll die!" they cried. As he was about to turn back, he heard, close to his ear, the voice of the youngest sister saying: "No! No! You don't know them. If you go back, they'll kill you. Just keep climbing."

Not knowing whether he had really heard the voice in his ear or not, M'hend started ahead. All he wanted was to get to the top of the rocks and breathe cool air again.

When he had nearly reached the summit, the girls began to scream once more. They went on for such a long time, and they sounded so piteous, that M'hend felt sorry for them, and stopped climbing.

"We're drowning! they cried. "Turn around and you'll see us."

But then in his ear he heard the girl at his house say: "No. Look straight ahead, and find the right path home."

Once again M'hend started to climb. Soon he was at the top. Without pausing, he quickly made his way down the other side. Now he could no longer hear the voices. He fastened the monster's sword into his belt, and set off in the direction of the mountains where he lived.

Now that the girls were not with him, M'hend was able to walk much faster. He got to his village in half the time it had taken him to get to the One Hundred and One Mountains. By the time he reached home his clothes were in rags and his skin was burned to a deep brown. After he had kissed his mother and grandmother, he went to the girl and laid the monster's sword on the floor in front of her.

"Your sisters are there and the sword is here," he told her.

"I knew they wanted to kill you, and I called to you and told you not to go back," she said.

"And I heard you!" cried M'hend. "You saved my life."

He sat down on the floor beside her and drew her close to him, and they were both happy.

RABBIT

BY
Shiga Naoya

ILLUSTRATED BY
ALLEN SAY

Ｗe keep a rabbit now and feed it oak and bamboo leaves. Weeds will be coming up soon and feeding the rabbit will be easier.

Once we raised rabbits in Yamashina and once in Nara, but I didn't think they were interesting animals to have around. At Yamashina, we let them have the run of the garden and they went under the house and lived beneath the livingroom. There was a large pond in the garden and often it was amusing to watch the baby rabbits play on the lawn around the pond. But in the spring, when many vegetables began to sprout in neighboring fields, our rabbits went under the hedge and began to ravage the crops until a farmer complained. We gave all the rabbits away.

In Nara, there were five or six Chinese parasol trees in front of the kitchen and a mud wall stood on either side of them. We stretched wire nets between the walls and kept a rabbit in the enclosure. Soon it made a hole in the ground and it seemed that she had given birth inside. When I dug up the hole to have a look, there were five little rabbits bunched together at the bottom of a deep, twisted tunnel. The ground was bedded-down not only with straw, but with fur the mother rabbit had torn off her own chest, exposing her pink flesh. Because we only wanted to raise rabbits and had no thought of eating them, we let them all go off into the woods of Kasuga. Since no one saw them after that, I suspect they were caught by either men or dogs.

The one we now have was bequeathed to us by the office of the local town council, where it was born. One day toward the end of last year, Kimiko, our youngest daughter, said, "May we keep a rabbit?"

"We'll have to eat it when it gets big," I replied. "You may keep it only if you will agree to this."

"I don't mind, because once we raise it Father will never be able to kill it."

"Oh, yes, I will kill it and eat it. Yes, I'll certainly eat it."

"That's all right," smiled Kimiko.

Without delay we made a box to put the rabbit in. We drove a square wood post into the ground in front of the dining room and made something like a serving tray, a foot and a half square, and nailed it flat on top of the stake. Kimiko came home cradling a tiny rabbit which couldn't have been more than a few days old.

During the day we put the rabbit on the traylike platform and, at night, we put it in a box on the concrete floor of the porch.

The rabbit ate voraciously and produced many little droppings that looked like black beans. Every morning we collected the droppings and buried them at the peony roots. Gradually the rabbit grew larger.

We put a small box on its side in a corner of the platform and the rabbit would run into it to hide every time an airplane went overhead or the sound of a blue magpie was heard. The rabbit constantly twitched the tip of its nose, but evidently depended on its hearing. Whenever there was the distant bark of a dog, its ears stood up at once. The twitching of its nose ceased. It became perfectly still. Sometimes it stood on its hind legs with one ear turned in front and the other ear turned back. Sometimes, stretched out in the sunlight, it had only one ear standing up out of laziness.

One morning a bedquilt was dropped down from the upstairs bow where it hung for airing. Startled by the noise, the rabbit jumped down from the platform and hid in the bushes. All in all it is an easily frightened animal. Or so I thought. There was a time when a cat hung helplessly by its front paw claws which were hooked onto the edge of the platform after trying to jump onto it. The rabbit peered timidly down at the cat from above, twitching its nose.

Once Kimiko was alone in the dining room and heard strange squeaking noises and rushed outside to see a dog chasing the rabbit. Seeing Kimiko the dog promptly made its escape, but now the rabbit was even frightened of Kimiko and she had a hard time catching it. A wound on the rabbit's forehead was still bleeding. The scar remains to this day.

I thought it was an animal that did not cry, but it too has a voice. I noticed later that it emits a low cooing sound when it is happy. When I go near it, it comes close to me and coos. When I imitate the cooing, it coos back. It turns out to be a more tamable animal than I thought. For some time now I have been staying up nights and when I went to the toilet the other night—it is located under the porch—I startled the rabbit and it scuttled under the porch step to hide. But he was waiting outside the door when I came out and circled around my feet in joy. It tried following me into the hallway so I chased it back and had to prop a board across the porch entrance so it wouldn't follow me.

Now that it's larger, we've discarded the tray-like platform. In its place we drove a supporting stake into the ground and built a three-foot square platform out of a rain shutter. When we took the rabbit out of its box in the morning, it frolicked on the new area by running, jumping, sliding, and missing its footing with one of its hind legs. When I went near it, it came up to me and, without provocation, bolted suddenly as a dog does. It seemed as if it wanted to play a run-and-chase game. It's also very much like a dog when it comes over and obstructs me trying to clean the platform. When I try to push it away, it crouches purposely and refuses to move. It also likes to be petted, especially when I massage around its neck. The rabbit puts its throat on the platform and sits perfectly still with its eyes closed.

Of the three times we have kept rabbits, this one is certainly the most entertaining. Because of the scarcity of food we cannot really keep animals. It's been a long while since our last pet and perhaps for this reason I take such an interest in this one.

It's become a pleasure in recent days to watch the rabbit on the platform through the dining room window. I realize that almost every gesture it makes is depicted in the Japanese paintings of old. I had known the gestures of the rabbit first in paintings. Watching our rabbit, Sōtatsu comes to my mind at once—his strokes deftly simple, expressing the essence of the rabbit in all its liveliness. It's curious that I did not think of Seihō's realistic rendering of the rabbit. I suspect that true form cannot be captured by realism. I find it interesting that a live rabbit is nearer by far to Sōtatsu than Seihō.

I had one of my children weigh the rabbit and it has grown to 5.4 pounds. By touching its back I can feel its thickening flesh.

This is another story, but the other day W., who

lives nearby, taught me a method of killing rabbits. A live rabbit had been given to him and since he had to kill it before eating it, he wrapped twine around the rabbit's neck and hung it from a nail outside and let it hang until it died a while later. W. said, It was dead without shedding blood.

But I cannot kill our rabbit. To tell the truth, together with Kimiko, I knew this from the beginning.

—Translated from the Japanese
by Allen Say and David Meltzer

RHUBARB AT HOME

BY

Howard Nemerov

Two boys have invented a baseball game
That works like a real one, or almost the same,

Though played in the yard and having for bases
This tree, that bush and that rock; it works on that basis

Till sooner or later there's one thing makes trouble
When somebody gets a base hit, triple or double—

And they get on base and they suddenly disappear!
You have to remember who's really where,

And if both boys don't remember the same
It means the instant end of that ball game.

For Jeremy gives Zander the word:
"Your guy's out on a force-play at third."

Which isn't at all as Zander had reckoned:
"He can't be, you dope, he hadn't reached second."

So what happens is one team, in tears, is the Sads,
And the other, in sullens and sulks, is the Mads,

And the Mads maintain that the Sads are beat,
While the Sads complain that the Mads always cheat,

And there's a wailing and screeching of Sads and Mads
Just under a window that happens to be Dad's,

Who comes down in his wisdom to settle the matter
By fooling the pitcher and conning the batter

Into some kind of compromise so totally sappy
It looks like no one will ever be happy,

Till Sad and Mad grin and agree it is Dad
Who is Bad. The moral to this is one that I had

Somewhere around here, in this pocket or that—
Oops, no, it was here all the time in my hat:

"Invisible base-runners"—that's what it says here—
"Must not be lost sight of nor let disappear."

TWO POEMS

Ron Padgett

I HAVE ANTS IN MY PANTS

I have ants in my pants
and they are wearing pants
and there are little tiny ants in those pants
Isn't that *odd*?

THE GIRAFFE

The 2 f's
in giraffe
are like
2 giraffes
running through
the word giraffe

The 2 f's
run through giraffe
like 2 giraffes

THE SAD STORY ABOUT THE SIX BOYS ABOUT TO BE DRAFTED IN BROOKLYN

BY

Grace Paley

I

There were six boys in Brooklyn and none of them wanted to be drafted.

Only one of them went to college. What could the others do?

One shot off his index finger. He had read about this in a World War I novel.

One wore silk underpants to his physical. His father had done that for World War II.

One went to a psychiatrist for three years starting three years earlier (his mother to save him had thought of it).

One married and had three children.

One enlisted and hoped for immediate preferential treatment. This is what happened next:

II

The boy who enlisted was bravely killed. There was a funeral for him at home. People sat on boxes and wore new sackcloth as it was one of the first of that family's bad griefs. They ate and wept.

Then, accidentally, due to a mistake in the filing system, the married father of three children was drafted. He lived a long time, maybe three months, and killed several guerrillas, two by strangulation, two by being a crack shot, and one in self-defense. Then he was killed as he slept in the underbrush for other people think they ought to act in self-defense too.

A couple of years later, the boy who had gone to the psychiatrist for three years and the boy in the silk underpants were reclassified. Because of their instabilities, they had always been against killing. Luckily, they never got farther than the middle airlane over the very middle of the Pacific Ocean. There, the mighty jet exploded, perhaps due to sabotage, distributing 133 servicemen in a blistery blaze to their watery graves.

As the war went on and on, the college boy became twenty-six years old. He was now in his eighth year in college. He could not remember the name of his high school when he applied for his first job. He could not remember his mother's maiden name, which is essential to applications. Nervousness ran in that family and finally reached him. He was taken to rest in a comfortable place in pleasant surroundings where he remained for twelve years. When he was about thirty-eight, he felt better and returned to society.

Now, the man with the shot-off index finger:

III

Even after four years, he didn't miss that finger. He had used it to point accusingly at guilty persons, for target shooting, for filing alphabetically. None of these actions concerned him anymore. To help him make general love, he still had his whole hand and for delicate love, his middle finger.

Therefore he joyfully married and fathered several children. All of them had shot-off index fingers, as did their children.

That family became a peaceful race apart. Sickness and famine didn't devastate them. Out of human curiosity they traveled and they were stubborn and tough like the feathery seeds of trees that float over mountain barriers and railroad valleys. In far places the children of the children of the man with the shot-off index finger gathered into settlements and cities and of course, they grew and multiplied.

And that's how at last, if you can believe it, after the dead loss of a million dead generations, on the round, river-streaked face of the earth, war ended.

DEAR PARROT

BY

John Phillips

ILLUSTRATED BY
ANNA DIBBLE

Nobody knows how the birds began. Not really. Not even the Parrot remembers.

Ornithologists base their theories upon the fossils of extinct birds and of creatures that came in time before the birds— eons and eitons and alautons ago. Like all scientists, ornithologists are learned men, but not so wise as the philosophers and the poets, who taught the scientists what to think. Aristotle, for instance, the ancient Greek who may have been the greatest thinker who ever thought, was so impressed by the parrots his pupil Alexander the Great brought back from the conquest of India some twenty-three centuries ago that he wrote a fine description of this bird for future ornithologists. As for the beginnings of life on earth, here are a poet's lines which describe them more intriguingly than any scientist has done:

> When fishes flew and forests walked
> And figs grew upon thorn,
> One night when the moon was blood,
> Then surely I was born.

That is from a poem about the Donkey. He resembles the Parrot only in that ignorant people have made both the subjects of tiresome jokes. A smaller relative of the Horse, the Donkey has ears which are supposed to be too long for his head and his head too long for the rest of him and therefore he has been considered funny-looking, or strange, or weird. That could explain why the poet makes the Donkey's birth under a blood-red moon seem a little scary, like Halloween. Nowadays, figs grow on trees, but the Parrot remembers when figs grew on thorny bushes and it was difficult to eat one. Back in the Jurassic period the forests didn't actually walk, of course. Sometimes it *looked* as if the forests were walking—or, anyhow, jumping around a bit—because they were full of dinosaurs and brontosauruses roaring about and knocking down the trees.

That Brontosaurus was a lizard-like beast, about as long as a middle-sized airliner and as heavy. When you visit the Natural History Museum, look for a reconstructed skeleton of the Brontosaurus or for a replica in plastic large as life with his eyes and gigantic mouth grinning down upon you. Think: When this animal roamed the earth he made a roar like thunder and the oldtime Greeks, who must have learned about him from their prehistoric ancestors, named him Brontosaurus, which meant Thunder Lizard in their language. He ate trees. His jaws were big enough to hold a rubber tree without much trouble; his teeth were sharp as spears and big as fire hydrants. He waddled through the primordial forests and just chomped on trees when he got hungry. Picture a herd of twenty or thirty Thunder Lizards slouching along with their mouths full of broad-leaved trees which they have pulled out of the ground

roots and all. No wonder it looked as though the forests walked. That's what the poet meant and what the Parrot saw, the first Parrot, for surely he was there among the fishes that flew.

Not the flying fishes we know that skim over the tropic waves—fishes that really flew over the land, the jungles, and the rain forests.

Most ornithologists believe the birds were reptiles or scaly fishlike snakey things that lived in the ocean until they crawled ashore and learned to fly. Ornithologists believe that uncountable centuries ago when these reptiles began to be birds they turned their scales into feathers.

The Parrot still keeps his scales upon his feet. Should you have the luck and the good taste to have a pet parrot of your own, he won't mind your examining his feet. The Parrot has been on earth so long that he is closer than most birds to the reptile, and this must be why he is so smart: He knows the secrets of the tortoise. If you invite your parrot to perch on your wrist, his leathery toes upon your skin will feel a trifle snakelike. If he and you are the friends you should be and you really trust each other, he will snakestep his way along your outstretched arm and perch upon your shoulder. Probably the Parrot's favorite spot is upon his friend's shoulder. While he's there, you may take a close look at the bright little feathers which grow in delicate layers that grow ever littler as they near his eye. The patterns of these feathers, each so intricately placed to overlap another, are the patterns of the scales of a fish.

Doubtless your parrot likes to have his head scratched. He will lower his head, rest his beak on your shoulder, and close his eyes in rapture as you gently scratch. Nothing, not even a mate to share his lonely cage, gives a tame parrot more pleasure. He will puff up his neck feathers so you may run your finger through his undercoat of downy feathers and bristling tiny pinfeathers. When the Parrot molts and renews his plumage, the old feathers drop out and the tightly rolled pinfeathers sprout and unfurl as ferns do and exactly where they belong in the feather pattern. It's something like, and yet a lot more complicated than, the way your new teeth replace the old ones.

Instead of teeth, he does his biting with a strong, curved beak. He does not chew his meal of fruits and greens and seeds; he grinds it down with grains of sand or gravel he stores in a compartment of his throat known as his *crop*. A tame and trusting parrot will eat right from your mouth. Place on your lip a sunflower seed, making the correct parrot noises as you do so. The courtly bird, who could easily with a careless thrust of that sharp beak mangle your lip, will pick up the seed so softly you hardly notice it.

Offer him a peanut roasted in its shell and a parrot accepts it with his foot. The foot becomes a hand and his toes, fingers to hold the peanut while he munches it, the way you'd eat a cookie. (If you know another bird that can do this trick, I'd like to meet him.) The Parrot breaks the peanut shell and while his thick black tongue spews shell fragments on your shoulder, he nonchalantly swallows the nut. He offers no apology for the mess; he knows it's the natural thing to do. In his tranquil fashion he will chomp up a carrot or a celery stalk; he will demolish a pencil or any other wooden beak-sharpener, and the shreds and splinters will drift down onto your carpet as if it were the rain forest's floor. It is the same with old feathers he plucks out while molting, the same with his excretory functions which he indulges whenever the urge is on him, no matter what he splatters with his wet green and white droppings or whom.

The scaly feet are fine for perching, too—for holding tight to a branch during a tropical storm—and for climbing. The Parrot is yoke-toed: two toes point forward and two behind. His beak serves as a third hand when he climbs a tree or a vine in the wild or, in captivity, a rope. In your own parlor just as efficiently up an upholstered sofa or a curtain to the very top, hitching himself up there with beak and toes.

Those feet are very bad for doing just one thing and that is walking; they simply weren't designed for pedestrian use. The Parrot loses all his style when he must move flatfooted across a floor with a slightly foolish rocking of the body. The claws that dig so well into cloth or a tree's bark only encumber him on a horizontal surface. He cannot scamper like a sandpiper nor waddle like a webfooted duck. The best he can manage is a droll flock-flocking walk as his curved claws strike and slide uselessly on the boards.

Sometimes when he's out of his cage and feeling at loose ends, a house parrot flock-flocks his solitary way down the corridors, searching for his friend. His eyes are keen but since they are set on either side of his head, he cannot see in front of him. To find out where he's going he has to turn his head to and fro, using one eye and then the other. When he comes to an open door, he cocks his head sideways to see if his friend is in the room. To make his presence felt he will commence to bite at his friend's shoe or subtly nip his ankle. He wants up on the shoulder: To make this perfectly clear he may well dance and shuffle a foot or two from side to side and fan out his tailfeathers. That's what he used to do in the rain forest to impress his mate with the elegance of his plumage. He keeps on with the parrot dance from side to side and cocks his head up at his friend. Now the pupils of his eyes shrink and dilate in black dots centered in the yellow circle of the iris. The black expands and contracts upon the yellow so wildly the effect is fairly psychedelic. This is the Parrot's way of winking at you and an important part of the whole performance that ornithologists call the courtship display. All of this activity is accompanied by a serenade of clucks, whistles, laughs, and croaks that only say, *Pay attention to me. I want up on your shoulder.*

Why all the fuss? you ask. Why doesn't the bird just fly onto the shoulder? If he's a healthy bird and his wings aren't clipped, why won't he fly? Because when a parrot gets used to a cage, he loses the habit of flying. There is no excuse for the wicked practice of clipping a bird's wings and no reason for doing this to a bird born in an aviary. An aviary is an enormous cage, roomy enough for a number of birds to fly around in and pretend they are free. Often an aviary contains trees or imitation trees with hollow trunks for the Parrot to nest in as he is accustomed to do in the wild. Captive birds have to lay their eggs somewhere and they use these contrivances, which do not fool the Parrot one minute. Still, he is an adaptable bird and plucky; he has the pride of his ancestors, he refuses to feel sorry for himself. He finds solace in knowing some parrots have lived more than one hundred years in captivity, and that is a lot longer than human beings who put him there.

A tame parrot flies the swift, direct flight of his brothers that dart through the tops of the rain forests. He is lazy, though, about flying; he had rather ride around on his friend's shoulder or even flock-flock along the floor than fly. The reasons he uses his wings at all are instinctive: (a) he feels neglected and wants attention; (b) he loses his grip while climbing; (c) a sudden noise, no more than popcorn popping, startles him and he takes to the air. The time to tell for sure that you are a parrot's friend is when the panicked bird is flying about the room in search of a safe perch and you stretch out your arm and he lands on it.

Out of doors it is risky to uncage a parrot. He is eager to explore the shady branches of a tree and he expects to clamber back down again to his friend. But what if a branch snaps off in the wind? If a robin is startled, he flies off to safety with other robins. A parrot startled in a backyard in Seattle or a rooftop in Chicago can only fly off into danger, and he will find no parrots there.

The North American weather is tough on a tropical bird. If he belongs to the great family of Amazon parrots, his basic jungle green that camouflaged him in the rain forest does not blend so well with the snow. He isn't a penguin; an African or a Latin background has not equipped him to survive our winters and he too easily expires of enteritis or pneumonia; a summer's cold hailstorm can do him in, too. Only a gallant exception like the Monk Parakeet thrives in bad weather: A smaller cousin of the Parrot, he comes from Argentina where the weather can be icy indeed. A few winters back some of these parakeets escaped in New York City—or were set loose on purpose by their cold-hearted owners. Far from expiring in the coldest winters New York has ever known, the Monks have nested and hatched until now their flocks are seen in all five boroughs of the city. If this business keeps up, the Monk Parakeet could replace the pigeon as boss bird of New York.

Now and then you read in the papers about a parrot who flies to a high place and will not be coaxed down. Firemen come with fireladders, but parrots don't use fireladders. On May 26, 1978, a blazing Red Macaw—who is another cousin of the Parrot but twice his size—would not abandon a linden tree in Jellicoe City, Indiana. He would not come down for the Fire Department, not for the Police Department, nor for the State Troopers, who were all calling to him, "Roger. Roger, won't you please come down?" This vain effort persisted until midafternoon, when school let out. Some passing fifth-graders noticed the glorious long-tailed bird. "Lookit!" they yelled. "It's Rajah." Straightaway the macaw responded by whistling a poignant melody that charmed all ears. The fifth-graders knew his name was Rajah and not Roger because he belonged to their home-room teacher, a kindly widow named Effie M. Rowe. Mrs. Rowe wears her silver hair in a tidy bun and she has a lovely smile. Though she looks a bit plump to have climbed to the top of a fireladder and carried Rajah home on her shoulder, that's just what she did. Next morning she and Rajah had their picture in the Jellicoe City *Banner*. It was Mrs. Rowe, the *Banner* states in its brief account, who taught Rajah to whistle "When I Grow Too Old to Dream," which is her favorite song.

All parrots can whistle, but not all can carry a tune. Most any parrot can produce the shrill sound of a sailor whistling at a pretty girl what once we called the "Wolf Whistle." It takes an uncommonly gifted and accomplished bird to render an air so exquisite as Mrs. Rowe's favorite. *When I grow too old to dream, your kiss will live in my heart. . . .* How sweet a song. A long, long time ago Mrs. Rowe must have sung it to Mr. Rowe, when they were courting. She must have sung it a lot and the song billowed from her comfortable bosom in a rolling contralto until Mr. Rowe—a young man with, I am certain, clean hands and a pure heart—implored her: "Effie, dear heart. Effie, will you be my wife?" I am sure Rajah has listened to the widow Rowe humming the tune through so many a solitary evening that by now it just whistles itself.

It is well that Rajah never aspired to *sing* the song. At least I trust he did not. Canaries can sing, but they cannot whistle and they seldom try. Parrots can whistle, but they cannot sing, though they far too freely try to. Once a parrot is moved to song, he squawks and screeches; he can screech a screech as nerve-wracking as the Peacock's. If you can't close your ears to the sound, it helps to remember the Parrot means to sing as beautifully as the canary or the meadowlark, and he actually thinks he can. This is the biggest mistake the Parrot makes. You just have to forgive him for it. Try to look at the problem from the Parrot's point of view.

Screeching and squawking, after all, are as much a part of the jungle sound track as the trumpeting of elephants and the nattering of monkeys. To the Parrot they are joyous halloos to inform the flock he is feeling tip-top and proud to be a parrot. In the rain forest the most active times of his day are also the most raucous: When the flock departs at dawn for the day's feeding and again at dusk while it settles down for the night, there is a great beating of wings and jostling of branches and parrots call out to each other. Thousands of miles away, alone in a cage, the captive parrot remembers.

So it is that the first thing in the morning, as he hears the sounds of a waking household, this parrot squawks. He means, *I'm a parrot, pay attention to me.* When night falls, he squawks at the first noise of his friend returning home, and he will scold you if you don't give the proper greeting. He will scold you if you do not open the cage and let him up on your shoulder, so that you both may sit a while and calm the day's passion. If you will only do this, he will make nothing louder than satisfaction-sounds while he preens his feathers. In a grateful impulse he will preen his friend's hair, too. Softly he processes your locks in his beak, a few strands at a time, to make sure they are free of mites and cooties. If you have just had a showerbath, he will help dry you by squeezing drops of water from your hair or your whiskers. In the contemplative silence all you can hear is his upper bill scraping upon the lower. He yawns perhaps or drops his head for a good night scratch. Back in the cage he perches on one foot, the other clenched into a yoke-toed fist: he relaxes his quill muscles and the feathers puff out, giving a slight potbelly but at the same time ennobling his profile so that it resembles a postage-stamp figure of the national bird of some emergent Caribbean nation. He is waiting for you to turn out the light and return him to his jungle dreams.

Certain people see a parrot and immediately ask, "Does it talk?" They loom over the unhappy bird and repeat the old imbecilic question, "Polly, want a cracker?" No sophisticated bird will tolerate so old-hat a name as that one, and the Parrot is nothing if not sophisticated. And to be called "it" is a flagrant insult: There are Male and Female parrots, cocks and hens, but, unlike chickens, it is hard to tell by their size and feathers. Among most Amazon species and the African Gray, Male and Female have the same dimensions and where plumage is concerned they are positively unisex. Their owners can only guess at their pets' sexes and they must always be prepared for a surprise. A parrot that for years was known as Harry may very well lay an egg in his cage one night and thereby change the name to Harriet.

Certain people don't understand parrots at all. "Does Polly talk?" they go on saying. "Hello, Polly. Pretty Polly." The bird snakesteps to the other side of his cage, and still these people won't take the hint. They stick their fingers into the cage and poke him as if he were a taxidermist's specimen. That scares him and he makes an angry noise; they poke again and then the parrot bites as hard as he can. His beak is his protection and he keeps it sharp enough to bite a finger to the bone. A tame parrot that is exposed to strangers who bedevil him does not stay tame for long.

The world knows the best-talking parrot is the African Gray. His head and neck are narrower and remind you more of his reptilian ancestors than his fuller-faced green cousins from South America. His wings and body are pale gray and slate gray and his tail-feathers a vermilion red—almost the colors of the Confederacy. He comes from Kenya and Tanzania and the slopes of mysterious Kilimanjaro, a mountain half as old as time. The Gray is at ease in all earthly and celestial tongues and has a mind-boggling repertory of sounds. A baby crying, a lady laughing. Hounds on a summer's night, a mile away, baying at the moon. Sneezing. Coughing. Burping. Snoring. It's almost spooky, the way the Gray associates sight with sound. He sees you reach for your handkerchief and he makes the sound of you blowing your nose before you can. Put a drinking glass under a faucet and he does the splashing of water before a drop of water has splashed.

If you speak directly to a parrot, any parrot, he's apt to cock his head and silently stare you down. He doesn't care a whit what you are telling him; he may be mildly interested in the sound of your voice. He understands what you're saying all too well: "Good morning," "Polly is a pretty bird," and the rest. Merely, he finds this patter unworthy of reply; so he stares at you and measures your voice. Later, when you are some distance off, perhaps in another room with your mind on other things, then, of a sudden, he will repeat to you distinctly and diabolically in imitation of your voice the silly things you told him. He does this quite simply to demonstrate the imbecility with which people treat parrots, how generally banal and empty he finds human converse. Happily, he would discuss with you those human ideas which interest him, such as the Binomial Theorem or the Sermon on the Mount, but nobody asks him about these. How odd that parrot owners—or parrot fanciers, to use the fancy name for them—fail to grasp this essential fact.

There are grown-up men and women so intent on heaping junktalk on their birds that they stay hours at a time by a cage in the dark so the parrot must listen without distraction as they repeat their mindless slogans. They expect this discriminating bird to memorize their twaddlement and say it back word for word—or "parrot" it, as we condescendingly say. Some so-called parrot fanciers go so far as to purchase phonograph records—masterpieces of junktalk, vapid and treacly sayings spoken by a vapid person in a treacly voice. "Good morning!" "How are you this morning?" "I am such a pretty bird." "Have a good day. . . ." You and I can always seize this horrible record and throw it out the window. The parrot can't. Caged and shut up in a dark room with this rot repeating in his ears, as if he weren't captive enough already, he has to be a captive audience, too.

At least the record doesn't teach him bad words, you say. How come parrots say bad words . . . ? Because he's forever hearing people say them. Through the millennia, in the ancient and the recent tongues, the Parrot has heard these words. The Parrot says our bad words for the same reason he says any words: to show how ridiculous we sound.

Few they are and greatly prized, but there is an elite corps of parrots who refuse to play the talk game. They will not talk junktalk, nor say bad words, nor condescend to any other form of human converse. Whoever hopes to communicate with this superlative bird must use the language of the Parrot, which is elaborate beyond our comprehending. It is at once inflectional and polytonic, monosyllabic and agglutinative; it encompasses the dialects and inflections, rhythms and tonalities of recorded human speech from Austro-Asiatic to Zulu-Kaffiresque. Further, it partakes of all the etymons of the Animal Kingdom from Aardvark to Zebra, as well as of the Avian and Piscine orders, not to say of the Cosmos. Small wonder the most patient parrot can hope to teach his friend at best no more than a rude *patois* of this language.

The discipline begins with the teacher perched on the shoulder of his pupil-friend. He sits the pupil down in a dark room, so there will be no distractions, and slowly, distinctly for hour upon hour he repeats the primal parrot sounds. No squawks nor screeches in this *séance*, nothing rancorous or raucous: rather the smaller nest noises of the forest, clucks and raspings of content and discontent, chirps and croakings simple enough for the raw human voice to copy. If several dozen lessons are passed to the teacher's satisfaction, a sweet enchantment sets in. The pupil gains a giddy confidence. Soon the ceremonial chittering of a parrot biting an apple issues from his slackened mouth. Lost in a parrot trance, the pupil proceeds to early courtship chatter, minor nest-building signals, wee burbles in the forest rain. His mouth discovers rapturous new involvements for the tongue and cheeks and lips; his larynx, uvula, salivary ducts, and by degrees his very tonsils are given over to medleys of puffing, popping, kissing, kvetching parrot speech. And should he be extraordinarily favored by his teacher, extraordinarily fortunate in his trance, the pupil—virtually a disciple now—will speak fluently in the mystic tongue-click language which long ago the Parrot taught the apricot-skinned Bushman nomads who wander the Kalahari Desert in faraway Botswanaland. The parrot friends vouchsafed this honor can be counted on the fingers of one hand.

Surely a finger will count the name of the Most Noble Hastings Sackville Russell, twelfth Duke of Bedford. The Parrot never had a better friend. His Grace, the Duke, maintained leafy parks and aviaries at Woburn Abbey, England. His Grace raised hundreds of parrots and parrotlike birds such as the Budgereegah—that spunky Australian parakeet who is quite the rage among the British, who have nicknamed him "Budgie." His Grace studied those birds all his life and put what he learned into a book which is respected by parrot fanciers the world around. His Grace loved his birds so dearly that he actually gave his life for them. He was defending a flock of Budgereegahs from a predatory

Sparrowhawk when his shotgun misfired and knocked him dead, aged sixty-five, into a bush at his estate near Tavistock.

Alas, his Grace. The Duke of Bedford was the last of Britain's great parrot-fancying aristocracy. The old traditions are crumbling. To keep up a decent aviary these days will cost you plenty, and British taxes being what they are, a Peer of the Realm is lucky if he can afford to keep a Budgie in a shoebox.

Old traditions are crumbling—and yet, and yet Britain's reigning Queen Elizabeth is a Budgie enthusiast. There are said to be aviaries still at Windsor Castle, but nothing like the old days. When Elizabeth was a little girl, her papa, King George V, kept a cockatoo in his bathroom, which bit up the royal bathtowels to Queen Mary's distress. Life used to be easier for Dukes and Kings, as the Parrot well remembers, because he honored with his presence the Houses of Tudor and Stuart, too. Henry VIII had his pet parrot and Charles II gave a parrot as a present to his girl friend, the lovely Duchess of Richmond.

Meanwhile, over in France in the House of Bourbon, King Louis XVI was giving parrots to his girl friends at the same time his Queen, Marie Antoinette, was giving parrots to her boy friends. The birds had too much self-respect to be used as tokens in this game of royal decadence. They took to flying through the palace of Versailles with a raucous squawking that spread scandal and consternation in the Court and acutely demoralized the Monarchy. The Parrots' indignant act was a little-known but precipitating factor to the outbreak of the French Revolution and the birth of Democracy in France.

The Parrot has watched Man in his folly the way he watched the Brontosaurus devour the trees, with curiosity. But Man has stuck it out longer on the planet than the Thunder Lizard did, and the Parrot has developed a tolerant affection for the two-footed, wingless schmuck whose record of prolonged calamity we call History. The Parrot is no name-dropper, but the fact is, he has known not a few historical personages and cultural movers and shakers.

The priest-kings of the Incas and the Aztecs, Manco and Montezuma, adorned their heads with parrot feathers. Columbus and then the Conquistadors brought back jungle-green parrots and flamboyant red and blue macaws to delight the Queen of Spain. The silk-gowned Mandarins of China sipped their tea while parrots perched upon their sleeves. The Roman emperors—the demented Nero most of all —were intrigued by the African Grays, who attended their banquets and chatted with the debauched guests in Caesar's Latin. The poet Ovid mourned the death of one of these imperial birds in an elegy composed in dactyllic hexameters and pentameters of incomparable perfection. Earlier still, in Greece, the parrots of Alexander the Great had of course already made friends with Aristotle. And seafaring Jews of Old Testament time—Jonah might have been among them—sailed from the Mediterranean Sea through the Pillars of Hercules and south along the African shore to the land of Ophir, where they beheld the Gray. They sailed home from Ophir with caged parrots to grace the palaces of King Solomon.

Now we have traced the Parrot all the way back to the Bible. I have saved for the last some information about the Most Important Person the Parrot ever knew, who was Noah. By the time Almighty God in His wrath decided to destroy His sinful creatures with the Flood, Noah was six hundred years old. Even by the Parrot's standards Noah was old. When God told Noah to build the Ark and save his family together with a Male and Female of every flying, walking, and creeping thing of earth, this was a tremendous responsibility for the old man. There were rumors that under the strain of it Noah had taken to drinking too much wine. Noah was the first person the Parrot had really liked. The Parrot felt sorry for his friend and wanted to help him. This is what happened:

After the Flood ended and the waters were abating from the face of the earth, after the Ark was grounded on top of Mount Ararat, Noah sent the Dove to bring back proof the land was dry once more. When the Dove came back with an olive leaf, Noah said, "Big deal. What good's an olive leaf?" A leaf from an olive tree that grew *above* the land was not proof enough for Noah that there really was dry land out there. "You're some stupid Dove," said Noah, who was over-wrought and unjustly blamed the Dove. The Parrot liked the Dove. She was pretty, with her dove eyes, and very idealistic. Unfortunately, when it came to practical matters, she was something of a chucklehead. The Parrot knew there must be some better evidence there was dry land somewhere beyond the waters. So the Parrot said to Noah, "Noah, I'll take care of it," and before the old man could stop him, he flew out the window of the Ark.

Why this story was omitted from the Book of Genesis, I cannot guess. I only know the parrots tell it; so it must be true. The Parrot was gone seven days and seven nights, and on the eighth day in the morning he returned with a roasted peanut in his beak. Noah knew at once there was dry land, because peanuts grow on vines and the vines spread over the dry earth. He knew at once there was dry wood, too, on the dry land, because you had to rub two dry sticks together to make a fire to roast a peanut on. Tears of relief and gratitude poured down the old man's cheeks. "Parrot," he sobbed. "My dear, dear Parrot! How glad I am!"

If you don't believe this story, please close your eyes tight and just imagine how the Parrot must have appeared to Noah that eighth morning:

A speck coming closer over the distant waters; jungle-green plumage or gray—or crimson, or yellow or blue, choose your own color—and swift-beating wings coming closer until Noah could see the peanut in the beak and the pleasant, amiable, comical face unique among birds to the Parrot and he could see the parrot wink of the parrot eye with its black pupil dilating psychedelically and cheerfully in a display for his friend Noah.

"Dear Parrot. Dear, dear Parrot," was all the old man could say, over and over through his tears. The bird flew onto his shoulder and offered the peanut. Noah ate the nut slowly, the first he had tasted in months. Fragments of the broken shell stuck in the old man's beard and the Parrot delicately preened them away.

ABRACADABRA: ON THE IMPORTANT QUESTION OF WANTING TO BE A GOAT

BY

George Plimpton

MEDORA: May I ask you something?

Of course. I knew you had something on your mind, watching you standing around fidgeting, with the heel half-in, half-out of your shoe. What seems to be the trouble?

MEDORA: I am bored with being me. I don't like being nine. I'd like to be fourteen for a change, just to see what it's like. Or even better, I'd like to be turned into something absolutely different—like a giraffe, or a hawk, or a dolphin jumping out of the sea. I know you can't arrange it, but I thought I'd talk to you about it, anyway.

Well, I'll tell you something that might make you feel better. People have always felt very much as you have—that from time to time it would be fun to be something else. I myself have always wanted to be turned either into a major-league baseball pitcher—even a little-used relief pitcher sitting in the sun with his legs stretched out in front of him from a bench far out in the bullpen—either him, or a bird called the hadada ibis, which is a large purplish specimen with a long curved beak who lives in Africa and sits on the speckled-barked limbs of the acacia trees and looks down to see what is happening as the animals come down to drink at the water holes. So you are not alone in wanting to turn yourself into something else. It is a wish as old as mankind. In fact, the Greek gods not only had the power to turn themselves into something else, but also to turn someone else, usually a quite innocent person, into an animal, or a bird, or a rock, or a flame.

MEDORA: I would not mind that. I think it would be fun to be turned into something without knowing what it was going to be. There'd be this terrific flash, wouldn't there? And you'd open up your eyes and discover you were something wonderful—like a black horse in the corner of a meadow.

Yes, but being changed into something else can be quite unpleasant. It is one thing to be a bird for a day, or a horse, just to see what it is like, but quite another if a Greek god gets angry at you and turns you into a hedgehog, especially if it happens on a day when you had planned to go on a Sunday picnic. Suppose someone like Zeus stood in the door one afternoon at three o'clock and turned you into a bureau. And afterward you would stand there on four wooden feet for a very long time and the only exciting moments would be when someone came and pulled open a drawer and put in some socks.

MEDORA: Who is Zeus? He doesn't live around here, does he?

Zeus was the king of the Greek gods. He sat on a throne on Mount Olympus. Beside him was a bucket of thunderbolts, into which he would reach from time to time to toss one down through the clouds onto the earth below. The next time a loud summer storm comes through, you can pretend that it is Zeus up there, playing with his thunderbolts.

Zeus's particular pleasure was to come down to earth and change himself into a cloud, or a flame, or different kinds of animals in order to chase after river nymphs.

MEDORA: What are river nymphs? Would I like to be one?

You might, since the river nymphs loved to swim. They were always near the water, sitting in the shallow streams, or lolling about the riverbanks, combing each other's hair, which was long and always glistening with water from their dips in the river pools. The trouble was that the river nymphs were so beautiful they were constantly being chased by the gods, especially Zeus. He would turn himself into all sorts of things to get close to them. Once, he fell in love with two river nymphs who were sisters—Antiope and Aegina. To get close to Antiope, Zeus turned himself into a satyr, which is a strange beast with the head of a man and the body of a goat, and he crept up to surprise her when she was asleep. As for Aegina, Zeus turned himself into a flame, some say, and others, a huge eagle, and he swooped down and carried Aegina off into the sky.

Aegina's father, Asopus, was very angry, as you can imagine, seeing his daughter being hefted up into the clouds, and he went running off after her, looking up and shaking his stick.

Zeus felt guilty and embarrassed at having been caught, and to keep from flying down and having to make excuses to the father, and feeling like a fool, he turned himself into a rock and Aegina into an island.

MEDORA: An island? Did the nymph's father realize that she had been turned into an island?

Probably not. The island was not shaped like his daughter to make it easy. It was just an island. If the father noticed, he may have said to himself, Odd, I don't ever remember an island there. But I don't think he said to himself, Oh, how awkward. There's Aegina, lying there in the sea, rather larger than usual.

MEDORA: Was it a large island or a small island?

I truly don't know.

MEDORA: Did it have a house on it? I would only like to be an island if it had a big house on it with enough room and beds for a hundred people. When I grow up, I want to be an architect.

I thought you wanted to be a black horse standing in the corner of a meadow.

MEDORA: Just for a while. Then I want to be an architect. Was Zeus the only one who could change himself into things?

Almost all the gods could do it. Often, the gods turned themselves into something else to keep from being bothered. Imagine what fun *that* would be—to have your younger brother hammering at the door of your room and being annoying, and from the inside you could say, "Go away, or I'll turn into a wolf in here, and if you don't believe me, look through the keyhole and I'll show you how different and long my teeth have become."

One of the very best at turning himself into different things was Proteus, whose job it was to guard the herd of seals that belonged to Poseidon, the king of the seas. Proteus could look into the future. He could tell you *exactly* what was going to happen tomorrow. The trouble was that many people knew he could do this, and they came around the seal rocks and bothered Proteus and very likely the seals he was supposed to be guarding. So Proteus tried to keep people away by turning into all sorts of things to frighten them off—lions, dragons, water spouts—and sometimes he turned himself into a seal so that, among all the other seals, it was impossible to tell which one was Proteus.

The trick, though, was to get your hands around Proteus's neck somehow, and never let go, no matter what he turned into, because he was really all bluff, like most people who pretend to be very ferocious, and while he might turn himself quickly from a lion, to a serpent, to a camel, to a dragon, if you could hang on, finally Proteus would give a great sigh and, giving up, he would tell you what was going to happen tomorrow.

MEDORA: I know what is going to happen tomorrow. I am going to feed my cat, Mr. Puss, and go to school. I don't have to hang on to the neck of a camel to know that.

You are very fortunate.

MEDORA: Tell me about some more gods who turned people into different things.

Well, one of the best gods at this sort of thing, or the worst, if you disapprove, was Dionysus, who was the god of wine. It has always seemed to me that he used his power quite recklessly and thoughtlessly. Perhaps that was because he was the god of wine, which can make you tipsy if you have too much of it, and you can be quite irresponsible. For example, Dionysus turned the two daughters of King Dieon into rocks because they refused to have a good time with him.

MEDORA: Yuk!

Absolutely. Then, another occasion, Dionysus tried to persuade the three daughters of King Minyas to go to a party in his honor. That seems simple enough, doesn't it, but the three girls said they had something else to do. They didn't want to go. So Dionysus first turned himself into a maiden, who came to the daughters and gently tried to persuade them to go to the party. No, said the daughters, they had something else to do. They couldn't go. So Dionysus lost his temper and he turned himself first into a bull, then a lion, and finally a panther to try to frighten the girls into going. It must have been like the doorbell ringing and a series of people dressed as animals arriving, wanting to take you to a fancy-dress party, except that these were *real* animals, long red tongues sliding over the end of their jaws, and they were hollering, "Hey, come on to the party, we're late."

Still, the three sisters wouldn't go, so Dionysus got so angry that he turned one of the sisters into an owl, the second into a screech owl, which is a smallish owl with a high, scratchy voice, and the third into a mouse— which was very difficult for her, suddenly having two owls for sisters.

MEDORA: I wonder why those sisters didn't go to the party?

I do not know. They were very stubborn. Perhaps they were waiting around for a better invitation. Certainly, after the word got around about what had happened, Dionysus had no trouble getting people to come to his parties. Why I suspect people came up to him on the street and said, "Just in case the mails are slow, and we haven't heard, are you having a party soon? Because we want to be *there*."

Once, Dionysus was captured by pirates who did not know who he was. When they tried to tie him up to the mast, the ropes kept untying themselves, a very spooky thing to see which should have indicated to the pirates that they were dealing with someone quite out of the ordinary. Certainly there was no doubt they had made a mistake, and a big one, when Dionysus suddenly turned himself into a lion right by the mast— an enormous lion who made the ship tilt under his weight when he crossed from one side to the other. The pirates were so frightened that they leaped overboard; as soon as their bodies hit the water they were turned into dolphins. There are those who believe—and I am one of them—that when dolphins leap from the sea, which they so often do, in long, grace- ful curves, they are looking for their pirate ship so they can get back to being sailors again.

MEDORA: I would like to stay a dolphin.

But wouldn't you like to be all sorts of things? Sometimes the gods played a game which was like a duel in which they changed shapes in quick succession—in which one would start out as an insect, and the other a song-bird, chasing the insect, and then the one who was the insect would change into a hawk, diving after the song-bird, and just as the hawk would reach for the song-bird with its claws, the song-bird would turn first into a large bush to confuse the hawk and get him thrashing around in the branches, and then the bush would turn suddenly into a snake, poised above the hawk with its tongue flickering, and the hawk—the tables being reversed—would have to do something quickly, like changing into a rock or a rainstorm, which was usually safe, in order to get out of trouble.

The most famous match of this sort was between Zeus and his first wife, who was called Metis. During this game, Zeus did something very tricky. He pretended to admire Metis's ability to change into different things. He stopped performing himself, but he kept egging her on. "Let's see you become an elephant. Oh, that's terrific! A crocodile. Splendid! An oak tree. Oh, my! Now let's see if you can do something very small— a fly!"

Metis was supposed to be very prudent and wise, but she was so carried away by the excitement of the game, and the flattery of Zeus, that she did exactly as he had asked . . . she turned herself into a fly . . . upon which Zeus opened up his mouth and, inhaling a deep breath, *zip*! he swallowed her!

MEDORA: Gross! Why did Zeus do a thing like that? That doesn't make it sound like a game at all.

Well, Zeus had found out something very disturbing—that if Metis ever had a son, that son would grow up and take Zeus's place as the king of the gods. Naturally, Zeus did not want that to happen. He liked sitting up there on Mount Olympus and throwing thunderbolts from his bucket and chasing after river nymphs, and other such activities. So he thought the best thing to do was to trick Metis and swallow her up.

MEDORA: Why didn't he smack her with a flyswatter?

Well, Metis was a very sensible goddess whose advice Zeus was anxious to have. So he wanted to keep her around, even if she was inside him. Besides, being swallowed by a god is not quite the same as being zipped in by an ordinary person. First of all, nothing drastic happens to you. You can wander around inside the god. I suppose it's like being in a very strange sort of apartment house. You can function quite normally, apparently, except that you cannot get out. If you wander up the throat, the god swallows, and it's like a great escalator sending you back where you started.

So Metis wandered around inside Zeus. She did not get especially angry with him for swallowing her. In fact, she would advise him on occasion—which was what he hoped. He could hear her whispering from time to time, a voice inside his head, and he would follow her suggestions.

Not only that, but Metis gave birth to a child. It was not a man-child, which Zeus was so scared of, but a girl whose name was Athena.

MEDORA: Didn't Zeus know that all this was going on inside him—this person having a baby and all that?

He certainly did. Especially when Metis sat inside Zeus's head and began weaving a fine robe and hammering out a helmet for her daughter to wear when she was born. Imagine the racket! Zeus began to have these terrible headaches, and they got worse after Metis's daughter arrived. Now there were two people traipsing around in there. In fact, the headaches got so bad that Zeus called for Hephaestus, who was the blacksmith of the gods, and he came with his tools to open up Zeus's head like a surgeon and out stepped Athena, Metis's daughter, full-grown, wearing the gown her mother had made for her, and also the helmet. She became Zeus's favorite daughter, Athena, the Goddess of Wisdom, though I would have thought that every time Zeus looked at her he would have been reminded of those terrible headaches.

MEDORA: Did Zeus ever get married again?

He certainly did. He married Hera, a beautiful goddess who became the Queen of Olympus. In fact, when Zeus fell in love with Hera, he did not do what people usually do: he did not write her a love letter, or call to her through a window, or write poems, or let her know through her friends that he was interested in meeting her. What he did was to turn himself into a bird called the cuckoo, and settle himself down by a path where he knew Hera would be walking by. Sure enough, she came along, and saw this bird which looked half-frozen, so she thought, and she picked it up and was holding it against her body to warm it when suddenly the bird turned into Zeus. Quite a surprise! I mean, to be holding a bird which suddenly turns into a large man with a beard—what would you do? Give a great yell and get quite angry, I would think. People do not like to be surprised in such a way.

But this sort of behavior was common among the gods, and Hera did not mind at all. She fell in love with Zeus, this bearded man who had suddenly materialized in her arms from a small bird, and they got married.

MEDORA: And they lived happily forever after?

Not really. Hera was very possessive of Zeus, and jealous. She disapproved when he went chasing after river nymphs. Unfortunately, she could not do very much about Zeus, because not only was he the king of the gods, but chasing river nymphs was not a habit that she could break him of. So she took her anger out on the river nymphs themselves, which seems somewhat unfair, because they were lovely, innocent creatures, whose only bad luck was to be so beautiful that Zeus became interested in them and wanted to scamper after them. In fact, very often Hera's jealousy was such that she would turn a particular river nymph into something else—knowing that her husband was only interested in a river nymph that looked liked a river nymph. For example, she turned the beautiful river nymph Callisto—whom Zeus was pursuing—into a large bear because she reasoned that Zeus was not interested in scampering after a nymph who had been turned into a large bear.

MEDORA: Did Callisto enjoy being a bear?

Not at all. One of the saddest things about Callisto was that although she had been turned into a bear, she could not get along with the other bears at all. She did not like their eating habits—eating berries, and breaking open beehives to eat the honey. She preferred tea and muffins. She did not like the *looks* of bears; in fact, every time she saw another bear, she turned and ran, forgetting as she swayed along through the forest on four paws that she was a bear herself.

One day she was skulking about in the woods thinking very unbear-like thoughts—such as what sort of curtains she would like to have in her kitchen—when she saw a young man coming toward her. He was carrying a spear, she noticed, and far more important, she realized that he was her own son, whose name was Arcas. She was so excited that it completely popped out of her head that she was a bear, and she went lumbering toward Arcas, intending to take him in her arms and find out how everything was at home.

Well, Arcas had no idea, of course, who this particular bear was, and he raised his spear to defend himself. Which is not surprising, is it? I mean, if you saw a bear rushing toward you across a lawn, you would not suspect it was actually your mother.

MEDORA: Only if she said so.

But you would not wait around for a bear to say such a thing. At least, Arcas did not. He raised his spear, and it would have been a very sad matter indeed had not Zeus happened to glance down from Mount Olympus and notice what was going on. He did the first thing that came to mind, and, as usual, it was rather startling. He did not turn Arcas's spear into a lily, or Callisto into a butterfly, which would have saved the situation. He did something far more extravagant. He snatched the both of them up from the forest and he flung them up among the stars, where they both became constellations. Callisto is the Great Bear, which we usually called the Big Dipper, and Arcas, her son, is the Little Bear, or the Little Dipper, whichever you prefer. You have seen both these constellations and now when you go into the night and look up, you will have learned something about them you did not know before.

MEDORA: It might be cloudy.

I'll tell you something else that is interesting about those constellations. Both of them seem to revolve slowly around the North Star, and neither dips below the horizon. The reason for this, the Greek myths say, is that Hera was very angry that Zeus had saved Callisto and Arcas, throwing them up into the night sky and making constellations of them. Hera felt shamed by seeing them up there. It was as if Callisto and Arcas had been rewarded instead of being punished. And so she went to see Oceanus, her foster-parent, who was one of the great powers of the sea, and asked him to honor her wish that at least the pair be kept out of *his* domain. Oceanus agreed. And that is why those two constellations turn around the North Star and you never see them dip below the horizon, as the other stars do, into the kingdom of the sea.

MEDORA: Why didn't Zeus change Callisto back into a river nymph at the very beginning . . . when Hera wasn't looking?

Well, Zeus, unfortunately, being very mighty, the king of the gods, was the sort of person who does a lot of damage and then tends not to pick up after himself. Heedless. If a nymph he was pursuing happened to turn into a bear, well, that was a shame, but there were always more nymphs to scamper after.

I am going to tell you about one of the most famous river nymphs and the consequences of *her* experience with Zeus. She had a very short name, Io, which, as you'll see later, was fortunate. She was beautiful, of course, and Zeus noticed her. So he disguised himself as a cloud this time, a sort of fogbank, and he meandered slowly up the river toward Io to get a close-hand look.

It was not a very sensible disguise. Hera was immediately suspicious —suspecting that if Zeus was fooling around in the middle of a cloud he was probably doing something in there that she did not approve of. So, as the mysterious cloud moved up the river, she decided to find out what was going on.

Sure enough, Zeus was up to something he should not have been. He was flirting with Io. When he heard Hera approaching, not wanting to be caught by his wife standing next to a beautiful girl, he did the first thing that came to mind: He turned Io into something—not into a rock, which the gods so often liked to do as we know, or a tree, or a bee, or a mouse, or a lily pad, or a trout in the river, or a dragon fly, but, instead, possibly because he picked the very first thing that popped into his mind, he turned her into a very large cow, looking rather startled, I would have thought, and what's more, a *white* cow, which is not a common sight at all. My own opinion is that Zeus wanted to turn Io into a swan floating peacefully on the river, and he got the color right but the animal wrong. He was flustered. Perhaps a brown cow would have fooled Hera, but certainly not a white one.

So Hera stood there, tapping her foot and glaring at her husband, knowing that he had been up to no good but unable to prove it. Knowing that the white cow was probably Io, Hera put a watchman named Argus up on a large rock above the riverbank to keep an eye on Io to make sure she was never turned back into a river nymph. Or, I should say, "eyes" because Argus had a hundred of them, all over his body, and you can imagine what a fine watchman he was because when he slept, only two of those eyes closed at a time. The rest blinked and moved and looked here and there and if they saw something strange, Argus would wake up and do something about it.

Io never came home that night. After a while her father went looking for her. He searched the riverbanks and he looked down into the bottom of the deep pools, thinking she had fallen asleep with her hair streaming in the slow currents. But there was no sign of her anywhere.

Then one day he happened to pass by a white cow standing on a riverbank.

What would you have done if you were Io, suddenly seeing your father coming toward you? How would you let your father know that you had been turned into a cow? Do you have any ideas?

MEDORA: I'd call out loudly, "Hey, Dad, I've been turned into. . . ."

No, that would not work. Because when you opened up your mouth to say, "Hey, Dad, I've been turned into a cow," you would find that the sound coming out would be as follows: "Moo!" And your father would look over to see a white cow calling out, "Moo!" and he would think nothing of it . . . certainly not that the cow was his daughter.

MEDORA: Will you give me time to think?

I don't think you can come up with the correct answer. So I'd better tell you. What Io did when she saw her father coming along the river was quickly to write her name in the mud down by the water. How lucky for Io that her name was so short! Writing a name with a hoof cannot be easy for any animal, but at least the name Io is simpler for a cow to work on in the mud than, say, the name Clytemnestra. Why the cow would hardly have written the first two letters of that immensely long name before her father would have hurried by on his search.

So Io did this—wrote her name Io, in large letters in the mud—and her father looked down and reading what the white cow had written he knew that finally, after all his wanderings, he had found his daughter. He was very excited in one way—the relief of finding her—but very disturbed in another, because what he had discovered was that his daughter was now a cow. What would you do if you discovered such a thing about your cat, Mr. Puss—that he had been turned into a bull, and had written his name, Mr. Puss, in the mud with his hoof to let you know what had happened to him?

MEDORA: Mr. Puss does not write. He would let me know if he had been turned into a bull by pouncing on a mouse. Then I would know

that he was really Mr. Puss. I would tell him to come home and
behave.

Well, what Io's father did was to go home and offer prayers up to Zeus,
pleading with him to turn his daughter from a white cow back into a river
nymph.

Zeus heard the prayers and feeling rather guilty about what had
happened to Io—after all, he had been responsible—he decided to do
something about the matter. The question was what? There was this odd-
looking monster-figure with his hundred eyes watching from his rock to
be sure nobody came around to fool with the white cow. The solution,
of course, was to find some way to put Argus to sleep so that Io could be
whisked away, turned back into a river nymph, and returned to her father.
But how could one get all those eyes closed—when only a few of them
slept at a time?

Zeus picked the god Apollo to do what he could do . . . very likely
not giving the matter another thought. Apollo was one of the cleverest
of the gods. Perhaps he would find a way.

So Apollo appeared by Argus's rock. He began to tell Argus a number
of very long, boring stories, and at times he'd shift and play some dull tunes
on a musical instrument made of pipes and reeds called a syrinx. Slowly,
one by one, Argus's eyes began to close. He yawned with his one mouth,
and said, "Ho hum."

Finally, Apollo told Argus the story of how his musical instrument,
the shepherd's pipes, had been invented. I do not know why he thought
Argus would be put to sleep hearing the story, because it is an exciting
story with an interesting change of a nymph (naturally!) into something
else. Would you like to hear it? Hey! You haven't gone asleep on me,
have you?

MEDORA: I was pretending to be Argus. I was pretending to see how
hard it would be to stay awake. . . .

Well, I was going to tell the story which is said finally put Argus to sleep,
but I'd hate to waste it on someone who already *is* asleep.

MEDORA: I will prop my chin up on my hand like this.

You look very attentive. Well, here's the story that put Argus to sleep.
It's about a nymph named Syrinx. She was beautiful and very much admired by various gods, and the spirits of the woods, and the satyrs; but

she would have nothing to do with returning their love. She preferred to hunt. Show Syrinx a rabbit, or a deer, or something to pursue through the woods, and she was off after them. She carried a bow made of animal horn; she wore a short huntress's tunic.

One day the god Pan was wandering through the woods when he spotted Syrinx—and as so often happens with these nymphs, he fell immediately in love with her. He hurried to her side to tell her so. But she would have nothing to do with him. She was not interested in what Pan wanted to tell her—all those syrupy words had little to do with what she liked, which was to chase after animals.

So she ran away through the woods. But Pan, who was quite angry, followed quickly after, meaning to catch her. Just as they reached the banks of a river and Pan was about to throw his arms around her, Syrinx let out a despairing cry to the water nymphs, lolling about in the water, to save her. They heard her, and just like that! they changed Syrinx into a tall tuft of reeds . . . which is what Pan grabbed within the circle of his arms. He let out a loud sigh of disappointment. One can hardly blame him —hugging what he thought was going to be a lovely girl and which turned out to be a clump of reeds. His sigh was so loud and long that the breath of it made a musical sound going through the reeds that he was holding in front of him. Do you know the sound that a blade of grass makes when you cup it between your hands and blow past it? A sort of snorting sound? Well, apparently the sound that Pan's breath made going through the reeds was much more melodious and sweet and it made him think of Syrinx, the nymph. So he said, "If I can't have you as a nymph, at least I can keep you and remember you by these reeds," and he cut the reeds and put them into little pipes of unequal length which he bound together into a musical instrument he called the syrinx.

Perhaps he was the first person to think of using reeds as part of a musical instrument—the reed that today we find in the mouthpieces of clarinets and oboes and English horns . . . the woodwinds. . . .

MEDORA: When do you think all those eyes of Argus began to close? About now?

Well, I don't think so. Because the story about Pan and Syrinx has always seemed an interesting one to me, at least. It has a good plot, with a chase in it, and also something is learned, which is a lively and useful combination which no one should fall asleep over.

So I think Apollo must have told some other stories as well, perhaps a very long one about the history of a vegetable, a turnip, perhaps, and forgetting in the middle, and starting over again right from the start, and maybe three or four voices telling it at the same time, perhaps both backward and forward, so that the effect was like the soft whine of insects on a hot summer day, or the drone of a schoolroom on a Friday afternoon.

Slowly the eyes of Argus began to close, one after the other. Think of all those eyelashes closed, lying like stitches against his skin, until finally there were just one or two open, dawdling, winking, and then they too were closed . . . and Argus was sleeping.

As soon as Apollo saw this, he leaped forward, up onto the rock, and he hit Argus very hard over the head with a sword. Perhaps all those eyes flashed open for an instant, but that was the last movement that Argus ever made.

When Hera found out about this, she was angry, and very sad, too. She had been fond of Argus. He had been a faithful watchman for a long time. So to honor him—even though he had failed to keep a proper watch on Io—she took all his eyes and she put them in the tails of her pet peacocks.

Have you ever seen a peacock spread his tail? The next time you do, you will see the blue eyes looking at you from the great sweep of his tail and you'll remember the story of Io.

MEDORA: So Io was turned back into a nymph as soon as Argus was gone, and everybody lived happily. . . .

No, that was not the end of Io's difficulties at all. Hera was so angry at what had happened that she sent down a large, ferocious insect called a gadfly, which chased Io for hundreds of miles around the Mediterranean Sea, year after year, buzzing and nipping at her, and keeping her on the run, until finally Hera felt she had been punished enough and allowed Zeus to turn her back into a river nymph.

So you see, since Io had not really done anything to deserve such a terrible experience—except to be so beautiful as to attract the attention of Zeus—it shows how complicated life can become if you have Greek gods around who can change themselves and other people into whatever they choose. It can be very risky.

MEDORA: Well, all right. I'll stay me for a while. At least until after supper. Then I might just change my mind.

SLEEP TIGHT

BY

James Purdy

Little Judd was about five years old when his sister Nelle mentioned the Sandman to him. Up until that time he had talked and thought mostly about fire chiefs, policemen, soldiers, and of course sailors because his father had gone to sea.

> " 'Your Daddy is sailing
> the ocean wide' "

Sister Nelle would sing in a fruitless endeavor to get him to sleep. But that was the one thing little Judd could not do. About dawn he slumbered for a few hours, but during the night, almost never.

Then, in despair, Nelle had thought of the Sandman and told Judd he would come and put him to sleep if the boy would get quiet and promise not to turn on the radio or play with his watercolors and stain the bedclothes.

"Sandman will come and make your eyelids heavy," Nelle had promised him. "But only if you will be good and lie quiet and still in your bed."

Then Nelle would sing him another song, this last one about the 'Red Red Robin who comes Bob-Bob-Bobbing Along, and Judd would grin when he heard the familiar words.

"Sing more about the robin, why don't you," he coaxed her.

Nelle would sing until she was hoarse, but it only made Judd more wakeful.

"There is no end to your repertory of songs, Nelle, I declare!" Mother said one evening after Nelle had come downstairs exhausted and pale from trying to put him to sleep.

"I should never have told him about the Sandman," Nelle confessed. "Now he is purposely keeping awake so he can meet him."

"Don't blame yourself, Nelle, where he is concerned," Mother comforted her. "Whatever we do with regard to little Judd is bound to go wrong." She sighed and took off and folded her apron and laid it in the dirty clothes basket.

Little Judd, as a matter of fact, had thought of almost nothing but the Sandman since Nelle had mentioned him. Yet, no matter how much he had questioned his sister about him, Nelle had been unable either to describe his appearance or explain exactly how he was able to put the grains of sand on boys' eyelids. Also, little Judd had wanted to know what sort of a box or sack the Sandman kept his sand in. Nelle was such poor help in filling out these details that the boy became much more wakeful than ever.

One night, long after his mother and Nelle had gone to sleep downstairs, little Judd heard a strange noise and, turning around, was sure he was looking straight at the Sandman himself, who had crawled in through the open window. He was a tall dark man wearing a sort of Halloween mask and he had long blue gloves on. There was also a large red wet spot on his chest.

He was breathing heavily and every so often he would double all up and hold his belly and say "Owww."

"Sandman?" little Judd inquired.

The dark man with the mask stared cautiously now at the boy while continuing to make his "Oww" sounds.

"Come on now, Mister, give me some of your sand, why don't you!"

The man hesitated for a moment, then came noiselessly over to the boy and sat down heavily on the bed beside him.

"Did you come tonight specially for me?" the boy wondered.

"Yes," the man spoke after brief hesitation, "you can say that, I suppose." He smiled ever so little, and began to touch the boy's shoulder, then stopped.

"You're sure you are him, though?" Judd spoke earnestly and loudly.

The Sandman nodded weakly in response and then put his finger to his lips and whispered *"Shhh."*

"Why don't you give little Judd then some of your sand?" the boy also spoke whispering.

The Sandman started to reply but was halted abruptly by the blaring sound of police sirens outside. His eyes closed and opened nervously as if with his nervous winking he conveyed the rest of his explanation.

But little Judd, who hated the long silence of the night, clapped his hands for joy at the tumult outside. He loved anything that broke the terrible quiet in which he was always tossing and turning and wondering where his father was as he sailed over the shoreless sea.

"I'll give you some sand, little Judd," the visitor spoke out now, "if you'll promise not to tell anybody I am here." Saying this, he stood up with difficulty. "Remember, though, if they ask you whether anybody paid you a call tonight, tell them *only the Sandman*. Hear? Now we'll see about giving you quite a little pile of sand. . . ."

"What is wrong with your chest, Sandman?" Judd questioned, staring at the stranger more closely. All of a sudden, little Judd took the man's hand in his. Then, after holding it tightly for a bit, he cried: "Why, see what you have did to my blanket! It looks like you had spilled my red watercolor paints all over it."

The visitor bent over lazily, and his half-opened lips touched briefly the boy's soft yellow hair.

"Now then, little Judd," the man began when he saw how calm the boy had become in his presence. "I will go into that clothes closet over yonder, you see, and I will get you some grains of sand. While I am a-getting them, though, don't you tell nobody at all I am here, dig?"

His eyes fell to where his hand was imprisoned by the boy's grasp. Pulling his hand free quickly, he walked over to the closet and opened the door. Turning about to little Judd before he went inside, he whispered in the softest tone yet: "I will go get you your sand now, Judd."

Below the front doorbell was ringing in alarm, and Judd could hear over that sound his mother calling out *"All right, all right"* in the same loud provoked voice she used after he had wet the bed and she would cry, *"We can't keep you in rubber pants, can we, I declare!"*

"Yes, officer," his mother's voice drifted up to him while he kept his eyes fixed on the closet door.

"No, we haven't heard a thing, have we, Nelle?" Mother went on in a soaring, scared voice.

Presently, Judd heard footsteps scurrying up the stairs and in no time at all Sister Nelle was peeking through the half-opened door. Meantime, outside, the whole neighborhood had come awake. . . . More sirens and police whistles shattered the air.

"What is it, Nelle?" Judd spoke slyly, still keeping his eyes on the closet door.

Nelle studied him carefully. "There's been a robbery," she began, but then stopped and looked suspiciously around the room. "Someone got shot," she said in a very low voice. "Anyhow, you had best go back to sleep, dear . . . it's all over." She acted queer as she spoke and her eye roved unsatisfied about the room.

Before she could go down again, heavy unfamiliar footsteps reverberated over the threadbare stair carpets.

A great man dressed in a blue uniform stood at the door, behind whom, looking white and little, was Mother.

"Everything seems to be all right in here," the police sergeant announced as if to the room itself. He crossed the threshold and his hand rested for a moment over the hinge of the closet door.

The sergeant smiled then at Judd. "You hear anything, sonny?"

"Just the Sandman," Judd replied in his accustomed sharp tone of voice. Nelle smiled embarrassedly at his reply.

The sergeant and Mother left the room.

"We can't be too careful, Mrs. Bond," the sergeant's voice came to Judd's ears as strong and loud as when he had stood by the closet door. "We'd like to search the yard again and the basement."

Judd heard his mother crying then, and Nelle went out into the hall, and her footsteps could soon be heard retreating downstairs. More sirens screamed, coming very close to home, and a man called something through a bullhorn.

"You can come out, Sandman," Judd whispered. There was no answer from the closet.

"Sandman," Judd whispered a little louder. "Come out, and give me some sand. I want to go to sleep. Please, pretty please!"

The upstairs was quiet now but down below he could hear people moving about and the sergeant was saying something comforting to Mother.

"You needn't be afraid, Mrs. Bond. He is probably a long way from here by now. . . . And our detail will remain here throughout the night."

Nelle's voice now rose up too: "It's all right, Mother. Please don't cry so hard."

"Sandman," Judd said out loud.

Just as he spoke the closet door came open wide, and the Sandman stared, rigid, into the room, but not really looking in the direction of the boy. The wet red circle on his chest had grown larger and covered almost all of his shirt. His eyes looked different also, like little bonfires about to go out.

All at once the Sandman pitched forward, and then, as if trying to break his fall, he twisted and landed face up on the floor.

"What on earth was that noise?" Mother cried from her chair in the kitchen. "My God, don't tell me. . . ."

Judd stepped over the Sandman, hurried to the door, opened it, and called down, "It's all right, Mama. I upset the big chair."

"All right, dearest," Mother replied, forgetting to correct him for being awake. "I will be up to see you presently."

Little Judd was the happiest he had been since the day he and his daddy had played Grizzly Bear together. His Dad had imitated a fierce bear and then just before he was going to bite him, little Judd had shot his daddy with a toy beebee gun, and he had fallen down and lain very still.

Little Judd now went into the closet where the Sandman had been hiding and got his toy gun. He shot the Sandman four or five times. But the Sandman did not play right, as his daddy had. Instead, he made strange sounds which were not too pleasant, and a kind of pink foam formed on his lips, which had never happened in the case of his dad.

Little Judd saw also that the Sandman was very black, and indeed he had never set eyes on anybody that dark except once when a parade had gone by near his house and a large file of dark men and women had shouted and screamed and waved flags.

"Where is the sand you promised me?" little Judd complained.

He looked at the nozzle of his gun and then studied the way the red wet spot on the Sandman's chest kept growing still larger. It was summer and the visitor had very little on except his thin stained shirt, and his blue trousers. His feet were naked.

He decided the Sandman had been playing with his watercolors in the closet, which explained the red, or was it he had shot the Sandman so hard he had hurt him with his gun. In any case, whatever it was, it made him want to do watercolors with the wet red that was coming from the Sandman.

"Judd?" he heard his mother's voice from below. "Judd, darling?"

He hurried to the door, opened it softly, and called "Yes" to her.

"You're sure you're all right, precious?" Judd made kissing sounds in reply and then said, cupping his hands so that perhaps only his mother would hear him: "The Sandman has been here."

He heard his mother laugh and put her coffee cup down with a bang.

Behind the closed door, little Judd made a drawing on his watercolor paper of a ship at sea and a sailor looking at the rough waves.

There was so much watercolor red, though, that his paintbox was suddenly flooded with it. It was the best watercolor he had ever used, thick and yet runny. No wonder Nelle had talked so much about the Sandman if he provided such good colors to paint with.

After a while, though, little Judd got tired. He had used up all his watercolor paper, and then, too, he noticed that the Sandman had quit making any more paint. Only from his mouth did a kind of pink something issue, but finally that stopped, too.

"Sandman, it's time for you to leave. The day is coming, and nobody wants your sand in the sunlight." Little Judd was looking at the orange light streaming through the window. "Sandman, go home," he repeated, "come back when it's dark and bring me a different color for my paintbrush."

Little Judd yawned.

It had been an unusual night, he knew, but something was not unusual: He had not slept a wink.

This began to puzzle him, for here the Sandman himself had spent the entire night with him, and all he had given him was red watercolors.

But again, as so often in the past, Judd felt very sleepy now that the day was actually coming. But his bed was too wet with the red watercolors which the Sandman had left there.

There was a strange strong smell in the room now, and a number of large black flies had entered the open window and came to rest on the face and chest of the Sandman. They buzzed and moved their feet in a slithery way, rose in the air, then came down to alight again on the quiet Sandman.

The buzzing of the flies and the strange sweet smell in the bedroom made little Judd uncomfortable. He felt he was going to be sick. He whimpered a little.

Then he began to realize that he had made a mistake, or Sister Nelle had not told him the exact truth. That is, the black man who lay there so still with the flies swarming on his mouth and chest was perhaps not a real Sandman, for if he was him Judd would have surely slept, and he would not have had red watercolors bestowed on him but golden grains of sand.

Then he began to cry very loud. He screamed finally as he had when he wet his rubber pants.

Finally, he heard Nelle's step outside the door.

"What is it now, little Judd," he heard her voice against the closed door.

"I have shot and killed the Sandman," little Judd replied. "He's all covered with watercolors and flies, and I have killed him."

"You try to get some sleep now," Nelle still spoke through the wood of the door. "It's only five-thirty in the morning. Use the potty under your bed if you have to, little Judd."

"I thought he was the Sandman, but I guess he ain't," little Judd went on speaking to his sister. "I shot him to death with my gun, I guess."

"Use the potty if you can," Nelle told him. Her voice sounded as sleepy as if she had dozed off leaning on the closed door.

"Shall I come in and help you, Judd?"

There was no reply.

"Little Judd!" Nelle cried.

"He's not the Sandman, that's for sure."

It was then that Sister Nelle opened the door. She stood a long time staring first at the dead man on the floor, then at little Judd, then at the bloodstains on the floor, and all over the many sheets of the watercolor paper. Then Nelle began to scream, at first a low scream, then a more prolonged, louder one, and at last she gave out from an astonished countenance many piercing cries which recalled both the sirens and the bullhorn. Little Judd screamed in response to her, as if it was a song they were singing to one another, echoing one another as they did when they sang together about the red robin.

THE CIDER RIVER FAIRY TALE

BY

Margaret Randall

In the mist at the end of the street, you can just see the tips of the trees, the bottom of the old stone wall, lines and corners of the buildings you know because you pass them every-day on your way to school.

It's all familiar. It's yours. But today it is covered in mist. Parts of your memory are covered, hidden. Only a part of the outline, an idea or two, emerges.

It's a misty day.

It's your first day of second grade. First grade was down this same street. Every day, past the same houses, the same trees. Past this block that ends in woods, the stone wall, the buildings where mommy says they make apple cider—ummm—so cold in the summer and so warm when you come in from winter snow.

Today the place where they make apple cider is half hidden by mist. But it's the building you pass every day. You hunch your shoulders and lift them again under the school bag swinging against your back.

The leaves are turning: golden, brown, orange, yellow, red. The red and gold leaves catch bits of sun coming through the little drops of water in the air. The brown leaves beneath your feet scrunch wet and sound a marching beat as you move along.

Suddenly you stop.

A group of people you've never seen before are walking, walking back and forth in front of the old stone wall, before the corners of the building you see in chunks through the mist. A boy about your age is holding his daddy's hand. Walking along, he takes two steps or a step-and-a-hop to keep up with each of his father's big steps. Like you when mommy's in a hurry. Maybe the man is walking fast to keep warm. His coat's not as woolly as yours, the one grandma got you for Christmas. The man is carrying a sign and you begin to read:

- - - - - - PAY
CIDER - - - - - - -
HAVE TO EAT - - -

The first word was real hard. The man turns and comes back toward you now. You try again to figure out that word on the second line: WORK - - -, like what daddy does in the city, mommy on her paper route.

Women, too, are walking back and forth. Together. The little girl with the long blond braid smiles at you. You smile back. Maybe she knows what - - CENT means.

"Hey, watcha doin' . . . ?"

"Walkin' with my mommy."

"What are the words?"

"So they'll give the workers more money. . . ."

A young boy shouts out: "Come on . . . Can't stop to talk. . . ." The little girl smiles, shyly. "Ask my mommy," she calls back over her shoulder as she falls into step again beside the woman in the green coat.

The man with the sign is coming back in your direction. The words on his front are the same as the words on his back. Now you see it says: DECENT . . . what does *decent* mean?

At school, you can't keep your mind on the lesson. You ask Mr. Bellamy why all the people are walking back and forth in front of the Cider Factory. What the signs say. . . . But Mr. Bellamy says it's lesson time. If you have six and you take four away. . . . You close your eyes. The leaves scrunch and a smile crinkles on the little girl with the blond braids. The word *decent* shines through the mist.

It's a warm spring day. Your body says hello to fingertips of soft air. It was a cold winter between second and third grades. Daddy couldn't fix your sled and there was no hot cider before bed. Never any apple cider at all that winter. Mommy kept telling you, "We're not buying cider. Supporting the workers on their strike. . . ." But *strike* means to hit something. You didn't see the cider people hitting anything, just walking back and forth with signs and children, old coats and river mist. This morning it's warm and green. The air's fingertips pull you from bed.

The air smells different as you enter the singing woods. Tiny white flowers peep around the rocks by the river. You wiggle out of your book pack and kneel to shed your shoes and socks. But the running liquid invites cupped hands instead of touching toes. You lean down and bring a splashing handful to your lips. The river is golden and it's not water. APPLE CIDER in little spurts, APPLE CIDER IN HAND-CUP-FULS, APPLE CIDER DOWN YOUR CHIN AND SHIRT. . . .

The old Apple Cider Factory is painted bright red. The people have stopped walking in front. They're back inside. The autumn mist has lifted and winter is gone, too. The little girl with the blond braids has grown just like you. She waves and smiles again from her perch at the top of the slide. Now you know her name, and you call out: "Heidi!" and she waves and smiles as she lets go and zooms down to run over to where you are. Lots of kids are playing beyond the big fence in the new school yard by the factory. As you walk up to the fence you can see that the sides of the slide are braced with boards and you can make out a word or two: WORKERS . . . EAT TOO!

TWO POEMS

BY

Tom Robbins

IF FRANKENSTEIN GROWS TOMATOES

If Frankenstein grows tomatoes
And Dracula farms beans,
If the Wolfman plants the croutons
That Kong puts on his greens,
If the Creature From the Black Lagoon
Loves carrots, peas, and hash,
If Godzilla peels the potatoes
Used in the Monster Mash,
If Vego the Giant Cauliflower
Eats people like a fiend,
Then what is keeping you, my dear,
From licking your plate clean?

THE ABOMINABLE SNOWMAN

The Abominable Snowman
Lives far from any city
Up in the Himalayas
Where snow falls like confetti.
Men climb far to look for him
Their ropes coiled like spaghetti
But though they've looked for years and years
They haven't found him, Yeti.

$\mathcal{A}$ BEDTIME STORY FOR EVOLUTIONISTS

BY

Michael Rogers

A very long time ago—so long ago that no one you know can really say it in words—every single person on the earth lived in the same place. It was a very hot, rocky place, with some flat areas with grass, and sometimes little bunches of trees.

This was so long ago that people hadn't even decided to wear clothes yet. That's right—no one wore clothes, and if you think that's funny, listen to this: They hadn't thought of clothes because they were mostly all covered with hair.

Now you're probably thinking of monkeys. And if you saw one of those people today, walking down the street, you probably would think he was a monkey that had gotten out of the zoo. But you'd be wrong, because they *were* people, even though they looked ten times stranger than the strangest person you'll ever see.

There were really two kinds of people in that big, hot land: There was another bunch, who looked a little different and had even more hair. And they had been in the warm country first, and thought they owned it. They were shorter and stronger and weighed more than the new people. They were also good fighters.

For a long time, the two kinds of people fought each other whenever they met, in the fields or in the jungle or on the rocks. If you could see them today, you'd think they looked pretty much alike, and you'd wonder why they didn't join together to fight all the other strange animals that lived then.

But they didn't. For some reason, they hated each other so much they couldn't help fighting. They fought for a very long time, and finally the newer people beat the older people. In fact, you and I and everybody we know are related to the new people. In a way, they were our parents.

No one is sure why the newer people won—they were weaker and threw smaller rocks. But they did win. Maybe they won because, besides throwing rocks, they learned to tell stories. Bedtime stories, like this one, which has already put you to sleep. Maybe successful species need their rest. Or maybe we just need stories.

RAT
OF
86th

BY

Anne Roiphe

You have to be rough, tough, and to swagger a little if you want to be a rat in the sewers of the city. It was eat or be eaten his father, Rat of 95th, had always said. You need guts, wits, a sharp tail, and sharp teeth if you want to last in the sewers. Rat of 86th had learned these things and more.

He stuck his nose up in the air and rustled his whiskers as if they were so many daggers. His tail he carried upright like a flag or pointed it in a nasty sort of way right out behind him. As he walked he often pranced on his hind legs and boxed the air with his front paws. That was to let anyone who might be looking know that Rat of 86th was no poor little creature. His palace, his underground castle lay on the corner beside the movie house whose bright-colored lights illuminated the darkness of the sewer entrance in a way that Rat found quite attractive.

The movie house was Rat's garden, his grocery store, his sanctuary. Early in the evening he would rouse himself from his untroubled sleep, sniff the nice damp air of his gutter, roll a bit in the moist rotting leaves he had saved from the previous autumn, scratch his back against the rough cement wall, jump over the egg carton he had saved for no particular purpose, and rise through the black bars of the sewer grate. Nose sniffing for dangers, legs prancing, whiskers whirling, he would dash into the movie theater. Running close along the lighted wall with the posters of coming attractions, past the ticket taker's left side, he would in a matter of moments reach the dark safety of the upper balcony. There he would pause. Courageous rat that he certainly was, his heart would pound, his paws tremble, and there was a rapid blinking of his eyes as he slowly recovered himself. He would grip his claws deep into the plush rug of the movie house till at last he would feel better. That run from home to balcony was enough to make anyone who was not a tiger or a lion seriously afraid. Being afraid and still making the run was the kind of thing that made a rat, a rat—Brave and Bold. That's what he would tell himself as his eyes were getting readjusted to the dark.

Once accustomed to his surroundings, Rat would begin his happy journey down from the second balcony to the orchestra. He didn't travel the main aisles. Like a lady knitting, he would go up one row and down another, gathering popcorn and candy along the way. He would stop at the end seat and, hidden behind the heavy wooden leg of the chair, he would munch in peace his wonderful bounty, his delicious treasure. He loved the sticky chocolate left on the wrappers of the Mounds bars. He liked the peanut butter taste of the remains of the Baby Ruth. Best of all were the small candies, gumdrops and chocolate-covered marshmallows that had fallen whole from the hands and laps of concentrating movie watchers. The buttery popcorn was often covered with dust and grime. So much the better—dust and grime is like salt to a rat, it adds to the flavor. He would bounce a piece on the end of his nose, juggle two bits between his paws (if he tried it with three they would all fall). He knew himself to be a fortunate and full rat.

He had been on his own for several years. His father, Rat of 95th, had certainly taken good care of him when he was a bit of a thing; but once his whiskers had grown long and his tail sharp and strong, his father had told him that it would not do for him to sit forever on the old ragged comic sheet his mother had made into a bed for her eldest son. It was time he was off.

He visited home, of course. He would often make his way through the underground pipes to 95th. He always brought his mother a tidbit. She was especially fond of Juicy Fruits and sour balls. The food at home was naturally more ordinary. It was nothing more exotic than people's garbage taken from cans late at night. It was usually things like lettuce, string beans, an occasional nibble of chicken or chinese egg roll. His mother and father felt that Rat had done splendidly for himself and were always very pleased to see him.

One night it was raining and the air was cold. The rain splashed into the sewer and rushed through the pipes. On the ledge, on the side where Rat had his home, he slept peacefully. Some man tossed a newspaper into the gutter on the street above. It blocked the drain for a few minutes till suddenly like a waterfall the rain pushed its way into the sewer, and black and muddy the water rose in the pipes till it quite covered the sides and slopped over the ledge. Rat woke with a start and found himself swimming for the sewer entrance. His two special leaves floated backward down the black pipe, down to the river. This made Rat sad. Things should always stay the same. He hated any kind of change and it grieved him even though all he had lost were two brown leaves with many holes in them.

He cautiously poked his nose out of the sewer and saw the crowd milling around the box office. He was wet and damp and a little sad. He knew he should not enter the theater when so many people were moving through the lobby, but because he had just lost his leaves he thought he was terribly hungry. Sometimes sadness just makes you feel hungry. He pulled himself up and started his frantic dash for the second balcony.

He was streaking ahead beneath a poster show-ing two gun fighters snarling at each other when a lady with white gloves, a big package, and an umbrella suddenly saw RAT. "AGGGHHH! A RAT! A RAT!" she screamed, dropping her package and pointing her umbrella. Rat felt a sinking in his stomach and tears came to his small beady eyes, but he knew his only hope was to keep on running as fast as he could. The people in the lobby turned and stared, and some saw him. "There, there he is," said a young girl with a mean mouth. "I'll get him!" said a man in line to buy his ticket. The man started to run through the hall. They ran around the popcorn and candy counter . . . up the first staircase. The bannisters were golden, the carpeting red plush, the steps were deep, and Rat had to jump each one and then pull himself up to the next. The man was chasing him. He would have been caught, but the man ran right past Rat and into the dark theater. He was just pretending to chase Rat so that he could fool the box office lady and get into the movies without paying for his ticket. Rat didn't know why the man had spared him, but he just kept on running till he got to the second balcony. There the usher, warned by the shouts of the people below, stood at the doorway. Rat dashed between her legs and as she screamed, "AGGGHH! the RAT!" he jumped into the darkness of the movie theater. The usher turned and shone her flashlight along the floor.

Rat knew that any moment the light would shine full on him and in terrible desperation he did something he had never done before, he leaped onto an empty chair. A lady had put her fur coat on that chair while she and her husband shared a box of popcorn. At first Rat was frightened for he thought the fur was a kind of rattrap he had never seen before. But then, as the usher gave up her search, he snuggled down into the coat and slowly dried his wet skin and gathered his shattered wits about him.

After he knew the danger was over, he opened his eyes wide and for the first time saw the movie screen and the beams of white light that came from the small window above his head. He had, of course, always listened to the loud voices, but he had never before realized that you could see people, scenery, buildings. He watched, becoming more and more interested each moment. Suddenly he was alive with excitement. It was wonderful, it was stupendous, it was beyond believing. How he loved the movies! He was sorry to have spent so much time on the floor. He should have thought of climbing onto a chair sooner. He soon lost himself in the story; it was a western and he stayed till the very end, jumping off the chair just as the woman picked up her fur coat, resting her pocketbook for one dreadful moment on his tail. Since it was dark, she was not upset by the fact that her evening's pleasure had been shared by a rat.

Hurrying along the floor, eating his way down, he rushed back into his sewer and spent the night dreaming, over and over again, the movie he had just seen.

After that he went to the movies every night. He would find a chair with a big coat resting on it and he'd curl up, only his nose, whiskers, and eyes showing. He would watch the same feature as long as it played. He saw gangster movies, monster movies (those scared him so much he'd have to put a paw over his mouth to keep from screeching!). He saw family movies, cartoons, travelogues, mysteries, spy stories. He loved them all. He would swagger about the sewer pretending he had a secret message for the President and fighting off imaginary villains one after another. When he visited his parents, he told them wonderful stories of the things he had seen on the large screen. They listened to him with respect. He was certainly their hero.

This happy life continued for a while when suddenly Rat changed into a sad sorrowful creature with whiskers that turned down and a tail that drooped. What had happened was this. One night a new movie came on the screen. A man had rumpled a nice cashmere scarf on top of his coat on the next seat. Rat settled in between the folds of the scarf and planned to enjoy himself as usual. The movie was about a man and woman who were traveling together when they were separated and at the end of the movie they found each other again. They ran into each other's arms and hand in hand walked off into the night. Rat started to cry and he couldn't stop. He was afraid the owner of the scarf would hear him sobbing and so he jumped to the floor and, once safely under the seat, he put his head between his paws and wept some more. Now why should a rough, tough rat cry like a baby? What ever was wrong? The movie, after all, had had a happy ending.

All the next day he was sad and the day after and all the following week. Each night he would dash into the movie theater but he could hardly enjoy the film. He felt so blue. One night as he was nibbling without his usual pleasure a barely-touched Sugar Daddy, it came to him. When he had seen the man and woman together at the end of the film he had felt horribly lonely. He had no one to share his adventures with. No one admired how tough and brave he was. It was time he found a friend.

So the next night he did not go to the movies. He had dinner with his parents and almost enjoyed the pizza crust left in the tin of a lazy housewife whose husband always had to send out for his supper. When the meal was over and he had waited until that time when most people are asleep, he surfaced to the street and started on a long walk. He passed many big buildings, many little ones with tempting garbage cans in front. He looked at them all carefully . . . he peered down each sewer grate. He found no rats at all. "I cannot be the only young rat in the world. There must be others." Brave and bold rat that he was, he felt a weakness in the knees and a sad sort of hurt feeling all over. He went on and on . . . block after block seemed empty of rats. Then he came upon a high wooden fence. He saw some small windows in the fence. How strange . . . whatever could be behind there. He jumped up on a car fender, scampered to the hood, and from there took a flying leap to the top of the fence.

What he saw below was a construction site, a marvelous rocky, wooden pile of things, some tractors, a crane, and a little wooden shack. It couldn't have been a better rat playground. He immediately climbed down to investigate. He soon heard shuffling, squeaking, and the tinkling of rat laughter. You can just imagine how glad he was. Before he followed the sound, he straightened each of his whiskers, smoothed his fur, and practiced a few prancing steps. He stood with one paw on his hip, chin up, the way he had seen tough guys do it in the movies. Then he rounded a big pile of rocks and saw climbing in and out of a small truck a pack of rats. Not just one or two, but many more. For a second, Rat Brave and Bold had a queasy feeling in his stomach. He thought maybe he should just go home. He was, in fact, quite shy. But he went on. "Hello there, I'm Rat of 86th," he bellowed, a bit louder than was necessary. Nobody turned, nobody cared. He felt a little sick and his head ached. He went closer. "Can I come and join you fellows?" he said, trying hard to keep his voice from trembling. "Sure," called a big black rat doing a dance on the truck's roof.

With a wild feeling of joy, Rat jumped onto the fenders and began to slide about. "I'm Rat of 92," said one. "I'm of 71," said another. "This is a little out of my neighborhood, but I like the guys here." "I'm Rat of 84th, I'm sure I've seen you around the pipes." It was just great . . . to be in the pack was the greatest . . . to be in a crowd was even better than going to the movies.

After a while he began to notice that he wasn't the biggest in the group. He wasn't the strongest and there was a wiry brown and white fellow whose teeth looked much sharper than his. That made him sad for a moment, then he remembered that he had surely been to more movies than all the others, and knew more things about the world. Besides, he was as brave as the bravest among them, or so he told himself. The leader rat was certainly the strongest of them all. He was Gray Rat of 93rd. Every now and then he would come up and punch Rat of 86th in the back, causing him to fall on his nose or head. That didn't make Rat of 86th happy but he knew he couldn't fight him, and he did so much want to be a part of the pack.

Every night after that, Rat would go to the movies, eat his customary dinner, watch a single film, and then join his new friends on the construction site. The building was making slow progress. The holes got deeper, there was even some more rubble and some puddles to splash in. There were piles of bricks to hide behind and pieces of cement. Foundation blocks made good bases for games of tag, hide-and-go-seek, and the like.

Now there was a group of girl rats that played each night in the construction site. They built houses out of little stones. They jumped over pieces of string. They giggled a lot and were sometimes mean to each other and sometimes they just sat and watched the boys do tricks. Sometimes they applauded. The loveliest of all of them was a girl rat called Beauty Salon. That's where she lived, eating nail polish and sandwich remains. Beauty Salon was the special favorite of big Gray Rat and none of the others talked to her too much or too long because if they did Big Gray would come over and give them a push or a nip in the back of the neck.

Rat of 86th just couldn't help himself. He knew he shouldn't really do it. But it was Beauty Salon whom he was always watching. Whenever he could, he would go near her, hoping she would notice him just a little. Actually, he wanted her to spend all her time thinking about him. He wanted her to worry about him, to wonder if he liked her, and to be very jealous if he talked to Stationery or Fish Market or any of the other girls.

Of course she ignored Rat of 86th because she knew if she paid any special attention to him, Big Gray would make garbage of him in no time at all. And it was true she noticed 86 a great deal. She liked his jaunty way of walking, she liked his intelligent eyes, and most of all she liked the way he obviously admired her. It makes a girl rat feel terrific if she's admired a lot. She spent a long time curling her whiskers and she hoped that the new Rat of 86th would appreciate her efforts. He did more than that. He began to pine away with love.

He didn't even enjoy Mounds bars or Hershey's chocolate kisses anymore. He couldn't sleep properly because he was always dreaming of Beauty Salon. He began to look thin, and his mother worried that perhaps he was sick. At the movies he was able to forget for a while, but when the lights came back on and he was forced back from the drama of the screen to the bleak reality of his own impossible love, he would droop his whiskers and slouch back to his sewer. There he would resolve to win the love of his life and do like any decent hero—he planned to triumph over his rival big Gray Rat. The question was how?

The building at the construction site was coming along. There was now a first and second floor, no walls, no windows, just a large cement frame. The rat pack would climb up and swing from the bare pipes. They had races along the outside ledges. They dashed about with loose wires in their teeth. They ate the remains of the workmen's lunch, snuffled in the last of the beer left in the bottom of cans. They left their paw prints all over the thick dust. This last was what led to Rat of 86th becoming a hero, a leader of the pack.

The workmen arrived early one morning and saw the pawprints clearly in the dust. "Rats," one said. "No doubt about it, rats." "Let's do them in," said another. "Right," they all agreed. Everyone wants rats to go somewhere else. All the workmen chipped in a little money and one of them went out and bought a box of rat poison. That night before they stopped work, they spread the little round biscuits all about the floor. "We're sure to find a mess of dead rats in the morning," they said as they left. Later, when the moon was high up in the sky the rats all gathered as usual at the construction site.

They climbed eagerly up to the floor where the workmen had spent the day. They looked forward to their usual pleasures of scavenging. It wasn't long before they discovered the delicious-smelling biscuits the workmen had left about. With high spirits they pushed each biscuit to the center of the floor and were just about to start nibbling when Rat of 86th took a good look at the little cake in front of his nose. Printed on the top he saw a skull and crossbones. It took him a second to remember where he had seen that sign before—on the flag of a ship carrying evil pirates about the sea—somewhere else, too, on a bottle in the medicine chest of an elderly lady who had turned out to be the murderer of fourteen people. She had poured something from the bottle into all her victims' tea. It was a wonderful movie, Rat remembered. But the sign of the skull and crossbones—a sudden feeling of cold passed over Rat . . . that sign meant death. "Stop, STOP, STOP," he shrieked. "These cakes will kill you. Don't, DON'T eat them. They have the sign of death on them." All the rats paused. They looked at Rat of 86th, they looked at their cakes, they saw the skull and crossbones, but never having been to the movies they didn't know what such a picture meant. They didn't know whether to believe Rat of 86th or not.

Big Gray Rat didn't like it at all. Somebody else was telling his pack what to do. Some smart aleck was trying to show him up. "I don't believe it," he said. "86th just wants you to leave all the sweets so he can sneak back here and have them all for himself. I'm not going to fall for such scare talk." And he picked up the biscuit in his paws and was about to gulp it down when Rat of 86th screamed, "Don't do it! Please, please don't do it!" There was something in his tone that made Big Gray pause and then take just a little nibble of the cake. He waited before sinking his teeth in for the second bite. In the next second, as all the rats stood around watching, he suddenly got a very funny feeling in his stomach and he thought for sure he was going to die.

He did crawl off into a corner and he was very very sick to his stomach, which was very unpleasant, but after just a while, he began to feel better and he stood up, a little weak but ALL RIGHT. All the rats were gathered around 86th listening to him tell the story of the pirate movie. He was their Hero, he was their new leader, he had after all saved all of them. They were pleased that Big Gray had only taken a little bite of the poison biscuit, but they weren't much interested in him anymore and there were some who even felt he deserved all those pains in his stomach he had endured. He went around pushing them, but nobody paid him any special attention.

Beauty Salon had been just about to swallow the poison when Rat had screamed his first warning. She trusted him completely and now she felt more than just the gratitude one might reasonably hold toward one who has saved your life. She felt moving within her, like full white clouds billowing over the ocean, tender feelings for Rat of 86th. Beauty Salon had never before felt such an aching of happiness as came with this love.

A night or so after the incident with the rat poison, Big Gray was sulking behind a stone. The rest of the rat pack were leaping and chasing over the fenders of the large crane that now stood to one side of the rising building. Rat of 86th was the acknowledged leader of the games, and whatever he did was copied by the others. He was really quite puffed with pride at his new position. He now hoped that Beauty Salon (whose soft eyes blinked at him whenever he turned toward her) would choose him. However, even though he was the leader of the pack and a Hero to all his friends, he lacked the courage to just walk up to the girl of his hopes. Every time his leaps would bring him near to her, his legs would tremble and he would turn his head away and rush by. He was a very shy hero.

She began to despair. Perhaps she was mistaken, perhaps he really admired Stationery, or Fish Market, or Notions, or any one of the other girls. Her curled whiskers started to uncurl at all those awful thoughts. Two large drops appeared in the corners of her eyes and wet the brown fur of her nice little pointed face. Rat of 86th in one of his somersaults saw those glistening tears and he became cold with terror . . . what could be wrong? Maybe she really loved Big Gray and hated 86th. In a sudden panic he rushed over to her, pulling a weed that had sprouted in the sandy bottom of the excavation site. He handed her the weed, which she clasped to her chest. He asked her to please, please go for a climb with him. She could only nod her agreement and followed him up onto the fender of the crane . . . up onto the cabin top, and then, in order to make certain they would be alone, Rat of 86th led Beauty Salon up the skinny neck of the crane and onto the very head piece which during the day opens and closes, its sharp teeth inside picking up and carrying things.

Those two rats sitting on the top of the crane

viewing their friends like so many small bugs beneath them told each other all their secrets. A light seemed to shine from each of them. Like neighboring planets in the sky they floated through the dark night till it became clear to them both that in the future they would share everything.

Big Gray sat behind his stone angry and bitter. At a certain moment he cast a despairing eye to the crane and saw Rat of 86th with the girl he had marked out for himself. He saw red, purple, and black. He was so angry that a noise like that of a motor winding up came from his throat. He leaped for the cabin of the crane. He had seen workmen operate the crane during the day. Murder, terrible murder was his ambition. Even as he jumped up the fenders, he saw in his mind bodies crushed on stone and himself dancing in joy about the ruins of his enemies.

He leaped up to the cabin and threw himself, with all the strength his anger gave him, against the gear shift in the cabin. He tried it once and nothing happened. He tried it again and he could feel the stick tremble; and a third time, the stick lurched forward and the mouth of the crane opened wide. Beauty Salon, who was sitting delicately with her little paws crossed on the edge, was thrown from the top of the crane and her small body hurtled through the air on its way to what seemed to be certain death. Rat of 86th managed to grab one of the teeth of the crane and hold on. He could have pulled himself to safety. But he saw Beauty Salon falling to the earth and he felt a terrible pain that he knew was grief. He remembered sad movies he had seen and he felt certain that life without Beauty Salon would be a pale sad thing . . . and so he shouted to the indifferent ground, "I will join you, my love. Let us not be parted even in death. It is a far better thing I do than I have ever done before. . . ." And with lines like that on his lips he let go his hold and fell after his love to the ground.

The rat pack stood frozen and watched as the two bodies tumbled toward them. Something so terrible that really lasts only a second can seem to take an hour. A long gasp of horror came from each rat. A high pile of sawdust had been swept up the day before by the neat workmen and it was into this soft pile of dust that Beauty Salon fell, followed seconds after by Rat of 86th.

They disappeared under the dust. The watching rats were silent, hardly daring to hope. Suddenly a head appeared, it was Rat of 86th, and he pulled up by a paw Beauty Salon. They were dazed, they were covered with yellow dust, but they were unhurt.

"Hurrah, hurrah!" cheered all the rats but Big Gray, who slouched off to another part of the city and was never heard from again.

When the sun started to come up over the East River, Beauty Salon picked up the weed she had been given and followed Rat of 86th.

After that, they went every night to the movies. They ate Hershey kisses, popcorn, orange soda, M & M's—to their satisfaction; and then together they would find an unoccupied chair in the upper balcony and, paw in paw, they would watch the feature film, the previews, and the shorts, and sometimes they would sit through the whole program twice.

B.R.M.TZ.V.H.

BY

Jerome Rothenberg

A poem from memory for Matthew Rothenberg's 13th birthday celebrated as a "bar mitzvah event" one month after the date three decades three years past my own

naming the day it comes
deep into March
Aquarius has shifted into Pisces
—Diane's time—
waters receded & warm days
hanging over San Diego
where never in my life I thought to end up
or thought to be here
standing in this western yard
to make bar mitzvah
as event—I stress—not
the ghost of ceremony
I recall from my own lost 13th year
middle of wartime & reports
first coming in that told
deaths of others curly-headed
cousins sacrificed
only their photos left to scan thru
later. "who is this?"
you asked
"a child" I answered
hair curled like your own
forget it
death's depressing after all
someone still dreams of

a universe benign & wakes
to stifled flesh
I wouldn't interrupt this day with
but wonder
how any sanity was possible
this century
o Matthew Matthew born once
in the glow of brother—Milton's—death
the mystery thus thrust
into our thoughts
—of light & dark
co-equals—
I was alone to greet you (as I hope
you will not be)
of those who shared the table
at our home back in the Bronx
by then I was
the one surviving
(as I knew it would be)
& thought: how could I
bring them to life for you
except the poems pictures
I began around
their deaths your life
fathers mothers grandmothers
set there as titles
ancestors the imagination made
the shades all poetry
recalls back to Ulysses in the pit
the voice of David out of Sheol
orphic Jew my master
de profundis I could see her wraith
—those mad poetic words!—
my mother enter in dark of
restless sabbaths
she who would call us "sweet face"
too much love
had spoiled her
I could never
answer that or answer
my father's angers

disappointments of his life in dry goods
peddling peddling
the old books forsaken
he dropped off in sleep & told me
"strange that it takes so long to die"
& she "the whole town's talking"
mysteries of death
& life
fantastic faces all we know
we love
bar mitzvahs happening
on sabbaths that divide
the day that Jesus died
from Easter
—Esther of my mother's name—
when all the dead arise
in mind they sing
song that first ushered in your birth
a man child son
grown old & beautiful
at last
"joy joy
"praise praise

STRAWBERRY TALKING

BY

Strawberry Saroyan

ILLUSTRATED BY
ARAM SAROYAN

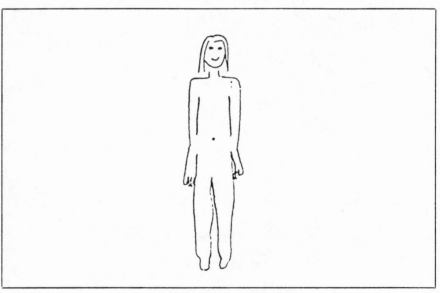

This is my first body.

Everybody has a body.

The mirror is looking at me.

Don't laugh without smiling.

The bee wants me.

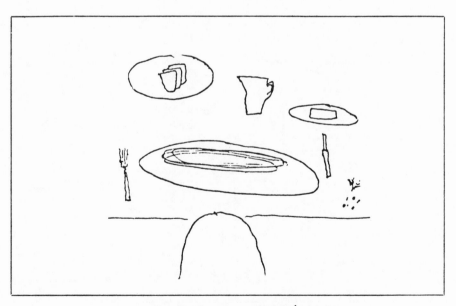

We eat pancakes and bread.
The flies eat crumbs.

Open your eyes so I can see you.

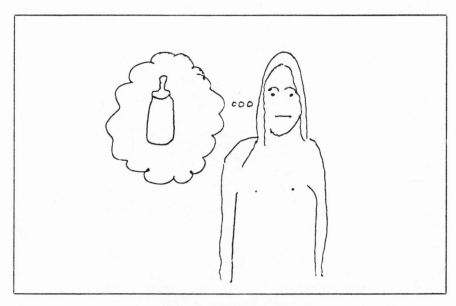

The bottle lost me.

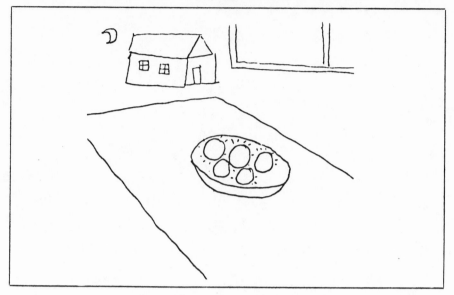

The sun's all gone — it's on the peaches.

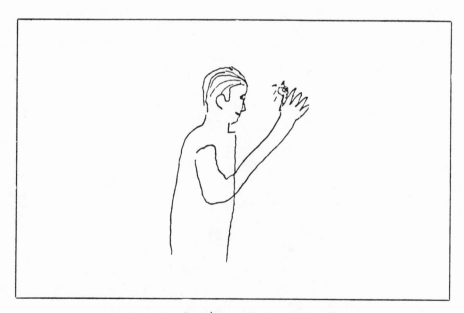

Benjamin found a snail on his head.
It was crying.

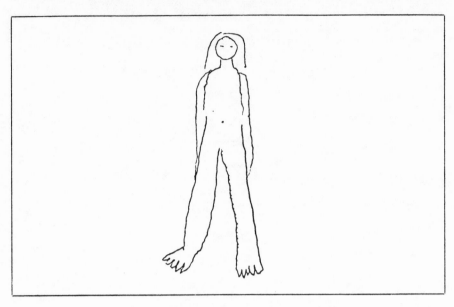

I have big huge legs — I grow them down.

Strawberry Saroyan is a little girl who lives
in California with her mother and father,
Gailyn and Aram Saroyan, and her baby sister,
Cream.

ABIYOYO

BY

Pete Seeger

AUTHOR'S NOTE: *In a book of African folk tunes, I came across this lullaby. A footnote explained that it was sung as part of a story about a monster. From that hint, I developed a new story for my own children, not realizing at the time how closely the symbolism hit home. Already the folk process in summer camps has produced new versions of it. I strongly urge any parent reading this to try telling stories by ear instead of always relying on the printed page. After retelling the old favorites, reshape stories from anywhere and everywhere (movies, novels, TV shows, anecdotes and riddles) and before long, you'll be making up brand-new stories. How? Start thinking, "What would happen if . . . ?"*

(Start by singing the song.)

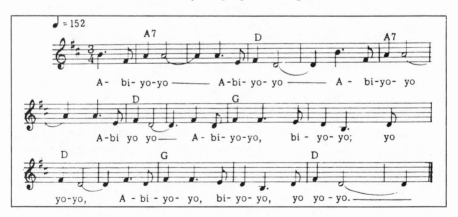

Once upon a time there was a little boy who played a ukulele. He'd go around town: clink, clunk, CLONK! Of course, the grown-ups would be busy, and they'd say:

"Take that thing out of here. We're talking. Git!" And they'd kick him out of the house.

Not only that. The boy's father would get in trouble, too. His father was a magician. He had a magic wand. He could go Zoop! with it, and make things disappear.

But the father was a terrible practical joker. He'd come up to someone just about to drink a nice glass of . . . something. Zoop! The glass would disappear. He'd come up to someone doing a hard job of work—maybe sawing a log of wood: zzt, zzt, zzt. Up comes the father: Zoop! And the saw would disappear. He'd come up to someone just about to sit down after a hard day's work, and zoop! no chair.

People got tired of all this. They said to the father: "You get out of here, too. Take your magic wand and your practical jokes and you and your son, just git!"

And the boy and his father, they ostracized them. That means, they made 'em live on the outskirts of town.

(Banjo starts a low, menacing strum.)

Now, in this town they used to tell stories. The old people used to tell stories about the monsters and giants that lived in the old days! They used to tell a story about Abiyoyo. They said he was as tall as a house, and could eat . . . people . . . up. (Of course, nobody believed it, but they told the stories anyway.)

But one day, one day, the sun rose, blood red over the hill. And the first people that got up and looked out of their window—they saw a great big shadow in front of the sun. And they could feel the whole ground shake *(stomp, stomp)*.

Women screamed. Strong men fainted. They said, "Run for your lives! Abiyoyo's coming!"

Down through the fields he came. He came to the sheep pasture and grabbed a whole sheep. Yeowp! He ate it down in one bite. He came to the cow pasture. Yuhk!

Just then the boy and his father woke up. I think they'd been up late the night before at a party. The boy rubbed his eyes and said:

"Hey, paw, what's coming over the fields?"

The father said: "Oh, son, it's Abiyoyo. Oh, if only I could get him to lie down. I could get him to disappear."

The boy said, "Come with me, father." He grabbed his father by one hand. The father grabbed the magic wand, and the boy grabbed his ukulele. Over the fields they went, right up to where Abiyoyo was.

People screamed, "Don't go near him! He'll eat you alive!"

There was Abiyoyo. He had long fingernails, 'cause he never cut 'em. He had slobbery teeth, 'cause he never brushed them. Matted hair, 'cause he never combed it. Stinking feet, 'cause he never washed them. He was just about to come down with his claws, when the boy whipped out his ukulele.

(singing)

> Abiyoyo, Abiyoyo
> Abiyoyo, Abiyoyo
> Abiyoyo, yo yoyo yo yoyo
> Abiyoyo, yo yoyo yo yoyo Abi. . . .

Well, the monster had never heard a song about himself before, and a foolish grin spread across his face. And he started to dance.

ABIYOYO, ABIYOYO

The boy went faster.

ABIYOYO, YO YOYO, YO YOYO
ABIYOYO, YO YOYO. . . .

The giant got out of breath. He staggered. He fell down flat on the ground.

Zoopy, zoop! went the father with his magic wand, and Abiyoyo disappeared.

People streamed out of their houses, and ran across the fields. They said: "Why, he's gone, he's disappeared!"

They lifted the boy and his father up on their shoulders: "Come on back to town. Bring your damn ukulele; we don't care." And they all sang:

> Abiyoyo, Abiyoyo
> Abiyoyo, Abiyoyo
> Abiyoyo, yo yoyo yo yoyo
> Abiyoyo, yo yoyo yo yoyo.

CARRIE

BY

Ntozake Shange

st. louis, 1957

& we waz a house fulla chirren who waz fulla the dickens 'cordin to grandma there waz me & my two sisters & my brother & my two cousins/ too smart for our own good & nothin but trouble for the ladies who looked after us while mama waz at work & papa went to the hospital.

we cd watch little rock & eisenhower or american bandstand/ then wait til waz the day for "colored" at the "Y" or play beat-em-up in the yard. or wrestle wid the white boys from texas down the street. i usedta like to dig holes in damp ground & line the worms up on the sidewalk/ my brother liked to set things on fire & my sister like to beat me up til i told on her/ then pull my top braid that wasnt pressed cuz it was summer & a waste of money/ til some of my hair wd actually come out in her hand/ my littlest sister liked to write "pussy" in nail polish behind the refrigerator & my cousins rode bikes up on the private catholic girls school til the police came/ they waz only twelve/ but the officer saw my mama waznt no reg'lar colored woman so he just warned her bout the attitude folks in st. louis had towards nigras & since she waz from the north & her chirren waznt "customed to tradition"/ he'd let it go on by/ this time.

well. we ran bernice off cuz she cdnt cook nothin but hard stiff grits & didnt 'low none of us to run up & down the stairs or rub the goldfish together. & she always tol' mama when one of them fresh boys wd come by to talk to me on the front porch. but she never cd figure out which one of us waz stealin her change & buyin snickers & new jack sets/ so mama thot bernice waz 'maginin things & fired her.

there waz a tree in the fronta the house/ alla us usedta sit by it & think of things to do. watch the earth roll under the clouds/ waz the only time we knew peace/ cuz in the house waz grandma raisin "cain" her own self/ cuz somebody rode down the street on the bike/ free-handed/ or somebody trampled mr. noble's carnations & it waz one of us/ so there waznt no calm in the house/ til regina came.

doin the slop. listenin to tina turner. eavesdroppin on roscoe & regina when they slipped to the side porch & waz feelin on each other. regina waz a high-school drop-out/ but she waz pretty wid spit curls & big bangs over her eyes. & she wore tight skirts & bernard's ring on a chain round her neck. she took us to summer high/ where the baddest basketball team for colored waz/ to see smokey robinson & the miracles sing "shop around" & she let us dance on the stage. when regina waz wid us/ even grandma let us alone. she waz so busy seein to it that roscoe didnt stay long & regina didnt forget she waz a lady/ grandma forgot all bout us/ then in the middle of little willie john & regina's friends showin us how to "french kiss"/ grandma came lookin for her fan. & mama fired regina for bein a bad influence.

the house got crazy. mama tryin to feed nine people & make lunches for five/put each one of us at a different bus stop. cuz a integration/ none of us went to the neighborhood school/ my own school waz 15 miles away/ so grandma tried to help/ & she got real nervous tryin to please mama/ & be in her room cryin cuz none of us wd mind. waz all the time sassin her. forcin her to cut switches off the hedges to whip our legs/ when we waz the only grandchirren she had.

i had had just about enuf & ran off a couple of times/ & mr. robinson at the pharmacy by the trolley stop always called mama to tell her what line i got on/ & then the trolley driver wd stop & let a police on/ who took me back/ & i came home from mrs. maureen's fulla beauty parlor gossip a child had no right to hear/ & when i tried to listen to blues on the radio/ somebody wd turn it off & 'cuse me of tryin my best to be a niggah. so mama went away for a while & daddy brushed our braids to a point like a dunce's cap & then patted them down. he gave us way too much money for lunch & told grandma she waz overworkin her heart so he wd have to get some one to come in til mama figured out whether she waz comin back.

it waz sposed to be a secret bout mama not bein sure whether she wanted to live wid us/ but i knew & cuz i didnt want the others to worry & cuz they were becomin bothersome/ i didn't say nothin bout/ & when carrie came i figured everythin wd always be awright.

carrie waz a big woman/ bigger than any woman on my mama's side or daddy's/ even aunt marie who waz sposed to have talked in tongues & run a farm all by herself cdnt have been as big as carrie/ & carrie straightened her hair so funny/ it made her look even bigger/ cuz she didnt curl it/ just ran a hot comb thru it/ so it pointed out in all directions/ like a white man's crew cut/ & she had pierced ears/ like aunt mamies who waz ninety & the ears liked ta touch her shoulders/ they waz so long & narrow/ but more n alla that/ carrie wore two house dresses at the same time/ one up til lunch & the other up til she went to her rooms on the top floor/ where the white folks who lived there before us/ left all this junk/ scrapbooks & crinolines & things/

carrie tied her dresses wid a rope/ a real thick rope/ not like one for hangin clothes/ but like one for makin a swing on a tree/ & she always wore it/ even when she changed house dresses/ & carrie wdnt use none of the bathrooms/ even tho there oughtta have been enuf for her/ cuz there waz one on each floor/ but carrie usedta say/ she liked the latrine in the cellar cuz that's what her mama had in arkansas/ & that's where she went/ of course my mama didnt know that.

mama didnt know that jeff usedta come round either/ & jeff waz a handsome ol man/ i cd even tell that/ he waz broad & brown & spoke good english/ carrie said that waz cuz jeff usedta garden for white folks fore the neighborhood changed & roughians like me cd move in/ & jeff wd bring carrie some carnations from mr. noble's yard every friday fore she got off work/ & sometimes they'd have a lil whiskey & laugh. carrie waz good to us.

she liked us/ almost seemed to understand how we were different people/ not just a bunch of smart aleck kids/ & we wd mind her & eat alla her food/ & i even learned to/ iron/ cuz carrie said the first thing a negro man wanted to know bout a woman sides cd she handle her licquor/ waz cd she iron a fine white dress shirt/ grandma thot carrie waz a lil crazy/ & maybe that she worked roots/ but compared to wilma who showed up the first time carrie disappeared/ grandma wd rather that strange actin one to stay/

wilma usedta get terrible nosebleeds every time i asked her why she didnt have no boyfriends/ & then she wd lie & tell grandma i asked her somethin bout sex/ & even grandma knew better 'n that/ cuz i waz a child/ & a woman gettin nosebleeds cuz she had to talk about sex waz silly & a strange woman waz much more reg'lar for grandma than a silly one/ cuz grandma wd getta talkin bout grandpa who'd been dead thirty years & she wd just be twinklin & massagin her bosom/ so everyone waz always glad when carrie came back & nobody asked her where she'd been/ we waz just so pleased to be able to smell her again & listen to all the stories bout her ex-husbands & her chirren/ carrie been married five times/ & had six chirren/ three dead/ one most dead/ one a dancer & one in the service/ the one in the service usedta send us pictures of him & german women near a wall/ & the dancer always sent photos of herself wid/ sure'nuf italians standin in a circle round her.

mama came home. we had a party/ carrie started bein more/ proper/ not cursin or drinkin so much/ & never mentionin men or jeff anymore/ it just waznt the same/ but the house sure did run good/ me & my sisters stopped fightin in the bed/ & i didnt run-off/ the boys stopped stealin things/ & my brother started makin up songs like chuck berry steada burnin up every thing/ we usedta play like we waz the shirelles & mama wd sing christian gospel songs like paul robeson not like the man at the church carrie took us to sometimes/ where we cd play tambourines & get a spirit. but.

jeff waz still comin round. mama scolded carrie soundly for entertainin in fronta her chirren. & she said one more incident & that wd have to be that. mama still didn't know bout alla carrie's husbands or bout the latrine & when she asked carrie to stop wearin that rope round her waist/ carrie looked at mama like she must be a crazy woman herself/ or a stupid one/ so mama never mentioned that again.

just bout the time vanita/ my very best friend/ got to wear stockings insteada anklets/ mama took us aside for a talk bout things women shd know/ & i checked everything she told me wid carrie/ & carrie said mama waz almost right/ but it waznt necessary to keep yr dress/ down/ yr knees locked/ & yr head high/ all the time/ just when some no good niggah came round did ya need to do alla that pre-cautionin.

carrie met jeff on the corner round from the house since mama came back/ & on fridays she stayed gone til monday mornin/ she came back just in time to help me get everybody's lunch together & make daddy's breakfast cuz mama skipped that meal for her figure/ n i waz gettin to be real important/ cuz carrie had shown me how to fix just bout everythin we ate/ how to starch clothes/ & wax the crevices on the stairway/ how to clean crystal & silver/ what to say when some one called/ i always used to shout/ "mama, it's somebody colored"/ or "daddy it's a white man"/ but carrie showed me how to be right/ & to sweep all under the bed & turn the blinds at midday so the sun wdnt bleach the furniture/ so when carrie didnt come this one monday mornin i figured i wd cover for her/ i cda done a good job too/ cept mama & grandma kept askin where waz carrie/ & wdnt let me do none of the stuff i knew how to do/ widout tellin me their way/ which waznt the way carrie showed me/ so i shouted back/ & got in a fight wid em/ for bein a impudence/ not havin respect/ & as i waz movin the glasses outta the dishwasher/ to pour juice/ for us/ my dumb brother dropped his shoe he cdnt tie in between my legs/ & all the glasses shattered cross the floor/ grandma held her heart/ cryin/ lord lord. please be careful/ & mama waz cursin & the phone rang.

mama said/ carrie where are you/ in between makin horrifyin faces at me as i swept up the glass/ & carrie musta been goin round the bush/ cuz mama kept sayin/ where are you/ til finally she looked sick & said "JAIL"/ well/ why/ & i know for sure carrie said/ "cuz i hadta cut this friend a mine"/ cuz mama kept sayin/ "cut a friend a yours"/ then she got very social workery & told carrie to come pick up her things & her last check cuz there waz no way in the world anyone cd expect her to let a criminal look after her chirren. carrie musta come while we were at school/ when i came home alla her things were gone/ but i found some of the rope she usedta tie round her waist by the latrine downstairs in the cellar.

my sisters & my brother & my cousins/ didnt even realize what had happened/ our losin carrie & all/

& i never mentioned my feelins to mama/ cuz then she wd just remind me/ that i always pick the most niggerish people in the world to make my friends/ & then she wd list mavis & freddie & charlenetta & linda susan (who waz really po white trash) so i didnt say nothin.

i just took carrie's place in the house/ & did everythin like she wda cept i did use the regular bathrooms/ & prayed for her like she prayed for the one of her chirren waz most dead.

cdnt see how anybody didnt know carrie wdnt cut nobody less they hurt her a whole lot. not less she hurt a whole lot.

SAUL'S PROGRESS

BY

Harvey Shapiro

1

I told my son:
"Stop trying to screw the monkey's tail
Into his bellybutton.
Originality
Is never its own
Justification.
Some innovations
Get nowhere."

"The Sunday monkeys are my friends,"
He said.
I was on my way down
From the heavenly city
Of the 18th Century philosophers.
He was on his way up,
Almost three.

2

"Moby Dick is smarter than
The other dicks."
A song to make the
Bad guys happy.
You sang it all day Saturday
With snot-filled nose

And clouded eye,
To raise me
To a fury.

3

You sit on the crest of a dune
Facing the sea,
Which is beyond sight.
Your anger at me
Makes you play by yourself,
Tell stories to yourself,
Fling out your hurt
To the wide sky's healing.
A red boat in one hand,
A blue in the other,
You begin singing songs
About the weather.
Cliff swallow, brilliant skimmer.

4

As if he were me, he comes bounding in,
All happiness. I owe him
All happiness. For these years at least.
When he smiles and says, a good time,
I have no notion who else
He has made happy with my happiness.

THE NIGHT THE BEARS ATE THE SLEEPING TROUT

BY

Adam Shaw

"You know those ducks in the lagoon right near Central Park South? That little lake? By any chance do you happen to know where they go, the ducks, when it gets all frozen over? Do you happen to know by any chance?"

—Holden Caulfield

Can't say that I know about the ducks, but a while ago I was walking along this creek, up someplace near where some of the water runs east and some runs west, and knew that, had he been with me, Holden would have asked about the trout.

With the powder deep on the mountain, and the village hushed below, the bears plowed down from the hills and through the glades, past cow-empty barns, down through shrub pine, and down through the aspen dark now in the night. They came singly at first and then in pairs, steady in the moonlight, in silence except for their footfalls.

The bears were brown except for crescent yellow moons on their chests.

Under the boulders, under the steady water, under the ice, the trout slept and did not hear the bears, for they had been asleep since Christmas. And did not hear the water, for it was their stream and their water.

The bears came down to the pool, singly at first and then in pairs. And gently, with their winter-furred paws, reached down to touch their moonshadows.

Which came up trout-filled.

Rejoicing, for they were not bad news bears, not at all, they ate the sleeping trout, all of them except for the very old ones who slept in the deepest eddies waiting for spring. Every spring.

And the bears padded back up over the hills, singly at first and then in pairs, and thus it was that, a very long time ago, the night the bears ate the sleeping trout came to pass.

THE WIZARD WHO INVENTED SILENCE

BY

Irwin Shaw

T he Wizard lived either in the Painted Desert, or the Petrified Forest, or on a houseboat in the Dry Tortugas, as the case may be. He was an ambiguous Wizard. He was known to like ladies and infants and was either monogamous, bigamous, or trigamous, as the case may be, and he had numerous sets of children, as the case may be.

He was a Wizard of Communications, transmuting sounds into messages or messages into sounds, as the case may be. He was acute of hearing and testy, particularly when within hearing distance of a Rock and Roll band over a transistor radio. He was not fond, he discovered, either of the sounds or the messages of which he was the master, although he was well rewarded for his work, since in his lifetime, which might have been in the past, the present, or the future, it was commonly accepted by men of intellect and feeling that the trouble with the world was that human beings did not know how to communicate with each other. There were many poems and novels and treatises and plays written on this subject and the writers of them were highly regarded by critics and educators and philosophers and other assorted people who knew how to read and write. The Wizard may or may not have received the Nobel Prize, as the case may be, for his work in Communications. He was not fond of the word, *Communications*. Ambiguity was his field, he was fond of saying, but his listeners felt that he was merely being witty, which is the prerogative of Wizards.

His crowning achievement, people believed, was the invention of a machine that transmitted ten thousand messages simultaneously at twice the speed of light, which Einstein had definitely proven was impossible. The Wizard had ambiguous feelings about Einstein, although he admired the way Einstein combed his hair.

As he grew older, or younger, as the case may be, the Wizard became progressively more annoyed with the sounds of children, of the animal world, of conversation, especially at cocktail parties, of little girls' squeals, little boys' whoops, the cawing of crows, the roars of lions, the song of the peacock, the whirring and thumping of machinery, and women saying over a martini glass, "You're looking so much better, dear, than last year."

One day, after hearing little girls squealing, little boys whooping, crows cawing, lions roaring, drills drilling, and women raising their voices to be heard over the clinking of cocktail glasses and saying, "My husband has lost interest in me," the wizard fell to doodling on a little pad and found that he had invented a riveting machine that riveted without making a sound, a vacuum cleaner that vacuumed with a whisper like a summer wind ruffling tall grass, a generator that generated with the light tinkle of a distant trout brook. Going from there, he designed a room in which children playing sounded like the faint trilling of birds in a faraway field of chrysanthemums and in which a party after the first night of a play sounded like a Gregorian chant being sung across the ocean in a cathedral in Jerusalem in the thirteenth century.

He was an acoustical Wizard as well as an ambiguous Wizard, but he was a practical and pragmatic man and he decided to put his discoveries to use. Among the many benefits he bestowed on Mankind was a silencer for the 155 howitzer and the hydrogen bomb, so that people could die in peace. He may or may not have been awarded his uncertain second Nobel Prize for this accomplishment.

There was nothing much he could do about the animal kingdom; the birds still cawed, the lions still roared, the peacocks still screamed, so he came to the conclusion that his efforts had to be focused on Man and Man's works, which was not a wholly inconsiderable piece of territory even for a Wizard.

With the help of a grant from the Order of Trappist monks, he was given a small town on which to experiment. By the use of mathematical formulae which no one could understand, he built a cunning dome over the town, under which a taxi driver leaning on his horn could not be heard, television commentators could only be followed by the deaf and dumb who had learned lip-reading from infancy, the pleas of lawyers in the courts could only be judged by the honesty or dishonesty of their faces, and the pronouncements of generals and politicians made one think of the sweet rise and fall of an infant's breathing in his crib.

A curious phenomenon was noticed after a while in the experimental town. No suicide was recorded in the town for an entire year, although the town was located in the Midwest, the practice of psychiatry was discontinued for lack of patients, children of four began to read Kant and Wittgenstein, divorces fell to zero per thousand population, and old men and women who had been bedridden for decades took to riding bicycles, their faces flushed with the rosy hue of youth. The writers who lived in the town did not write a single novel, play, or treatise on the modern tragedy of lack of communication and instead wrote odes to the beauty of young women and the joys of family life.

The benefits of the dome were not lost on his fellow citizens and the Wizard was hired to continue his work on a more ambitious scale. New York City, which could not scrape up the money to pave the West Side Highway, floated bonds to erect an enormous dome, to the Wizard's specifications, covering Manhattan, Staten Island, the South Bronx, Brooklyn, and Queens. There were many anxious moments, as was to be expected, as the work went on. What had succeeded in a small town under the auspices of the Order of the Trappist monks, was a different story, people said, from a gigantic endeavor in a city of eight million under the auspices of the Board of Aldermen and the Chase National Bank.

But the day came when the Wizard made his final mathematical calculation and said to the workmen under his direction, "Please put that last section of laminated nacre there," and stepped back and watched for a moment and said, "It is done."

There was a moment of trembling silence, then a soft hush, then, in the busy city, a gentle, pleasant buzzing, as of a few drowsy bees foraging in fragrant clover across the river in New Jersey. There was unheard applause, although all over the city people could be seen clapping their hands together. Taxi drivers, knowing what to expect, did not bother to touch their horns. Policemen smiled. Men touting for porn movies and massage parlors threw away their leaflets because they could not command the attention of passers-by. Con Edison engineers, emerging noiselessly from their ghostly manholes, looked like fairytale giants rising from the earth. The divorce rate fell and the rate of suicide, even as it had done in the small town in the Midwest, and after a while Madison Avenue, where the advertising agencies were located, was almost deserted. In the discotheques, couples waltzed dreamily to an inner music, humming to themselves, and in the subway the trains slid by like small boats in the tunnel of love in the old Coney Island. At basketball games and hockey matches in Madison Square Garden, with the shouting gone, the players looked like friezes on the walls of Cretan palaces, graceful and figures of myth. The offices of the psychiatrists on Park Avenue were all for rent and the sale of anti-ulcer medicines was discontinued completely. Wives and husbands were seen walking arm-in-arm, and nobody left the city for the weekend.

The keys of the city were offered to the Wizard by a grateful mayor, but the Wizard was too busy working on the last details of this new concert hall to attend the ceremony. Before he had begun the hall, it had been rented, for the night of the Fourth of July, by the most popular Rock group in the world, The Unholies, and the Wizard had to work overtime to prepare the auditorium. He was standing at the back as the Unholies, with their spangles, their beads and pendants, their drums, cymbals, electric guitars, and microphones, strutted onto the stage. There was a small sound from the audience, which was standing and gesticulating wildly at the appearance of the musicians. The sound was like the sleepy tapping of cicadas among the sage and lavender and thyme bushes on the Mediterranean coast of France on a lazy summer afternoon.

The musicians began to play. Their motions were familiar to the crowd. But the sound was the rapturous measured harmony of Mozart's *Eine kleine Nachtmusik*.

The Wizard smiled briefly, then slipped out.

It was said that he had disappeared, but from time to time it was reported that he had been seen, quadrigamously or cinquagamously, as the case might be, at Niagara Falls, or in the tumult of the Sook of Istanbul, or in the Eastern lands where peacocks were bred, as the case might be.

THE FASTEST MAN IN THE WORLD

A KID's FABLE BY
Sam Shepard

The wind moved down through the center of town. One of those quick winds that appears and disappears. Just like that. All the crabapple trees looked like they were about to snap. Then they'd spring back, straight as a post. Their red leaves barely moving. Just like nothing ever happened. Just like it was a regular old ordinary day in the sun.

The wind came up again, blowing down through the main street even stronger than the last time. Like it was trying to outdo the last time. Except this time everything came loose. All at once, everything in town that wasn't nailed down was blowing, sailing, flying down the main street.

It was all over in a flash. The last thing to go was a giant golden banner hanging by ropes between two telephone poles. In black letters the banner read: "TODAY—THE FASTEST MAN IN THE WORLD." That was all it said. It took off like the tail of a Chinese kite. Even after the wind had stopped a long time the banner was still soaring way out over the eucalyptus trees. It kept going across big open fields until it finally dropped on a beach where nobody was.

The people in town were glad to see the wind go. They never knew who had put the golden banner up to begin with so nobody missed it. Everything that had been torn off by the wind was put back. Everything that was broken was fixed. All the people were more than happy to get back to normal.

That night a truck rolled into town. A brown pickup truck with a few dents. The driver was a skinny little man in a plain gray suit and a blue baseball cap. At that moment he was the only one in town who knew who he actually was. Nobody else knew. Nobody else even cared. All the houses were glowing with the blue lights of TVs. The voices of television were heard through the streets. Hardly any real people's voices were heard. One of the only real people's voices was the voice of the little skinny man. He was talking to himself very softly. At least it sounded like he was talking to himself, but actually he was talking to the wind. He was driving very slowly past all the glowing blue houses. His eyes were taking everything in. He kept talking the whole time and the wind (which was now a slight breeze) was talking back. The two of them had been friends for a very long time.

"It doesn't seem to me as though anybody got the message here," said the little skinny man to the wind.

"Well, it's been very difficult to get them to understand my language. I almost blew my head off today and nobody understood a thing."

"Didn't anybody ask where I'd be appearing?"

"Not a soul."

"Very strange."

"I even went so far as to put up a banner. In their words. In their own language. I don't think anybody even saw it."

"Well, we'll just have to give them a little free demonstration in the morning. Maybe that'll snap them out of it."

"I sure hope so."

The morning came in as clear and as bright as any morning the people had ever seen. In fact, it was so clear and so bright that some of the people even thought something was wrong. There was no wind at all. Not even the slightest breeze. Not a single sound was in the air. The people decided to go on about their business anyway. That it was just another funny change in the weather. They all put on their jogging suits and started jogging down the main street. This was something that everyone in town did. No matter how old or how young, they all jogged.

The little skinny man was watching from his pickup truck as they all ran past him. Nobody even saw him. He'd been sitting like that all night long. Wide awake. Very still. Waiting for the people. As they all ran past in their fancy jogging suits, the little skinny man slid out of his truck and followed them down the street at a shuffle. He was still wearing his blue baseball cap and his plain gray suit.

At first he was content to keep a good distance from the people. He didn't want to scare them. He only wanted to show them something very simple. His face was glowing now with a special kind of excitement. His whole body could hardly restrain itself from what was about to happen.

The people were now reaching the outskirts of town, where there wasn't anything much except a golf course. They usually ran around the golf course once and then headed straight back home where they all took showers and ate big breakfasts and read each other the newspaper.

It was on about the seventh fairway that the little skinny man caught up to them. He just joined them like he was another ordinary person who lived in the town. Just like them. They all smiled at him very politely, although secretly they wondered why he was wearing a plain gray suit and a baseball cap. Nobody jogged in a plain gray suit and a baseball cap. The little skinny man was also very polite and remarked about the wonderful weather and how it was a perfect day for running and how he'd heard through the grapevine that the fastest man in the world was coming to town that day.

"The fastest man in the world!" they chimed in almost the same breath.

"Yes, that's right." He smiled at them with a smile like lightning. "Faster than almost anything you can name. So fast he almost disappears. As fast as a shooting star."

Everyone broke down laughing at the little skinny man. In fact, they laughed so hard they all had to stop jogging. They fell down on the grass, holding their sides, rolling around, kicking their feet at the sky, and giggling their heads off. The little skinny man kept jogging in place. He kept smiling the whole time. He flipped both his blue tennis shoes off, high into the air. The tennis shoes landed in the very center of all the laughing people. As soon as that happened the people stopped laughing. They stared at the shoes. Then a shimmering golden light pulled their eyes toward the bare feet of the little skinny man. The feet were shining like light bulbs. Nobody could take their eyes off the feet. The feet were dancing. The feet were singing, they were so happy to be out of their shoes.

Then an incredible thing happened. The golden feet rocked straight back on their heels, pointed all their flashing toes at the sky, and took a gigantic leap that sent the little skinny man a hundred and twenty-five feet straight into the air. As he shot up into the sky a shower of red sparks floated down on all the people. But none of them were scared. It was much more fantastic than any fireworks they'd ever seen. They followed the flying body of the little skinny man until he landed in a peanut-shaped lake, sending all kinds of white swans and ducks screaming for their lives. As he hit the lake his legs started churning like a crazy propeller. The water gurgled up in blue bubbles, throwing huge waves out over the trees. A high, shrill whining sound came from the center of the lake. Like the sound of a thousand bees getting closer.

Now the people were scared. They all stood up when they heard that sound and they gathered close together just in case something awful might happen. All they could see from the lake was the burbling water and a pulsing golden light. The light kept turning brighter and brighter until it finally got orange. The sky kept getting darker and darker until it finally got gray. The people were getting more and more frightened. Suddenly the light exploded out of the lake. The people jumped. Some even screamed. The light raced out clear across the golf course, cutting a golden path straight into town where nobody was. Then they saw all the lights in their houses go on. One by one. Until every house in town was shining with light. The sky was almost black by now. The people had the strangest feeling, seeing their houses lit up and nobody in them. Almost as though they were dead and had been brought back to life. They watched their houses and imagined they were watching themselves from a distance. Imagined it must be night time now in the town and all the people must be getting ready for bed. Imagined some of them were watching television and doing all the things they all do at night in a little town like that. Then all the lights in the houses suddenly went out again. And everything was pitch black except for a tiny speck of golden light heading straight back toward them. It was coming toward them at a much faster speed than the speed of light. It was as though it was already as close to them as it was far away. As though it was both places at once. When it reached them it stopped. It just hovered like a humming-bird right there in front of them. Then it changed. In a flash. There was the little skinny man standing there in the same place the light had just been. He was picking his teeth with a toothpick and smiling at them with a smile just like lightning. The same smile he always had. He made a few smacking sounds as though he'd just finished eating something delicious. He pointed with the toothpick to the tallest tree. The people's eyes followed. High up on the very topmost branch they saw the little skinny man doing a dance. He was clapping his hands and knocking his knees together, but nobody could hear any music. Quickly their eyes turned back. There he was, still on the ground. Still picking his teeth and smiling. He pointed again with the toothpick but this time straight up to the sky. Again, the people looked up and what they saw they could hardly believe. There was the little skinny man running full blast right across the whole sky. He seemed to be chasing something, but nobody could tell what it was. His mouth was wide open and each time he came to a star he swallowed it whole. He made a big circle around the sky gobbling up every star in sight and each time he swallowed a star the sky got a little bit darker. As the sky grew darker and darker the little skinny man got brighter and brighter until it looked as though he might explode from the light he was eating. Finally there was only one star left in the sky. The Dog Star. The people prayed he wouldn't eat it, but he did anyway. Just gobbled it up like a donut. When that happened the little skinny man was the only light in the sky. In fact, the light was so bright that the people all had to turn their eyes away. When they turned back again it was daytime. The little skinny man had disappeared. All they saw was the sun. The same giant sun they'd seen every day of their lives.

It was right then, at that moment, that they all remembered this was the same morning they'd all started jogging. They looked around at each other in their fancy jogging suits and nobody said a word. There was no reason to say a word. They started walking very slowly back toward the town. Before they knew it, they were running. But it wasn't just an ordinary run. Their legs were flying out in front of them. The old people were running as fast as the kids. As they raced back into town an old brown pickup truck was just leaving. Nobody even noticed. The truck moved slowly out to the open highway and disappeared over a low hill. Everything was very still for a while. Then, very gently, the wind came up just on the outskirts. It moved out through the fields, making all the grass wave. Then it swooped down to the beach where nobody was and picked up the big golden banner that was still lying there from the day before. The banner leaped high in the air and stretched itself out, almost as though two people were holding it at either end. It just hung there in midair for a long while with the words in black letters: "TODAY—THE FASTEST MAN IN THE WORLD."

STORY FOR DEAD OF WINTER

BY

Alix Kates Shulman

*S*now had been falling hard for *hours by the time Robin got into bed, pulled up the covers, and said, "Tell me a story, Sara."*

Sara put on her storytelling voice and began:

There was once a time, before the great snow, not so long ago, when every child from five years on, from Maine in the East to California in the West, got up early each weekday and went to school. Schools were places where children learned to write and read, subtract and add, answer and ask. Everyone went, no one questioned it. Even children too young to attend got together at home and played School. Until the great snow, when my story begins. . . .

That weekend (when my story begins), white flakes filled the air, whirling up as well as down, gusting through the days and nights from Friday to Sunday. The world was as white as baby teeth. In the mornings you couldn't tell the streets from the sidewalks, and even the biggest plows had trouble getting through. When the radio announced the schools would be closed on Monday, no one was surprised. There had always been snow holidays in our part of the country, with snow so high you couldn't open the front door and banks sometimes so deep the youngest stepped in up to their necks. But no one could remember a snowfall to match this one.

At first all the children rejoiced. Another holiday! No more school! The days were filled with snowballs, igloos, forts, sliding, sledding, snow people. The younger children went to sleep at night to dream snowball dreams and got up early to make them come true. Prudent parents ate their breakfasts listening to the radio for official announcements that the schools were opening again. But the younger children dashed straight outside and the older children, seeing the white-filled sky, went back to sleep. By noon they joined the youngsters outside building snow people of every size. They stayed out as long as there was sun, for there was little time to play in snow when school was on.

But after a week, two weeks, a month, the novelty wore off. There was something wrong with so much snow. Even the children sensed it. No longer did they rush out to play before finishing breakfast, but waited till the sun was high. Sometimes they searched the sky for a sign that the snow was letting up, but there was no sign.

Now snow people lined the streets, or what had looked like streets before the snow. Some of the snow people had lost their heads; others were frozen to ice. The children, growing tired of the snow, ignored the snow people and moved indoors. There they turned to cards and Bingo and Monopoly. They played for hours. They watched TV. They all slept later and later in the mornings, secretly waiting for the weather to break.

Who could blame them? Who would not grow tired of cards and Bingo, TV and Monopoly? Parents, forced by school closings to leave their jobs to stay home with the children, didn't know what to do. Some hired sitters and kept their jobs; but when they returned home in the evenings, often the children were in tears. "Read to us!" they cried. Only dimly now did they remember school. Some of the youngest ones began to forget how to read. Even the older ones remembered less and less.

More weeks went by and still the schools stayed closed. Some of us, remembering milder years, continued to tune in the official radio station every morning waiting hopefully to hear new news. But gradually even those of us who once believed in official announcements stopped listening. School? Deep down we feared it was over. Like the libraries, parks, and public pools we had learned to do without and then forget, school was a habit too easily broken. When the snow ended the schools remained closed. For repairs, said some. For Spring Vacation, said others. Whatever the reason, the habit of school was lost. People felt the loss but did nothing. Nothing had become the new habit.

Now, for many children, old and young, those large, low rectangular buildings with clocks and water fountains in the corridors and lunchrooms and gyms in the basement turned up only in dreams. There, at night, the children romped through light green rooms with row after row of desks and chairs, with books and plants on the tables, and maps and chalkboards on the walls, and teachers ready to answer their questions. But in the daytime they forgot.

Then one day an unusual thing began to happen. Some of the older children began to join the youngest ones whenever they played School. Everyone got to play teacher, but often the older ones instructed the younger ones. No one knew how it began or why. Some claimed it was because the older children were tired of always being nagged to read aloud the same old books or tell how to spell or answer the same old questions. Whatever the reason, Doctor and Store, Bingo and Monopoly, fell out of favor as everyone started playing School.

Everywhere, little groups of young began to gather around an older child until he or she agreed to teach them how to shape the letters of the alphabet, how to form the words, how to name, count, add, subtract, carry, borrow, ask, answer. Groups formed to talk about dinosaurs. Others told nothing but riddles. In our neighborhood a boy and girl with a drum and kazoo began a chorus that learned thirteen songs in perfect three-part harmony. Some of the elders agreed to tell stories to the young if they wanted to hear—especially stories of the bygone days when everyone went to school.

"And now to sleep," said Sara abruptly, in her normal voice. She kissed Robin on the nose and turned off the light.

"But what about the South?" said Robin brightly, sitting up. "And the West? Didn't they still have school where they didn't have snow?"

"Good point," said Sara. "However . . . by Spring word had spread all the way to California that snow had closed down most of the schools in the East, and that brand-new plans were under way. Not to be outdone, Californians soon came up with a totally different scheme for closing schools without regard to snow. For, you're right: there was hardly ever any snow in California. They voted to stop collecting taxes. Without money, they couldn't pay teachers and without teachers, they too had to close the schools." Again Sara slipped on her storytelling voice:

Ohio and Florida were next. Soon, all over the country new plans were devised for closing down the schools. All over the country children rejoiced at first, then turned to cards, TV, and Monopoly, then grew bored with these, and finally, recalling little moments in green rooms, remembered school only as a game they played or as a place they dreamed. All over the country, people developed new habits and new ways to learn.

Nowadays, when those of us who still remember gather with the young to tell our stories, we tell them of those times not so long ago when every child from five years on, from Maine in the East to California in the West, got up early each weekday and trudged to school. Until the great snow when my story begins. . . .

Sara consulted her watch. "And now, good night," she said, "this time, really. I've got to hear the news in one minute." She blew Robin a fast kiss and left the room.

In the dark, Robin watched the white snow ripple through the black sky and fill the window. It was piled so high on the window ledge that Robin had no doubt the schools would still be closed the next morning. How long had it been falling? It was getting harder and harder to remember now, thought Robin, slipping softly as snowflakes into a deep sleep and a green dream.

BEDTIME STORIES

BY
Charles Simic

(for R. E.)

1

The great toy-maker made toy-judges.
He wound them up to a screech.
Then he made a toy-torturer.
He made a toy-executioner.

But he forgot to make toy-victims.
There was just you and me.
And we were cold. And I had a bad cough.
And you had one leg shorter than the other.

2

All the lost ones gathered
To make a forest. Autumn,
And someone's reporting a disappearance
For every last one of them,

Has each twig, leaf, root,
Described and then dimly outlined
By a police artist . . .
The old woman in crisp, funereal silks.

3

When a tree falls in a forest
And there's no one around
To hear the sound, the poor owls
Have to do all the thinking.

They think so hard, they fall off
Their perch and are eaten by ants,
Who, as you already know, all look like
Little Black Riding Hoods.

4

You got something in your left eye.
It's a step-ladder.
Very tiny. Very interesting.
There's a bucket, too, and a man
In white overalls. He's got a brush!
He's going to paint your eye black.

I make kiss-like noises
To scare him off.

5

This must be that famous cottage
Where the wolf swallowed grandma.
Only now there's a Chinese Laundry on one side,
And a poolhall on the other.

And if it isn't, how come
When they open its narrow door at night,
The light falls on its fours and crawls off,
And behind it the posse of someone laughing,
        someone crying herself to sleep?

OLE AND TRUFA: A STORY OF TWO LEAVES

BY

Isaac Bashevis Singer

The forest was large and thickly overgrown with all kinds of leaf-bearing trees. It was in the month of November. Usually, it's cold this time of year and it even happens that it snows, but this November was relatively warm. The nights were cool and windy but as soon as the sun came out in the mornings it turned warm. You might have thought it was summer except that the whole forest was strewn with fallen leaves—some yellow as saffron, some red as wine, some the color of gold, and some of mixed color. The leaves had been torn by the rain, by the wind, some by day, some at night—and they now formed a deep carpet over the forest floor. Although their juices had run dry the leaves still exuded a pleasant aroma. The sun shone down on them through the living branches and worms and flies which had somehow survived the autumn storms, crawled over them. The space beneath the leaves provided hiding places for crickets, field mice, and many other creatures who sought protection in the earth. The birds that don't migrate to warmer climates in the winter but stay behind, perched on the bare tree limbs. Among them were sparrows—tiny birds but endowed with much courage and the experience accumulated through thousands of generations. They hopped, twittered, and searched for the food the forest offered this time of year. Many, many insects and worms had perished in recent weeks, but no one mourned their loss. God's creatures know that death is merely a phase of life. With the coming of spring, the forest would again fill with grasses, green leaves, blossoms, and flowers. The migrating birds would return from far-off lands and locate their abandoned nests. Even if the wind or the rain had disturbed a nest, it could be easily repaired.

On the tip of a tree which had lost all its other leaves, two still remained. One leaf was named Ole and the other, Trufa. Ole and Trufa both hung from one twig. Since they were at the very tip of the tree, they received lots of sunlight. For some reason unknown to Ole or Trufa, they had survived all the rains, all the cold nights and winds, and still clung to the tip of the twig. Who knows the reason one leaf falls and another remains? But Ole and Trufa believed the answer lay in the great love they bore one another. Ole was slightly bigger than Trufa and a few days older, but Trufa was prettier and more delicate. One leaf can do little for another when the wind blows, the rain pours, or the hail begins to fall. It even happens in summer that a leaf is torn loose—come autumn and winter and nothing can be done. Still, Ole encouraged Trufa at every opportunity. During the worst storms when the thunder clapped, the lightning flashed, and the wind tore off not only leaves but even whole branches, Ole pleaded with Trufa:

"Hang on, Trufa! Hang on with all your might!"

At times during cold and stormy nights, Trufa would complain: "My time has come, Ole, but you hang on!"

"What for?" Ole asked, "without you, my life is senseless. If you fall, I'll fall with you."

"No, Ole, don't do it! So long as a leaf can stay up it mustn't let go. . . ."

"It all depends if you stay with me," Ole replied. "By day I look at you and admire your beauty. At night I sense your fragrance. Be the only leaf on a tree? No, never!"

"Ole, your words are so sweet but they're not true," Trufa said. "You know very well that I'm no longer pretty. Look how wrinkled I am! All my juices have dried out and I'm ashamed before the birds. They look at me with such pity. At times it seems to me they're laughing at how shriveled I've become. I've lost everything, but one thing is still left me—my love for you."

"Isn't that enough? Of all our powers love is the highest, the finest," Ole said. "So long as we love each other we remain here, and no wind, rain, or storm can destroy us. I'll tell you something, Trufa—I never loved you as much as I love you now."

"Why, Ole? Why? I'm all yellow."

"Who says green is pretty and yellow is not? All colors are equally handsome."

And just as Ole spoke these words, that which Trufa had feared all these months happened—a wind came up and tore Ole loose from the twig. Trufa began to tremble and flutter until it seemed that she too would soon be torn away, but she held fast. She saw Ole fall and sway in the air and she called to him in leafy language:

"Ole! Come back! Ole! Ole!"

But before she could even finish Ole vanished from sight. He blended in with the other leaves on the ground and Trufa was left all alone on the tree.

So long as it was still day, Trufa managed somehow to endure her grief. But when it grew dark and cold and a piercing rain began to fall, she sank into despair. Somehow she felt that the blame for all the leafy misfortunes lay with the tree, the trunk with all its mighty limbs. Leaves fell but the trunk stood tall, thick, and firmly rooted in the ground. No wind, rain, or hail could upset it. What did it matter to a tree, which probably lived forever, what became of a leaf? To Trufa, the trunk was a kind of God. It covered itself with leaves for a few months, then it shook them off. It nourished them with its sap for as long as it pleased, then it let them die of thirst. Trufa pleaded with the tree to give her back her Ole and to make it summer again, but the tree didn't heed, or refused to heed her prayers. . . .

Trufa didn't think a night could be so long as this one—so dark, so frosty. She spoke to Ole and hoped for an answer, but Ole was silent and gave no sign of his presence.

Trufa said to the tree: "Since you've taken Ole from me, take me too."

But even this prayer the tree didn't acknowledge.

After a while, Trufa dozed off. This wasn't sleep but a strange languor. Trufa awoke and to her amazement found that she was no longer hanging on the tree. The wind had blown her down while she was asleep. This was different from the way she used to feel when she awoke on the tree with the sunrise. All her fears and anxieties had now vanished. The awakening also brought with it an awareness she had never felt before. She knew now that she wasn't just a leaf that depended on every whim of the wind, but that she was a part of the universe. She no longer was small nor weak nor transient, but a part of eternity. Through some mysterious force Trufa understood the miracle of her molecules, atoms, protons, and electrons—the enormous energy she represented and the divine plan of which she was a part. Next to her lay Ole and they greeted each other with a love they hadn't been aware of before. This wasn't a love that depended on chance or caprice but a love as mighty and eternal as the universe itself. That which they had feared all the days and nights between April and November turned out to be not death but redemption. A breeze came and lifted Ole and Trufa in the air and they soared with the bliss known only by those who have freed themselves and have joined with eternity.

PANTOUM FOR DEAD ANIMALS

BY

Lorna Smedman

You can make a dead bird drink water
from a birdbath or a cup—
only those who died while flying thru a cloud
though, the rest are just dead.

From a birdbath or a cup
water evaporates.
Though the rest are just dead
bunches of dry bones,

water evaporates
out of squirrel bodies buried in the corner of the yard.
Bunches of dry bones'
molecules rise to the clouds.

Out of squirrel bodies buried in the corner of the yard
energy scatters into birch trees,
molecules rise to the clouds,
and these make shapes of more strange animals.

Energy scatters into birch trees'
bark, stamps on white paper,
and these make shapes of more strange animals,
some who howl, bite, gesticulate,

bark. Stamps on white paper
ask if
some who howl, bite, gesticulate,
even young children, know the answer.

Ask if
you can make a dead bird drink water.
Even young children know the answer:
only those who died while flying thru a cloud.

BUMBLEBEE

BY
Patti Smith

is a game that i made
for toddy and linda
for when we were little
but we still play it

all you need is a pillow
to serve as a satchel
and maybe a bed
to serve as a mountain

one hand in your pocket
your head is bowed over
and with your free hand
throw over your burden

like a good soldier
over your shoulder
then you start walking
round in a circle

thinking of nothing
then you start humming
buzz-a buzz buzza
nothings the matter

round in a circle
in the realm of the one
the buzz of the bee
the radiant drone

follow the leader
thru good and bad weather
til no ones the wiser
now your together

HECTOR LEAVES HOME

BY

Isaac, Jason, and Ted Solotaroff

Hector Cruz was born in the slums of New York City on New Year's Day, 1975. He grew up at the Cathedral School of St. John the Divine, where his parents had brought him at an early age because they were trying to give him a better life. By 1977 he was all grown up and at the height of his cool. He was still single, had three girl friends who chased him to exhaustion and vice versa, and lots of buddies who envied his long, lean body, his speed, his courage, and his very enjoyable life.

When Hector was still young he had watched his parents and older brothers and sisters disappear into a huge machine that sucked up everything it came near. From then on, Hector had to make it on his own. He continued to live at the Cathedral School, where he had the run of the kitchen and a cozy place just off the English room, B-24, which being in the basement was warm in winter and cool in summer. Living so close to the English classes, Hector had become literary. Along with nibbling at the children's classics and devouring a dictionary, Hector found that *The Lord of the Rings* particularly appealed to his taste. Hector sat in on most of the English classes, but his favorite one was English as a Second Language. Hector disliked grammar, like all normal students, but when the teacher read a good story to the class Hector was all ears.

So much for Hector's day life. On Friday afternoon he never went to classes. Instead, he spruced up his dark gray coat and white shirtfront, groomed his hair and whiskers, did his loosening up exercises, and practiced his dance steps. At eight o'clock sharp, he ambled up to his date's place on the third floor. His Friday night girl friend was named Maria. She was his favorite one because she was sleek and pretty and a terrific dancer. But she made Hector impatient because she liked to stay home and talk and cuddle with him, while he was eager to get off to the Open Trap, a popular hangout of the school and church younger generation who danced the Scurry and the Scamper there.

On this particular evening Hector and Maria were trying a new step when there was a thump and some yelling outside of the concealed entrance to the Open Trap. Big Lenny, the doorman, came running in and shouted, "The Pack is outside." Instant panic. Some of the braver ones peeked outside and saw several huge dark figures stalking up and down. One of them, who had very prominent front teeth, stepped forward and shouted, "Come out, you little creeps."

"Cool it," Hector said as calmly as he could. "We're not bothering you."

The leader of the Pack, whose nickname was Purr, snarled back, "We'll cool your face."

Lenny, who was the strongest one, shouted, "Try it!"

At which point Purr and the others in the Pack began butting the wall. Hector, who knew a bad scene when he saw one, immediately led Maria toward a secret exit. Outside, they darted down to the basement and into Hector's place. Though he tried not to show it to Maria, Hector was upset. So much so that he stayed home Saturday night with Juanita, another of his girl friends, telling her of his various narrow escapes.

By Monday morning Hector had regained his cool. Just in time too. As he was traveling upstairs, thinking that he would slip into the Science class and see what was cooking, he suddenly heard a loud curse. With his superb reflexes Hector pivoted and reversed his field as a long, bristly object swept past him. "There you are," he heard a voice roar. "Take that!" But Hector was gone.

Now he had to be careful. His enemy, John the janitor, was on his case again. This was more frightening than the amateur efforts of those monsters in blue blazers who were always trying to capture him with their pathetic scraps of bologna and cheese. John seemed to forget about Hector for weeks at a time, but when the janitor spotted him, the next few days were likely to be trouble.

Still, as usual, Hector refused to lie low. In fact, that

very afternoon he dropped in on Maria and suggested they visit the French class. As they skipped along the first floor corridor, Hector was so busy flirting with Maria that he didn't notice John and the identical machine that had made his parents disappear. The large white nozzle was already rushing at them when Maria saw it. She shrieked and froze. Hector immediately shoved her out of the way of the terrible wind that was sucking them forward. Maria raced into the French class. In a tight corner, Hector faked one way and went the other. John swung the nozzle around, but once again, Hector was gone.

"You damn little pest," John hissed, and chased after him down the hall, picking up a broom on the way.

Maria was so frightened she darted right past the French teacher, Madame DuPont. *"Un souris,"* exclaimed Madame DuPont to the class. Actually she wasn't very frightened because she came from Marseilles. Bobby Greenfield, the mouse-hunter of the class, quickly sized up the situation and yelled for John.

His first swoop of the broom stunned Maria. John was moving in for the kill when several of the children who owned gerbils began to protest. Madame DuPont was sympathetic. She picked up Maria, cooed a few French words over her, and placed her unconscious body in a Kleenex box. Bobby Greenfield persuaded her to let him take Maria to Science class for purposes of observation. He was already planning a medical career.

Hector waited for hours and hours at Maria's place. He began to fear the worst because it wasn't like Maria to stay away this long; she liked to hang around her home instead of looking for action like he did. That evening he began to search for her. He first went to the French room but the door was closed and he couldn't wriggle through it. He tried to call to her but not too loudly because he was afraid John might hear him. He went from floor to floor calling Maria in a voice as low as he could make it but he had no luck. He had asked all of his friends and even his other girl friends but no one had seen Maria since that morning. He was going slowly home when he thought he heard a little voice coming from the Science room. Could it be Maria? He called her name in a loud brave voice. She answered. He asked her what she was doing in there. She said she was in big trouble.

"What trouble?" asked Hector.

"They caught me," Maria said.

"No sweat," said Hector, having regained his cool. "I'll get you out."

But, as he soon realized, he had a lot of problems. It took a whole day just to figure out how to visit her during recess and after school because the Science teacher always closed the door when she went out. Luckily the Science room was in the basement and had a window at ground level. It had bars on it which would have been all right with Hector if the window hadn't been closed. Hector hung out in the vicinity as much as he could, shivering in the cold air. He had never gone out of the school much before and wasn't used to the cold. It was scary to be outdoors, but exciting too.

Finally, on the fourth day, Mrs. Pepstein opened the window because one of the monsters was playing with a Bunsen burner. Seeing his chance, Hector scooted into the room and hid behind a radiator. The warm air made him drowsy and since he had a few hours to kill anyway, he calmly took a nap.

When he awoke the classroom was empty. He slipped down the radiator and jumped to the floor. "Here I am, Maria," he said, hoisting himself up on the teacher's chair so that he could talk to her easily.

"Hi Hector," she said, but she didn't seem to be as happy to see him as he had expected.

Hector paced around the chair, stroking his whiskers while he thought of a plan to free Maria from the cage in which she was kept on the teacher's desk. Finally he figured out that if he got hold of Lenny, who had also escaped from the Pack, the two of them could lift the hook that held the door of the cage. "Okay Maria," he said. "I'll go get Big Lenny and we'll have you out of there before you know it."

"Don't bother, Hector," she said quietly.

"What do you mean, 'don't bother.' You're my girl friend."

"I just don't want to leave. I like it here. At least for the time being." She motioned to the cage, which Hector now noticed had been fixed up nicely by the class. They had put in an exercise wheel, a styrofoam floor, a dish of water, and plenty of lettuce.

"This is a nice place," admitted Hector. "Except for one thing, the most important one. You can't get out."

Maria shrugged. "That's not the most important thing."

"What is?"

"Feeling safe. Being taken care of instead of chased."

"I'd rather be chased than caught," said Hector in his braggiest voice. He motioned to the open window. "I'd rather be out there than in here." He began to pace back and forth again. He'd never run into a situation like this before.

"That's you," Maria said. "Not me. Besides, you're just as much locked up in doing your thing in the school as I am in here. Except that I'm safer."

Hector turned away. He had known this in his head for the last few days of being outdoors. Now that Maria had said it, he realized it was true. But he couldn't admit it to Maria. "You're just waiting for them to bring you some nice fat guy from the Church crowd so you and him can live happily ever after."

"You'll never understand me, Hector," Maria said.

Hector let her have the last word. He had his own decision to make. Cathedral School was too small for him. He had no future except to get so fat and old that he would finally be killed by John. He hoisted himself up the radiator and through the bars. He was outside now and free and on his own. He moved warily away from the school, than darted across 110th Street and out into the world.

BABY GRAY AND THE BLUE FAIRY

BY

Terry Southern

Donkey was less bad than many supposed. It was rather that he was seen on occasion sporting with Pigman and Bad Baker, and that very often he brought up their names as points of reference in the discussion at hand. And yet, if Pigman and Bad Baker were to be feared for their wicked cunning, surely even so was the Donkey as well, for his foolishness and his great great pride.

Baby Gray was a true baby gray-fur, so tiny and dear that she just sat in the forest all day in a little bundle and stared ahead. She was too small to play, and her thoughts were warm and furry things that meant nothing; so she would just crouch in the sun in a bundle of goodness—though from time to time, she might cry out in a very small voice: "See me in my fur suit!" Then she would crouch there, waiting for someone to come and do something to her . . . a kiss or a pinching, she didn't know which, she was so tiny and dear. She was called Baby Gray-Fur.

All the smallest and dear of the forest—Mouse, Good Toad, Cricket, and others—would come to see Baby Gray sitting there in her goodness. Toad gave her a bowl of sweet pudding.

"This is for your goodness!" he said and rushed away.

Baby Gray seemed pleased and sat there by it for a long time, purring, until finally old Pigman came rooting by, his red eyes all gleaming, and put the bowl of sweet-pudding upside down on top of Baby Gray, thinking to have a fur pudding for himself.

"I'll just wait for a bit before having this fur pudding," said Pigman, and off into the forest he went, rooting about for more mischief.

Now Baby Gray was inside the bowl of pudding and was becoming a true Fur Pudding.

"Peek! Peek!" she cried in a tiny voice. "Pique! Pique!" And, by chance, Blue Fairy was just passing.

"You're *not* to be in there!" said Blue Fairy, and she turned the bowl right side up and sat Baby Gray on the ground again. Baby Gray was so small she hadn't learned to clean herself and so just sat there in a little bundle of pudding and goodness, purring.

"You are very small," observed Blue Fairy, after she had washed off the pudding, *"and* very dear! I advise you to take up painting. Now then, go to Real Painter. Ask for the true earth colors, Good Umber and Flower Green, and then for the smallest brush ever. I say to you: Take care! A kitten must be very cautious!" And saying this, Blue Fairy sparkled a great deal and vanished in a silver mist.

Baby Gray was alone again in the forest and she sat very still. Without the pudding on her, she was smaller than ever.

Silly Donkey came prancing by then, and nearly stepped on Baby Gray-Fur.

"Real Painter!" she cried, for she knew nothing about anything.

"Real Painter?" snorted the Donkey. *"I'm* not Real Painter! I'm Proud Donkey! See how I leap about!" And he did a little dance on his hoof-feet while Baby Gray watched, though she was so small she could hardly see him, and just sat there blinking.

When Donkey grew tired of the dance, he said crossly: "See here, I've no time to waste on such a tiny fur! I've my own affairs to tend!" And he snorted and pranced about.

"Real Painter!" cried Baby Gray-Fur.

"Real Painter!" said the Donkey, quite annoyed. "You'll not find Real Painter *here!* Real Painter lives at River's Edge, everyone knows as much! *That* way! *That* way!" he cried, pointing with his hoof-feet, then stamping crossly. "Bah! I've no time for such a tiny fur!" And he pranced off into the forest.

Baby Gray scampered to River's Edge, fast as she could, and was soon in the studio of Real Painter.

"Real Painter!" she cried.

And Real Painter was there all right, wearing a big beard that was all covered with blue paint.

"Why it's the kitten, Baby Gray-Fur," said Real Painter, politely enough, but his words sounded strange, as though his mouth might be full of paint.

"Give me true earth colors!" cried Baby Gray, "Good Umber and Flower Green, and the smallest brush ever!"

"Ah yes," said Real Painter, rubbing his hands together, ". . . just so."

"These on advice of Blue Fairy!" cried Baby Gray-Fur.

"Certainly," said Real Painter, reaching for a pot of oily paint. "Now this oily paint is your Flower Green. Here, I'll just . . ." and then he leaned forward and put the pot of oily paint upside down on top of Baby Gray.

"Peek! Peek!" she cried inside the pot.

"Good!" said Real Painter, his red eyes gleaming as he snatched off the beard, "now I'll just wait for a bit and then have a nice Flower Green Fur Pudding!"

And if Baby Gray hadn't been inside the paint pot, she would have seen that it was old Pigman himself—who had somehow learned of her plan, gotten to the studio earlier, and hidden Real Painter in the cupboard.

"Yes," said Pigman, "I'll just wait-for-a-bit, before I have a nice Fur Flower Pudding!" And off he went into the forest, rooting about for more mischief.

"Peek! Peek!" cried Baby Gray inside the paint pot, because it was so awful being in there.

After a minute, Silly Donkey came into the studio.

"What! No one here in the studio?" said Donkey, prancing about on the wooden floor with a terrible clatter.

"Peek! Peek!" cried Baby Gray.

"Who cries Peek-peek to Donkey?" he demanded. "I've my own affairs to tend!"

"Peek! Peek! Pique! Pique!"

"Who cries Peek-peek from paint pot?" demanded the Donkey, and he did a little dance of wrath to show his annoyance. But, in leaping about so wildly, he upset the pot with one of his hoof-feet, and there was Baby Gray-Fur, in a heap of oily paint.

"Peek! Peek!" she cried, for it was a sticky mess.

"Bah!" said the Donkey, very irate, because he had gotten some of the paint on his hoof-feet. "Now look at my hoof-feet! And I've my Donkey affairs to tend!" He was doubly cross now and continued his dance of wrath, making a great clatter on the floor.

This noise gave Baby Gray a good fright, and she crouched

as small as ever she could, in a little bundle of goodness and oily paint. "Pique! Pique!" she cried.

By chance, Blue Fairy was just passing the studio and heard these baby gray cries and all the donkey clatter. She came in at once.

"Who cries out?" she said. "And what is all this donkey clatter?" Then she saw Baby Gray, a bundle of oily paint, and rushed to her.

"You're *not* to have this oily paint all in your fur and on your fur-face!" said Blue Fairy, and began to give her good cleaning.

Meanwhile, Donkey kept dancing wildly about, because, in his foolish pride, he thought an audience was gathering for his dance.

"Silly Donkey!" cried Blue Fairy. "What's the meaning of this—oily paint on the Baby Gray-Fur!"

"Who interferes with the Donkey Dance!" demanded the Donkey, without even looking up. "See how I leap about!" And he did a mad dervish and fell on his head.

"Bah!" said Donkey, getting up, "it's this oily paint on my hoof-feet gave me that fall!" Then he saw Blue Fairy there giving Baby Gray good cleaning. "Good!" said Donkey. "You, Blue Fairy, give me a hand getting this oily paint off my Donkey feet. I've my affairs to see to and I'll not be wanting to waste more time here in the studio!"

"You Great Silly!" said Blue Fairy. "You've given this fur kitten a fright with your clatter!"

"*Kitten?*" said Donkey, really annoyed. "What kitten?"

"This is Baby Gray-Fur!" said Blue Fairy. "A true fur kitten! None so small and dear—and now all *sopping!* Pique and improper, I say to this affair!"

"Bah!" said Donkey, stamping about. "That's no kitten! That's a sticky mess of oily-paint fur! I've no time for such a goo! I'm off to my Donkey affairs!" And he pranced away into the forest.

But Blue Fairy went on and gave Baby Gray *good cleaning.* Then she took her back and sat her in the sun again where she was safe and warm, inside a magic circle she had drawn. And there she sat, very still in a little bundle, and in a few minutes she had forgotten about how she had been all sopping with pudding and paint, and just sat purring, waiting for someone to come and do something to her . . . a kiss or a pinching, she didn't know which. That's how tiny and dear she was, you see.

BEFORE YOU WERE BORN

BY

Scott Spencer

ILLUSTRATED BY
COCO DUPUY

There's a time of your life only we remember
It's the nine long months from March to December
You were our child, though we did not know you
We loved you like crazy, though we couldn't show you
While time and nature brought you closer and closer to us.

When we knew you were in there, we laughed and we cried
Tears of happiness we couldn't stop if we'd tried
Champagne toasts and shouts of joy
What did we care if you were a girl or a boy?
While time and nature brought you closer and closer to us.

At first it was a matter of trust
You were really no larger than a speck of dust
But soon you were growing, doubling and tripling
We started choosing your books—Potter, Sendak, and Kipling
While time and nature brought you closer and closer to us.

Could you hear our voices as we talked in to you?
You probably don't remember—or maybe you do
We called out your names, for then you had fifty
Names like Ryder and Oudia and others quite nifty
While time and nature brought you closer and closer to us.

In a world of billions, of every color and race
We loved you the most—without even seeing your face
Without hearing your voice or feeling your hand
Without touching your hair and combing each strand
While time and nature brought you closer and closer to us.

We kissed you and called you and asked you to come
So we could show you the trees, the stars, and the sun
And when you finally joined us—lo and behold
To us, you were already nine months old.

VERSES FOR THE WALL BY YOUR BED

BY

William Stafford

WHEN YOU GO ANYWHERE

This passport your face (not you
officially, your picture, but the face
used to make the passport) offers
everyone its witness: "This is me."

It feels like only a picture, a passport
forced upon you. Somewhere this oval,
sudden and lasting, appeared. It happened
that you were behind it, like it or not.

You present it—your passport, your face—
wherever you go. It says, "I'm a little country,"
it says, "Allow this friendly observer
quiet passage," it says, "Ordinary," it says, "Please."

LESSONS IN THE WORLD

At the school where spiders learn
there is a sewing machine
finer than silkworms have
for their wandering.

And they all have a touch we lack,
a breaking in two of time:
one way for regular days,
another for important things.

They aim their heads down a line
that appears because they aim,
and comes true because they're so small
and know forward steadily.

ONCE WHEN I WAS LITTLE

They said, "See you tomorrow." And
they left. It began to get dark.
It was nice of them, to say
that—they didn't have to.
While the night went on, I thought—
"Maybe, tomorrow." The night was long.
When they came back, as I hoped,
they couldn't understand my joy:
"You promised! You promised!"

FAR IN THE WORLD

There are warm places. In Alaska for miles
there are coalfields—frozen sunlight
you can stand on while you freeze to death.

In some countries God has walked, but
not recently. They guard those places
with machine guns.

A man named Bartram found a tree down South
and sent a seed to Benjamin Franklin. No one
has ever found that tree again.

DRAWING

BY

Saul Steinberg

HOW TURTLES TAP DANCE

BY
James Stevenson

...A-FOOSH A-FOOSH

...FUTA-FAH...FUTA-FAH

...SHLOOOP - SHLOOOOP

...CH-CH-CH-CH-CH...

...TIPY TAP.. TIPY TAP...

RAPATAPARAPATAPARAPATAPA

KLONKA - KLONK - KLUNK - KLONK - KLUNKETY - KLONKETY......KA..KLONKA ...... **KLUNK!**

THANK YOU
THANK YOU

Z Z ZZ

HOW MUCH IS THAT FROGGY IN THE WINDOW, OR, BEAUTY IS ONLY WART-DEEP

BY

Peter Stone

Sing a song of CENTIPEDES, REPTILES and SLUGS,
Of OCTOPI, HORNED TOADS, SCORPIONS, WOMBATS and all
    those other things with supposedly ugly mugs;
All those lowly creatures who are seldom, if ever, taken
    home and kept as pets
Because of their unappetizing silhouettes.
We've been taught by Mr. Disney that things are cute if they resemble a
    bunny or a fawn,
And ugly and disgusting if they come up from beneath your lawn.
Beauty being what it is, residing in the eye of the beholder,
It's difficult to appreciate something that looks as if it
    just crawled up from under a boulder.
It's sad, alas, that beasties who appear a trifle unusual or,
    as some would say, bizarre,
Aren't extremely popular.
The actual number of living things that suffer from our
    finicky disapproval is more than ample.
For example:

JELLYFISH, despite their name, don't appear to be too tasty,
Probably because their complexion's pasty.

Then, too, we tend to distrust anything with tentacles
Instead of denticles.
But they come in extremely exotic hues and colors,
With appendages that look like egg noodles (spaghetti #9
      from Muellers).
But appearances notwithstanding, we really should applaud
      the jellyfish.
They're good to their families, which, considering what they
      look like, is really quite unsellyfish.

Now let's take the crawly, grabby, spiny LOBSTER—
Certainly he's more appealing than your average Chicago mobster.
He's got large pincers and beady eyes,
And is very valuable (priced according to size).
It's fair to say that if lobsters were soft and furry, and if
      large claws and beady eyes were standard
      equipment on a kitten,
Then "Dick Whittington and His Lobster" might well have been
      written.
All of which is very, very unjust to most crustaceans
And their relations.
The truth is they make really excellent pets.
(True, they have an awful lot of legs, but so do the Rockettes.)
They never bark, whimper, whine, screech, howl or mewl,
And seldom ever drool.
They don't attract ticks and fleas,
And when you walk them in the street they don't have to stop
      every few minutes at fire hydrants and trees.
And just think, they don't require a big back yard to spend
      the day in.
All they need is a pot to play in.

SNAKES are actually very cuddly.
The reason people don't like them is because they move too
      sudd'ly.
And don't have arms and legs like other reasonable folks,
Which makes them the butt of all sorts of cruel and unusual
      jokes.
And their scales appear rather slimy and slippery

Which they're not, but that doesn't keep them from being
     skinned to make belts, bags, boots and other
     frippery.
All of which I find terribly unfair because, let's face it,
     snakes could be a lot more scary.
They could be hairy.

If teeny ANTS were more attractive
They wouldn't have to be so active.
But, on the other hand, I've never known an ant, who, just
     because she wasn't cuter,
Had to go without a suitor.
Which means that more than a few, and probably even many,
Are turned on by long antennae.
They move in a group, and sometimes actually in an army,
And anyone who gets in their way when they're hungry is
     incurably (and terminally) barmy.
But taken one at a time (and once in a while in pairs),
They are civil, down-to-earth and rarely, if ever, put on airs.
Their manners are good, they chew their food well and they
     never take outsized bites,
Which certainly could never be said of their second cousins,
     those unacceptable termites.
But when you're blue, an ant can really make you want to sing
     and dance.
Especially when he's in your pants.

SPIDERS are really quite adorable.
The idea that people go around stepping on them is absolutely
     deplorable.
They eat flies, fleas, aphids, gnats, mites and other things
     that we're told not to,
But someone's got to.
True, you don't want to fool around with a black widow,
But even they can be very friendly (unless you call them
     "bub" or "kiddo").
You can always tell a spider because they invariably have
     eight legs.
(Which is four more than tables unless they're gate-legs.)
And as for some of them being excessively hirsute, well,
     that's not exactly a crime.
(If it were, my uncle Morrie would be doing time.)

So don't you think spiders can be forgiven for leaving the
    corners of your room all webby?
Mebbe.

We could have also mentioned NEWTS, SHREWS, SMELTS, CROWS,
    HYENAS, POTATO BUGS and LEECHES,
And one or two things we've all regretted stepping on on
    beaches.
But the list is much too long to go into here
Of all those things we ignorantly fear.
Why, oh why must we endlessly conform?
Why must we prefer things that sit up and beg, to things
    that swarm?
Why do we fondle things that purr and are covered in fuzz
Instead of things that buzz?
Why is someone who skins a cat treated like a traitor,
But not for doing it to an ALLIGATOR?
Is it merely because it isn't as pretty
As a kitty?
Let's face it: our reaction to VULTURES, SNAILS, SHARKS, MOTHS,
    MOLLUSKS, LOCUSTS, ARMADILLOS, WORMS, COCK-
    ROACHES and, last but not least, LIZARDS is much too
    namby-pamby.
Maybe things would have been different if only Uncle Walt had
    given us "The Night of the IGUANA" instead of
    "Bambi."

PAUL'S STORY

BY

Barbara Szerlip

ILLUSTRATED BY
BARBARA SZERLIP

Seated on the floor, Paul began his story. Only Yura and the cat were there to hear it, and the cat was busy making herself comfortable by the heater for a nap. No matter. Yura closed her eyes, the better to listen.

"We used to come to San Francisco quite often, riding in the big Buick. We always had a Buick, dark navy blue, four-door, with really nice upholstery inside, the *real* stuff, you know. Fuzzy mohair, like an overstuffed chair. In fact, it still had its blackout blinds from the war. It would take twelve, fourteen hours to go 350 miles—there weren't any freeways. I remember it used to be six hours to the halfway point, some place like Paso Robles. We'd pack all our stuff the night before, get up in the dark, leave at four in the morning. I remember there always being dew on the ground, and not eating breakfast.

"They didn't tell me it was a *special* trip this time, but my parents must have arranged it beforehand. I'd overheard them talking . . . how my hair grew funny out of my head, too many cowlicks, and turning in the wrong direction. How I didn't have the right skin tone. Plus my eyes were bad and I was scrawny. But I was too busy searching around for *Chan pee mui* to pay much attention."

Paul laughed. "*Chan pee mui** was my favorite.

"Grant Avenue was one big cobblestone alley to me, Chinatown just a maze of streets, but a maze where I knew I'd

* Plums preserved with orange peel.

be treated to incredible meals in polished wood rooms, with dragons waiting at the bottom of my food and grown-up chopsticks. There'd be *ha gow, so mei, gai bow, tow sau,* beef jerky cured in honey and soy, baskets of boy- and girl-shaped cookies hanging in store windows that were horrible to eat but looked really nice. The queues were gone, but a

lot of people still wore slippers, and older men sat around storefronts smoking pipes. There were a lot of little ladies who looked like my grandmother.

"I'd get really tired walking up those hills, having to lean forward as if fighting a great wind. Then, when we'd get to a visiting place there'd be *stair*-hills, higher and higher, until I felt like Phan-ku, trying to keep up with the space between Heaven and Earth. It was always this climb!

"I grew up 'poor' in a five-room house. It always amazed me that our friends and relatives lived in these tiny two- or three-room apartments. The staircases were musty with cooking and old carpets. It wasn't a *foul* smell, but I would think, 'Boy, these places are funny!' There were a lot of banisters to slide down. We'd always bring something with us, lychees, tea wrapped in paper. When the grown-ups smiled down, pinching my cheek, I'd wait like a stoic for the inevitable '*Nui toi!*'* 'I'm *not* a little girl,' I'd growl, indignant. 'I'm a little boy.' "

"Confusing the demons," Yura offered.

"One afternoon my mother said, 'we're going to see someone, just you and I.' Where had my father, my sisters and brother disappeared to? We walked toward the center of Chinatown. . . ."

Stalls of bitter melon, persimmons, neat bunches of scallions, flowering bok choy, pomegranates ("Chinese apples"), water chestnuts, lavender-edged ginger like smooth-skinned, arthritic hands. Past cages of live frogs and turtles. Past the open doors of sweatshops, with their sewing machines, women, and racks of identical blouses. Past the movie theater where illustrious warriors did battle every afternoon at one o'clock. Past babyfist scallops, abalone in iridescent shells, giant prawns and miniature shrimp, pale sea bass, bright salmon, and fish without English names. Cages of chickens with corn-colored legs and clipped beaks kept watch over unrecognizable comrades: trays of gizzards, livers, thighs, breasts, feet, hearts. Behind the counter in a laundry was . . . Grandmother! emptying dryers and wrapping the folded piles in sky-colored paper. There she was, the pale jade bracelet on her wrist. If only Paul could get close enough to see if it was beveled along the inside ("the way bracelets are *supposed* to be"), to be sure. "Be brave," her eyes said. Past pigs' feet and milky squid, flat, circular ducks hung through the neck and fat-glazed. Brine-cured radishes and crates of live snails. Lily flowers and black fungus for

* Cantonese for "little girl"; a greeting used to deter evil spirits, which wouldn't waste their time on females.

soup. Army-colored mung beans and sacks of ancient mushrooms. Stalks of fresh sugarcane.

Didn't these places ever close? Did these Chinese sleep standing up, their hands continuing to make change, iron collars, trim vegetables and fish out of habit, a somnambulist's dance? Paul would stay up late, wake early, trying to catch the shops unaware, dark and resting, the way he sometimes tried to trick his reflection in the mirror. "I'm going to move my right arm," he'd concentrate, then suddenly, swiftly, he'd move his left, watching to see if his reflection could be caught in a split-second delay. But the shops, like the mirror, were always attentive.

"I was holding my mother's hand, me! who thought myself so independent! We entered a door, began climbing stairs, the banister above my shoulder, then another door, and a yellow room with wooden wainscotting. 'Afterward we'll have dim sum,' my mother kept saying.

"I sat on a stool without undressing. The doctor looked at my ears, my eyes, inspected my hair, pinched my skin. He and Mother whispered a while, then he wrote out a prescription in black ideographs on a square of paper big as a tabletop. It looked like a window crowded with dark birds. It was over. Simple. Then we went to the herb store. . . ."

The herb store!

"Oh yes!" Yura burst out, already picturing how the doctor's bird-writing would fly off the giant prescription in search of its likeness scattered on jar labels and ceiling-high drawers. "Ginseng and sea horses!"

"True enough," Paul smiled, spurred by Yura's enthusiasm. "Ginseng and sea horses. Also mistletoe leaves for nervous afflictions, Solomon's Seal for lazy appetites and to slow the heart, pomegranate bark for the intestines, cockscomb for dysentery, China root for skin disorders, burdock against pneumonia and scarlet fever, dandelion juice for curing snake bite, quince for gout and cholera, unripe persimmon juice for hypertension, rhubarb for diarrhea, orchid bulbs (powdered and mixed with sesame oil) for burns, reed grass to counteract poison, chrysanthemum flowers for digestion, antelope horn and tortoise shell for spasms, watermelon rind for diabetes, ground pearls for insomnia, not to mention spotted lizard tails (one male and one female per dose) for asthma."

"Forget lizard tails," Yura said.

"Then, of course, there was licorice root that had been enclosed in a bamboo case and buried for one winter in a cesspool."

"Ugh."

"Dried toad venom for curing ulcers and tumors."

"Ugh." Yura's enthusiasm was waning.

"Hedgehog hide for hemorrhoids, sea lion genitals for those who wanted children."

"Stop!"

"Silkworm cocoons for night cries and deafness."

"What did *you* get?"

"I don't know. Whatever it was, it ended up as a broth. I knew it was medicine because I was the only one in the whole family who had to drink it. It was Paul's, right? It was Saong's, my Chinese name.

"Grandmother was an expert on those things. She kept a bottle of roots and herbs soaking in brandy in the closet of our house, and brought it out to rub on our bruises and sprained ankles. Sometimes she'd heat up a paste from it, rub it on my forehead and chest with a slice of ginger.

"At certain times of year, she'd take me into the yard to get one of the chickens we raised. We'd tie its legs to the faucet, tilt its head back, and kkkkkk. . . ." Paul moved his thumb across his throat with a grimace. *"Bok suey gai,* unseasoned white chicken set on a dish with three tiny cups for the deities, and special chopsticks. We'd also do *Bi Sun* for Chinese New Year and Double Ten. I had to hold the paper money with both hands, thumbs on top, and bow, making smoke in the four directions."

Yura watched Paul's face, listened as the story grew in him, the remembering softening his eyes, his mouth. She had known Paul a long time. When he spoke about himself, it was of things he was in the midst of, current, everyday things, and even then there was a reticence, not a sense of privacy so much as a concern that the subject would not be of interest.

"That was wonderful," Yura said, impressed. She had asked for a story to light up the rainy evening and her sour mood, a rare request usually ignored by friends it was asked of.

But Paul wasn't finished. He was warming to his subject as to one of his grandmother's tonics. He stretched his large-boned, muscular body across the floor, arms above his head, hands flexed, as if waking from a good sleep, and addressed his thoughts to the ceiling.

In one of the places where his parents went looking for jade, there was an immense ivory tusk. Back in the Ortega Street house, it sometimes crept into his dreams, small enough to balance on the palm of his hand, or other nights swollen and full as a landscape he could wander through for weeks without reaching the end. It was painstakingly carved with details of cherry trees, bridges where a youth on horseback might stop to offer directions to a disguised Immortal, pagodas that rose high above swirling clouds which capped the nearby mountains. Stairways, guarded by fierce stone lions, led to the river where junkets pulled up onto mudbanks busy with lichen and crabs. Shaded beneath wind-swayed ginkgos, three monks could be seen conferring on matters of importance. The whole intricate arch balanced on a rosewood stand, backed by shimmering brocade.

It was all he could do to keep from touching it. He could not imagine that someone had *made* such a thing, fashioned it, at the risk of his eyesight, by hand. It must have always been, a fossil etched by generations of earthworms.

There was one place that always had moon cakes, not just for the New Year. The thing that prompted Paul's desire was not so much the hidden egg yolks or fruit or nuts or slivers of meat, but the boxes they were packed in. There, on the lid, was Grandmother as she must have looked when she was an "educated young lady" in Hong Kong, being carried up flights of stairs in a sedan chair. When the jeweled phoenix was taken from her hair, the dark, thick bundle would fall below the backs of her knees! The embroidered chrysanthemums and peacock feathers of her coat were edged with waves and lavender clouds. One voluminous sleeve was pushed back to reveal a velum hand, the delicate wrist (circled by a beveled bracelet) bent to cradle a snowy rabbit. She divided the sky into day and twilight. Behind her, Heng-o's* Palace of Great Cold (said to be built of cinnamon trees) could be seen, shining on the temple roofs far below. Paul could tell from her expression

* Goddess of the Moon.

that this majestic floating was a method of transportation that pleased her. (And one no doubt better suited than a sedan chair for covering great distances.) It was nice to imagine Grandmother traveling to California like that, but she had made the long, long journey by boat, her dowry lashed in trunks below deck.

"That was in 1896. Grandfather and Great Grandfather had a general store up in the foothills. They traded gold, sold supplies to grubstakers and miners. Had stock in the Pacific Railroad. They must have been very well off to contract Grandmother as a bride.

"One day, Great Grandfather got into an argument that became a fight. Maybe the man's neck broke when Great Grandfather threw him from the porch of his store, maybe his head hit the hitching post, or a rock. The Sheriff acknowledged it as self-defense. But a group of men in the local bar were organizing to 'lynch the China-man.' Friends came by with a wagon to warn the family. There wasn't time for the strongbox, the intricate dowry furniture and linens, the railroad certificates. They grabbed a few supplies, emptied the cash register. Grandmother's arms were full with her firstborn, just a few months old. They managed to get away just in time.

"Uncle George always told people he was born in Chinatown and that the records had been destroyed in the 1906 fire. The family wanted no traces of having been in Marysville. Self-defense or not, a white man was dead and a Chinaman was responsible.

"So the family became 'invisible Chinese' in Chinatown, where my mother was born. Grandmother worked shelling shrimp for a penny a pound, worked in sewing factories . . . she used to make silk frogs, beautiful ones, bound with cord. And crochet stuff. She made one hell of an adjustment.

"I don't know how my parents met. All I know about my father is that he was raised in Kwantung Province, where he went to cooking school, and that he left for the Golden Mountain about 1915. I saw a photo of him on a boat, taken just after the First World War. He was on his way back to China to visit his other family, the one he'd left there and couldn't send for because of immigration. My mother was probably this beauty walking around Chinatown. She was. I've seen photographs I can't believe! She was small-boned, short, weighed about ninety pounds. I'd never lose my father in a crowd, he was always bigger than everyone else—and that wasn't a child's fantasy, it was a fact. Big head, good-sized shoulders. His hands—pshwwww."

Yura studied her friend's strong, thick fingers, hands that dwarfed hers. When she'd first met Paul, his tied-back hair hanging almost to his waist, she'd mistaken his broad features for American Indian.

After a few moments, Paul turned and smiled. Yura knew that his father, the giant who could make perfect sugar roses, was long gone, as was Grandmother, and that Grandfather had died before Paul was born.

"I can turn a good story, eh?" he teased.

"You didn't. . . ."

"No, it's all true," he assured her, laughing.

It was late, close to midnight. Both the rain and Yura's difficult mood had cleared. "Are you famished?" she asked.

"Let's go." Paul pulled on his boots.

"You'll let me treat you, of course, after all that," Yura said firmly, knowing it was hopeless.

It was a fifteen-minute walk to Chinatown, and they knew of a place that served wonderful duck rice porridge until two o'clock in the morning.

QUEEN MAB

BY

Paul Theroux

There was only one rule in Crumm. It was this: No one was allowed to open the door in the wall that encircled the mountain. What you could see of the mountain was steep and terrible. Usually the top was hidden in cloud, but on certain days the summit was visible—a crater, with a column of smoke, and sometimes fangs of fire rising from it. It was an old mountain which, on the sunniest days, was seen to have the black fury of a volcano.

The people in Crumm were glad that a wall prevented them from going near the mountain. The wall protected them from danger; so the rule—about not opening the door—was taken to be a good rule.

The wall was high. On its top, spikes like spearheads and knives were fixed, and the stones in the wall were as forbidding as cruel men's faces, which howled like skulls when the wind passed by them. The weeds that drooped from the cracks of these stones were like ragged beards. The door itself was wooden, and plates of iron gave it the look of a warrior's armor. The doorknob was tarnished, for no one had ever touched it, let alone turned it and tried to open it.

Apart from the walled mountain, Crumm was the most ordinary town. It was so ordinary that from time to time people left it and went to other places, where there was more sun, or more snow. When these people returned they said that in other towns there was no mountain, no wall, no door.

We are lucky, said the townsfolk of Crumm: We have a mountain.

It is a terrible mountain, said the others.

But the wall protects us, said the townsfolk.

If the wall protects you from the mountain, said the others, you might just as well not have one. You are like everyone else.

The townsfolk said: We are not like every other town. We have a rule in Crumm which says that the door to the mountain wall must not be opened.

It is a terrible mountain, said the others.

But the rule protects us, said the townsfolk. Other towns do not have this rule.

It was true. Apart from this rule, Crumm was like every other town in the world. And the rule was observed. Who would dare to approach that howling wall on a windy day, when the ragged beards of weed were flapping, and take the blackened knob of that armored door in his hand and twist it and open it? The very sight of the mountain—the smoke and flames—was enough to make grown men turn their backs on it and think of something important that was to be done indoors.

When people died in Crumm the word *death* was never used. They said, *He has gone through the door.*

Not far from the wall, there was a coal yard, and the strongest, toughest worker in this coal yard was a girl named Mable. She was fifteen years old.

I'm big, said Mable, and I'm still growing!

She wore a leather apron and heavy boots, a greasy hat and gloves. She sang in a warbling voice as she worked:

> My name is Mable,
> And I am able
> To heave a ton of coal!

The girls in the coal yard admired her; the women were a bit afraid of her; the boys and the men hated her, because Mable could throw a lump of coal farther than anyone. Sunday was lump-throwing day. Friday night was for beer drinking, and though Mable was not allowed to drink beer she sang to the older coal-heavers and, between songs, pulled the bottle caps off with her teeth. No one in Crumm, man or woman, could do that.

I'm big, said Mable, and I'm still growing!

She was happy, and she felt that nothing important would ever happen to her. To be the best coal-heaver in Crumm was certainly a great thing, but every day there was more coal to heave, and one ton of coal was much like another. She thought of leaving Crumm, as others had done. She even thought of taking up a new occupation.

I can do anything I want, she said. I'm smart enough to be a brain surgeon, pretty enough to be queen, and tall enough to be a telephone pole.

It was then, as she looked around for a new occupation, that she noticed the door in the wall.

She persuaded herself that the wall was not made of stones like cruel men's faces; that the door was not faced in armor. No one had ever opened it. The rule about not opening it had been made so long ago, the townsfolk of Crumm could not remember who had made it, or why. There might be something wonderful behind the door, or if not—and if the guesses were correct—there was death. Either way, it was not coal-heaving.

So Mable approached the door. This frightened the other coal-heavers much more than when they had lump-throwing contests or when she yanked bottle caps off with her teeth. Mable saw fear on the others' faces. This delighted her. She touched the doorknob and even pretended to turn it.

My name is Mable,
And I am able,
To walk right through this wall!

One day she tried to turn the knob. She was amazed: The knob would not turn. She stood there gasping, but nothing happened.

The townsfolk of Crumm were relieved when they saw the difficulty she was having. They were secretly glad that the door could not be opened, and they felt safer than ever.

But this angered Mable. Nothing had ever defeated her before. So, instead of trying to turn the knob, she gathered some tools from the coal yard: a pick, a shovel, an ax, a crowbar, and a ten-foot beam. She piled these beside the door and worked for a full day. She no longer thought about what she would find on the other side of the door; she only knew that this door had to be broken down or she would never be happy again.

And one day, with the eyes of Crumm upon her, she beat the door down.

She put her tools aside and stepped through the door. No sooner had she done it, than the door was made whole again. The townsfolk saw Mable disappear. Some wept, some ran away, some prayed, some said: Mable got too big for her boots. And everyone said that Mable had got just what she deserved.

Mable, meanwhile, had entered a passageway. There was a lozenge of light at the far end, but before she reached it, she met two rather surprised princes.

They said they had never expected to see anyone enter through the door—they had given up hope. We have good news for you, they said. You will be our queen.

They asked her name, and when she said Mable, they replied: We will call you Queen Mab.

At the end of the passage was a throne room, and beyond it an entire kingdom: friendly animals, adoring people, sunshine, and everything one could ever want. The palace was filled with rooms, and in each room was treasure, or a banquet, or music. The princes and all the people in the kingdom fell at Mable's huge feet and said: Queen Mab, you are our queen—we have waited so long for you to rule us.

But there was little to ruling these people. You ate and drank, played music or danced, listened to poetry, watched television. Anything you liked. Mable laughed: It was so much easier than coal-heaving!

But there is one thing, a prince said the morning after Mable arrived.

And what is that? she asked. By now she wore a crown instead of her greasy cap, and a scarlet cape instead of a leather apron, and silk slippers instead of boots.

That door, said the prince.

Mable winked at the prince. She said: I know what you're going to say. Don't open it.

You are apparently a wise queen, said the prince. If you are truly a wise queen, you will not open that door.

That's what they told me in Crumm, said Mable.

This is not Crumm, said the prince.

This is certainly not Crumm, thought Mable.

This is a different door, said the prince.

I can't open it, said Mable.

Oh, you can open it, said the prince. But you must not.

We have no rules, said the prince. You can do anything in this kingdom, even open that door.

The door was narrow and, like all the other doors in the palace, it looked as if it was made of beaten gold. There was no doorknob; a gold chain was fixed to it.

It is not hard to open, said the prince. But you should not even think of doing it.

I won't, said Mable. And why should I? she thought. I have everything I want.

So, as Queen Mab, Mable ruled the kingdom in the easy way she had discovered. Nothing was required of her but to enjoy herself, and she spent her days in idleness and great luxury. I am queen, she said, and looking in a mirror she saw how she had changed. She wore silks trimmed with fur, and even her face and figure were different and queenly. She could barely remember how she had once looked, as a coal-heaver in Crumm. There is nothing I cannot have, she said; nothing, nothing.

In the course of time, she thought of the door in the palace which the prince had advised her not to open. But he was a prince, and she was queen. He was her servant, she the ruler.

She summoned the prince.

I command you, she said. Open that door!

The prince went to the door as he was told. He grasped the gold chain and tugged. He turned purple from the effort.

Finally, he said: I cannot do it.

If it is impossible, said Mable, then why did you advise me not to open it?

It is impossible for us, said the prince. But you are powerful. You can do anything. But power is nothing without wisdom.

You mean, I alone can open the door? asked Mable.

You alone, said the prince. But if you are wise you will not.

Bring me the wisest man in the kingdom, said Mable.

A wise man was brought to her. He was old and feeble, but his eyes glittered like an eagle's.

I command you, said Mable. Open that door!

The wise man smiled. I cannot open the door, he said. I am too weak.

Mable said: If you were strong, would you open the door?

If I was strong, said the wise man, I would be king.

Answer your queen! demanded Mable. Would you open that door?

The wise man said: I would obey the wishes of my people.

Take him away, cried Mable. And she thought: I will have him beheaded in the morning.

That night, she went again to the door. There was no one

nearby, and she wanted to see what great secret awaited her behind the door.

From the depths of the palace she heard a faint whisper saying, Queen Mab, Queen Mab! It was perhaps the wise man scratching his dungeon wall and croaking her name. Queen Mab!

But my name is Mable, she said, and I am able. . . .

She touched the chain and tugged it. Just as she applied pressure to it, it opened. There was darkness; she peered into the darkness. A figure faced her. The figure was dressed in a leather apron, and heavy boots, a greasy hat and gloves. There was coal dust on the figure's face, and Mable saw at once that it was herself, as she had been. Out of pity she went to this silent sorrowing creature and raised her arm to comfort her.

The door slammed shut behind her. She was no longer in darkness, but standing in Crumm, in the old clothes she had always worn.

Nothing had changed. Did I say nothing? No. It was a cloudy day in the coal yard, but when the sky cleared, Mable saw that the mountain was gone from Crumm.

THE INTERESTING STORY

BY

Rachel and Tony Towle

FOREWORD

MY FATHER IS A POET—HIS NAME IS TONY TOWLE. HE EATS STEAK AND BEANS FROM A BOWL, WITH WATER FROM THE SINK, AND LETTERS FROM THE TYPEWRITER, AND GREEN FROM THE GLASS. CLOUDS COME INTO THE ROOM AND RAIN AND FILL THE GLASS WITH JELLYBEANS AND CLOUDS.

CHAPTER I

SALLY CAME IN, SAYING "THERE IS KINGSLEY, WITH A BOOK WHICH ON THE SECOND PAGE SAYS 'MRS. COOKIE BAKED ANOTHER COOKIE.'"

"DUCK," SHE SAID, AND ANOTHER COOKIE FELL OFF THE TABLE ONTO A GREEN WORM EATING AN APPLE. "UGH!" SAID MRS. COOKIE, AND NIB-BLED A GREEN WORM-COOKIE. SALLY SAID, "TRY A CREAMPUFF, TOO." BUT IT WAS ONLY A YELLOW CLOUD. MRS. COOKIE TASTED IT THEN, AND FLOATED IN THE AIR, AND THE WORM FLOATED AFTER HER, SHOUTING "YOU STOLE A CLOUD! NOW THE RAIN WON'T FALL AND THE FLOWERS WON'T HAVE ANY WATER" AND SHE DRANK A RED CLOUD AND NIBBLED ON MRS. COOKIE AND THOUGHT: "IF THIS IS MRS. COOKIE WHERE IS MR. COOKIE?" "WELL," SAID SALLY, "MR. COOKIE IS OUT MILK-ING THE COOKIE COW AND GETTING SOME MORE COOKIES FOR OUR DINNER."

THE WORM FINISHED MRS. COOKIE. THE CLOUDS SUDDENLY STARTED RAINING AND THE WORM SAID, "NOW THE FLOWERS WILL GROW AND SO WILL MRS. WORM," AND HE DISAPPEARED FOREVER. "THE BOOK IS FINISHED," SAID MR. COOKIE, "AND NOW WE WILL HAVE OUR DINNER OF COOKIES IN THE RAIN."

CHAPTER 2

"AFTER THE RAIN STOPS, WE WILL GO OUTSIDE AND HAVE ICE CREAM FOR OUR DESSERT AND TOOTHPICKS FOR OUR FOREST, AND LEAVES FOR OUR SEATS AND SKY FOR OUR HATS," MR. COOKIE CONTINUED, AND DISAPPEARED IN THE FOG THAT HAD COME WHILE THEY WERE TALK-ING, AND THEY HAD THAT FOR DESSERT. BEDELIA ASKED TONY TOWLE: "ARE YOU GOING TO TAKE RACHEL TO THE PARK TODAY?" "SHE AL-READY WENT TO THE COOKIE-PARK-FOREST AND CLIMBED IN IT HIGHER AND HIGHER UNTIL SHE CAME TO THE TOP OF HERSELF ABOVE THE CLOUDS, AND THERE WAS THE EATEN MRS. COOKIE, SO RACHEL ATE MRS. COOKIE AGAIN, AND AGAIN."

MRS. COOKIE, THOUGH SHE WAS SOMEWHERE ELSE, SAID "I WILL NEVER AGAIN EAT A CREAMPUFF, FOR I KNOW THAT IT WILL BE A YELLOW CLOUD THAT I CAN'T SEE AND I CAN'T BAKE." MR. COOKIE SAID, "WHAT HAS HAPPENED TO ME? I HAVE SHRUNK INTO A TINY BROWN CRUMB AND HAVE BLOWN AWAY TO THE TOP OF THE MOUNTAIN, HIDDEN FROM TONY TOWLE, WHO IS EATING BEANS FROM A BOWL, AND COOKIES TOO! IT IS A GOOD THING THAT HE SPEAKS FRIENDLY TO ME. I THOUGHT HE WAS A GIANT WHEN HE SAID 'HELLO THERE, MR. COOKIE,' WITH HIS MOUTH FULL OF ELECTRICITY. HE DRIPPED BIG BLOTCHES ON HIS SHIRT AND THE SHIRT JUMPED INTO THE RIVER OF SPARKS AND CLOUDS TO WASH." "ARE YOU FINISHED NOW, MR. COOKIE?" ASKED MRS. COW, POPPING HIM INTO HER MOUTH. "NOTHING HE SAID WAS TRUE, YOU KNOW, BECAUSE THERE ARE NO SUCH THINGS AS GIANTS AND BESIDES, THERE ARE NO MOUNTAINS IN COOKIE LAND, AND ANYWAY HE TALKED TOO MUCH." "HMMM . . ." SAID MR. GIANT, THOUGHTFULLY POPPING MRS. COW INTO HIS MOUTH AND GOING AWAY TO CRY AND SLEEP ON THE MOUNTAIN OF TWINKIES, WHERE PEOPLE TWINKED YOUR NOSE UNLESS YOU WERE A GIANT.

"WHAT A MESS HE'S GOING TO BE," SAID KABAZZA. THEN THE RAIN TURNED A DISGUSTING PURPLE SOMERSAULT AND LANDED ON ME, AND

MELTED ME, SO I MOVED IN WITH MR. AND MRS. WATER AND WE RAN DOWN THE MOUNTAIN AWAY FROM THE GIANT, AND BROUGHT THE MOUNTAIN'S DIRT WITH US, TO SOME FLOWERS WHICH HAD DROPPED INTO A YARD WITH NO DIRT, SO WE PUT SOME DIRT TO THEM SO THEY WOULD MAKE SOME SENSE. "WHAT A MESS," SAID KABAZZA AGAIN, AND ATE MRS. COOKIE AGAIN AND THOUGHT, "IF TONY TOWLE IS A POET, WHAT IS IRMA TOWLE?" "AN ACTRESS," SAID MRS. WATER, "AND WHAT ARE YOU?" "I AM A STUFFED DOLL, I AM IN BOOKS, AND YOU ARE IN THE SAME BOOKS BUT ONLY AS RAIN AND ICE, YOUR NAME IS MRS. WATER." SO HE DRANK MRS. WATER AND MR. WATER RAN ALONE IN HIS RIVER DOWN THE DIRTY MOUNTAIN.

CHAPTER 3

"NOBODY WILL DRINK ME, BECAUSE I'M ALL DIRTY!" AND HE KEPT RUNNING AND FELL INTO A POOL AND GOT CLEAN, AND GOT OUT AND RESTED NEXT TO THE POOL ON THE DIRT IN THE GARDEN AND SAID, "I'M GLAD I'M CLEAN NOW." AND THE VEGETABLES SAID, "HOW CAN YOU BE CLEAN LYING ON THE DIRT?" BUT MR. WATER HAD GONE AND THE VEGETABLES GREW, AND SALLY GREW UNTIL SHE WAS A BIG DOLL WHO HAD A LITTLE DOLL OF HER OWN, NAMED RACHEL, WHO WAS SO TINY THAT YOU COULDN'T SEE HER, BUT YOU COULD HEAR HER LITTLE DOLL CALLING FOR MRS. COOKIE: "I WANT A COOKIE, MRS. COOKIE, WITH HER GINGERBREAD SKIRT, AND. . . ." A TINY WHITE FROG GOBBLED HER UP AND RAN OFF INTO A YELLOW CLOUD, WHERE A MILKWEED WENT INTO HIS NOSE AND GOT CAUGHT, AND HE CALLED DOWN TO MR. COOKIE FOR A HANDKERCHIEF, BUT MR. COOKIE WAS LOST, SO THE FROG SNEEZED OUT RACHEL'S DOLL'S LITTLE DOLL, WHO HAD A LITTLE DOLL WHO CHASED THE FROG INTO THE GIANT BLUE GIANT, WHO WAS SLEEPING. IN HIS DREAM HE WAS FIGHTING WITH A GIANT, AND HE WON, SO HE GOT A LITTLE BLUE DOLL FOR HIS PRIZE. AND HE GAVE IT TO HIS CHILD, THE GIANT BLUE COOKIE, WHO SAID "THANK YOU, PAPA." AND THE BLUE DOLL GAVE HIM A NIBBLE.

CHAPTER 4

NOW ALL THIS WHILE SALLY WAS LAUGHING TO HERSELF, READING ABOUT THE THINGS WE WROTE ABOUT, BUT IT WAS A DIFFERENT THING WHEN SHE CAME TO A TOMATO WHO WAS COUNTING HER SEEDS. "THAT'S TWENTY-FOUR!" SHE SOBBED, PICKING UP A TOMATO HANKIE WITH THIRTY-THREE SEEDS AND A LUMP, WHICH HER LITTLE DOLL

SLEPT ON. KABAZZA PICKED SOME TOMATOES AND THE GIANT PICKIED SOME COFFEE BEANS. "HOW DO YOU <u>PICKIE</u> SOMETHING?" ASKED MR. COOKIE. "LIKE PINCHING," SAID THE BALD-HEADED GIANT, AND HE BEGAN TO PICKIE MR. COOKIE UNTIL HE WAS ONLY CRUMBS. "<u>THIRTY</u> CRUMBS," SOBBED THE TOMATO. "THAT'S A LAUGH," SAID MATILDA THE LUMP, RISING UNTIL SHE WAS AS BIG AS THE SUN RISING IN A PAN AS SMALL AS THE MOON.

"LOOK, MR. GIANT," SHOUTED THE LUMP, FOR SHE WAS BRAVE, "YOU SHOULDN'T HAVE . . . OOF!" SHE HAD BUMPED INTO THE YELLOW CREAMPUFF RAINCLOUDS, AND STICKS, COFFEE GROUNDS, AND FROGS SOON COVERED MR. GIANT. "WHAT A MESS," SAID SALLY, "I THINK YOU NEED A BATH." SHE PICKED UP THE BOWL OF SOAPY WORMS AND GREEN FROG-BUBBLES; MR. GIANT SCREAMED AND JUMPED INTO THE PURPLE VASE, AND THERE HE GREW, A GIANT DIRTY FLOWER.

CHAPTER 5

ON THE OTHER SIDE OF THE MOUNTAIN, TONY TOWLE WAS HAVING SLICES OF MATILDA THE TOMATO. "DO YOU THINK THAT'S NICE?" ASKED MR. WATER FROM HIS GLASS. "WELL, YES, BECAUSE I LOVE TOMATOES," AND HE DRANK A GLASS OF WATER. RACHEL WALKED IN WITH MRS. COOKIE, WHO HAD ADOPTED A COOKIE WHO NEEDED A HOME. "YOUR HOME IS DESSERT!" ROARED THE GIANT POET, BUT SALLY SAID: "NO, NO, YOU MUST NOT EAT HIM, YOU SHOULD BUILD HIM A CANDY HOUSE, LIKE THE ONE FOR MR. AND MRS. COOKIE AND RACHEL." "ALL RIGHT," SAID THE GIANT, AND FELL ASLEEP IN THE CANDY CLOUDS. THE COOKIE WAS HAPPY; HE GAVE THE GIANT A KISS AND ADDED A CANDY CLOUD OF SMOKE FOR THE CHIMNEY AND A GREEN JELLYBEAN FOR THE DOOR. "AND AN ICING-BLOCK FOR THE CHIMNEY," MUMBLED THE WORM, GOING BY ON A CLOUD OF CREAMPUFF CRUMBS. "WHAT'S AN ICING-BLOCK?" ASKED THE MOON. "A BLOCK OF ICING," SAID THE WORM, AND WOKE UP. "WHERE AM I?" HE ASKED. "ON THE MOON, SILLY," SAID THE MOON. "WHAT A MESS," SAID SALLY, "I'D BETTER GIVE YOU TWO A BATH; PASS THE SOAP, MR. COOKIE." AND SHE SCRUBBED MR. WORM INTO TINY WORMS, AND THE MOON INTO THE SUN, WHICH SHONE LIKE ICING. "YUM YUM," SAID MRS. NIGHT, AND ATE THE MOON WHO WAS THE SUN AND EVERYTHING GOT DARK. THEN THE MOUNTAIN ATE MR. NIGHT AND MRS. NIGHT RAN BEHIND THE SUN. "MY GOODNESS," SAID

MRS. COOKIE, "THIS IS A VERY STRANGE DAY AND NIGHT." THEN MRS. COOKIE DISAPPEARED. THE GIANT SNORED, AND EVERYBODY DISAPPEARED.

MORAL

"WELL," SAID MR. COOKIE, "I HOPE MRS. COOKIE COMES BACK AGAIN TO TELL US THE MORAL." "THAT ISN'T NECESSARY," SAID MR. MORAL, "YOU SEE, AS I AM MR. MORAL I CAN TELL YOU THE MORAL. BUT I AM EATING A PICKLE NOW SO I WILL <u>NOT</u> TELL YOU THE MORAL." "LISTEN MR. MORAL," SAID MR. COOKIE, "IF YOU WILL NOT TELL ME THE MORAL . . ." "QUIET, MR. COOKIE," SAID MR. MORAL, "I'M THINKING OF ONE NOW . . . A GIANT BIRD COMES DOWN . . ." "OH HUSH, MR. MORAL," SAID MR. COOKIE. "<u>MRS.</u> MORAL KNOWS THE REAL MORAL, NOW LET HER TELL IT." "THANK YOU, MR. COOKIE," SAID MRS. MORAL. MRS. MORAL AND HER SON SOON PUT THEM TO SLEEP WITH A WONDERFUL MORAL. "HOW DID YOU LIKE IT?" SHE ASKED. BUT THE GIANT BIRD FLEW DOWN AND ATE MRS. MORAL. "THAT IS THE MORAL," SAID HER SON, AND DISAPPEARED. "THE BIRD WAS THE BIRD OF NIGHT," CAME HIS VOICE FROM BEHIND A CLOUD, "AND MR. AND MRS. COOKIE ARE REALLY ALIVE." "AND STALE AS A COOKIE'S GRANDFATHER!" SAID MR. MORAL, WHO HAD TRIED A LITTLE OF THEIR ARMS, "AND TERRIBLE WITH PICKLES BESIDES." MR. PICKLE JUMPED FROM THE CLOUD OF JELLYBEANS INTO MR. MORAL'S MOUTH: "HOW DO <u>PICKLES</u> GO WITH PICKLES?" "IS THAT THE MORAL?" ASKED SALLY. "NO, SILLY," SAID MR. PICKLE. "WHO ARE <u>YOU</u> TO CALL SALLY SILLY?" DEMANDED KABAZZA. "I MUST BE THE REAL MORAL," HE REPLIED, "FOR MR. MORAL IS CRUMBLING INTO SHREDS OF WORMS AND BEANS, SO THAT IS NOT THE MORAL, BUT I WILL LET THE MOUNTAIN EAT YOU BECAUSE YOU TALK SO MUCH." SO THE MOUNTAIN ATE KABAZZA, AND THAT MAY BE THE MORAL. "IT IS <u>NOT</u>," SAID KABAZZA FROM THE MOON, "YOU DON'T EVEN KNOW WHAT A MORAL IS!" "IT IS A PICKLE," SAID MR. PICKLE. "NO," SAID THE MOUNTAIN, "IT IS A THING THAT TELLS YOU A LESSON."

THE
END

REPORT FROM OUTSIDE THE CLOSET

BY

Chögyam Trungpa

He rose from his chair. He walked toward the closet. I watched him. He opened the closet door and shut himself in the closet. It was turning five o'clock and he had had his tea, but I'm not sure why he shut himself in the closet. Me or the chair or the atmosphere might have been disturbing to him; but on the other hand it might have been inspiring to him in some way.

There was an occasional sound from the closet. But the closet door seemed functionally all right. It was doing its job. Although the room was dark owing to overcast weather, the inside of the closet must have been still darker.

What would happen next? Maybe he didn't want me to be here to watch him come out of the closet. It might embarrass him. But on the other hand he might regard this as a victory of some kind which he *wanted* me to witness.

I wonder how *he* would write this story, perhaps approaching it from an entirely different perspective. He might think that *I* would be embarrassed if he came out. On the other hand he might feel it would be some kind of victory for *me*. Not only that but he would be able to witness my victory.

I became increasingly impatient. I felt I should do *something*. I reviewed in my mind all sorts of things I might do with regard to his being in the closet. I thought of opening the closet, quite casually of course, and asking him if he might need something. . . . How could he do this to me, using me in this way, making a fool of me. Then I realized with sudden relief that in fact he was making a fool of him*self*.

As I was lost in these thoughts abruptly the closet door opened. Still munching his tea biscuits, he came out of the closet and sat down in his chair. Slowly he reached for the teapot and filled his cup. I wasn't quite sure how to relate to him. The tense silence of those few seconds was almost too much. For some reason I felt I had to defend myself. But defend what? I wracked my mind. Trying to be as nonchalant as possible, I decided to address him. I poured myself a cup of tea.

"Well?" I said.

"Well, what?" he said, as though nothing had happened.

CHILD POEM

BY
Anne Waldman

To you, child of pure form
stream-lined child
butter-smooth child
myself in flesh and place
musical child with hungry belly
candy bars!

child with wire-haired terrier
child between two adults in a blue car
little girl whose father goes to a factory
bold child in red tights
ballerina!
to all of you

to you child who can suddenly read
and to you child who has been reading

Let me tell you about the hero who
pierces dragons and rides his bed
like a horse
he pierces them with the sound
of the radio
"argh argh argh" go the dragons
"she bop she bop" goes the radio
then he jumps back under the covers

or the princess who is forever
combing stars out of her hair
"O those nasty stars, tangling
up my gorgeous hair!"

to you child with enormous pockets
full of money
quarters that jangle as you strut
around the juke box sticking out
your chest—give us a kiss!

I am a Greek child with Greek vocabulary
I am the river child dancing like an eel
I am a moon child,
the moon is sometimes plastic
I am the purring clock

does a fish eat spaghetti?
does the television ever go to sleep?
are there comic books on Mars?
of course not, stupid
I am lighting up the day like chrysanthemums
is the rain singing or weeping?

take a pen and stab the poem
don't shoot each other with cap guns
talk to that tree, she'll understand

Dear Child: keep reading
don't be lazy

toad child
kitty child
mouse child
why are baby animals so cute?
is it their button noses?

I'm the stinging scorpio child
I'm the aries baby ram
I'm the pisces fish child

I'm the flying machine
I'm the choo-choo train

I'm the skinny bookworm child with glasses
I'm terribly smart, I'll pass the test, ha!

I'm the overweight kid, I love cookie meat
I'm everyone's darling heart throb girl

I'm the buddha baby
I'm so holy I'm a sugar saint
I'm as holy as swiss cheese

No, I didn't do it, Miss Morris, she did!

I'm the tattle tattle tattle tattle tattle tale child

I'm the silky hair gypsy child
I'm the pin-the-tail-on-the-donkey child
I'm running into the ocean now, catch me if you can

O goodness, there's a rat in the kitchen
will he eat the chicken?

Please put the next line into Chinese:
"she has two tiny-moth eyebrows"

and put the rest of this one into Spanish:
"fetch la leche at the bodega, por favor"

and here's one for the Japanese language:
"I like your green kimono with wasps painted on it"
or
"My blue sleeve is wet"

In French I would like to say
"The sun looks like a fried egg"
"le soleil ressemble à . . . ."
what's "fried egg" in French?
I know the word for "french fry"
it's "pomme frite," but
"The sun looks like a french fry"?
sounds dumb

In German please say the word for "please"—
"bitte"
sounds like "bitter" without the "r"

I am pouring the milk in every direction

language has a life of its own
child of language: where is your root?
language has left the light to play on the pictures

good-bye, language
hello again, words
how many words can I learn today?

Is there a word for "growing up"?
"maturing" sounds awful
In Italian let's say
"basta, basta"
that means "enough, enough"
who wants to grow up? not me!
basta, basta!

I'm the eating-hotdog child
I'm the no-mustard-please girl
I'm the yes-relish-thank-you boy
more potato chips
more ice cream

I'm the fancy cowboy
I'm the more-fancy-than-the-cowboy cowgirl

every day's a holiday
whoopee
baby Ada on the table stomping her shoes
whoopee

Let's put some rocks in this poem
let's get some rock n' roll in this poem
let's put a roller coaster in this poem
let's put our coats on in this poem

it's cold in here brrrrrrrrrr

now it's getting hot, let's take
our coats off

I'm all the signs of the zodiac
I'm the gemini double child
half angel, half monster
grrrrrrrrrr

I'm the terribly serious child
no horsing around in this poem
my horse is thirsty and needs a barrel of H_2O

Let's tell some stories in color:
a green girl went to a red store to
buy some blue paint
"I'm painting the sky blue," she said
"How silly," the yellow salesgirl said
"The sky is blue today already,
why don't you paint it pink?"

"You're the silly one, yellow girl,
the sky's very pink today"
They looked out the window and indeed
the sky was extremely pink, then it turned greenish
and before they knew it, it was a deep maroon
and soon it was all black
"Come to think of it the sky's a lot of colors,"
the green girl said
"maybe I'd better go paint the ocean . . ."

I'm the meanie I'll pelt you with a snowball
on your way home from school

I'm the pea-shooter and I never miss a shot

I love soda, I love soda

more sugar, more toothaches, more lollipops please
more more more

I'm a child and I say MORE

I'm very good I'm raking the autumn leaves

why can't these toys put themselves away?
why can't the clothes jump into the closet?
shoes, do your stuff!

why won't it stop raining so we can go out
why why why!

I want to be a sailor when I grow up
I'd ride in a big boat with enormous sails
we'd go to Yokohama, we'd go to Cape Town
we'd go to Bristol, Bombay, Singapore

we'd go to San Francisco!
I'd kiss the girls and make them cry

I want to be an actress when I grow up
I'd break some hearts
boo hoo

I want to be a professor
I want to be an ambassador

I want to be a priest
I want to be an atheist

I want to be a dog catcher
I want to be a modern dancer

I want to be a big hairy athlete
(good luck, kid, don't hurt your feet)

Dear Child: to you, this poem
dear dolphin child: for you, a poem

and waves coming and waves coming coming and waves coming and
waves coming water splashing and big wave coming water splashing
and waves coming and waves coming coming and waves and you
splashing

dear strange mystery
and be you upon this boat of life forever child

> boom boom
> clap clap
> moo moo
> honk honk
> giddyup giddyup
> splash!

ADELIE PENGUIN

BY

Tony Walton

ILLUSTRATED BY
TONY WALTON

ADELIE PENGUIN

HAS DOZENS OF COUSINS

WHO LIVE IN THE LARGE PENGUIN POOL AT THE ZOO

THEY ALL LOOK ALIKE

SO THEY ALL HAVE THE PROBLEM

OF TRYING TO FIGURE OUT WHICH ONE IS WHO

THE THING WITH THEIR NAME ON

THAT CAME ON THEIR CRATES WITH THEM

SOMEHOW WAS LOST WHEN THE LAST OF THEM CAME

NOW ALL OF THEM SEEM

SO EXTREMELY IDENTICAL

NONE OF THEM KNOWS JUST WHO GOES WITH WHICH NAME

YESTERDAY ADELIE

WANTED TO CLARIFY

ALL OF THE MUDDLE SHE HAD IN HER HEAD
UNABLE TO LABEL
HER NEAREST AND DEAREST
SHE PONDERED AND PUZZLED AND HERE'S WHAT SHE SAID:

"PHOOEY AND FISHBUBBLES
DRAT AND DARNATION
WHY <u>DOES</u> EACH RELATION SEEM SOMEHOW THE SAME ONE
THIS BOTHERS ME BADLY"
SAID ADELIE SADLY
AND CRIED AS SHE TRIED TO DECIDE HOW TO NAME ONE.

"PERHAPS IF A PENGUIN
COULD DRESS LIKE A PERSON—
THEN WHICH ONE WAS WHICH WOULD BE EASY TO TELL
YOU COULD GUESS WHO WAS WHO
BY THE CLOTHES THAT WE CHOSE
BUT WHAT COULD WE WEAR THAT WOULD FIT ON US WELL?

"WE COULDN'T WEAR TROUSERS
NOR EVEN NICE UNDERTHINGS
IT'S PROBABLY BEST JUST TO SETTLE FOR SHIRTS
WITH LOVELY LARGE LETTERING
SHOWING DISTINCTLY
THAT THIS SHIRT IS SUSIE'S OR THAT SHIRT IS BERT'S.

"TOP HATS WITH OUR NAMES ON
MIGHT HELP WITH THE PROBLEM
AND LOOK RATHER SMART WITH OUR SHINY TAIL COATS
BUT HOW COULD WE SEE
WHEN OUT DIVING AND SWIMMING
WE'D JUST HAVE TO DO ALL OUR TRAVEL IN BOATS.

"THERE <u>MUST</u> BE A SOMEWHAT
MORE CIVILIZED SYSTEM
IF ONLY WE SOMEHOW COULD START TO EMPLOY ONE
PERHAPS I SHOULD LINE UP
EACH PENGUIN AND LIST THEM
ACCORDING TO WHICH IS A GIRL OR A BOY ONE.

"THE BIG ONES ARE BOY ONES
THE GIRLS ARE MORE DELICATE
SHY ONES ARE FEMALES WHILE BOY ONES ARE BOLD."
(THESE WERE ALL THINGS YOU SEE
DEEP IN HER MEMORY
THINGS SHE HAD READ ABOUT
THINGS SHE'D BEEN TOLD.)

"GIRLS ARE OBEDIENT
BOYS ARE MORE MISCHIEVOUS
MOST BOYS ARE MUSCULAR—FEMALES ARE FRAIL
GIRLS ARE MORE SENSITIVE
BOYS ARE MORE COARSE OF COURSE
ONES WITH BIG FLIPPERS ARE CERTAINLY MALE."

ALL OF THIS RIGMAROL
ADELIE SANG ALOUD
WHILE SHE ARRANGED HER RELATIONS BY SEX—
SOME SHE WAS RIGHT ABOUT
MOST SHE GOT BADLY WRONG
STILL SHE SANG
AS SHE HUNG
ALL THEIR NAMES
ROUND THEIR NECKS:

"THIS MUST BE SUSIE
SUSIES ARE SENSIBLE
SANE AND RESPONSIBLE—MYRTLES ARE MEEK—
THIS MUST BE MAISIE
FOR MAISIES ARE LAZY
BUT PROUD OF THE PRETTY PINK BUMP ON THEIR BEAK.

BERTIE AND SPIKE
ARE ALIKE IN THEIR CHEEKINESS
BOYS ARE <u>ALL</u> CHEERFULLY CHEEKY YOU SEE.
CHARLIE'S A CHATTERBOX
MAISIE'S A LAZY LOX—
WHICH ONE IS ADELIE?
MERCY! THAT'S ME."

OH THAT OUR ADELIE
COULD HAVE BEEN BORN TODAY
KNOWING THAT MOST OF THAT CLAPTRAP'S ALL WRONG—
WE ARE NOT TINKERTOYS
VERY FEW GIRLS OR BOYS
FIT INTO FORMULAS FOUND IN A SONG.

MOST OF OUR MAKE-UPS
ARE MAGICAL RIDDLES
MUDDLED UP MIXTURES
OF SHADOW AND LIGHT
FOR WE ARE ALL BORN
WITH SO MANY FINE SHADINGS
NOT EVEN A PENGUIN
IS <u>JUST</u> BLACK AND WHITE.

THE GENIUS AND THE SPOILED BRAT

BY

Claire Nicolas White

Matilda was the youngest of four children and when she was a small baby her brothers and sisters spoiled her to death. Then, when they had thoroughly spoiled her the two oldest went off to college and boarding school. Home on vacation they called her "a spoiled brat" and scolded their mother. "Why did you spoil Matilda so, and why did you give her that creepy name, and why does she have blond curls instead of plain straight brown hair like ours?"

Now poor Matilda would sit all alone in her room, quite abandoned. Her big brother John used to come home from school, throw her up in the air, and let her play his French horn if she didn't spit in it. Then her sister Anne would take her into the attic and dress her in costumes from the trunk and let her try on her own necklaces and earrings. Then the youngest brother, Luke, would play difficult games with her but he always won and she'd say, "No fair!" and would tip over the Parcheesi board in a rage. When the two oldest left even Luke felt a bit lonely. He'd wander around the house, looking bored, until suddenly he took up carpentry. Then he disappeared into the barn, working until dark.

Matilda sat in her room and looked out over the dry winter fields. She wished Luke would come in and play a game. Even if he won, it was better than nothing, but nowadays he was always too busy. "I have work to do," he would say, looking very old and important. Lately he had had paint on his fingers.

"What are you making, Luke?" But he said, "None of your business," in an unfriendly sort of way.

Matilda had dressed her doll in a pink silk gown, silk stockings, sunglasses, and high-heeled shoes and she herself had on a green velvet dress with gold buttons, white socks with tassels, and yellow moccasins. They could go to a party like this if someone asked them, but who?

Then she saw a strange procession coming out of the barn. Her father and Luke were carrying a large, unwieldy object toward the house. She could not imagine what it was. They carried it up to the porch and tried to get it through the front door but it wouldn't fit. "We'll have to take down the door," Father said.

"Heavens, it's so big. Where shall we put it?" exclaimed Mother. Curious, Matilda ran downstairs.

"What is it?"

"A surprise for the spoiled brat!" Luke had that important, slightly disagreeable expression again but he seemed terribly excited and little smiles kept creeping about the corners of his mouth. Father took the door off its hinges and the huge object just about slid through the opening in the wall. It was made of wood, with something that looked like a chimney sticking out of the slanted top. Then Matilda saw the front of it, the compartments, the tiny stairs, the doors with hinges and door-knobs, the lighting fixtures in the ceilings. "It's a dollhouse!" cried Matilda, and clapped her hands with delight.

The only room big enough to put it in was the living room, if they moved out the bookcase and father's big armchair. "We'll just have to sit on the sofa together," said Mother, but when they did they looked very odd, as if they themselves were oversize.

Matilda was in seventh heaven. She plugged in the lights and brought down her entire doll family to see their new palace. "Who shall be the owner?" she thought as she looked over her collection. "Gollywog has lost the buttons of his jacket and Pinocchio is so stiff he can't go up the stairs. It will have to be a lady. Pupetreena is too big and Maggie is too young . . ." The obvious candidate was the doll with the pink silk dress, the sunglasses and silk stockings, called Evelyn. She was just the right size and had the right air of dignity and elegance. One suspected that she actually dyed her hair a brighter shade of red. She moved into the house without further ado and the other dolls seemed to take it for granted that she was their queen, though Maggie was heard to mutter under her breath something about her being a "spoiled brat."

"Quiet there, Maggie. Some of us just happen to be spoiled and there's nothing we can do about it. It's something you're born with," Matilda scolded. She put her little cast-iron stove in the kitchen, and a tiny silver tea set on a table. She also found a Mexican carpet for the living room, and out of an ad for an art book that had come in the mail she cut reproductions of paintings by famous artists such as Van Gogh and Modigliani and glued them to the walls. The doll's trunk with all her clothes in it was put in the attic and though the two straw chairs her grandmother had brought her from Chinatown were too small, they seemed just right in the children's room, upstairs.

"Children?" thought Matilda. "Heavens. She isn't even married yet, but I guess it's better to be prepared."

The next day when Luke returned from school, Matilda was already busy with her house, which was quite what he expected. As a matter of fact, whenever he saw her doing anything else from now on he would say reproachfully, "I guess you don't really care about the house, do you? I guess I'd better give it to someone else."

She was busy making red silk curtains for the living room and said to Luke, "Since it's an extra special size house, it needs extra large furniture, and where am I going to get it do you think?"

Luke had to admit that it was a problem. "I'll have to make it myself, I guess," he said, and cheerfully he once more disappeared into the barn.

They were both very busy. Matilda made towels, sheets, and blankets, and decided to hire a cook for the doll who did not look like a typical housewife, too dainty somehow. There was a slightly dumpy doll dressed like a peasant from Brittany in a white bonnet, a green dress with an apron, striped stockings, and wooden shoes. She had cozy pink cheeks and assured Matilda in a thick accent that she cooked only the best French dishes. Her name was Clementine.

That evening Luke came home with an elegant sofa upholstered with red velvet, a piece of mother's old evening dress.

"It's just what I had in mind and it matches the curtains," said Matilda. That night the doll slept on the sofa under a throw of pale blue wool. In the morning Clementine brought her a steaming cup of *café au lait*.

Bit by bit Luke furnished the house. First a good size double bed for the doll, with a carved head board, springs made of woven string, a quilted cotton wool mattress covered with striped ticking. Next a dining-room table with room for five guests and chairs with woven string seats; a grandfather clock, very real, with one of father's discarded dollar watches as a face and with brass pendulums; a cabinet with little doors, painted yellow, installed over the cast iron stove in the kitchen; another chair for the living room with a red velvet seat and a curved back rest; a bathtub cast in plaster, with faucets and a shower curtain, and last but most elaborate, a coffee table with carved boxwood legs and an inlaid marble top.

In school, Matilda told her friends, "I have an awfully good carpenter!" and when they came to see the dollhouse they were amazed. "How does he do it? Everything looks just like real. He must be a genius."

Luke just happened to overhear them. "A genius?" he thought. "I wonder . . . perhaps I am," and once more he went to the barn. That night he put up a freshly painted sign along the road by the mailbox. DOLLHOUSES MADE TO ORDER it said in bold black letters.

Pretty soon the telephone began to ring. "Is Mr. Gordon in? Are you the gentleman who makes dollhouses?"

"I guess you mean my son?" said Mr. Gordon, who felt suddenly rather out of things. A Mrs. Pereira wanted her own house copied in miniature for her daughter's birthday. Though Luke mumbled that he could probably invent her a better house himself, he took on the commission for fifty dollars plus materials. The next afternoon he went off on his bicycle with pencil, pad, and tape measure.

Mrs. Gordon, the children's mother, sitting on the sofa in the living room, noticed a lot of activity in the dollhouse. Gentlemen callers came, one after the other, and Evelyn received them in the parlor. Her knitting lay beside her on the sofa and on the coffee table stood a tray of glasses, one of those miniature bottles of liqueur, and a bowl of Rice Krispies in the way of crackers.

The gentlemen callers had all been dressed for the occasion by Matilda, the cavalry officer's buttons sewn on, Pinocchio's nose filed down to a less outrageous size, but somehow none of them looked quite right in the elegant parlor: too young, too odd, too small, or too shabby. Matilda went to the attic where some discarded dolls of her sister Anne lay face down on a bed spring. Among them was a gentleman in a Tyrolean costume. He had, unfortunately, lost his wig, but his porcelain head had a dignified, pink look, as if he were a cheerful and dependable character. Matilda took him downstairs and with some black wool she made him a splendid wig, a bit long over the ears. Dressed in his jacket without lapels he seemed quite "Mod."

That evening at dinner Matilda told her mother, tossing her head in the direction of the dollhouse and with a sigh of satisfaction, "She's engaged." In the little parlor one could imagine the young couple whispering till late into the night as the contents of the bottle of liqueur on the coffee table miraculously diminished. Matilda had to set her alarm at midnight so as to send the gentleman home, put

Evelyn to bed, and turn off the lights. As she tiptoed into the dark living room where the lights glowed cozily in the miniature house, she thought she heard a rustle and saw Evelyn quickly sit up straight. Her head had been resting on her fiancé's shoulder and on his jacket there was one telltale red hair.

But Evelyn still seemed restless. "She needs to get out a bit," Matilda decided and at night, when her mother and father wanted to sit down on the sofa to read the papers, there was no room for them. A whole party of dolls had gathered there and was looking at television.

"They're at the movies," Matilda apologized.

"But how about us?"

"Couldn't you sit in the kitchen till the movies are over?"

Grumbling, her daddy went to his workbench in the cellar to fix an old chair, but he returned to complain, "All my tools are gone. Where did Luke put them all?" Luke was still at work in the barn. He was paneling the library of Mrs. Pereira's house, a very painstaking job.

"Dolls!" mumbled Mr. Gordon. "As if people weren't enough trouble!"

And indeed, the situation was getting out of hand. The following evening, when Mrs. Gordon wanted to set the table, Matilda came rushing out of the parlor to stop her.

"Wait, wait! They're not quite finished!" Under the dining-room table she had set up a whole photographer's studio with a sign tacked to the table leg saying "Eveline, fashion model. Posing from four to six." The cavalry officer was the photographer, his camera, a miniature Japanese one Anne had bought once at the World's Fair, was set on a tripod, and draped in one of Mrs. Gordon's silk handkerchiefs, lit by a pocket flashlight, Evelyn was posing glamorously.

"She needed a career," Matilda explained. "They'll be through at six."

"But in the meantime dinner will get cold," complained Mrs. Gordon.

"Can't we eat in the kitchen?" There was nothing else to do. Now the dolls were everywhere: on the sofa, under the table, and their house occupied half the parlor.

"This is impossible!" Matilda's father exclaimed. "Whose house is this anyway?"

"I'm very sorry," Matilda said. "But what can I do? They have a right to live too you know!"

When Mrs. Pereira's house was finally finished it was May. She invited Evelyn and all her friends to a housewarming, at which Evelyn announced blushingly that she was to be married in June and showed off a tiny ring, Luke's latest masterpiece. Mr. Pereira's neighbor, a certain Judge Lowander, was so impressed by the house that he commissioned Luke to build a treehouse for his sons, "With a rope ladder you can pull up through a trap door, and make it strong enough for me too so that I can use it as an escape when my wife has tea parties." This new engineering problem was a challenge worthy of Luke's ingenuity, and he set right to work.

Evelyn's wedding invitations were in the mail. Matilda went to New York with her mother to shop for the dress, but there was very little choice in such a small size. Matilda fretted and worried, and finally they were going home in the train without having found just the right thing. Matilda began to cry.

"Now really, it's silly to cry over a doll dress," her mother soothed her.

"Silly? But you don't know Evelyn. She's so elegant and fussy and she's getting married only once in a lifetime. Why are dolls discriminated against so? New York is full of stores for people, but there are practically none for dolls."

Mrs. Gordon sighed. "I guess I'll have to make her a dress myself. I was planning to make myself one, but it will have to wait." It turned out beautifully, with a train, a tight bodice, and leg-of-mutton sleeves. Evelyn was satisfied.

On June fifth, doll guests arrived from all over the neighborhood, with presents for the new couple. The church was under the piano. The wedding bells were tied to the rocking chair so that they clanged all the while that little Francis Pereira sat rocking herself on it. Matilda herself, who had practiced for weeks, played "Here comes the bride" with two hands. In the kitchen a buffet table was set up on a board resting on two bricks covered with white napkins: a marzipan pig, a bowl of currants, chocolate chips, lots of birthday candles stuck into little cubes of cheese, and a small wedding cake baked by Matilda, iced with cream cheese and decorated with silver sprinkles.

The next morning, when Mrs. Gordon came down to start breakfast, she saw a small cardboard mailbox in front of the dollhouse and on it was written: MR. RICHARD WAGNER, PNTR. "What does PNTR stand for?" she asked Matilda.

"Painter, of course." And pretty soon Mr. Wagner was cozily installed in the attic of the dollhouse with an easel (formerly the photographer's tripod), a tiny sketchpad, and a paint brush made of a toothpick with a tuft of Matilda's own hair tied to it with thread. His model was no other than the glamorous Evelyn.

Luke in the meantime ran into some engineering problems. He had decided to build a platform halfway up a cluster of three tall trees in a wooded area behind Judge Lowander's house. The problem was to get the boards up there and to fasten them to the trunks. He devised a pulley to hoist them into position, and perched on a rather delicate limb, distributed orders to the Judge's two sons, aged eight and ten, who were rather clumsy and kept hitting each other over the head with the boards by mistake. When the platform was finally built, he found that when the wind blew, it swayed back and forth with the trees, creaking ominously, but surprisingly resilient and solid. He had left a hole in the center of the platform, which was actually the front door of the house, through which one climbed into it by the rope ladder ordered from L. L. Bean. He then made the four walls out of marine plywood, with windows closed off with screen netting and a marine plywood roof. The two little boys were allowed to hand him the nails and to hold things in place and finally, when the time came to paint, they begged for brushes, painted each other entirely white, then dribbled the whole can down the trunk of the tree so that it looked like a birch. "You're the clumsiest, silliest fools I've ever seen!" Luke shouted at them, as he hung precariously onto a branch, painting the outline of the windows green. Then the two little boys got mad and, each taking hold of one of Luke's feet, began to pull.

"Help, don't!" cried Luke, but too late. Reaching for a branch to steady himself, the can of green paint he was holding slipped and splattered onto the heads of the two boys. They began to cry and fled to their mother. "Good riddance!" muttered Luke, who was now able to put the finishing touches to his house in a more professional manner. Though the white tree trunk looked rather startling, he was pleased with his job.

When Anne, their older sister, came home for summer holidays, she found a doll in her bed and the room full of bunches of buttercups and dandelions.

"What is this?" she exclaimed, and Matilda rushed in to explain.

"It's Evelyn. She's in the hospital having a baby."

"Not in my bed, she isn't! And besides, didn't she just get married only last week?"

"A week is a long time for a doll."

"A baby every week! My goodness, there's going to be a population explosion."

And indeed, when their older brother came home from college, Evelyn was having another baby in his bed, Mr. Wagner had painted so many pictures that the walls of the dollhouse were covered with them and they were now overflowing into the parlor, which became "The Gallery," and strings were tied between the legs of tables and chairs on which the diapers of the doll babies were drying. As he tripped over one of them, Mr. Gordon, Matilda's father, cried out, "This is too much! I'm moving out of this house!" He slammed the front door and drove away into the night.

Matilda went quietly to bed, but after a while Mrs. Gordon heard her sobbing loudly.

"What is the matter?" she asked her, trying in the dark to find the head of her own daughter between those of a teddy bear and a big green frog made of cuddly terry cloth.

"I want my daddy!" she sobbed.

"You want too many things," said her mother. "If you take the whole house for your dolls, where are we supposed to live?"

"It's not me, it's Evelyn. She never thinks about anyone but herself."

"In that case, perhaps it's time for you to put your foot down."

"But she gets so upset!" hiccoughed Matilda desperately. "What can I do? She's very spoiled, you know!"

"Go to sleep now. Daddy went to a meeting. He'll be back," and she tucked Matilda in gently.

The next day they were all invited to a party for the unveiling of the treehouse. All the neighbors were having drinks on the lawn, then Judge Lowander led the way to the woods, a glass in his hand, looking very elegant in pink trousers, a white jacket, and a yellow bow tie.

"Now, my dear friends, I shall show you where I plan to retire from the world." And while Luke kept his fingers crossed and held his breath, the Judge, who was very large and heavy, began to climb the rope ladder into the treehouse. It creaked, and the Judge's face got alarmingly red, but he finally hoisted himself safely through the hole. His smiling face appeared at one of the windows and the guests cheered and clapped. He pulled up the rope ladder so that nobody could follow him and then waved good-bye at the people below, who went home, thinking the Judge was a rather unfriendly fellow after all. As they drove home in the car, Mr. Gordon felt a little hand slip into his.

"Daddy?" It was Matilda, looking up at him. "Wouldn't you like Luke to build you a house like that?"

"Why?" said Mr. Gordon, puzzled.

"Then you could pull up the ladder and no dolls would be able to follow you."

Mr. Gordon laughed and hugged his little girl.

"I've got news for you, my dear. I think you need to get away from your dolls for a while so I'm taking you all to Grandma's to spend a month at the beach."

"Really?" Matilda smiled and put her cheek against Daddy's hand. "I'm so glad. It's been such a lot of work. I guess Evelyn will just have to do without me. After all, she does have a husband to spoil her."

As for Luke, he had so many commissions to build more doll-houses and treehouses that he sighed, "I too will be glad for a month's rest. It's rather exhausting to be a genius."

THE STORY
OF
A STORY

BY

Elie Wiesel

When I was your age, my son, I heard this tale from my father who heard it from an unknown beggar who had come in our village during a cold winter night:

There once was a poor unhappy man. Not knowing which way to turn in his sorrow, he sought advice from rebbe Israel, the celebrated Master of the Good Name. The rebbe welcomed him warmly and said: "Stay with me, at my side; look and listen, and above all be silent."

And time passed slowly. Our hero, still poor, still unhappy, did not leave the Master's side for many weeks, many months. From dawn to dusk, often late into the night—and even until dawn—he sat with rebbe Israel Baal-Shem-Tov, listening to him speak in his wisdom, listening to those who confided in him, only listening.

One day after the morning prayer the Master turned to him and smiled: "Now you may leave; start your journey today; you will go from village to village, from marketplace to marketplace, and everywhere you will tell and retell the tales you have learned here; they will bring you good fortune and happiness, you will see, go."

Thus the hero of our tale became a teller of tales, and nothing else. In every village, he would recall the teachings of his Master, and spin breathtaking stories for men and women, and children of course, who gathered around to listen: they showed their gratitude by giving him a warm meal, some old clothes, or even, on rare occasions, a small coin. Thanks to him and his tales, their existence seemed less dreary and their future less gloomy; thanks to him and his wondrous parables and anecdotes his listeners came to believe that miracles were still possible. That even in the midst of misery and suffering it is given to men and women, and children too, children especially, to dream strange and sunny dreams.

After many years, the teller of tales arrived in a lost village. He walked immediately to the inn where, according to his custom, he went from table to table telling local people and visitors his most moving stories, hoping to earn a few coins which he desperately needed. But his listeners were either misers or penniless; or was it that they were deaf? or drunk? Sadness came over our hero. He was hungry. And thirsty. And his purse was empty. So in his heart he spoke silently to his Master: What shall I do, rebbe? what am I to do? You promised me good fortune and happiness, what has become of your promise? On the verge of tears, he barely heard the innkeeper say to him: "I have an idea for you. Our village-lord is crazy, I mean he's crazy about stories . . . he pays money for stories: one piece of silver for a story he has heard only once, one golden coin for a story he has never heard. . . ."

Without wasting a second, our teller of tales ran to the palace and asked to be received. When the servant heard what his trade was, he showed him right away into a room where the village-lord was already waiting with food and drinks on the table. "Please begin," said the village-lord. Summoning all his talent, all his memories, our hero began. Unfortunately, his host knew all his stories. Our hero felt uneasy. He shut his eyes and implored his Master to come to his aid. He remembered an old parable, another one, and yet another about sick people in need of recovery, lonely people in need of beauty; all for naught; the host knew them all. Drained by his efforts, the visitor felt too weary to rise and take leave. For a long time he remained seated, facing the village-lord who grew impatient, even exasperated. Then all of a sudden, in a sort of daze, the teller of tales recalled an incident he had long kept buried in his memory: Rebbe Israel was talking with a stranger in tears, comforting him, saying: "Do not be sad; you have made many mistakes and have committed many sins, but you will repent, will you not? You will do your part and God will do His: He will forgive you, I promise you." The stranger whispered: "How will I know that I have been forgiven?" "It is simple," replied the illustrious wonder-rebbe. "One day someone will tell you *this* story; on that day you will know."

The teller of tales fell silent. Overwhelmed, the

village-lord burst into tears of gratitude and gave him one hundred golden coins. And from that day on they remained friends, bound by their common knowledge of the Master of the Good Name.

The teller of tales continued to wander around the world and tell his stories—all but one, the most beautiful of all, which he kept for you, my son, for you alone.

—translated by Mary Gimbel

A *SHORT STORY*

BY

Robert Wilson

It's good to see you again. Thank you, I'm glad to hear you say that. May I go in? Yes, but don't stay too long. You don't want her to know. Mm. The only crook I know for this job is. . . . You tell Herman he has a job. I'll take care of that too. I'm not a judge. I'm not the captain. Oh, I'm so sleepy. What was that old man? I can't do that. That scene in the kitchen was carrying things too far. It was a nightmare from beginning to end. Keep breathing, the evening is shot anyhow. Okay? Okay. It's a nostalgic nite cap. It looks terrific on your wall and ceiling.

He's the boss. He has the connections. Who's the boss? He's old. Why is he wasting my time? I don't think she likes you. That doesn't make any difference. I don't believe you. Well, there are a lot of memories here. Huh? Oh yeah. Got you. No hard feelings; water over the dam. Oh, ah. I understand. Do you? Stick to it. Follow instructions. The end. You don't get anywhere with something like that. Did you? Did you? Did you? Did you? Yes . . . ah ah . . . who are you anyway? Don't come near me, I'm seeing you for the first time. I'm giving it all back to you, all you've ever given me. Would you do me a favor would you kill would you please would you please kill me? What goes on?

Let's go. At ease. Yes. Sit down. Have you a light? I'm sorry. What do you want of me? Yes. Let's go. Sit down. Beautiful. Beautiful. We have to get started with this thing. Thank you. You have to be firm with him. Then you desire *discipline*. That's why you're here. Are you a lawyer? He sure is. One of the biggest conglomerates in the state. Will you kindly get the hell out of the way. That's an absolute I absolutely believe. Well, it does to me.

Is that it? Nope. I don't care for sentimental reasons. (*Character laughs.*) The man who dares to take the man into account; I stood for every kind of persecution. Let's talk about that later. We've got it. There aren't any of us upset. Mrs. Miller is not going to like that. Mooo (means to stop). Don't go out there. Everybody get rid of their Ouija boards.

Thank you, sir. See you again. Take me to the golden gate. Just remember this is total war. How could I steal your idea? I want to apologize for acting like this. There's no need to apologize. Thanks. Great. That's their bad luck. You look wonderful. What was he, a king or something? That's the most ridiculous thing I've ever seen in my life. Up to now I was interested in going into the contest. Registration 2, 1, 4. Yeah, yeah. I came in on it in the middle. Just take care. Ah shut up. If you have a clean white room you have to put something in it—put the smelliest stuff in the building in it. I want to see an artist given a room to do what he wanted.

Why am I late? Oh my god, we're late. Yeah, that's right. 505 is the number. Oh what an honor, I'm very flattered. *I'm* very flattered.

For heaven's sake, you can't stay in this room all day worrying. Well, I've been practicing for an hour. Come on in, fellows. I don't know. Another mad world. My compliments on your dress. Now we're not talking. Now you're talking. I tried. I feel better already. It's no time to be funny. Calm down. Avanti. They never give me any rest. This came special delivery. Oh, have you heard the circus is in town? I don't understand. Where can I contact you? Well, just don't stand there, tell me. Hm. Hm. Lady. Lady.

And. The. Gentleman. Certainly. I'll bet on this. I'm pulling out. Men have died for less than this. Leave me out of this. Okay. A very sensible discussion. I'll contact you. Maybe. Third time is lucky. I invite you to talk with me instead. Thanks. How would you like it if I talked? People are more inclined to read the written word. I'll be watching you, Mrs. Miller, from my room upstairs. It can't be 5:30. It can't be. Okay. Don't say another word. Let's go to sleep. Why are you crying? My darling, I've tried reaching you all night long. Okay. Okay.

You belong to me, you're fine. You don't understand. Of course, you silly little goose. Wait. Give me a baby. Wait. Please give me a fair shake. This way. Hot dogs. Please let him come. Please. Don't leave me. Why are you so mean to us? Huh? I've had enough. Hey you. See, I told you. Now you know what it's like.

You can take it back inside. Yeah. Get up front and find out. Coming down. Give me that. Stop that. Get high. Get ready. All right, I'm not what I thought you are. We had an appointment, the two of us, today. I was helping mother with some. I was happy working with you too. Pithy. You will give me much pleasure. How did it go? All right, I guess. The war is over. So long. Good, huh? What a waste. You're right. There you are. Thanks. How do you like that?

I love you. And you're my dear and oh how I . . . what do you do when you are alone so much and they don't even ever know you're around?

THE COLD IN NORTH DAKOTA

BY

Larry Woiwode

In North Dakota the first thick-foot freeze sometimes came before Halloween, and with the first heavy snow the world of our countryside was turned upside down. All the color was in the sky. I wanted to walk there the way I walked the fields and streets and byways of packed dirt in distant seasons, like my uncle who walked on his hands, but that wasn't the same, quite. I wanted to crawl across the curling clouds the way insects and flies crawled across our ceiling.

"Just be happy you're a boy," my father said.

The snow deepened and drifted and then on an afternoon when most of the county schools had been called off, including the one where our father worked, as my brother and I were getting into our bulky clothes to go to the farmhouse at the edge of town, Bendemeer's, to get our daily quarts of milk, he'd walk into the kitchen and say, "You boys wait," and take down his long brown canvas coat, lined with fleecy sheepskin, put it on over his suit jacket, pull on his floppily-buckled overshoes, his cap with furry earflaps that tied, his mittens and gloves, turn up the collar of the coat so it rainbowed above his cap, check and adjust us again, and then say, "All right, now let's go."

The air was so white we couldn't see the hedge around the house, or, after we'd walked a ways, the house itself. An unbound sheet went plunging and groaning around us, and only when the wind blew it off to one side and made it seem the ground had slipped under our feet, only then were we aware of the snow—spiraling at our eyes, over our foreheads, tautening the skin there and turning it numb, dripping from eyelashes, and gathering in powdery lines along the scarves he tied under our eyes with *his* eye on our shrinking well-beings; without them, a gust of this wind could make you gag, and that could lead to coughing, which could lead, through the throat and chest diseases, down to a room in the closest hospital, or worse, as I'd learned; and though the wool folds of the scarves smelled like wet dogs and sprouted bristles where our nostrils and mouths were galaxied and gasping behind, putting me in mind of monsters I imagined, they did the job.

"It looks like this is going to be a real blizzard," he said, and dragged his feet to plow the snow aside and blaze a path that we could navigate knee-deep, while we floundered in his wake, protected from the worst of the noise and swirl of it, and held the tails of his coat to keep in touch with his direction through this wind-blown afternoon that had become half night. By the time the gray buildings of Bendemeer's uprose above the blowing sheets, the bristles on our scarves were icicles, and our boots went squeaking over the frozen linoleum of their back porch up to our quarts of milk. Columns of white pushed above the tops of the bottlenecks, lifting the printed paper caps up with them, and were like three tipped tophats in a row, seen from the inside. He took the empties from a milk carrier he'd fashioned for us out of an orange crate, dropped the full ones into their rack of wood sockets, and with a backhand of his mitten sent the tophats whirligiging off into the mingling whitenesses.

"Let's get back before this gets worse," he said.

If this or a blizzard like it kept up, the roads were soon smothered and blocked, and in the middle of the morning-half of school a team of horses would appear at the end of the street, pulling a hayrack mounted on sleigh runners hewn from wood beams. The bearded driver was wrapped in horse blankets to his fur hat, and balanced himself with a foot against the mast of the rack's front upright, on a heaped load of golden threshing straw. Its glinting mound halted at the schoolhouse doors, the horses nodding at the reins and blowing frost from their heads, and then began to tremble as faces and hands appeared to those of us who looked on from the basement windows cut into diamonds with protective, metal-wire mesh. Our classmates dug caves to keep warm on the trip to town, they said, and the rest of the day were scratching themselves and picking straw out of their clothes.

And when the day outdoors was turning deep blue, the

horses would appear outside again, stomping and filigreeing the air with their steam, and there wasn't one classmate I held as a friend, it seemed, who didn't run out and do a disappearing dive into the straw. And then the golden load of it murmured out of town with the secrets children always share at that hour. "I wouldn't care if I froze, if I could ride home in a hayrack once," I said to my brother, as we watched it diminish along the fencelines of the white-frozen plain.

"Just be happy you live in town," he said.

The parochial school was across the street from us, a pair of snowdrifts away, and on the worst of the winter mornings he and I were the only ones there, other than The Sisters of the Presentation Order, who taught us. It was his second and my first year. I'd poke my finger into the jelly of the hectograph and see if printing came up on it purple blue. Or stick my tongue against the diamond mesh outside and try to pull it loose without losing a ribbon of skin. Or peek from sneaky angles in the Sisters' wimples to see if they really had hair (and what *hue?*) under that shinily-pressed white band with its flying black hood. Or listen to the youngest of them tell stories—as she gripped the big beads of her belted rosary in the lap of her floor-length skirt—about boys who'd displeased God by disobeying their parents, teasing animals, or receiving First Communion in a state of mortal sin, and how they were then struck by lightning, she whispered, or evaporated up out of their yards.

Or we scattered seeds and crumbs she gave us over the snowbanks for birds, wiped and washed the classroom slates, cleaned the erasers on a revolving brush in the German janitor's diabolical boiler room, emptied the pencil sharpeners and scraped Crayola shavings from their metal spirals that chewed up wax and wood, and had our fifth piano lesson that week. And then the Sisters, black fluttering birds themselves, had us kneel with them on the floor of the chapel-auditorium as they prayed for the safety of those who weren't with us, and for fairer weather for the remainder. They helped us on with our sweaters and scarves and coats, smelling of hand cream and the pink medicinal soap they passed out to their classes twice a year, and the scent of their touch clung to us through the towering whiteness to the warmth of our home.

We'd moved into a new house that year. Most of the upstairs was a maze of boxes and unpainted walls, but there *was* an upstairs, with three rooms and an attic, besides all of the finished rooms on the ground floor that we lived in, and so much space we all felt freer, but all more alone. Privacy.

It had a bathroom, too, the first one we'd had, and I didn't miss one bit those icy midnight runs to the outhouse, or cold pee pots on the nipping porch; I'd had whooping cough, galloping pneumonia, tonsilitis two winters ago, strep throat and tonsilitis again last fall, and, finally, this winter, my tonsils out.

My brother and I sat at our bedroom window and stared out at the snow.

"Let's get out the sled and go sliding," I said.

"Don't be stupid. That klunker'd sink three feet in this stuff."

"Where's the hedge?"

"Underneath all this. Where do you think?"

"Maybe it went away south."

"Dummy, it has *roots* in the ground. It stays there."

"Is it dead, then?"

"Probably it's hibernating."

"Did Jack Frost do that?" I asked, and scratched the spikes of ice fringing our windowpane.

"There's no such thing as Jack Frost."

I told him the storytelling Sister said that Jack Frost was an elf who had a red suit like Santa Claus, and icicles hanging from his nose. I left some cookies out for him one night, I said, and in the morning they were gone. "There was water there."

"Dad ate them."

I pushed him in the chest and we scuffled around, fell on the bed, and started heading toward the region of fratricide.

"Stop that!" a voice cried, and our mother appeared in the door in a flash, flushed to her flying hairline. She brushed back a blackish swirl. "How many times have I told you two how *angry* it makes me to see you fight? Shame on you! Both of you! It's wrong, and you know it; it's a sin! It's even worse when a pair of brothers engage in it. Oh, *you!*"

"Well, he hit me," I said. "When I was just———"

"We weren't really actually fighting," my brother said. "We were ah—practicing double tumbles on the mattresses." He hung his head.

"Forbidden," she said. "Also, you know if you lie to your mother at this time of year, Santa might hear of it." The hoof-taps on the housetop. "He has spies."

We both understood this, and fell back on the bed and started moaning and rolling around on the covers.

And now that she'd been our mother, she became herself. "It's stopped snowing," she said. "Did you see?"

"Yes! Yes!" we said, and went to the window.

"Isn't it lovely to be in? Well, now, anyway. When it was coming down it was like brooms across the ceiling!"

"It'll be great for sledding," my brother said.

"Yes," she said. "Why don't you two get out in it and enjoy it?"

"Well, if we went out in it now," I said, "that klunker'd sink three——"

"Hey, I just told him that and now *he's* saying it. Tell him to stop! Tell him to quit being so—quite so *ob*-stinate!"

This was a word she sometimes used to reprimand us, and hearing it come at me now as it did in his voice dimmed my vision with unbrotherly black-and-blue thoughts.

"And now we're back to where we started to begin with," she said. *"No fighting."*

And having hung that in the air before us, like a coat on a hook, she disappeared.

We dressed and went outdoors. He waded ahead, holding his elbows high, and I watched a wide halo tremble around him as he moved with the telltale plunges of people who moved through my dreams. He stopped at a snowdrift taller than our father and turned to me. We stared at one another over our scarves. Then the big bare tree in the corner of the yard, with its black limbs branching out over us, cracked, and a handful of ice came scattering down on our red-and-blue sledding caps.

"Are you afraid?" he asked.

"Yes," I said. For I was sure, as the Sisters told us, sometimes in warning, that God and Jesus and Mary and the angels were watching over everything all of us ever said and did, and one of them might decide to appear.

"Maybe God's underneath all this," I said. "Let's dig Him up."

"Don't be stupid," my brother said, and jerked a fuzzy thumb straight up. "He's there."

"Let's dig a cave, then, and hide in it."

"You can't until the crust freezes."

"Let's make a snowman, then."

"You can't until the snow packs, goon."

"Well, what can we do?"

"Go inside," he said.

I struggled over to a white swelling across the yard, dragged myself up on top of it, got my feet underneath me, felt my legs tremble on the trembling, hidden, insubstantial hedge, and then threw out my arms and dove. Dove into a crystalline darkness that supported me. I could fall forever through its enveloping folds. I felt afloat.

"How is it?" my brother called.

"Better than the lake," I cried, and pulled myself out of the glittery grave into sunlight. "Try it and see!"

He did, I did it again, we did it together, and when the snow that was packed into our overshoes and around our collars and cuffs had melted, and then started to freeze again, we finally ran for the house, leaving ragged slashes filled with shadow along the hedge, as though dozens of us had been diving and the sum of our exaltation was preserved by the cold and yielding North Dakota snow.

That night, when I was sure everybody else was asleep, I got out of bed and went to the window. Jack Frost? The yard was silvered by a gold-colored moon, and then the light at the neighbor's went off, closing them behind a blank wall, and the wind came up. It blew along the side of the house and broke in waves on the wing of our bedroom, making the storm windows and the panes in front of me hum with an animal sound that other parts of the house seemed to pick up.

I didn't know what time it was when I woke, and hardly felt the throbbing above my eye; the window was printed with polar flowers, plumes, and frosty continents, except for where my forehead had rested. That spot had been left untouched, or so I reasoned, to keep from waking me up. I dove under the covers, into the warm cave my brother made, and rode home in hayracks of snow.

The next day was Christmas Eve. My brother and I dressed in our burdensome clothes and took the crate toward Bendemeer's. Before we got to the football field at the edge of town, we heard hooves on the road behind us, and then a team of horses came jogging up, pulling a shed, almost like an outhouse, mounted on sleigh runners of wood. There was a glass window at the front and below the window a thin slit for the double reins. A stovepipe stood above its shingled roof and trailed a loose sleeve of smoke across the sky. These rigs replaced the hayracks, now that real winter was here, and I'd heard from my friends how the stoves inside that burned coal and wood and kept them warmer than the furnace at school, or so they claimed, were perfect for popping popcorn on during the long ride in from their farms. They sometimes rode for hours, they said. The red-faced farmer had probably picked up presents for some of them in town.

The horses passed us and cut along the white-wooden goal-posts of an almost unremembered season, bringing the sled skimming around behind them, their hooves muffled now in drifts, their backs steaming through the burlap packed under their harnesses for warmth, and headed toward the sun that stained the fields and pastures and scattered clumps of trees across the plain, for as far as we could see on the encircling horizon, orange-golden.

"I wish it was winter all the time," I said.

"If it was, the farmers couldn't raise crops and we'd starve; 'd be the end of it."

"Well, I wish it was Christmas more often."

"Christmas is when Jesus Christ was born."

"I know that."

"Well, we've each got only one birthday, my dear."

I said that Jesus could do or have whatever He wanted, because He was God, but my brother said He couldn't; that's why He died on the cross, he said.

"That's another God," I said. "There are three of them."

"I see you haven't been paying attention in catechism again, dunce hound."

"No sir! I mean, I have too!"

"Then you know He was crucified."

"He was not!"

"Yes He was."

"How come?"

"What do you mean, 'How come?' " he said, in a way of mimicking me that made me feel my zipper was unzipped. "That's what the Bible says."

"Bull-loney!"

"He died for our sins."

"He didn't die for mine!"

"Bull-loney."

"I've never sinned."

"If you haven't, don't worry. You will."

He went toward Bendemeer's singing Christmas carols as he went, and his breath made gray bells in the air that his high voice rang within. It didn't seem possible that the Christ Child was the crowned and bony, bleeding man nailed to the crucifix above our bedroom door.

My brother got our three quarts of milk and I let him carry them alone.

A block from the house, I saw our father come out the side porch and took off on a run. He was at the back of the car when I got to him, trying to get an old Army blanket on or off a brown-paper-wrapped box in the trunk. He whirled in surprise and blue smoke fumed around his face and earflaps as he deliberated. Then he said my brother was right.

"Then why have Christmas, Dad? Why pretend it's fun?"

"We rejoice that Jesus, who was the son of God and also God Himself—a member of the Trinity, of course—came to earth as Man, to be the savior of us men here."

I heard my brother come on a clattering run with the milk, and the trunk lid slammed down in a frozen crush.

I went inside to see my mother. She'd been brought up in another church, I knew, and had her own ideas about religion and God; she was at the kitchen stove stirring syrup that was about to candy, so she couldn't stop and talk, she said, but as I tugged my way out of my chrysalis of clothes, she told me that Jesus, who was born with the animals and shepherds around Him, did indeed die on the cross. "But that's a reason to celebrate," she said "Look at His precepts."

So there, I thought.

I went to bed early that Eve of The Night. My brother soon followed, wearing long wool socks over his cold-prone feet, and started whispering under the covers about the box in the trunk, which he was sure held a sled; it was the right size, he whispered, if it was a long sled, and if we each had our own this winter we wouldn't have to take turns all the time, or do those breath-crushing bellyflops across each other's backs. He was speculating about styles and sizes when his whisper dimmed and the regular sound of his breathing drew him into sleep.

I heard singing and went to the window. Loudspeakers had been hung outside the church a block away, and the choir was singing Christmas hymns into a microphone; they'd sing until midnight mass. Their voices spread a silver substance, heavier than the snow, it seemed, over my senses, and the confined area my sight controlled.

> *It came up-po-on a mid-night clear,*
> *That glorious so-ong of old . . .*

I whispered along with them as I stared out at our white lawn in the light of the street lamp.

> *Away in a manger, no crib for His bed,*
> *The lit-tle Lord Jesus lay down His sweet head . . .*

I was positive I wasn't one of the ones who caused Him to die. I didn't even know He was dead. But my mother, too, said everybody was responsible. On His birthday, did they forget?

> *Joy to the world! the Lord is come!*
> *Let Earth receive her King!*

Cold rose from the floor and I couldn't hear singing. If that had happened to Jesus, then what would become of me, a dreamy, sinful child from an unheard-of village in a rural vastness on this whirling world? The wind came up and a lightning rod cable at the corner of the house slapped against the siding in the cold air, and then the street lamp started to swing, tilting its light over the snowbanks, and there was a sound at the window. The wind, the sudden snowflakes tapping there, were asking to touch me.

I went into the living room. The Christmas lights and the shimmer of the tree in the alcove of the bay window filled the air with the firelight of many-colored, interchanging beams. I thought I heard voices, and then felt such a hush of interior silence I was sure I'd imagined them. I went to the tree and there, beside the mound of packages I'd watched accumulate over a month, was an addition smelling of varnish and runners painted red. My brother was right, again. A new sled. A *Flexible Flyer,* long enough to hold an adult lying flat, or seat three my size. Three.

Farther over, beneath the boughs at the center of the tree, overlaid with a host of different colors, was the Bethlehem scene, spread out and arranged on cotton rolls. The Night Visitors. The camels, cattle, and lambs. The stable with Mary and Joseph in shadow. The Infant on straw with His arms outstretched. I imagined layers of flakes like lace curtains unrolled, coulees of snow folding into one another, cold bells ringing their insides across the frigid air, crystals that rose from the landscape and glowed above it in silver dots. . . .

The tree lights guttered around my vision and rainbows swam. I couldn't understand it. Why Him? It wasn't fair to any of us. It was a crime.

I went into the kitchen and looked up at the row of coats on the rack above the oil heater, and decided I might as well start dressing up to go out into the cold.

"Say! What do you think you're doing?"

The bulk of my father was dark in the doorway, with the light from the living room shining around behind him.

"I don't know."

"Are you all right?"

"Yes," I said. "I guess."

He came and put a hand over my forehead. "Mmmm," he said, "You're probably still troubled or worried, or whatever, over what you asked today."

"Yes," I said.

"You needn't worry about anybody as willing as He was to accept His station in life. If He did complain, it wasn't more than once. That's a happy man."

I felt myself rise above his shoulders, and then his hands and arms as he gathered me in, then the stride of his feet underneath me, and started thinking about Christmas morning, the gifts under the tree, the new sled, and had just enough time before I reached the bottom of sleep in that North Dakota night, in the warmth of the wide white bed where he tucked me in closer to my brother, to thank Jesus for my father.

Notes on the Contributors

CHINUA ACHEBE is the author of *Arrow of God* and *A Man of the People*. He teaches at the University of Nigeria. "The Drum" was first published in 1977 by Fourth Dimension Publishers in Nigeria.

HELEN ADAM is the author of *Selected Poems and Ballads* and *Turn Again to Me*.

ALICE ADAMS is the author of *Families and Survivors* and *Beautiful Girl*.

MAX APPLE is the author of *The Oranging of America and Other Stories* and *Zip*.

ISAAC ASIMOV is the author of over two hundred books, including *How Did We Find Out About Comets?*, *From Earth to Heaven*, and *To the Ends of the Universe*.

GORDON BALL edited *Allen Verbatim: Lectures on Poetry, Politics and Consciousness*.

PAULÉ BARTÓN (1916–1974) was a Haitian poet and storyteller. In 1960, he was arrested by the Duvalier dictatorship, and after four years in prison, he emigrated, first to Jamaica, then Trinidad, and finally Costa Rica. He made a living raising goats.

PETER BEARD is a photographer and author of *End of the Game*.

ANN BEATTIE is the author of *Secrets and Surprises*, *Distortions*, *Chilly Scenes of Winter*, and *Falling in Place*.

BILL BERKSON is the author of *Blue Is the Hero* and *Parts of the Body*.

PAUL BOWLES is the author of *The Delicate Prey* and *The Sheltering Sky*.

JOE BRAINARD is a painter and the author of *I Remember*.

HAROLD BRODKEY is the author of *First Love and Other Sorrows*.

MICHAEL BROWNSTEIN is the author of two volumes of poetry, *Highway to the Sky* and *Strange Days Ahead*, and a novel, *Country Cousins*.

ED BULLINS is the author of *Four Dynamite Plays* and *The Theme is Blackness: The Corner and Other Plays.*

REED BYE is the author of a book of poems entitled *Some Magic at the Dump.*

HORTENSE CALISHER is the author of *Herself* and *Eagle Eye.*

NORRIS CHURCH is an artist living in Brooklyn.

ANDREI CODRESCU is the author of *The History of the Growth of Heaven* and *The Life and Times of an Involuntary Genius.*

JOHN N. COLE is the editor of *The Maine Times* and is the author of *Striper: A Story of Fish and Man.*

ROBERT COLES is the author of *Children in Crisis.*

ROBERT EMMET COLES wrote "An Eskimo's Cautionary Tale" with his father when he was thirteen years old. He goes to school in Concord, Massachusetts.

BETTY COMDEN is co-author with Adolph Green of *On the Town, Singing in the Rain, Bells Are Ringing,* and *On the Twentieth Century.*

EVAN S. CONNELL is the author of *The Connoisseur, Mr. Bridge,* and *The Long Desire.*

PETER COOK has co-authored and appeared in *Beyond the Fringe, Good Evening,* and *Bedazzled.*

ROBERT COOVER is the author of *Pricksongs and Descants* and *The Public Burning.*

GREGORY CORSO is the author of *Happy Birthday of Death, Elegiac Feelings American,* and *The Japanese Notebook.*

JONATHAN COTT is the author of a book of poems, *City of Earthly Love,* and is the editor of *Beyond the Looking Glass: Victorian Fairy Tales, Novels, Stories and Poems.*

MYRNA DAVIS is the author of *Bouquet,* a collaboration with her husband, Paul Davis.

PAUL DAVIS is a painter and poster artist.

GEORGE DENNISON is the author of *Lives of Children* and *And Then a Harvest Feast.*

ANNA DIBBLE is an artist living in Peru, Vermont.

ROSALYN DREXLER is the author of *I Am the Beautiful Stranger* and *The Cosmopolitan Girl*.

ANN DRUYAN is the author of *A Famous Broken Heart* and is one of the co-authors of *Murmurs of Earth*. She is also a writer for the television series, *Cosmos*.

ROBERT DUNCAN is the author of *Opening of the Field*, *Roots and Branches*, and *The Truth and Life of Myth*. "The Honey Moon Bees and the Busy Man's Garden" is taken from *Cat and Blackbird*, which was written in 1954 and originally published in 1967 by White Rabbit Press.

JACK DUNPHY is the author of *John Fury: A Novel in Four Parts* and *Nightmovers*.

COCO DUPUY was born in New Orleans and now lives in New York City.

RICHARD EBERHART is the author of *Collected Poems 1930–1976*.

RALPH ELLISON is the author of *Invisible Man* and *Shadow and Act*. "A Coupla Scalped Indians" first appeared in *New World Writing* in 1956.

GLORIA EMERSON is the author of *Winners and Losers: Battles, Retreats, Gains, Losses and Ruins from a Long War*.

LARRY FAGIN is the author of *Rhymes of a Jerk* and *I'll Be Seeing You*. "Landscape" was first published in 1972 by Angel Hair Books.

JULES FEIFFER is a cartoonist and the author of the play *Little Murders* and a novel, *Ackroyd*.

AARON FELTON, the son of David Felton, was twelve years old when he illustrated "Boogers." He lives in Salem, Oregon.

DAVID FELTON is Faith and Morals Editor of *Rolling Stone* magazine.

LESLIE FIEDLER is the author of *Love and Death in the American Novel* and *Freaks*.

DICK GALLUP is the author of *The Wacking of the Fruit Trees* and *Where I Hang My Hat*.

DAVID GATES is a musician living in New York City.

WILLARD GAYLIN is the author of *Caring* and *Feelings: Our Vital Signs.*

MARY GIMBEL is Associate Editor of Rolling Stone Press and Advisory Editor of *The Paris Review.*

ALLEN GINSBERG is the author of many books including *Kaddish and Other Poems, Planet News,* and *Mind Breaths: Poems 1972–1977.*

NIKKI GIOVANNI is the author of *Gemini, Spin a Soft Black Song,* and *Ego-Tripping and Other Poems for Young Readers.*

HERBERT GOLD is the author of *Fathers, The Man Who Was Not With It, Waiting for Cordelia,* and *He/She.*

ETHAN and ARI GOLD (twins) were seven, and their sister NINA was nine, when they illustrated "Teddy the Spy."

PAUL GOODMAN (1911–1972) was the author of many books, including *Kafka's Prayer, Growing Up Absurd, Utopian Essays and Practical Proposals,* and *The Empire City.* "Likely and the Dragon," written as a play for marionettes in 1947, is published here for the first time. Goodman subsequently wrote a prose version of this play, using the same title, which appears in *Adam and His Works* (Vintage Books) and in Volume Three of *The Collected Stories and Sketches* (Black Sparrow Press).

ROSE GRAUBART is an artist who has exhibited at the Philadelphia Museum of Art. Her short stories have been published in many magazines.

HANNAH GREEN is the author of *Dead of the House.*

WINSTON GROOM is the author of *Better Times Than These* and *As Summers Die.*

DONALD HALL is the author of *Riddle Rat* and *Ox Cart Man.*

OAKLEY HALL is the author of *The Pleasure Garden, The Adelita,* and *Report from Beau Harbor.*

JOHN HAWKES is the author of *The Cannibal, The Lime Twig,* and *The Passion Artist.*

SOPHIE HAWKES, the daughter of John Hawkes, did the illustrations for "Two Shoes for One Foot" in 1968. She currently attends New York University.

BOBBIE LOUISE HAWKINS is the author of *Fifteen Poems* and *Back to Texas.*

EDWARD HOAGLAND is the author of *Notes from the Century Before, The Courage of Turtles,* and *African Calliope: A Journey to the Sudan.*

ANSELM HOLLO is the author of *Sojourner Microcosms: Poems New and Selected, 1959–1977.*

DAVID IGNATOW is the author of *Say Pardon, Facing the Tree,* and *Tread the Dark.*

JOHN IRVING is the author of *Setting Free the Bears* and *The World According to Garp.*

JILL JOHNSTON is the author of *Marmalade Me, Gullibles Travels,* and *My Father in America.*

JOHN KEATS is the Romantic poet. The stanzas of "There Was a Naughty Boy" are two of four verses that the poet, while on a walking tour of Scotland, wrote in a letter to his young sister Fanny. As he explained to her: "I am ashamed of writing such stuff, nor would I if it were not being tired after my day's walking, and ready to tumble into bed so fatigued that when I am asleep you might sew my nose to my great toe and trundle me round the town, like a Hoop, without waking me."

ROBERT KELLY is the author of *The Loom, In Time,* and *The Mill of Particulars.*

KEN KESEY is the author of *One Flew Over the Cuckoo's Nest* and *Sometimes A Great Notion.* "Little Tricker the Squirrel Meets Big Double the Bear!" is one of a series of stories the author is writing under the pseudonym Grandma Whittier.

JAMAICA KINCAID is a writer who was born in the West Indies and now lives in New York City.

MAXINE HONG KINGSTON is the author of *The Woman Warrior* and *China Men.*

GALWAY KINNELL is the author of *Book of Nightmares* and *Body Rags.*

CHRISTOPHER KNOWLES is a writer, a visual artist, and a performance artist living in New York.

JOHN KNOWLES is the author of *A Separate Peace* and *Spreading Fires.*

RUTH KRAUSS is a poet as well as the author of *A Hole Is to Dig* and *I'll Be You and You Be Me.*

JULIUS LESTER is the author of *Black Folktales* and *Revolutionary Notes.*

DENISE LEVERTOV is the author of *Jacob's Ladder, Relearning the Alphabet,* and *The Poet in the World.*

BARRY LOPEZ is the author of *Desert Notes: Reflections in the Eye of a Raven* and *Of Wolves and Men.* "Whirlwind Woman" and "Coyote Shows How He Can Lie" are retellings of Arapaho and Jicarilla Apache tales, respectively, and are taken from Lopez's collection of Coyote stories entitled *Giving Birth to Thunder, Sleeping With His Daughter,* published by Sheed Andrews and McMeel, Inc. in 1977.

WALTER LOWENFELS (1897–1976) was a poet, anthologist, and social critic. He was the author of *The Suicide, Some Deaths, The Revolution is to Be Human,* and *Reality Prime. Be Polite to the Grass: Letters to My Twelve Grandchildren* was his last completed work. (Printed by permission of the Estate of Walter Lowenfels, Manna Lowenfels-Perpelitt, Literary Executrix.)

ALISON LURIE is the author of *The War Between the Tates* and *Imaginary Friends.* "Molly Whuppie" is taken from *Clever Gretchen,* a collection of feminist folktales. It was first published in *Horizon* in January 1978.

LEWIS MACADAMS is the author of *City Money, Live at the Church,* and *The Poetry Room.*

NORMAN MAILER is the author of *The Deer Park, Why Are We in Viet Nam?* and *The Executioner's Song.*

HARRY MATHEWS is the author of *The Sinking of the Odradek Stadium and Other Novels.*

PETER MATTHIESSEN is the author of *Far Tortuga* and *The Snow Leopard.* "Tukum the Swineherd" has been adapted by the author from his book *Under the Mountain Wall,* published by Viking Press in 1962.

MICHAEL MCCLURE is the author of the play *The Beard* and several volumes of poems, including *Jaguar Skies, Antechamber,* and *Rare Angel.*

DAVID MELTZER is the author of many books of poetry, including *Two-Way Mirror* and *Six.*

LEONARD MICHAELS is the author of *Going Places* and *I Would Have Saved Them If I Could.* ETHAN MICHAELS was nine years old when he illustrated "Moe."

MARILYN SUZANNE MILLER is a writer for *Saturday Night Live* and is working on a novel.

FRANK MODELL is the author of *Stop Trying to Cheer Me Up!*

N. SCOTT MOMADAY is the author of *House Made of Dawn.*

JAN MORRIS is the author of *Conundrum, Travels,* and *Destinations.*

WILLIE MORRIS is the author of *North Toward Home, Yazoo,* and *The Last of the Southern Girls.*

MOHAMMED MRABET was born in Morocco of Riffian parentage around 1940. He is the author of *The Boy Who Set the Fire, The Big Mirror,* and an autobiography—taped and translated from the Moghrebi by Paul Bowles—entitled *Look and Move On.*

SHIGA NAOYA (1883–1971) was the author of many short works and the novel, *A Dark Night's Passing.*

MICHELE NAPEAR is a painter who lives and works in New York City. The artist dedicates her illustration to her father, Harold Napear, who read her the Keats poem when she was a child.

HOWARD NEMEROV is the author of *The Collected Poems of Howard Nemerov.*

HOWARD NORMAN (who translated Bartón's poems) is the author of *The Wishing Bone,* and *Incidents of Travel Toward Hudson Bay.*

PAT OLIPHANT is the author of *An Informal Gathering* and a forthcoming collection of cartoons.

RON PADGETT is the author of several volumes of poetry, including *Great Balls of Fire* and *Toujours L'Amour.* Since 1969 he has worked with Teachers and Writers Collaborative and numerous poets in the school's programs.

GRACE PALEY is the author of *The Little Disturbances of Man* and *Enormous Changes at the Last Minute.* "The Sad Story About the Six Boys About to Be Drafted in Brooklyn" originally appeared in *I-KON,* Volume 1, Number 3.

JOHN PHILLIPS is the author of *The Second Happiest Day.*

GEORGE PLIMPTON is the author of *Out of My League, Paper Lion,* and *Shadow Box.* He is a founder and the editor of *The Paris Review.*

JAMES PURDY is the author of *Malcolm, Jeremy's Version,* and *Narrow Rooms.*

MARGARET RANDALL, an American poet living in Cuba, was the co-founder and co-editor of the Mexican bilingual literary magazine *El Corno Emplumado.* Her books include *Part of the Solution: Portrait of a Revolutionary, Cuban Women Now,* and *Doris Tijerino: Inside the Nicaraguan Revolution.*

TOM ROBBINS is the author of *Another Roadside Attraction* and *Even Cowgirls Get the Blues.*

MICHAEL ROGERS is the author of *Mindfogger* and *Biohazard.*

ANNE ROIPHE is the author of *Up the Sandbox* and *Long Division.*

JEROME ROTHENBERG is the author of *Poems for the Game of Silence* and the editor of *Technicians of the Sacred, Revolution of the Word,* and *A Big Jewish Book.*

ARAM SAROYAN is the author of *The Street* and *O My Generation and Other Poems.* His daughter, STRAWBERRY, wrote the text for "Strawberry Talking." "That is," says Mr. Saroyan, "she said these things, and I was struck by them and wrote them down, during the spring and summer of 1973, when she was two and a half years old and just beginning to talk."

ALLEN SAY is a photographer living in San Francisco. He has done illustrations for children's books and is the author of *The Bookkeeper's Apprentice.*

GEORGE SCHNEEMAN is a painter who shows with the Holly Solomon Gallery in New York City. "Landscape" was first published in 1972 by Angel Hair Books.

PETE SEEGER is a songwriter and singer, and is the author of *The Incompleat Folksinger.* "Abiyoyo" was first published by Fall River Music, Inc., in 1963.

NTOZAKE SHANGE is the author of *For Colored Girls Who Have Considered Suicide/When the Rainbow is Enuf.*

HARVEY SHAPIRO is the author of *Battle Report, This World,* and *Lauds: Poems.*

ADAM SHAW is the author of *Sound of Impact* and is at work on a novel.

IRWIN SHAW is the author of *The Young Lions, Rich Man, Poor Man,* and *The Top of the Hill.*

ALLEN SHAWN is a musician living and working in New York City.

SAM SHEPARD is the author of many plays, including *The Tooth of Crime, The Curse of the Starving Class,* and *Buried Child.*

ALIX KATES SHULMAN is the author of *Memoirs of an Ex-Prom Queen* and *Burning Questions.*

CHARLES SIMIC is the author of *Dismantling the Silence* and *Return to a Place Lit by a Glass of Milk.*

ISAAC BASHEVIS SINGER is the author of *Old Love, Shosha, Satan in Goray, The Spinoza of Market Street,* and several works for children, including *Zlateh the Goat and Other Stories.*

LORNA SMEDMAN has studied at the Jack Kerouac School of Disembodied Poetics at Naropa Institute in Boulder, Colorado.

PATTI SMITH is the author of *Babel* and has released several albums including *Horses, Radio Ethiopia,* and *Easter.*

ISAAC SOLOTAROFF was a third-grade student at the Calhoun School in New York City when he collaborated with his brother and father on "Hector Leaves Home."

JASON SOLOTAROFF was an eighth-grade student at Cathedral School in New York City when he wrote an early version of the story in 1977.

TED SOLOTAROFF, the editor of *The Red-Hot Vacuum* and founding editor of *American Review,* contributed some guidance and continuity to the story.

TERRY SOUTHERN is the author of *Flash and Filigree* and *The Magic Christian.*

SCOTT SPENCER is the author of *Preservation Hall* and *Endless Love.*

WILLIAM STAFFORD is the author of *The Rescued Year, Allegiances,* and *Stories That Could Be True.*

SAUL STEINBERG is the cartoonist and artist.

JAMES STEVENSON is a reporter and cartoonist for *The New Yorker* magazine.

PETER STONE is the author of *1776*.

BARBARA SZERLIP is the author of *Sympathetic Alphabet* and *The Ugliest Woman in the World and Other Histories*.

PAUL THEROUX is the author of *The Great Railway Bazaar* and *The Old Patagonian Express*.

RACHEL TOWLE, the daughter of TONY TOWLE, co-authored "The Interesting Story" when she was eight years old. She goes to school in New York City.

TONY TOWLE is the author of *North* and *Autobiography and Other Poems*. "The Interesting Story" was originally published in 1977 in a privately printed edition.

CHÖGYAM TRUNGPA is a Lama of the Kagur lineage of Tibetan Buddhism. He is the author of an autobiography, *Born in Tibet*; a book of poetry, *Mudra*; and *Meditation in Action, Cutting Through Spiritual Materialism*, and *The Myth of Freedom*.

ANNE WALDMAN is the author of *Fast-Speaking Woman, Journals & Dreams*, and a record with Giorno Poetry Systems.

TONY WALTON is a production designer for film and theater who has illustrated Oscar Wilde's *The Importance of Being Earnest* and *Lady Windermere's Fan*.

JOHN WESLEY is a painter whose work has been shown at The Robert Elkon Gallery and the Whitney Museum.

CLAIRE NICOLAS WHITE is the author of a novel, *The Death of the Orange Trees,* and a book of poems.

ELIE WIESEL is the author of *Dawn, Night,* and *A Jew Today*.

ROBERT WILSON is the creator of theater pieces such as *Deafman Glance* and *Einstein on the Beach*.

LARRY WOIWODE is the author of *What I'm Going to Do, I Think* and *Beyond the Bedroom Wall*.

Drawing by Joe Brainard